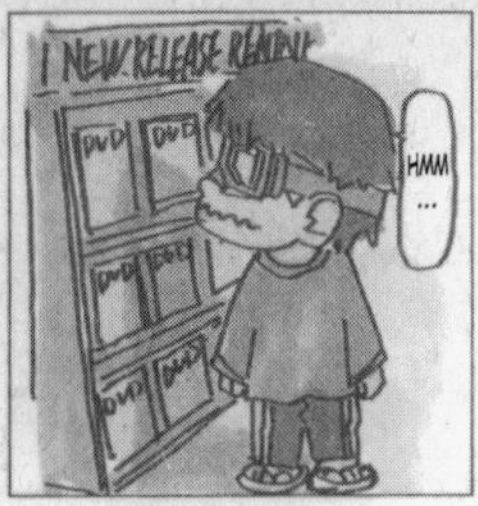
NEW RELEASE RENTAL
DVD
HMM ...

岸本斉史

Recently, DVDs have become prominent at movie rental stores. Certainly, DVDs are nice because unlike videotapes, you can just rent one disc and not have to choose what kind of audio track you want or whether you want subtitles or not until right when you watch it. That's really great, but...DVDs don't include coming attractions before the main feature. That's what I was looking forward to...

—Masashi Kishimoto, 2002

Author/artist Masashi Kishimoto was born in 1974 in rural Okayama Prefecture, Japan. After spending time in art college, he won the Hop Step Award for new manga artists with his manga **Karakuri** (Mechanism). Kishimoto decided to base his next story on traditional Japanese culture. His first version of **Naruto**, drawn in 1997, was a one-shot story about fox spirits; his final version, which debuted in **Weekly Shonen Jump** in 1999, quickly became the most popular ninja manga in Japan.

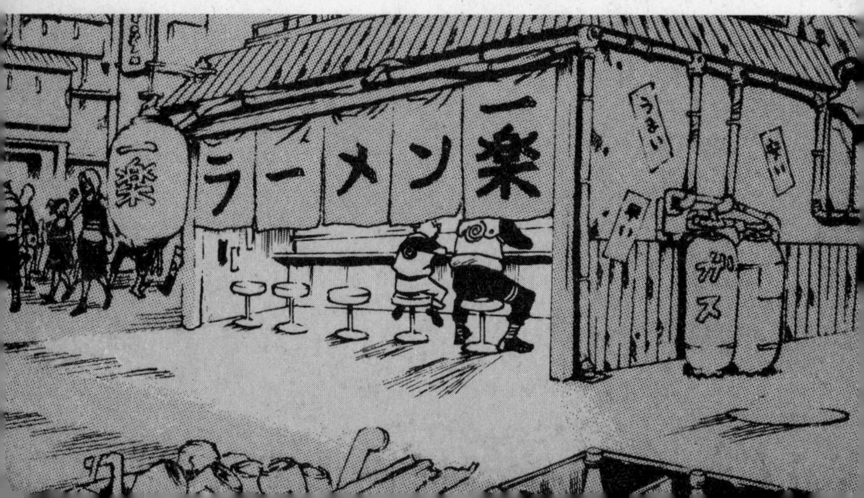
一楽
ラーメン一楽
うまい

NARUTO VOL. 12
The SHONEN JUMP Manga Edition

This graphic novel contains material that was originally published in English in **SHONEN JUMP** #45-47.

STORY AND ART BY MASASHI KISHIMOTO

Translation & English Adaptation/Mari Morimoto
Touch-up Art & Lettering/Heidi Szykowny
Additional Touch-up/Josh Simpson
Design/Sean Lee
Editors/Frances E. Wall & Pancha Diaz

Managing Editor/Frances E. Wall
Editorial Director/Elizabeth Kawasaki
VP & Editor in Chief/Yumi Hoashi
Sr. Director of Acquisitions/Rika Inouye
Sr. VP of Marketing/Liza Coppola
Exec. VP of Sales & Marketing/John Easum
Publisher/Hyoe Narita

Printed in the U.S.A.

Published by VIZ Media, LLC
P.O. Box 77010
San Francisco, CA 94107

SHONEN JUMP Manga Edition
10 9 8 7 6 5 4 3 2 1
First printing, December 2006

viz media
www.viz.com

PARENTAL ADVISORY
NARUTO is rated T for Teen and is recommended for ages 13 and up. This volume contains tobacco use and realistic and fantasy violence.

THE WORLD'S MOST POPULAR MANGA
SHONEN JUMP
www.shonenjump.com

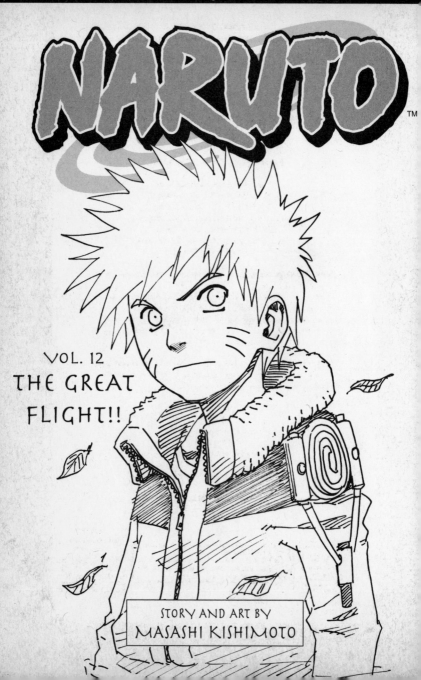

SHONEN JUMP MANGA

NARUTO™

VOL. 12
THE GREAT
FLIGHT!!

STORY AND ART BY
MASASHI KISHIMOTO

SAKURA サクラ

Smart and studious, Sakura is the brightest of Naruto's classmates, but she's constantly distracted by her crush on Sasuke. Her goal: to win Sasuke's heart!

NARUTO ナルト

When Naruto was born, a destructive fox spirit was imprisoned inside his body. Spurned by the older villagers, he's grown into an attention-seeking trouble-maker. His goal: to become the village's next *Hokage*.

SASUKE サスケ

The top student in Naruto's class, Sasuke comes from the prestigious Uchiha clan. His goal: to get revenge on a mysterious person who wronged him in the past.

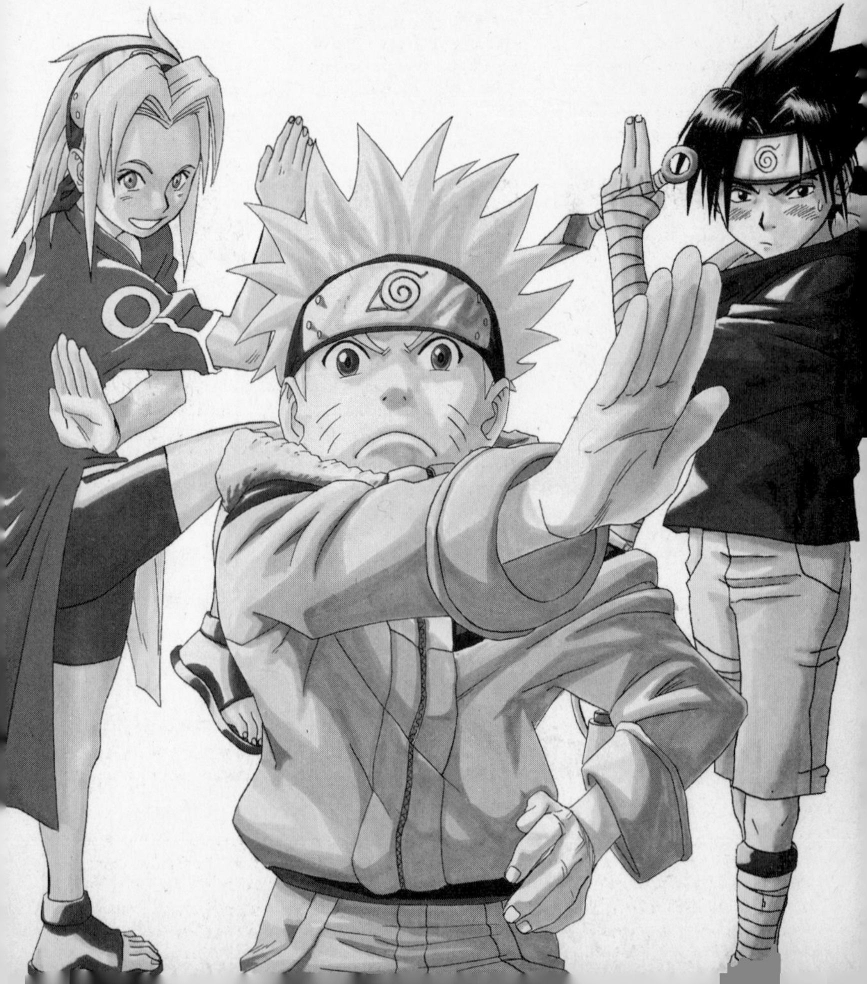

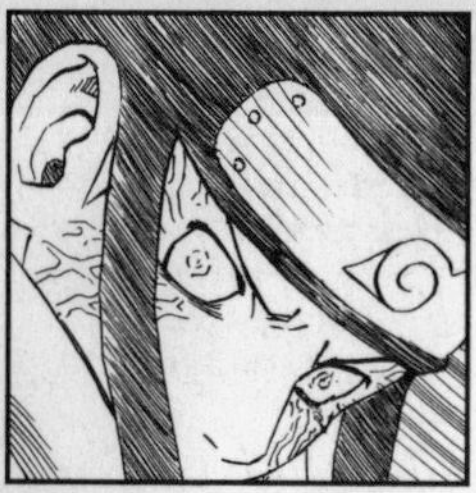

Neji ネジ
Part of the Cadet Branch of the Hyuga Clan, as opposed to the Main Branch to which Hinata belongs. Neji is widely considered to be a genius.

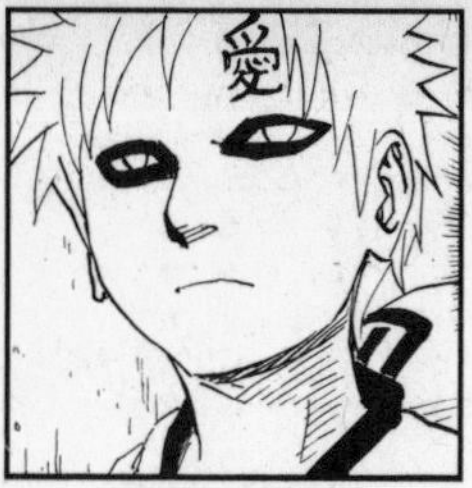
愛

Gaara 我愛羅
Bloodthirsty Gaara is one of the scariest ninja competing in the Chûnin exams.

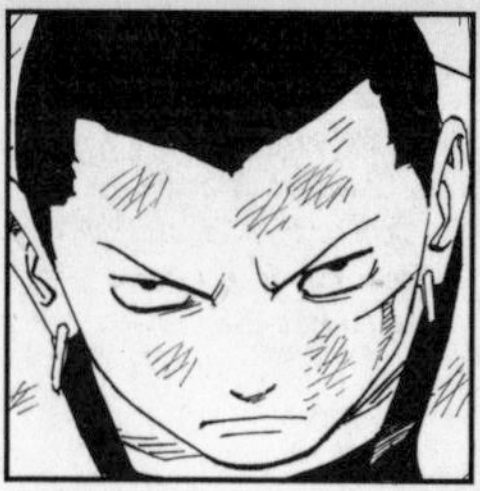

Shikamaru シカマル
One of Naruto's classmates. He specializes in the Shadow Possession jutsu, and is a skilled ninja despite his lazy demeanor.

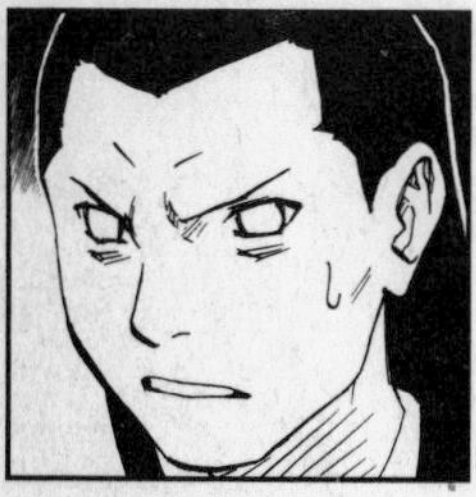

Hyuga Hiashi
日向ヒアシ
The head of the main branch of the Hyuga family and Neji's uncle.

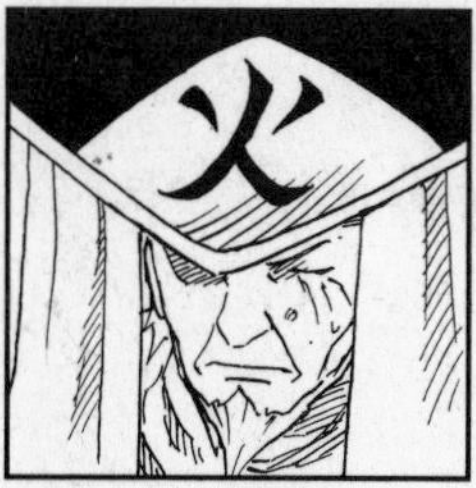
火

Hokage 火影
The leader of Konohagakure. He was retired, but stepped back into the position when the fourth Hokage was killed by the nine-tailed fox spirit.

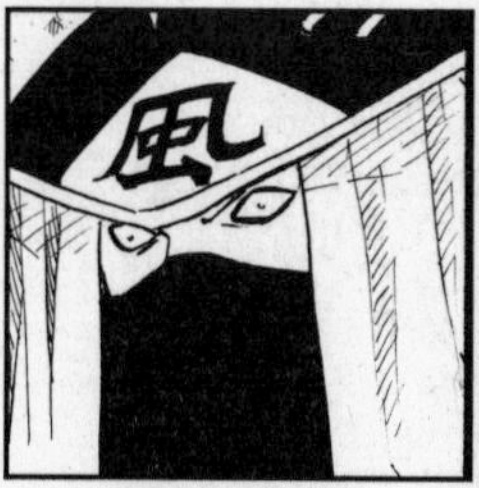
風

Kazekage 風影
The leader of Sunagakure (the Village Hidden in the Sand) within the Land of Wind.

THE STORY SO FAR...

Twelve years ago, a destructive nine-tailed fox spirit attacked the ninja village of Konohagakure. The *Hokage*, or village champion, defeated the fox by sealing its soul into the body of a baby boy. Now that boy, Uzumaki Naruto, has grown up to become a ninja-in-training, learning the art of *ninjutsu* with his teammates Sakura and Sasuke.

The preliminaries of the Third Exam are over and Sasuke, Shino, Kankuro, Temari, Shikamaru, Naruto, Neji, Gaara and Dosu have all passed and remain in the running. During the month of preparation time before the finals, Naruto trains with Jiraiya and brilliantly manages to draw out the Nine-Tailed Fox's chakra. The final round begins amid the swirling intrigue of Orochimaru and company. In the first battle, Naruto squares off against Neji, but...?!

NARUTO

VOL. 12
THE GREAT FLIGHT!!

CONTENTS

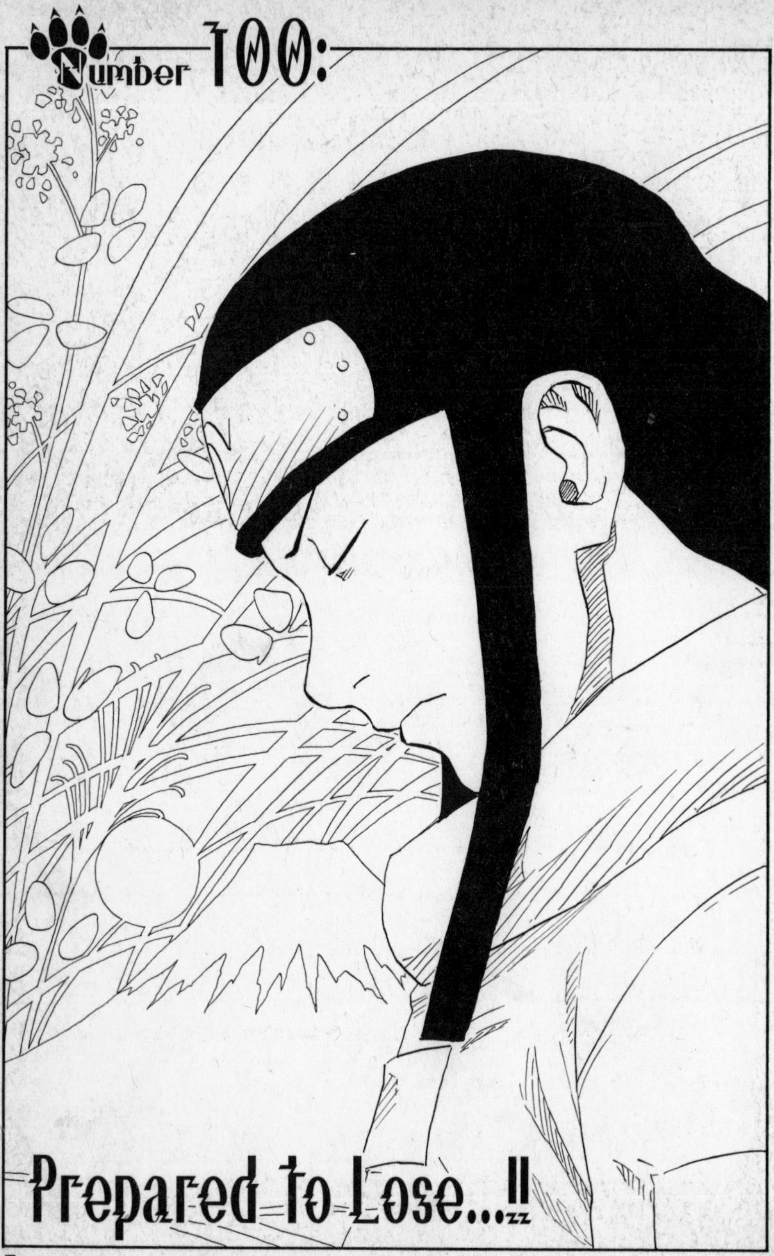
Number 100:
Prepared to Lose...!!

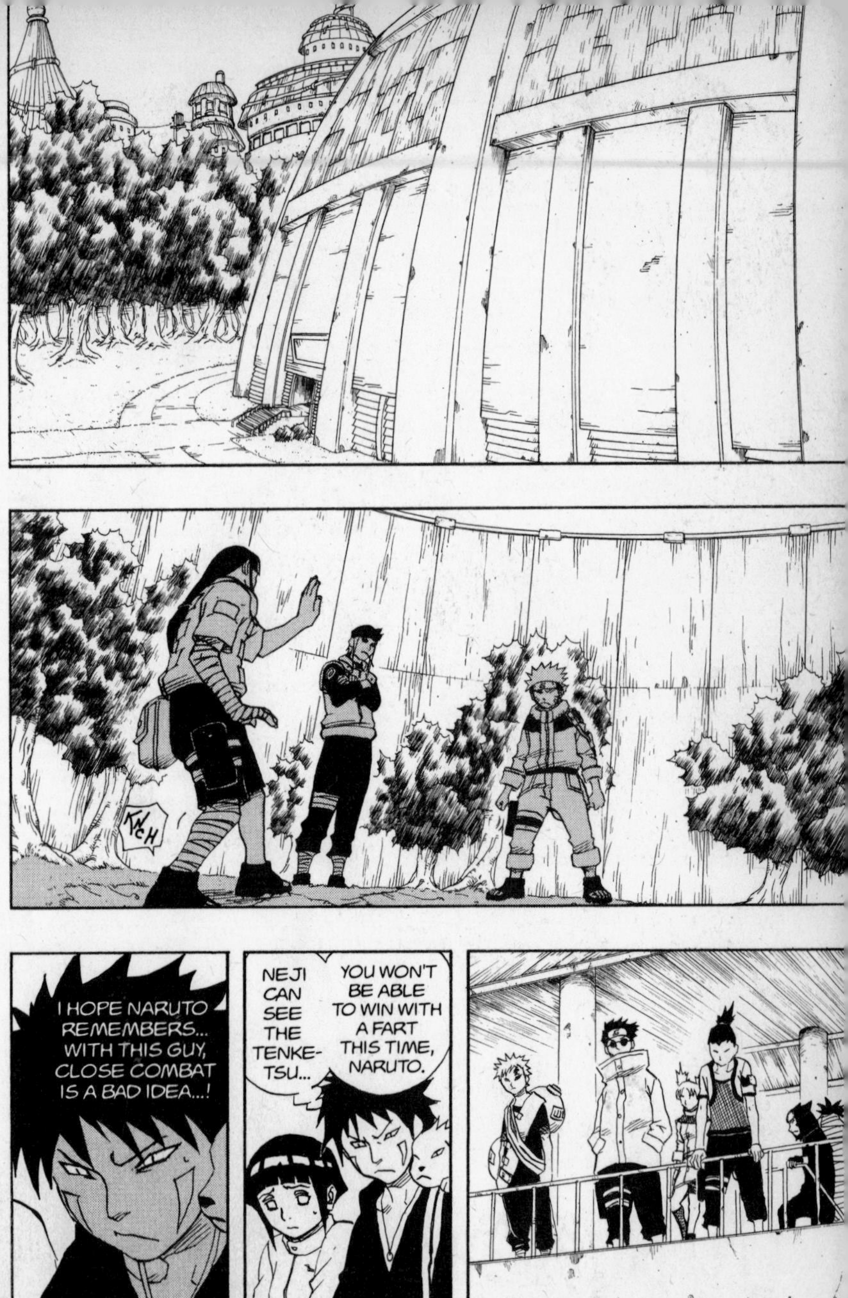
KNCH
YOU WON'T BE ABLE TO WIN WITH A FART THIS TIME, NARUTO.
NEJI CAN SEE THE TENKETSU...
I HOPE NARUTO REMEMBERS... WITH THIS GUY, CLOSE COMBAT IS A BAD IDEA...!

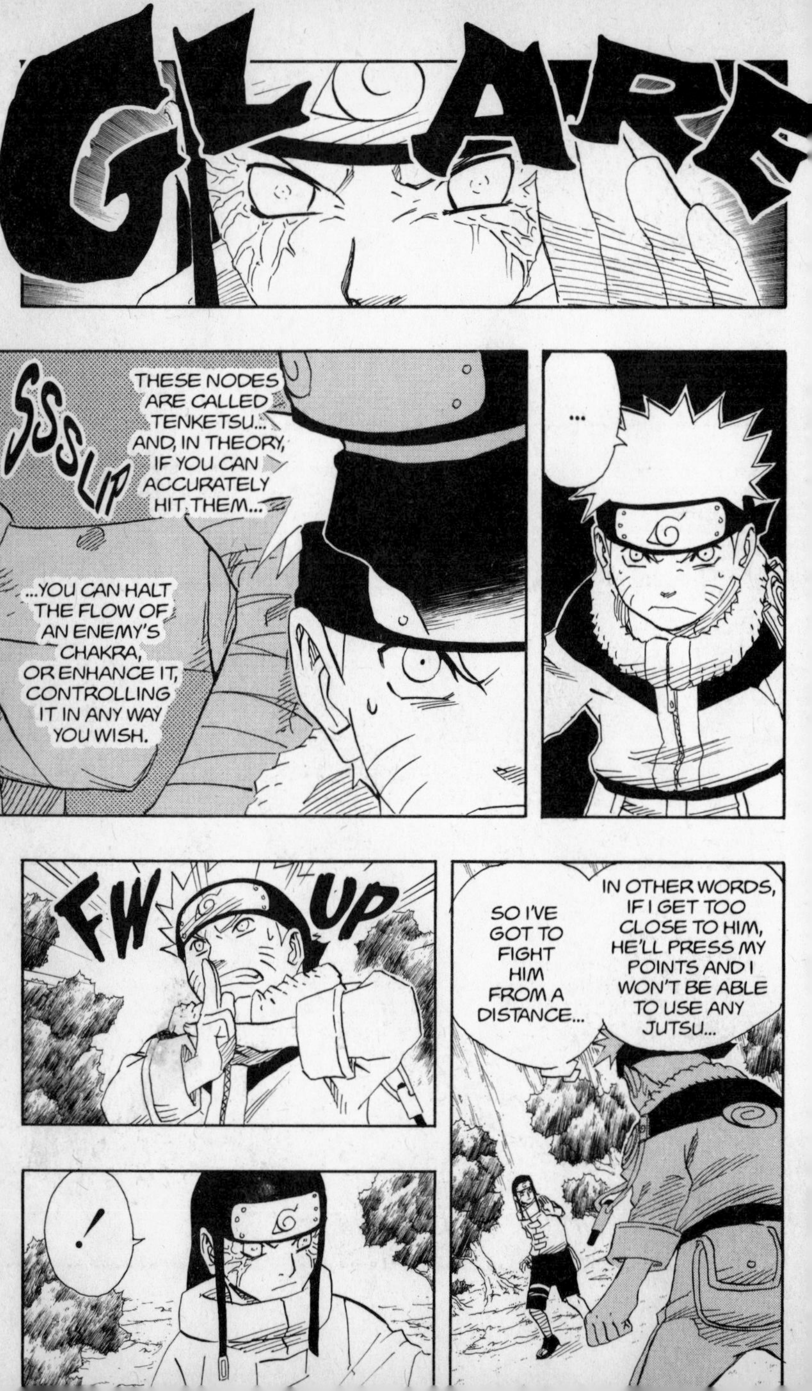
GLARE
...
SSSLIP
THESE NODES ARE CALLED TENKETSU... AND, IN THEORY, IF YOU CAN ACCURATELY HIT THEM...
...YOU CAN HALT THE FLOW OF AN ENEMY'S CHAKRA, OR ENHANCE IT, CONTROLLING IT IN ANY WAY YOU WISH.
IN OTHER WORDS, IF I GET TOO CLOSE TO HIM, HE'LL PRESS MY POINTS AND I WON'T BE ABLE TO USE ANY JUTSU...
SO I'VE GOT TO FIGHT HIM FROM A DISTANCE...
FWUP
!

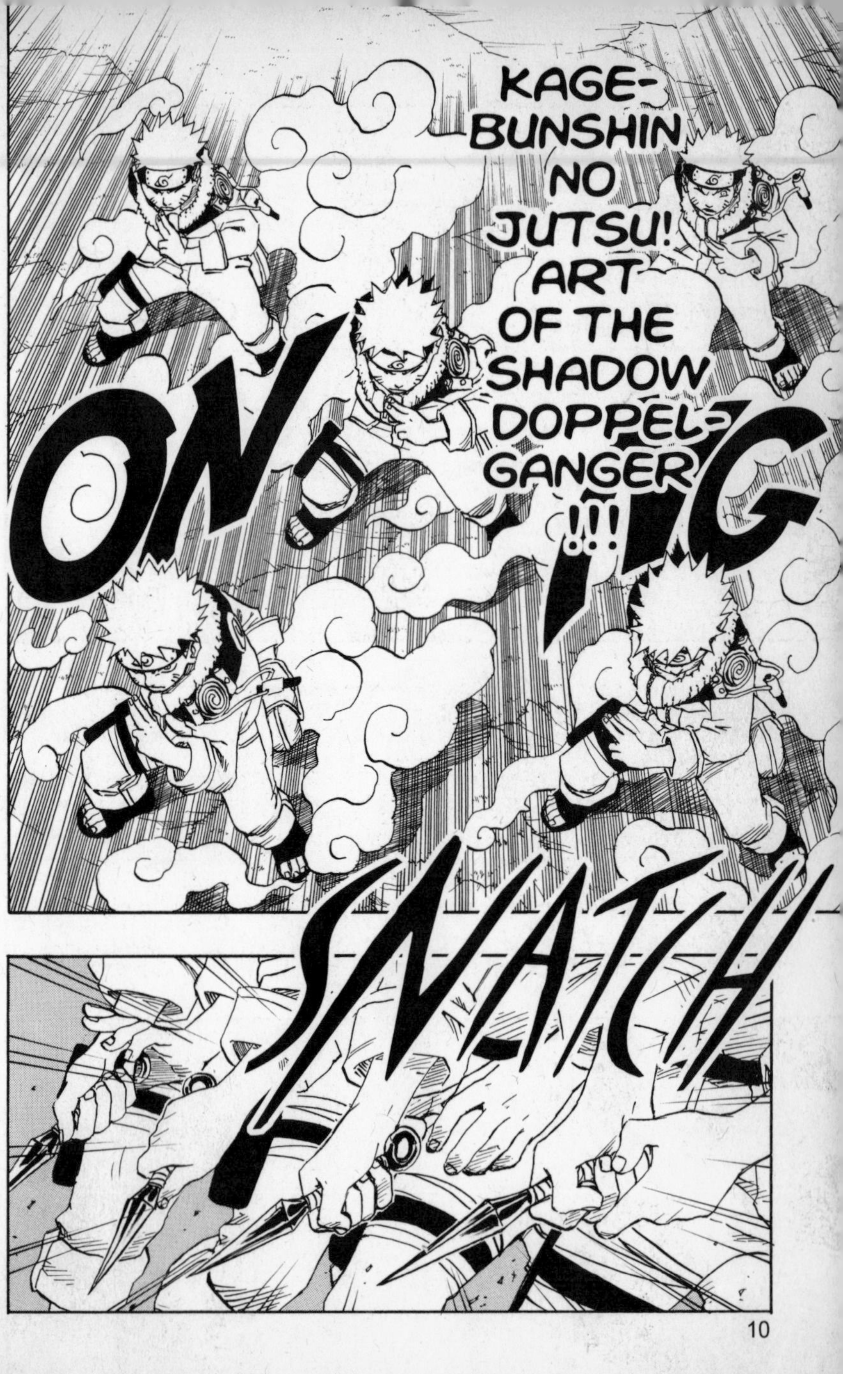
KAGE-BUNSHIN NO JUTSU! ART OF THE SHADOW DOPPELGANGER!!!
SNATCH

READ THIS WAY

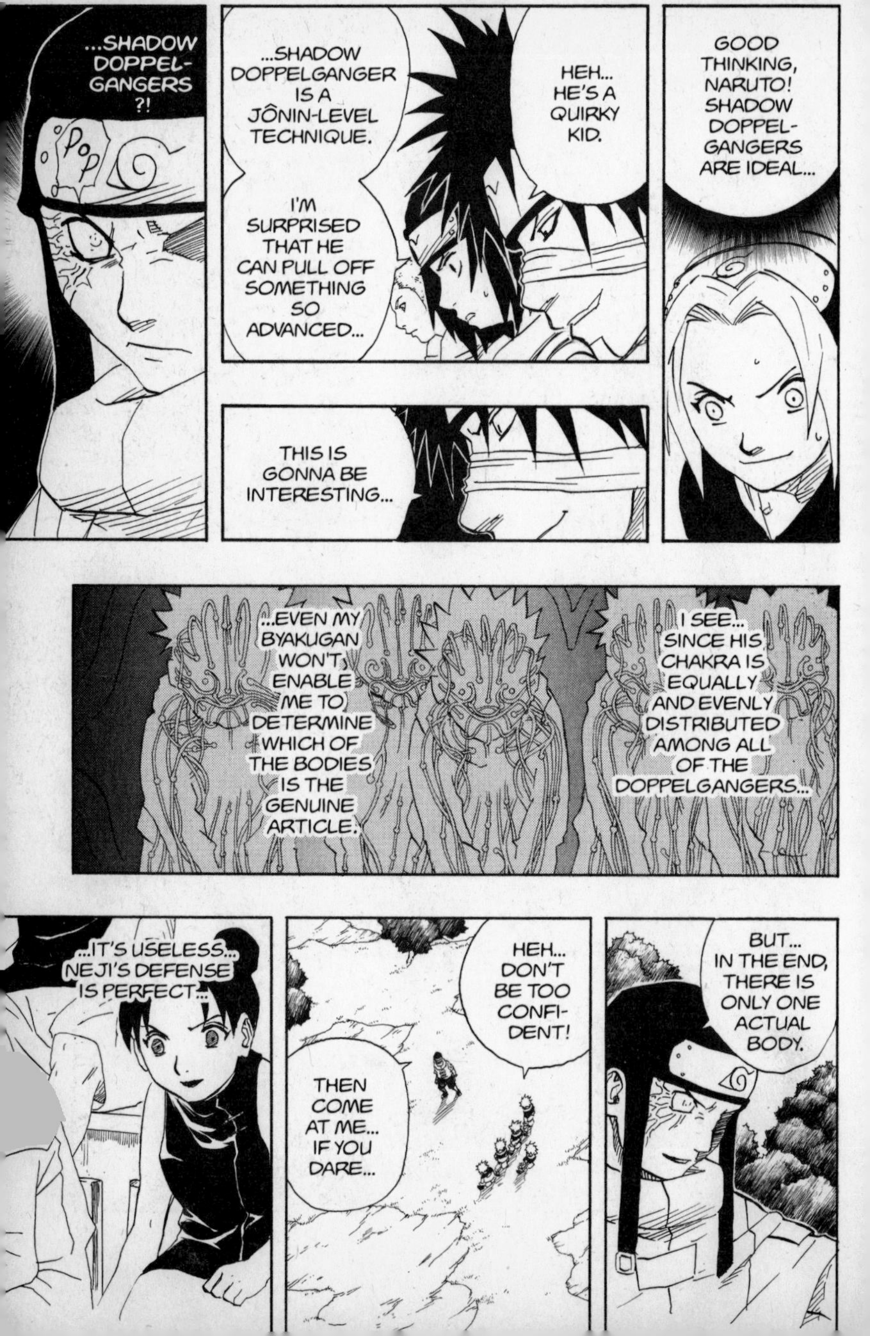
GOOD THINKING, NARUTO! SHADOW DOPPEL-GANGERS ARE IDEAL...
HEH... HE'S A QUIRKY KID.
...SHADOW DOPPELGANGER IS A JÔNIN-LEVEL TECHNIQUE.
I'M SURPRISED THAT HE CAN PULL OFF SOMETHING SO ADVANCED...
THIS IS GONNA BE INTERESTING...
...SHADOW DOPPEL-GANGERS ?!
POP
I SEE... SINCE HIS CHAKRA IS EQUALLY AND EVENLY DISTRIBUTED AMONG ALL OF THE DOPPELGANGERS...
...EVEN MY BYAKUGAN WON'T ENABLE ME TO DETERMINE WHICH OF THE BODIES IS THE GENUINE ARTICLE.
BUT... IN THE END, THERE IS ONLY ONE ACTUAL BODY.
HEH... DON'T BE TOO CONFI-DENT!
THEN COME AT ME... IF YOU DARE...
...IT'S USELESS... NEJI'S DEFENSE IS PERFECT...

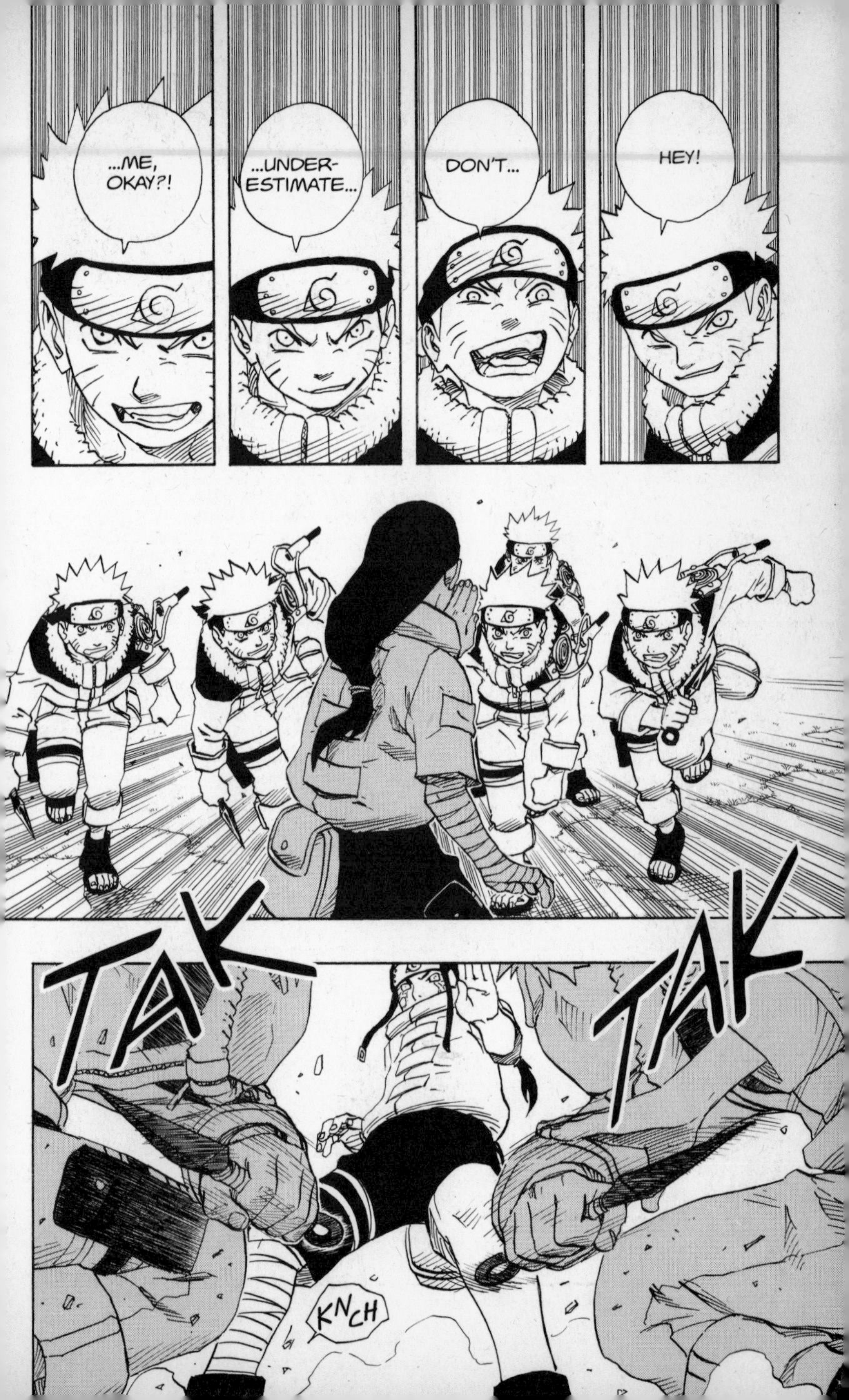
HEY!
DON'T...
...UNDER-ESTIMATE...
...ME, OKAY?!
TAK
TAK
KNCH

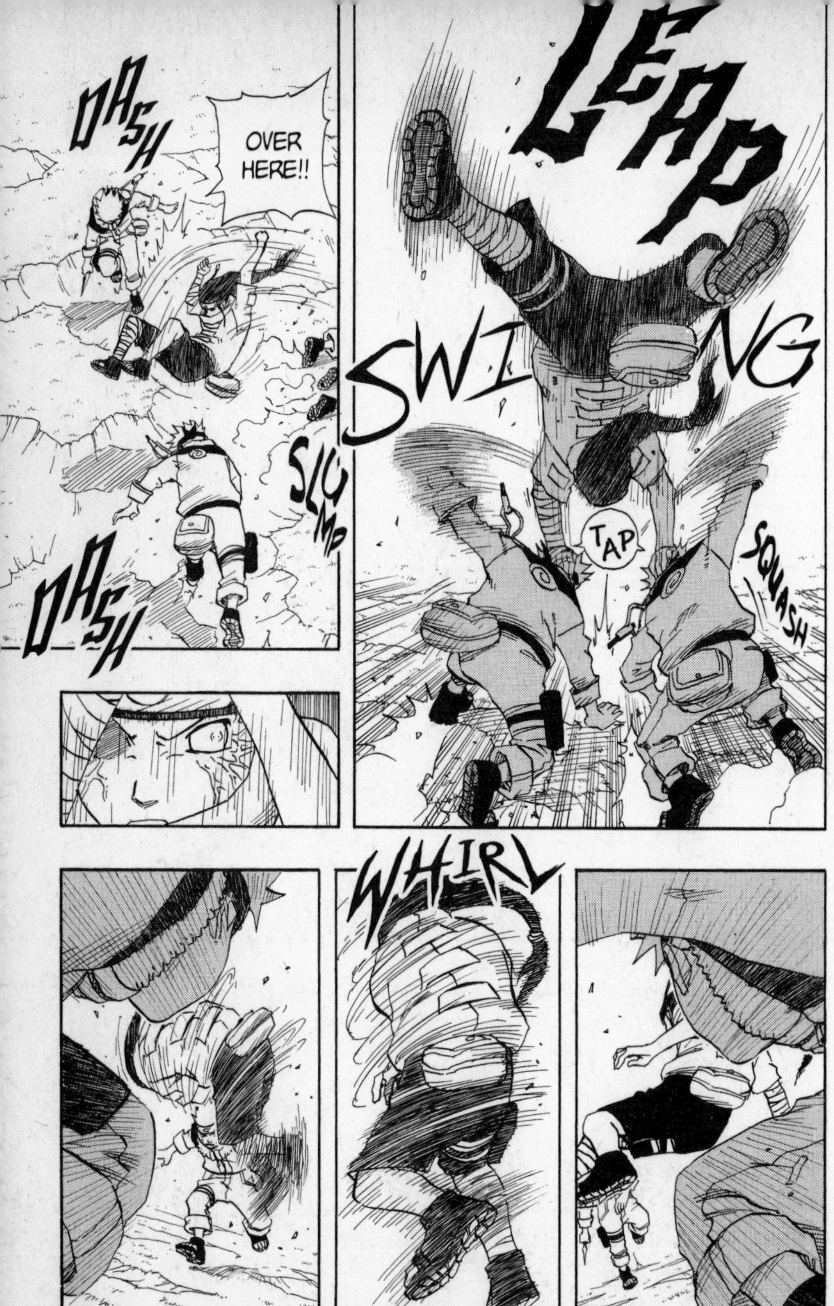
LEAP
SWING
SQUASH
TAP
OVER HERE!!
DASH
SLUMP
DASH
WHIRL

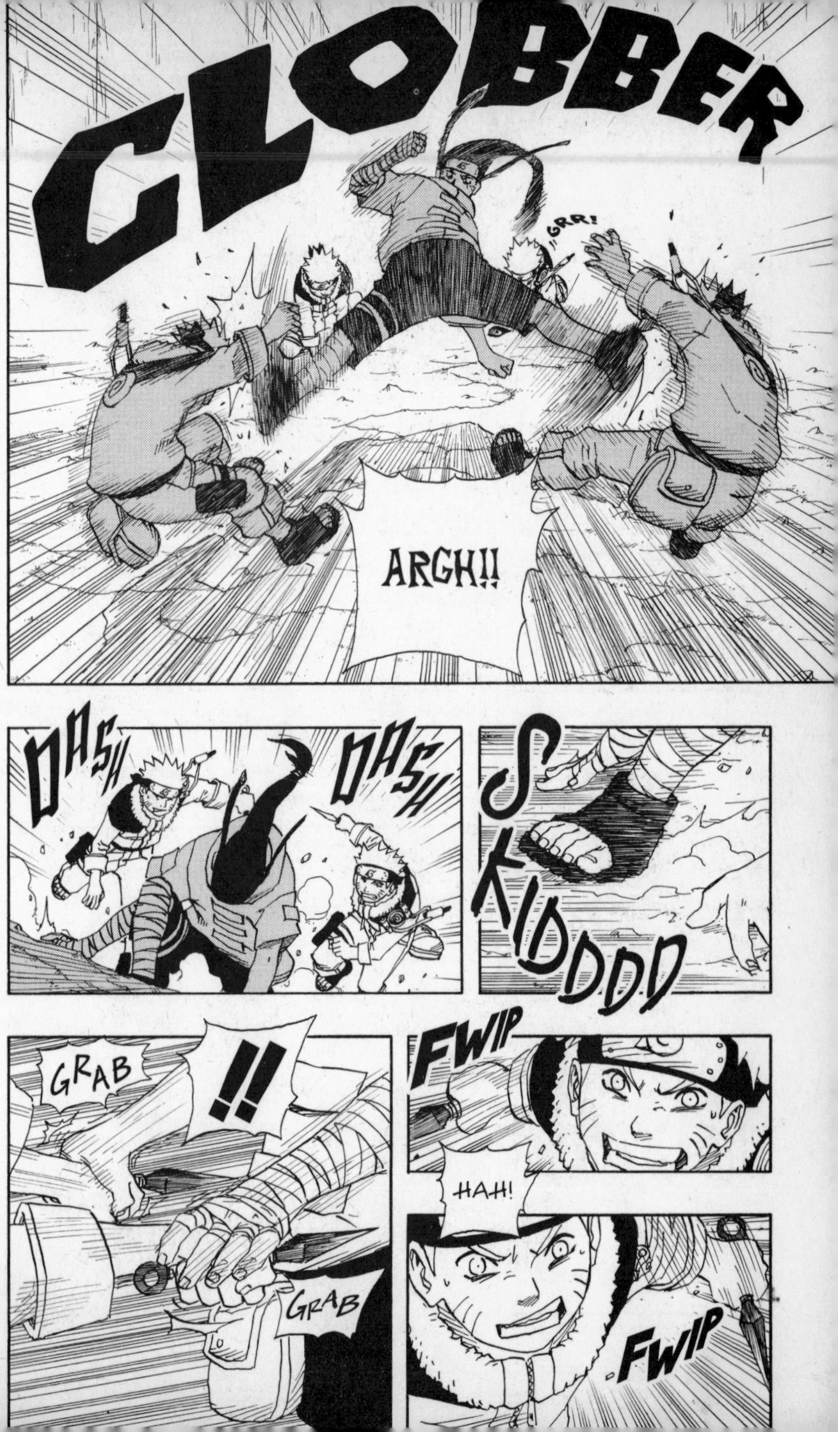
CLOBBER
GRR!
ARGH!!
SKIDDDD
DASH
DASH
FWIP
HAH!
FWIP
!!
GRAB
GRAB

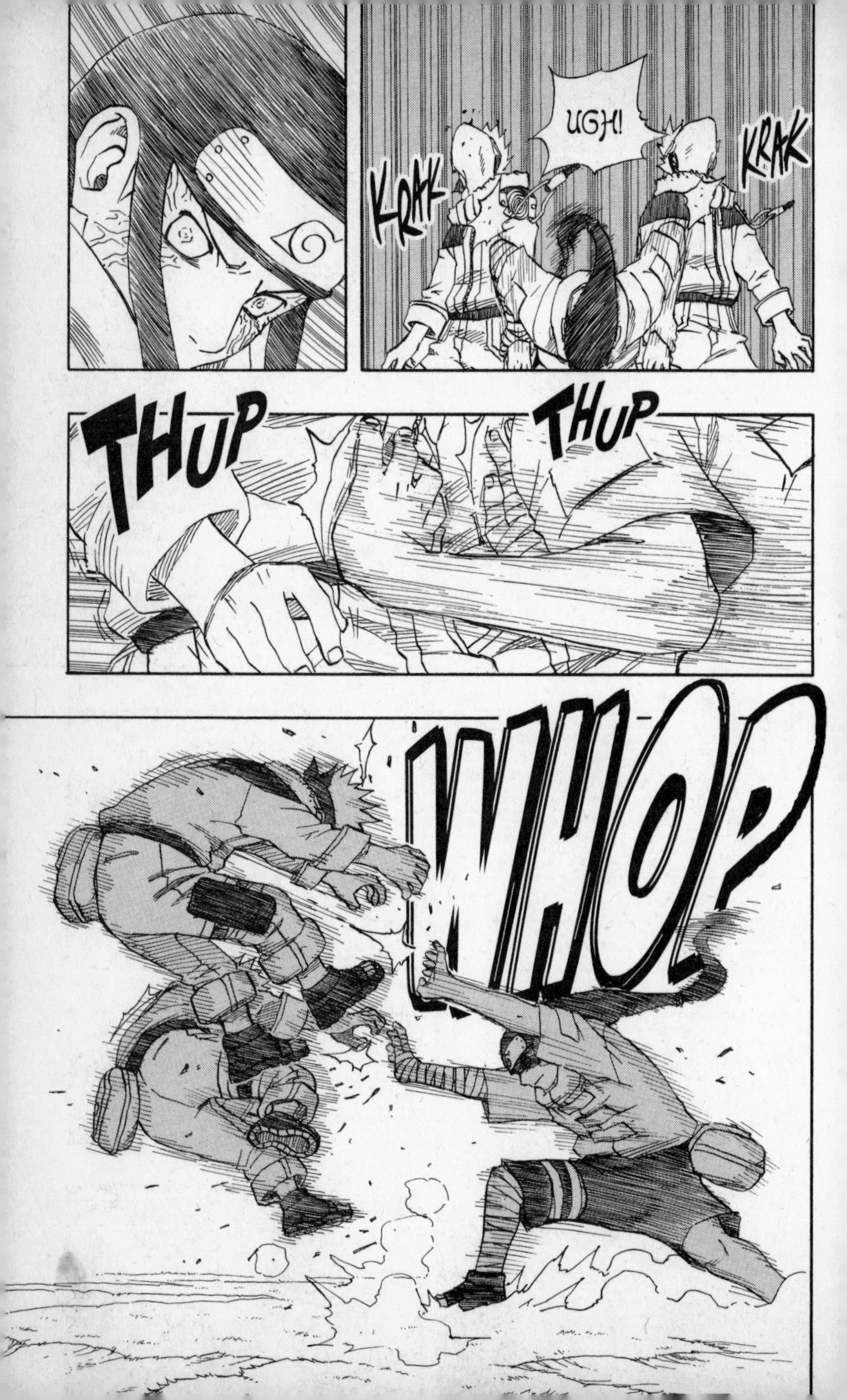
KRAK
UGH!
KRAK
THUP
THUP
WHO?

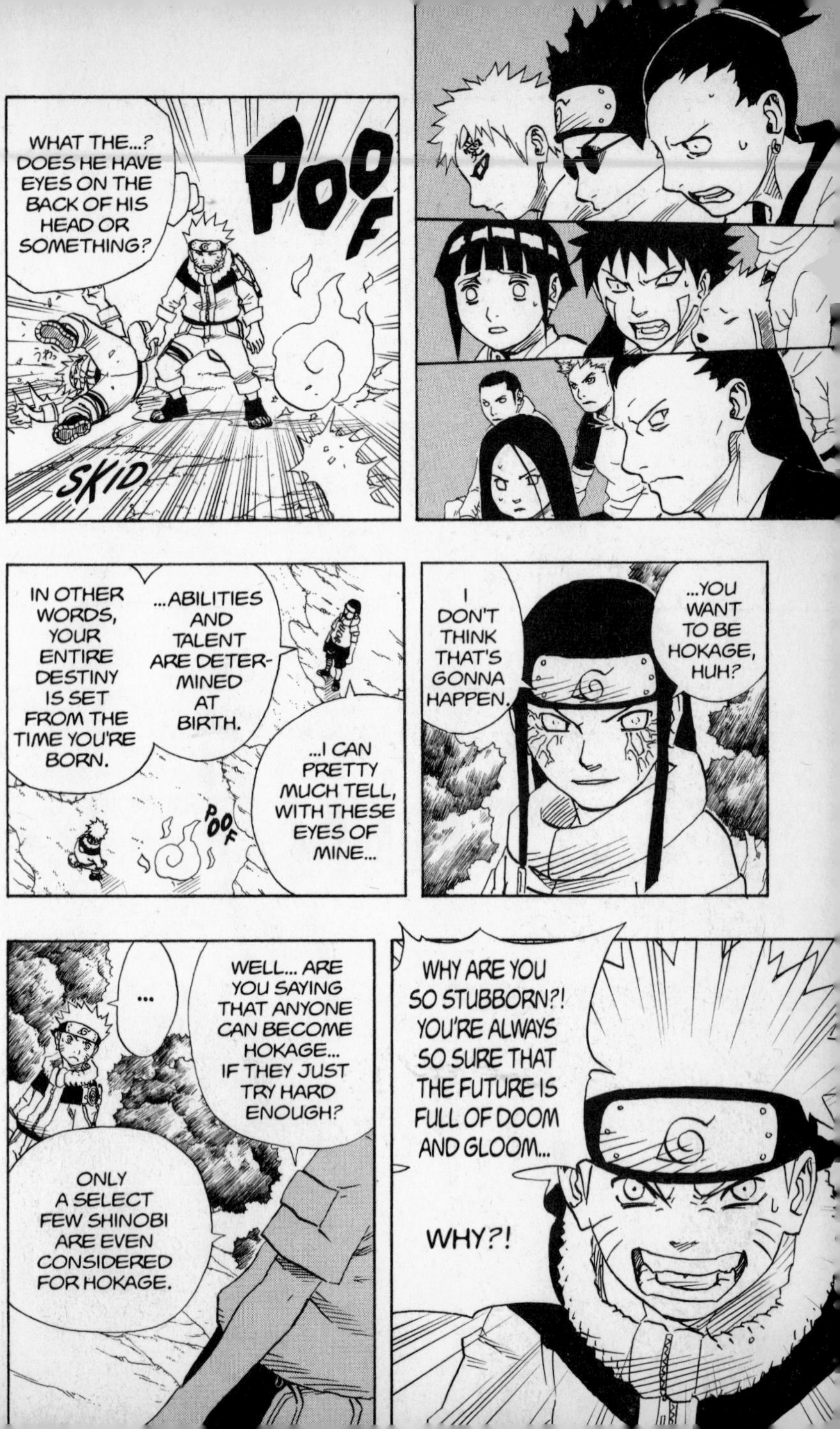
WHAT THE...? DOES HE HAVE EYES ON THE BACK OF HIS HEAD OR SOMETHING?
POOF
SKID
...YOU WANT TO BE HOKAGE, HUH?
I DON'T THINK THAT'S GONNA HAPPEN.
...ABILITIES AND TALENT ARE DETERMINED AT BIRTH.
IN OTHER WORDS, YOUR ENTIRE DESTINY IS SET FROM THE TIME YOU'RE BORN.
...I CAN PRETTY MUCH TELL, WITH THESE EYES OF MINE...
POOF
WHY ARE YOU SO STUBBORN?! YOU'RE ALWAYS SO SURE THAT THE FUTURE IS FULL OF DOOM AND GLOOM...
WHY?!
WELL... ARE YOU SAYING THAT ANYONE CAN BECOME HOKAGE... IF THEY JUST TRY HARD ENOUGH?
...
ONLY A SELECT FEW SHINOBI ARE EVEN CONSIDERED FOR HOKAGE.

READ THIS WAY

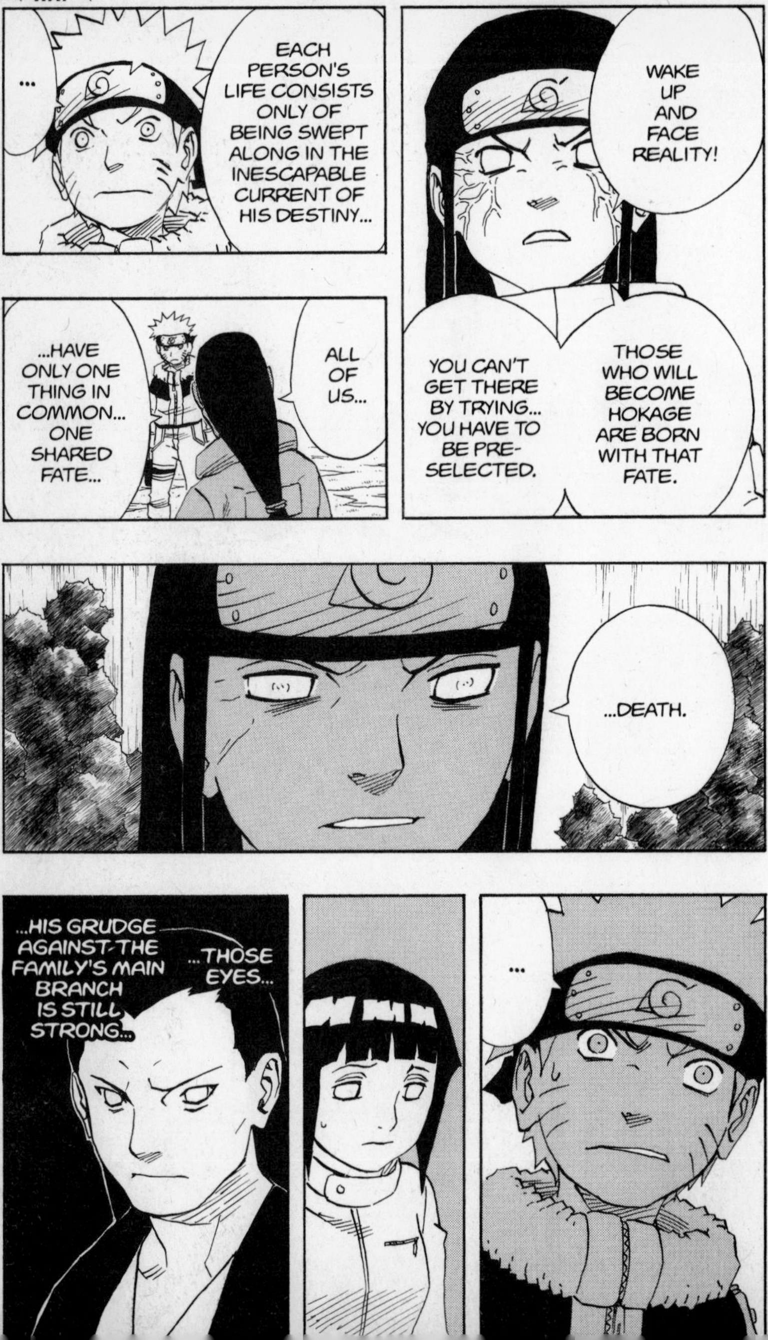
WAKE UP AND FACE REALITY!
THOSE WHO WILL BECOME HOKAGE ARE BORN WITH THAT FATE.
YOU CAN'T GET THERE BY TRYING... YOU HAVE TO BE PRE-SELECTED.
EACH PERSON'S LIFE CONSISTS ONLY OF BEING SWEPT ALONG IN THE INESCAPABLE CURRENT OF HIS DESTINY...
...
ALL OF US...
...HAVE ONLY ONE THING IN COMMON... ONE SHARED FATE...
...DEATH.
...
...THOSE EYES...
...HIS GRUDGE AGAINST THE FAMILY'S MAIN BRANCH IS STILL STRONG...

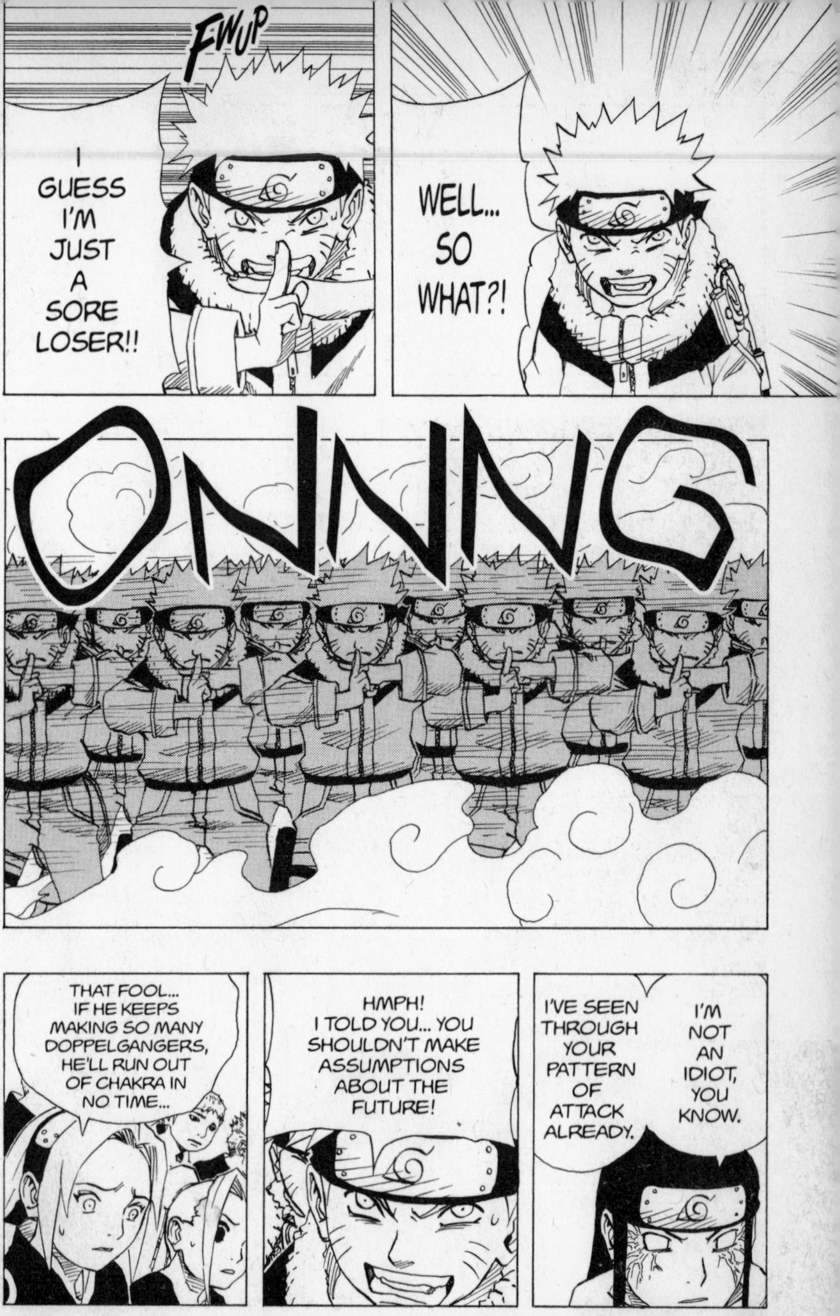
WELL... SO WHAT?!
FWUP
I GUESS I'M JUST A SORE LOSER!!
ONNNG
I'M NOT AN IDIOT, YOU KNOW.
I'VE SEEN THROUGH YOUR PATTERN OF ATTACK ALREADY.
HMPH! I TOLD YOU... YOU SHOULDN'T MAKE ASSUMPTIONS ABOUT THE FUTURE!
THAT FOOL... IF HE KEEPS MAKING SO MANY DOPPELGANGERS, HE'LL RUN OUT OF CHAKRA IN NO TIME...

READ THIS WAY

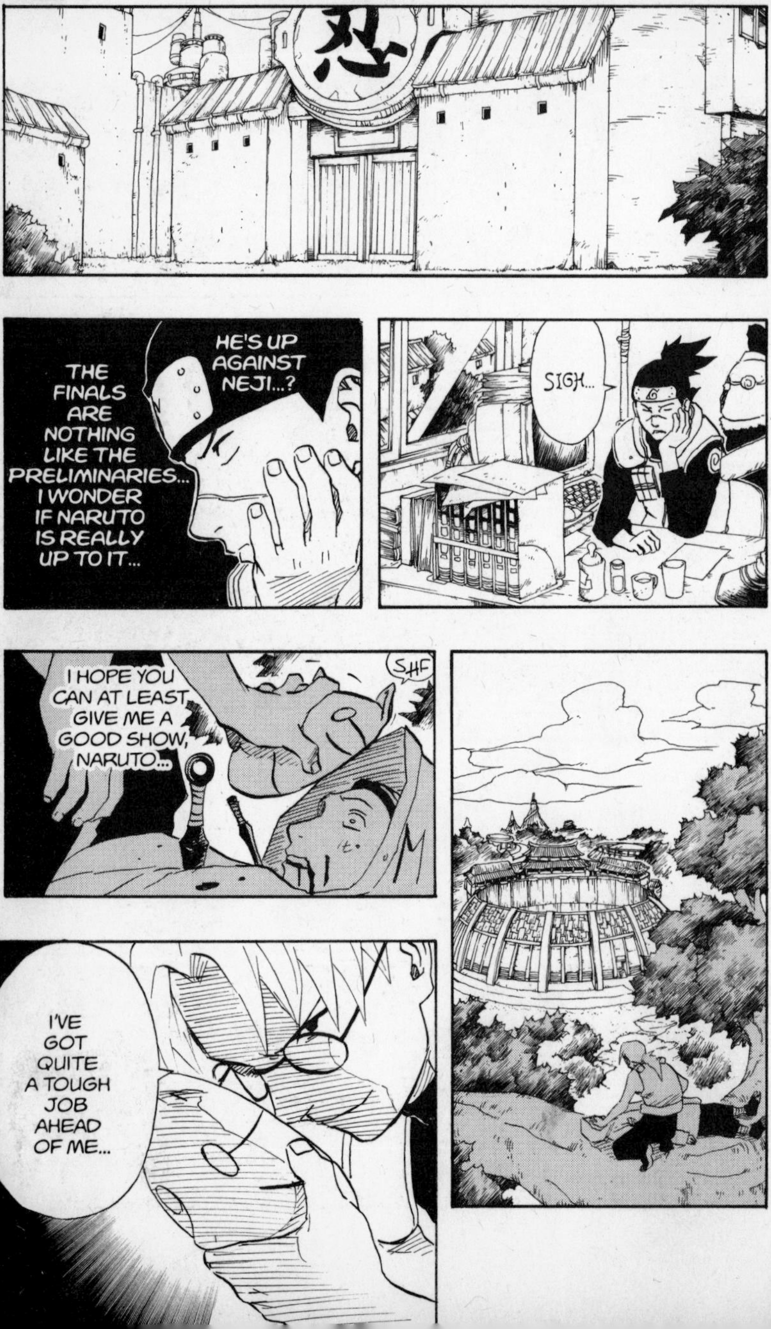
SIGH...
HE'S UP AGAINST NEJI...?
THE FINALS ARE NOTHING LIKE THE PRELIMINARIES... I WONDER IF NARUTO IS REALLY UP TO IT...
SHF
I HOPE YOU CAN AT LEAST GIVE ME A GOOD SHOW, NARUTO...
I'VE GOT QUITE A TOUGH JOB AHEAD OF ME...

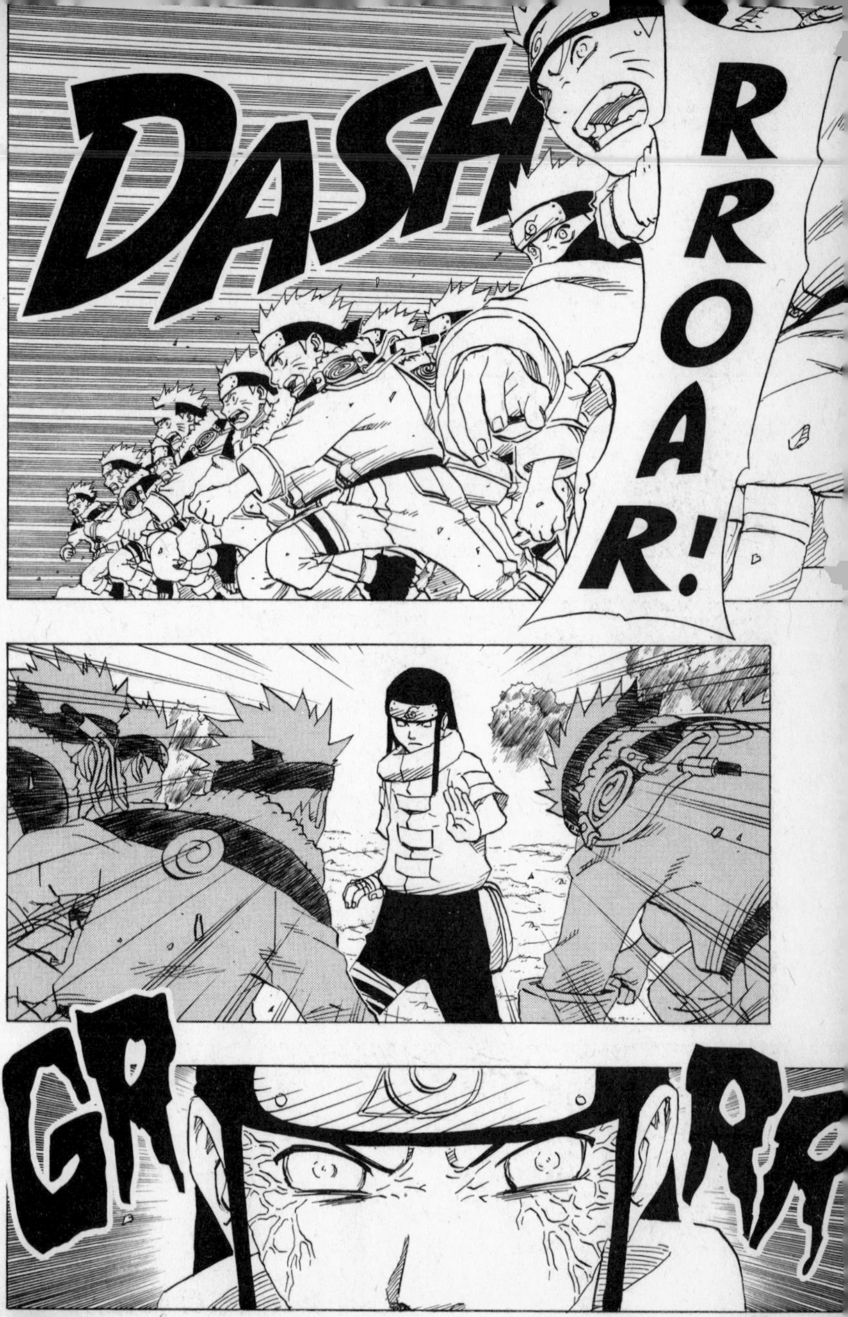
RROAR!
DASH
GR RA

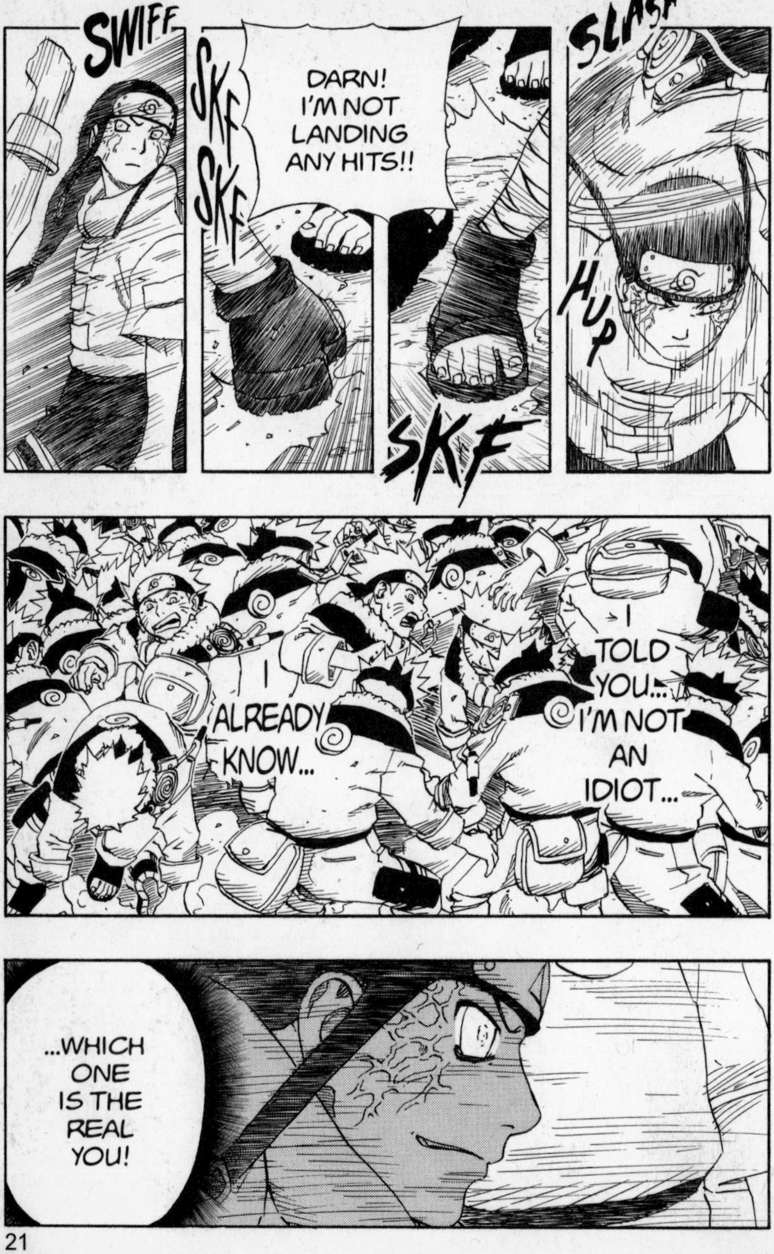
SLASH
HUP
SKF
SKF SKF
DARN! I'M NOT LANDING ANY HITS!!
SWIFF
I TOLD YOU... I'M NOT AN IDIOT...
I ALREADY KNOW...
...WHICH ONE IS THE REAL YOU!

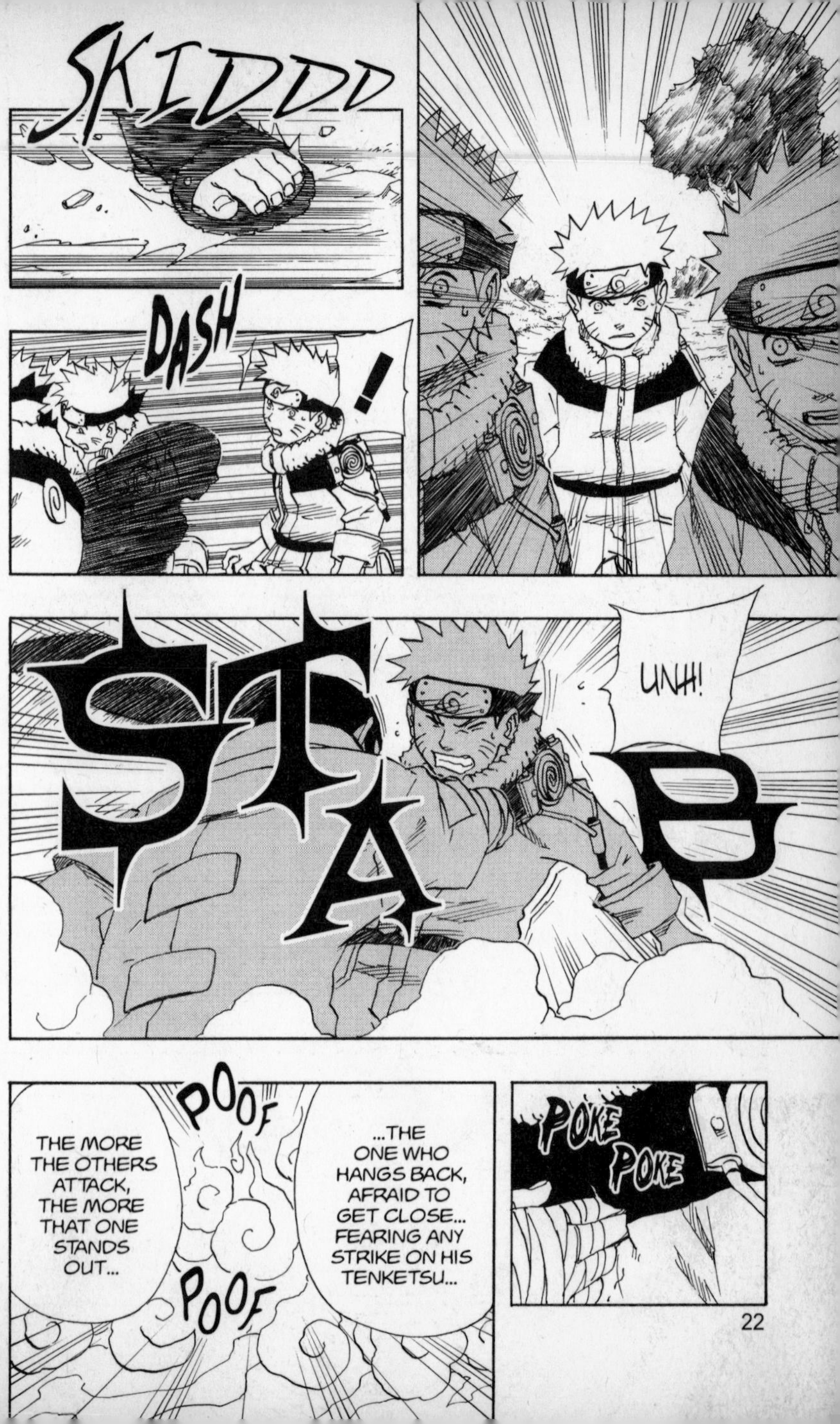

SKIDDD
DASH
!
STAB
UNH!
POKE
POKE
POOF
...THE ONE WHO HANGS BACK, AFRAID TO GET CLOSE... FEARING ANY STRIKE ON HIS TENKETSU...
THE MORE THE OTHERS ATTACK, THE MORE THAT ONE STANDS OUT...
POOF

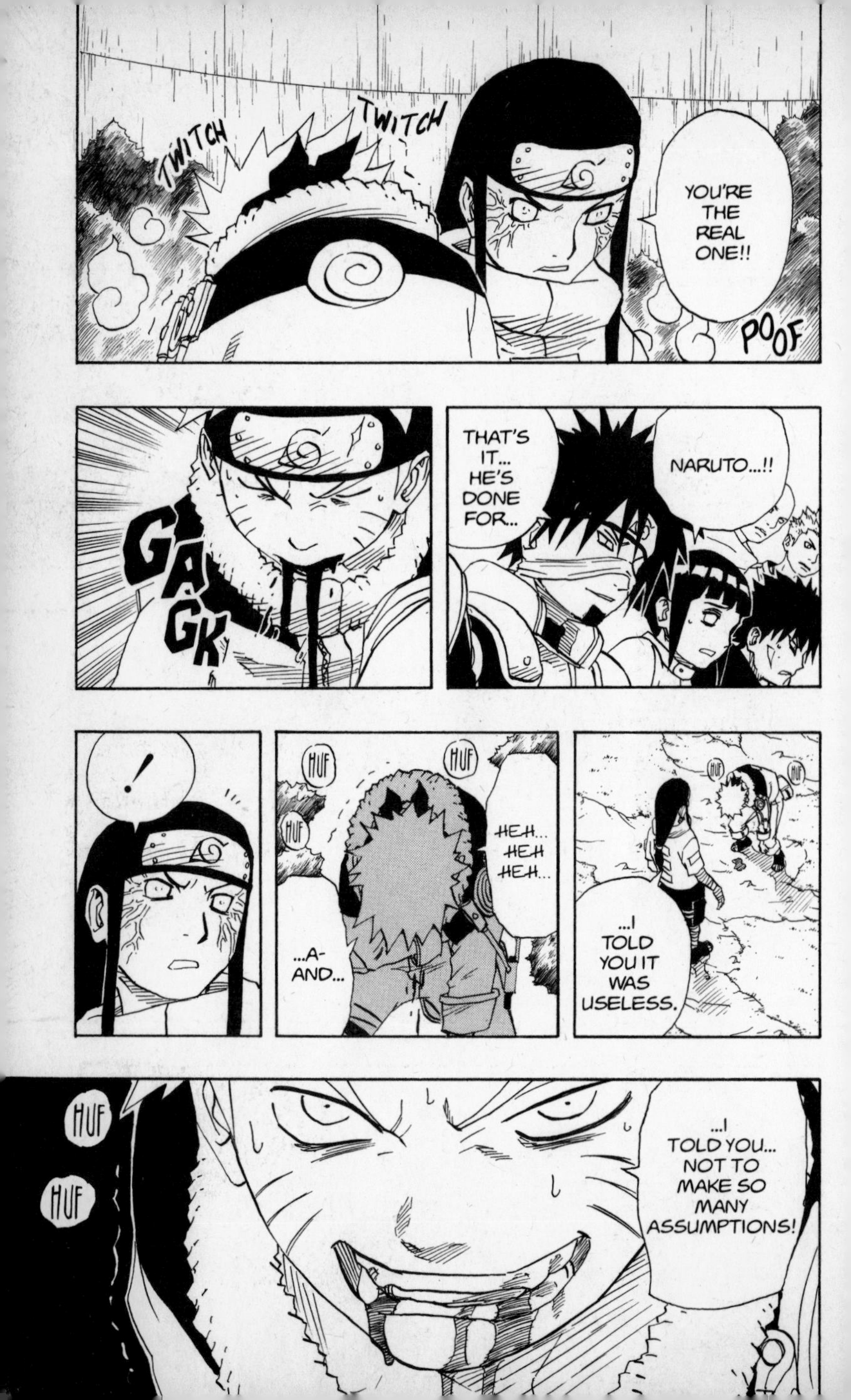
TWITCH
TWITCH
YOU'RE THE REAL ONE!!
POOF
NARUTO...!!
THAT'S IT... HE'S DONE FOR...
GAGK
...I TOLD YOU IT WAS USELESS.
HUF
HUF
HUF
HUF
HEH... HEH HEH...
...A- AND...
HUF
!
...I TOLD YOU... NOT TO MAKE SO MANY ASSUMPTIONS!
HUF
HUF

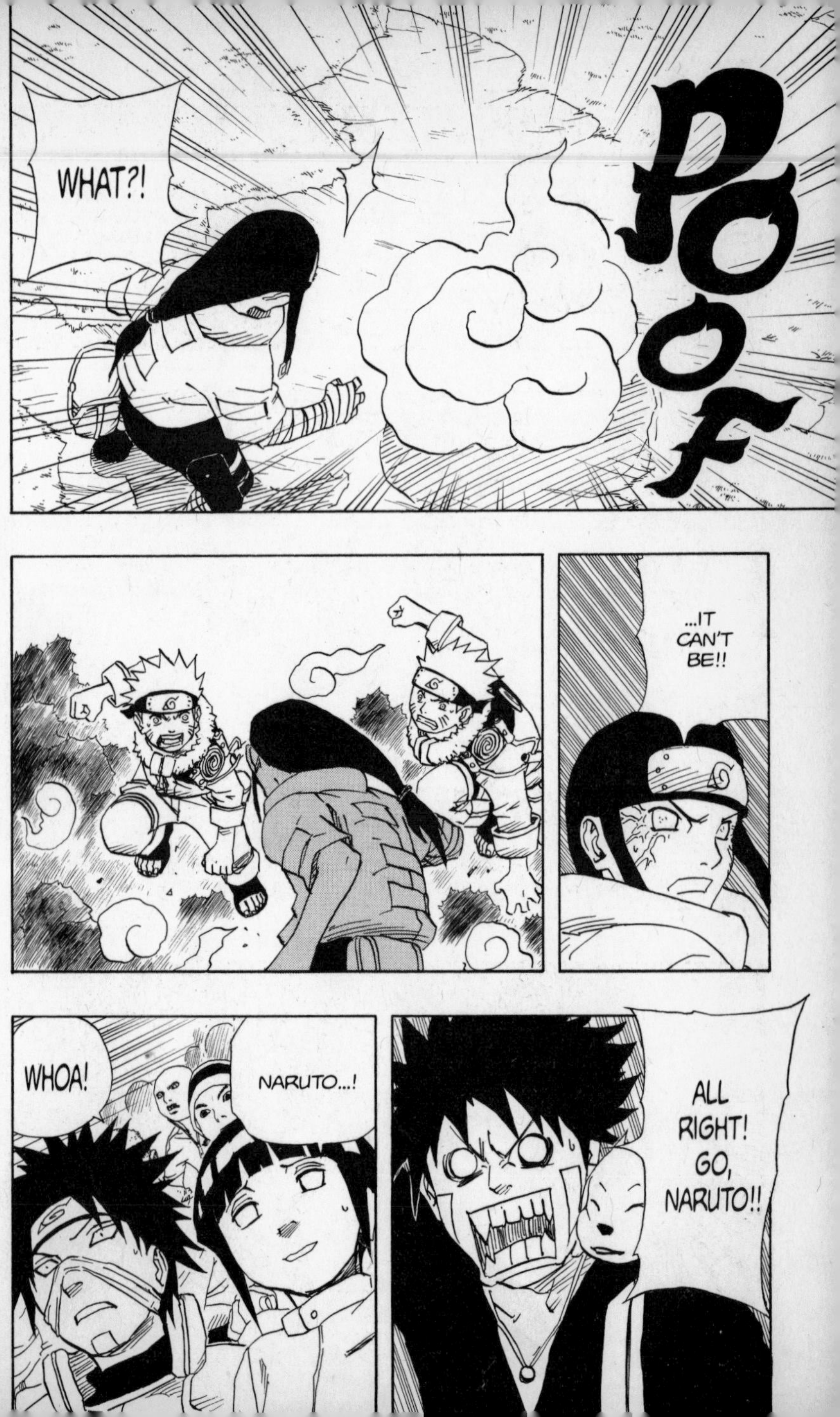
POOF
WHAT?!
...IT CAN'T BE!!
ALL RIGHT! GO, NARUTO!!
NARUTO...!
WHOA!

READ THIS WAY

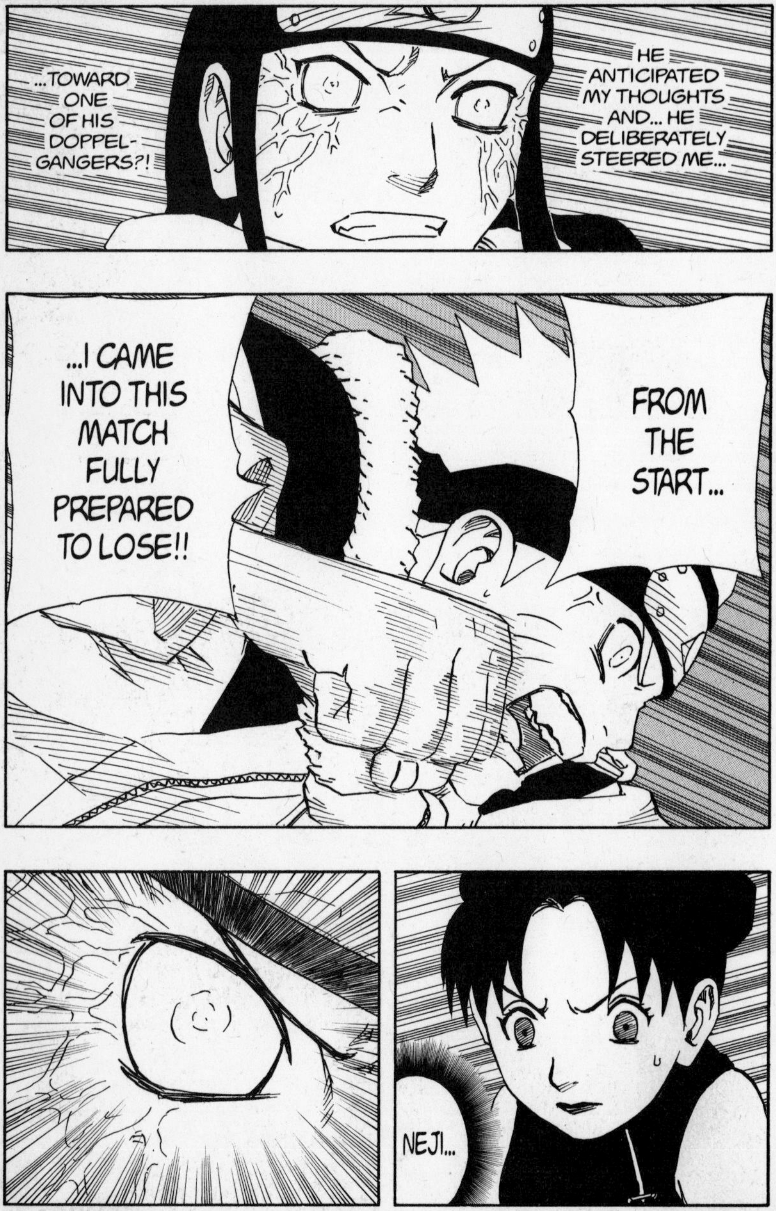

HE ANTICIPATED MY THOUGHTS AND... HE DELIBERATELY STEERED ME...
...TOWARD ONE OF HIS DOPPEL-GANGERS?!
FROM THE START...
...I CAME INTO THIS MATCH FULLY PREPARED TO LOSE!!
NEJI...

A MESSAGE FROM KISHIMOTO MASASHI TO ALL OF HIS ASSISTANTS

I CAN'T BELIEVE IT'S ALREADY BEEN OVER TWO YEARS SINCE WE STARTED WORKING ON *NARUTO*! I WANT TO EXPRESS MY SINCERE GRATITUDE TO ALL OF YOU, WHO ALWAYS LISTEN SILENTLY TO MY SELFISH, UNREASONABLE DEMANDS AND CATER TO MY EVERY WHIM.

I HAVE BECOME KEENLY AWARE OF THE FACT THAT MANGA IS NOT SOMETHING ONE PERSON CAN CREATE ALL BY HIMSELF. I HONESTLY BELIEVE THAT YOUR HARD WORK IS WHAT HAS ALLOWED *NARUTO* TO COME THIS FAR WHILE MAINTAINING SUCH HIGH STANDARDS OF QUALITY. I TRULY THANK YOU FOR EVERY SINGLE WEEK WE'VE WORKED TOGETHER!!

AND SO, TO ALL OF YOU READERS OUT THERE... STARTING WITH THE NEXT BONUS PAGE, PLEASE ENJOY THE COMMEMORATIVE *NARUTO* SECOND ANNIVERSARY DRAWINGS BY MY INSPIRING AND DEDICATED ASSISTANTS!

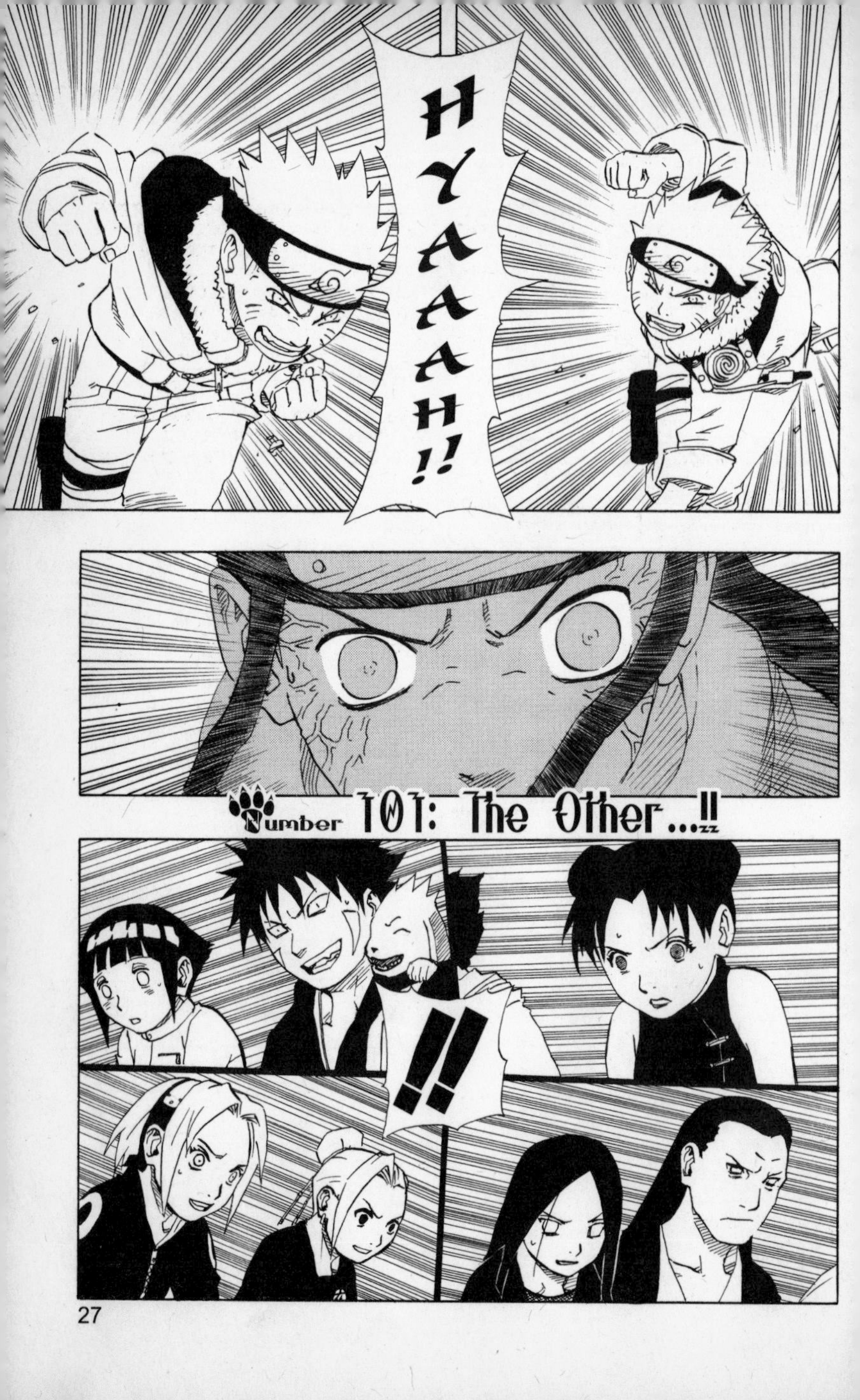
HYAAAAH!!
Number 101: The Other...!!
!!

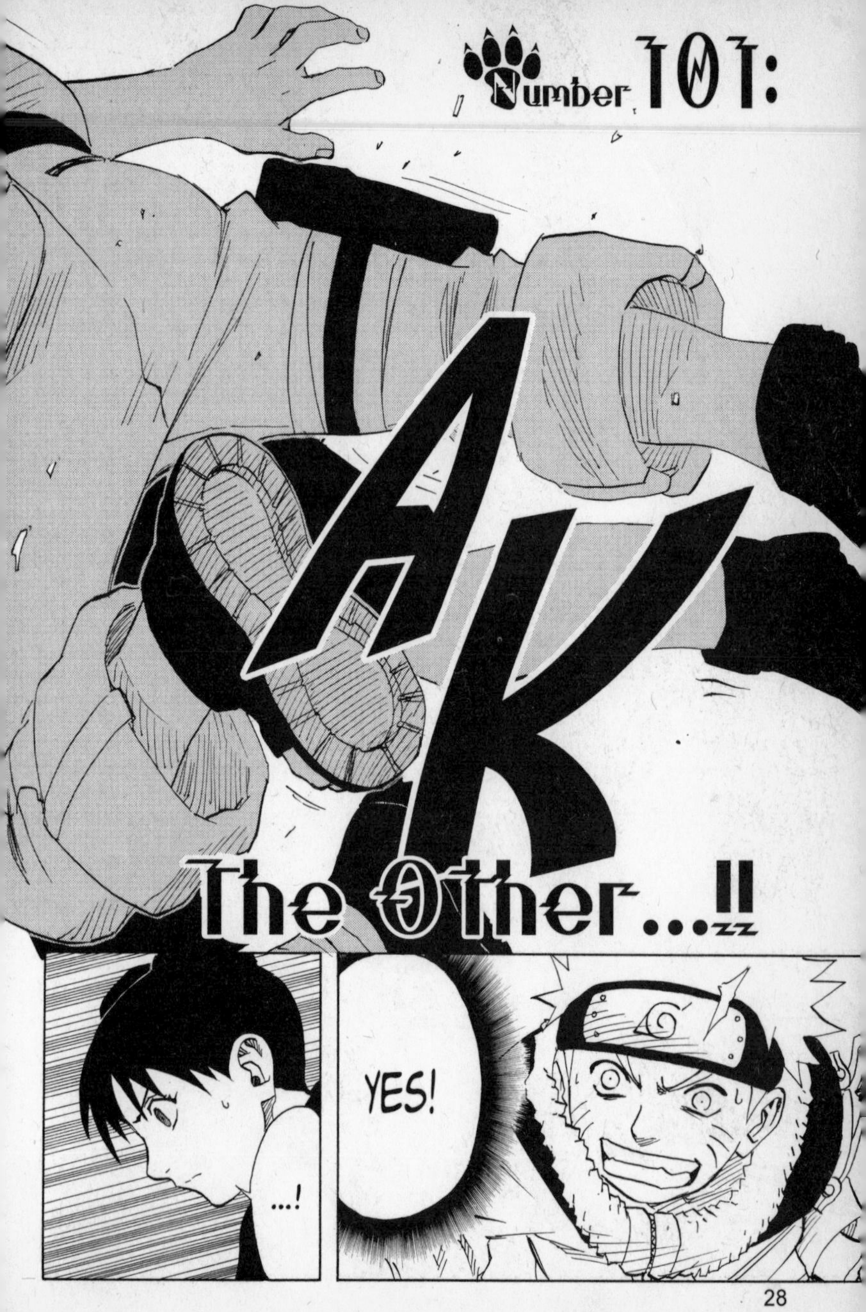
Number 101:
The Other...!!
TAK
YES!
...!

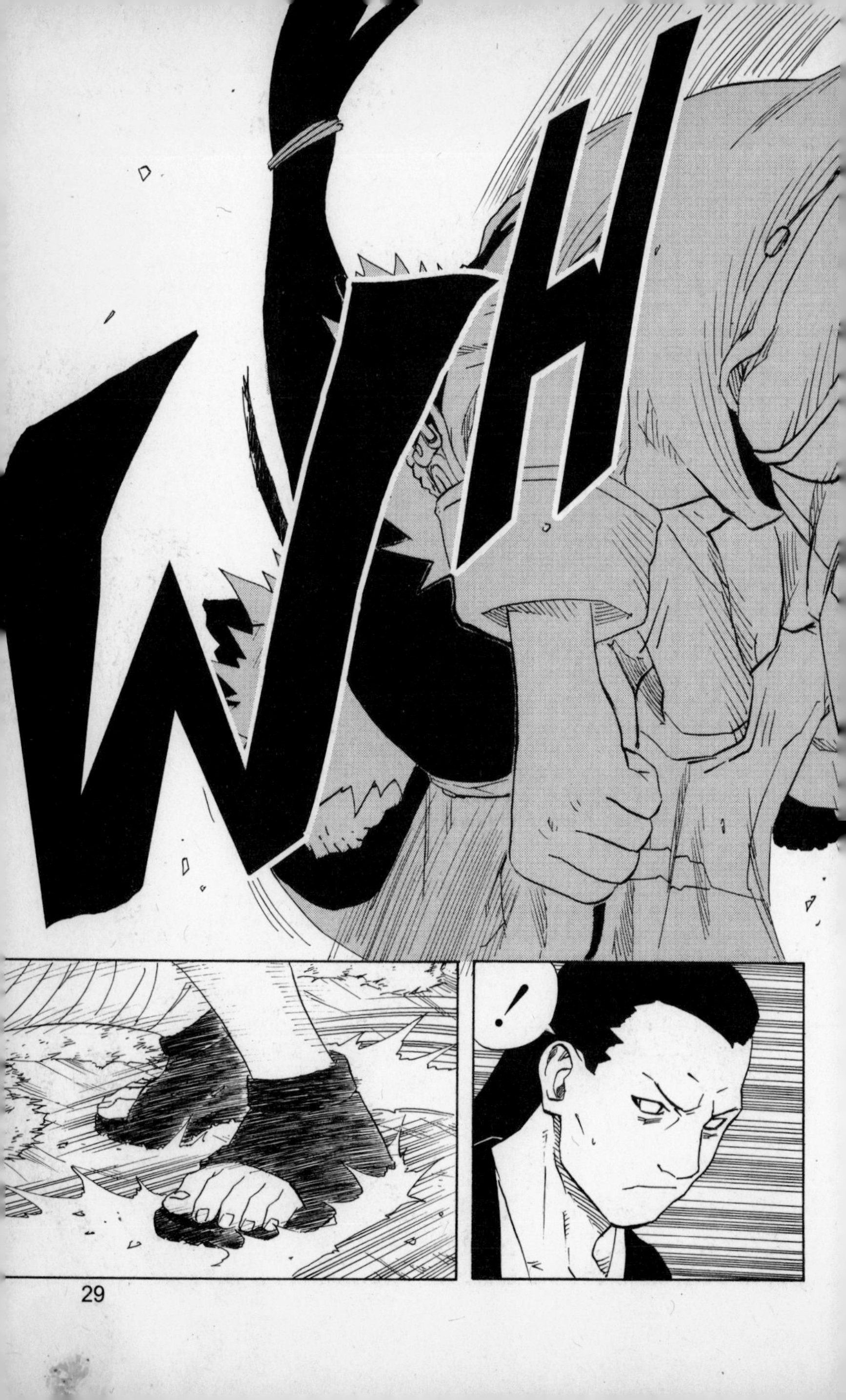
WH
!

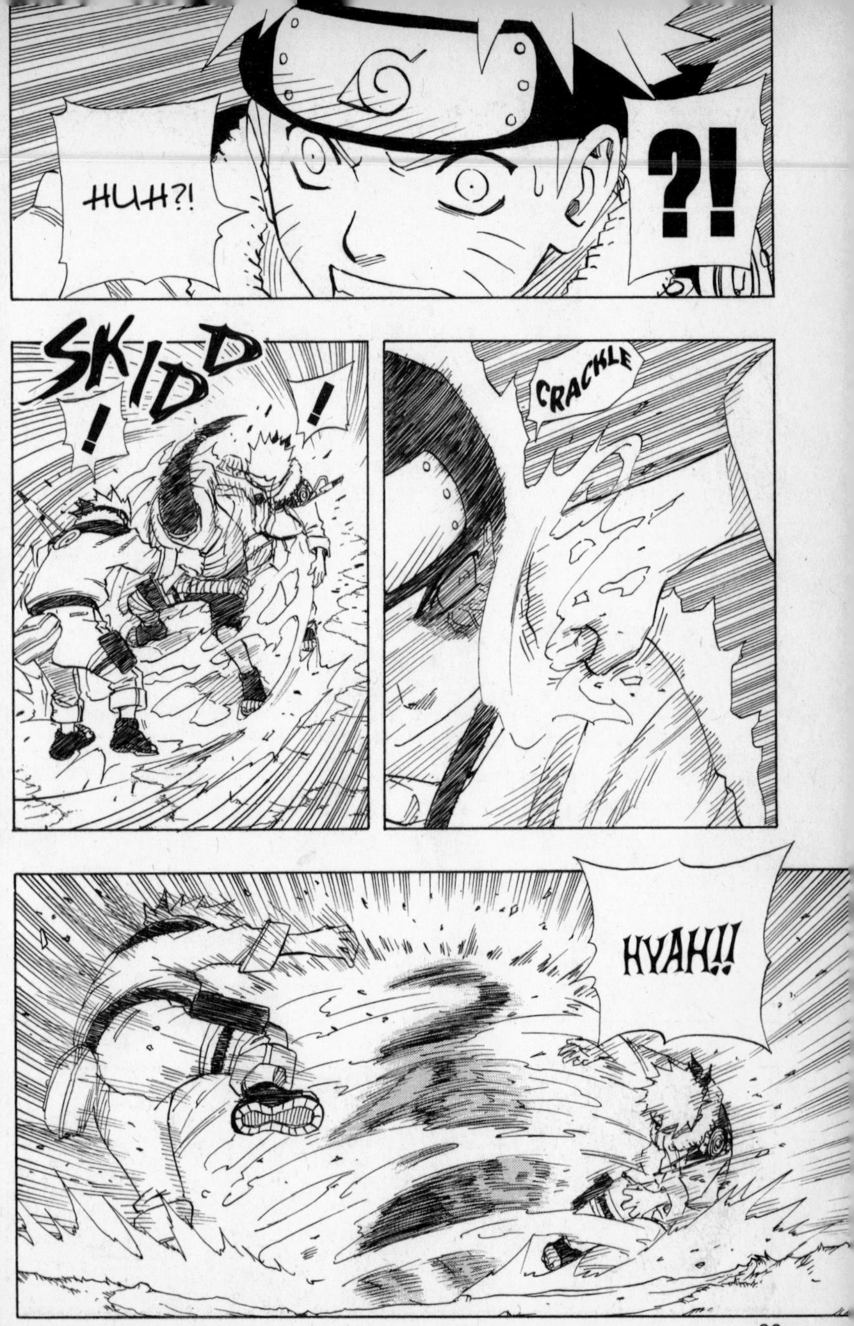
?!
HUH?!
CRACKLE
SKIDD
!
!
HYAH!!

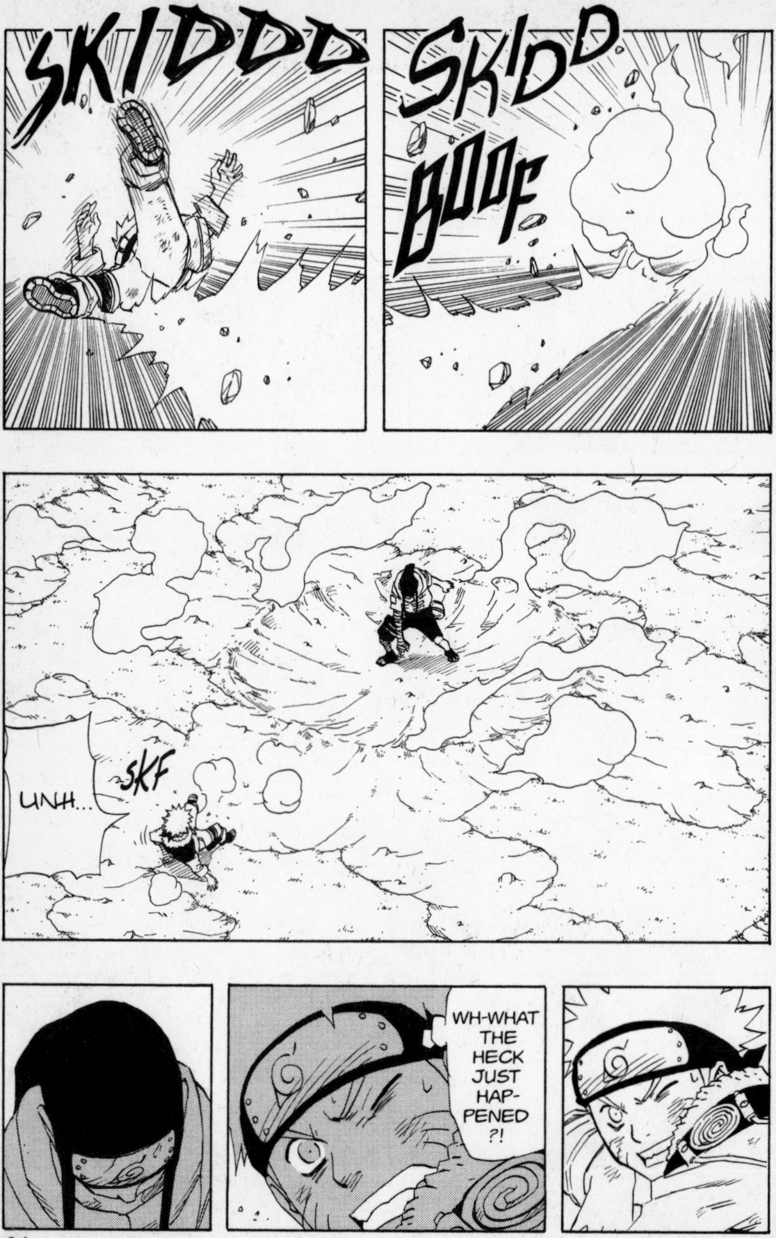
SKIDD
BOOF
SKIDDD
SKF
UNH...
WH-WHAT THE HECK JUST HAP-PENED ?!

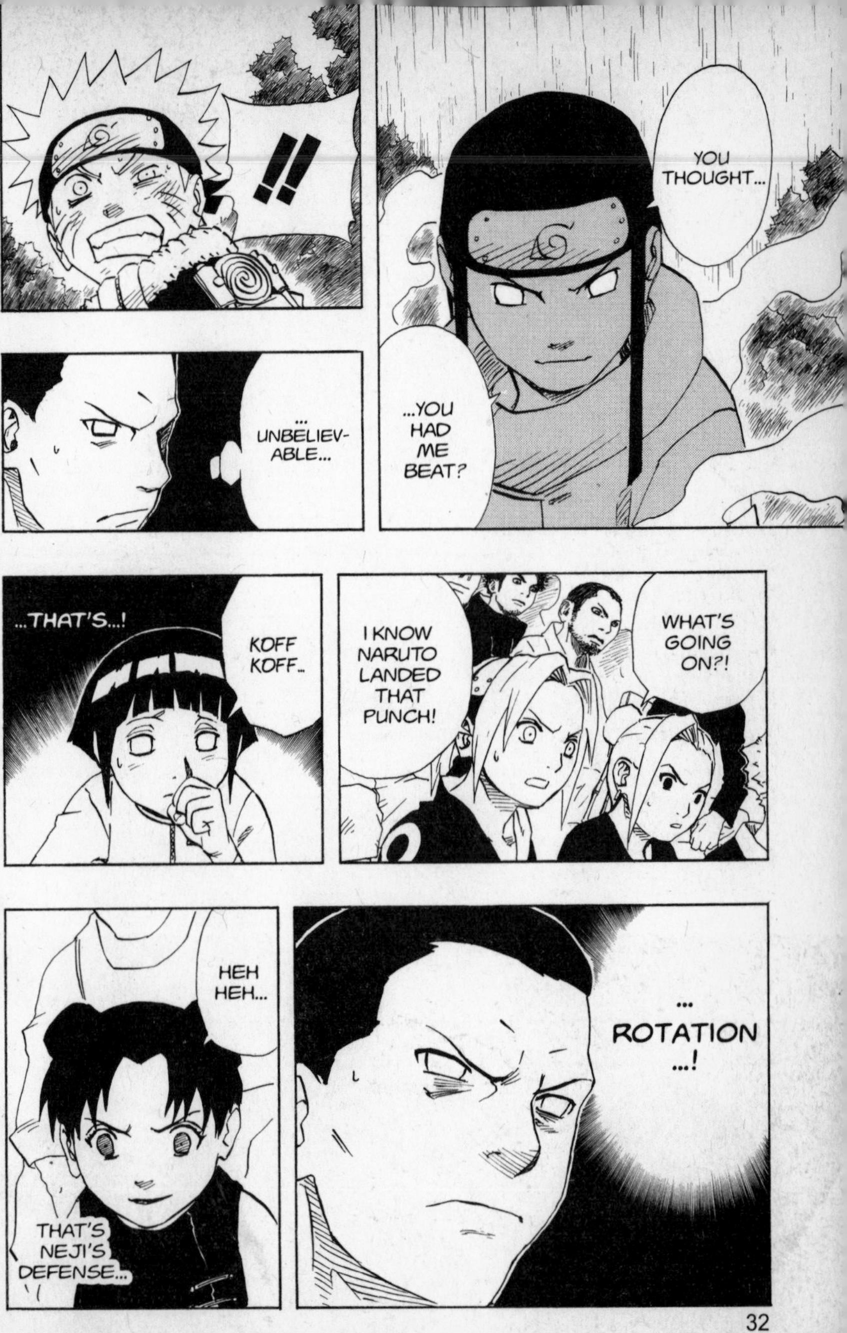
YOU THOUGHT...
...YOU HAD ME BEAT?
!!
... UNBELIEV-ABLE...
WHAT'S GOING ON?!
I KNOW NARUTO LANDED THAT PUNCH!
KOFF KOFF..
...THAT'S...!
... ROTATION ...!
HEH HEH...
THAT'S NEJI'S DEFENSE...

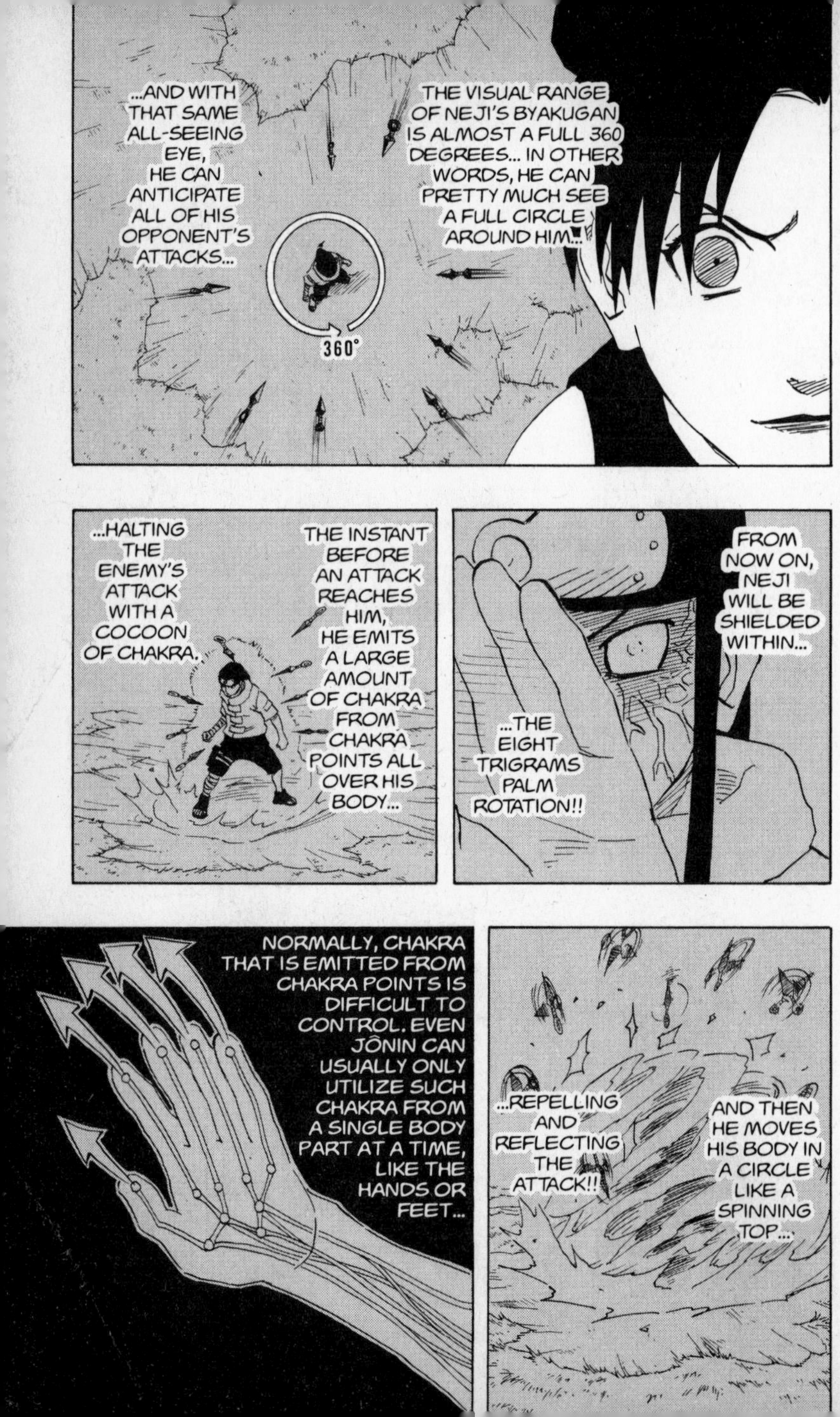
THE VISUAL RANGE OF NEJI'S BYAKUGAN IS ALMOST A FULL 360 DEGREES... IN OTHER WORDS, HE CAN PRETTY MUCH SEE A FULL CIRCLE AROUND HIM...
...AND WITH THAT SAME ALL-SEEING EYE, HE CAN ANTICIPATE ALL OF HIS OPPONENT'S ATTACKS...
360°
FROM NOW ON, NEJI WILL BE SHIELDED WITHIN...
...THE EIGHT TRIGRAMS PALM ROTATION!!
THE INSTANT BEFORE AN ATTACK REACHES HIM, HE EMITS A LARGE AMOUNT OF CHAKRA FROM CHAKRA POINTS ALL OVER HIS BODY...
...HALTING THE ENEMY'S ATTACK WITH A COCOON OF CHAKRA.
AND THEN HE MOVES HIS BODY IN A CIRCLE LIKE A SPINNING TOP...
...REPELLING AND REFLECTING THE ATTACK!!
NORMALLY, CHAKRA THAT IS EMITTED FROM CHAKRA POINTS IS DIFFICULT TO CONTROL. EVEN JÔNIN CAN USUALLY ONLY UTILIZE SUCH CHAKRA FROM A SINGLE BODY PART AT A TIME, LIKE THE HANDS OR FEET...

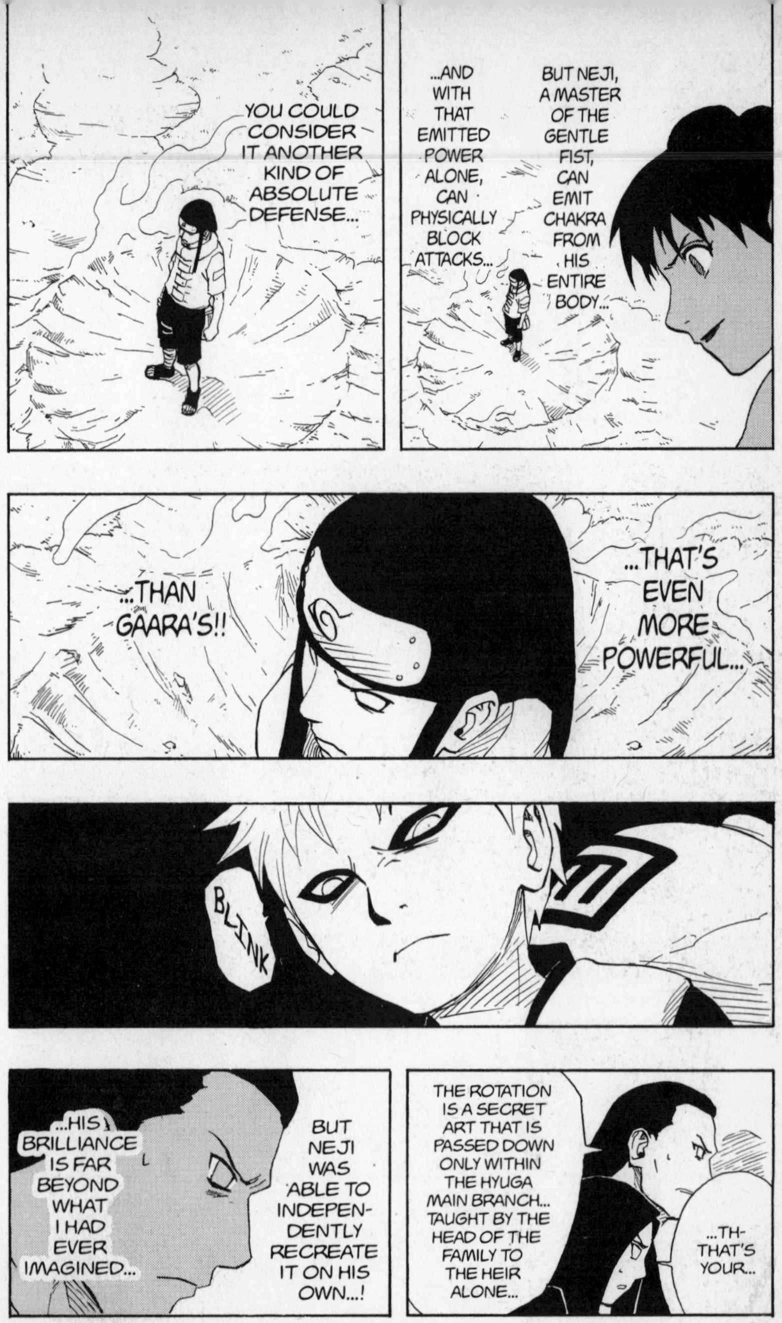
BUT NEJI, A MASTER OF THE GENTLE FIST, CAN EMIT CHAKRA FROM HIS ENTIRE BODY...
...AND WITH THAT EMITTED POWER ALONE, CAN PHYSICALLY BLOCK ATTACKS...
YOU COULD CONSIDER IT ANOTHER KIND OF ABSOLUTE DEFENSE...
...THAT'S EVEN MORE POWERFUL...
...THAN GAARA'S!!
BLINK
THE ROTATION IS A SECRET ART THAT IS PASSED DOWN ONLY WITHIN THE HYUGA MAIN BRANCH... TAUGHT BY THE HEAD OF THE FAMILY TO THE HEIR ALONE...
...TH- THAT'S YOUR...
BUT NEJI WAS ABLE TO INDEPEN- DENTLY RECREATE IT ON HIS OWN...!
...HIS BRILLIANCE IS FAR BEYOND WHAT I HAD EVER IMAGINED...

READ THIS WAY

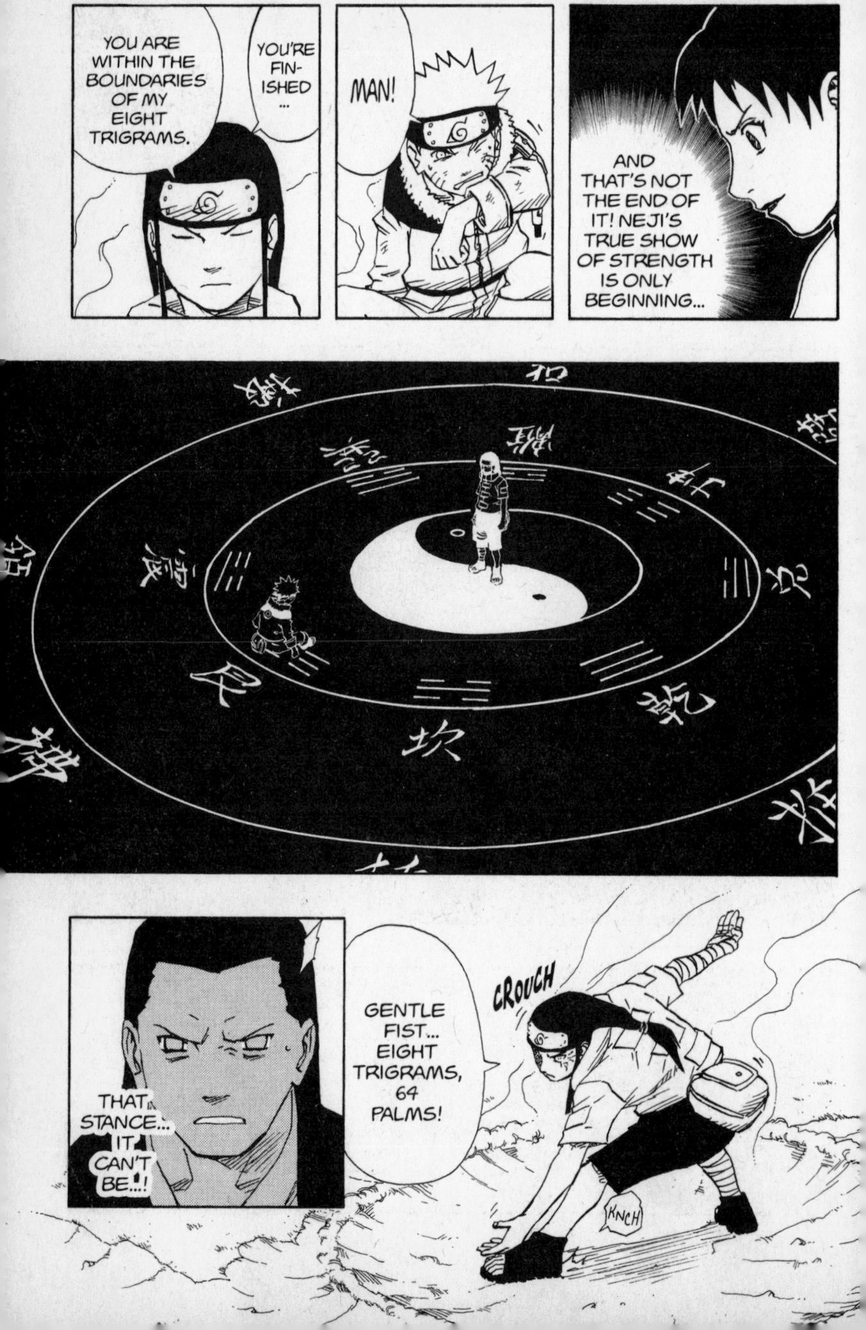
AND THAT'S NOT THE END OF IT! NEJI'S TRUE SHOW OF STRENGTH IS ONLY BEGINNING...
MAN!
YOU'RE FIN- ISHED ...
YOU ARE WITHIN THE BOUNDARIES OF MY EIGHT TRIGRAMS.
CROUCH
GENTLE FIST... EIGHT TRIGRAMS, 64 PALMS!
KNCH
THAT STANCE... IT CAN'T BE...!!

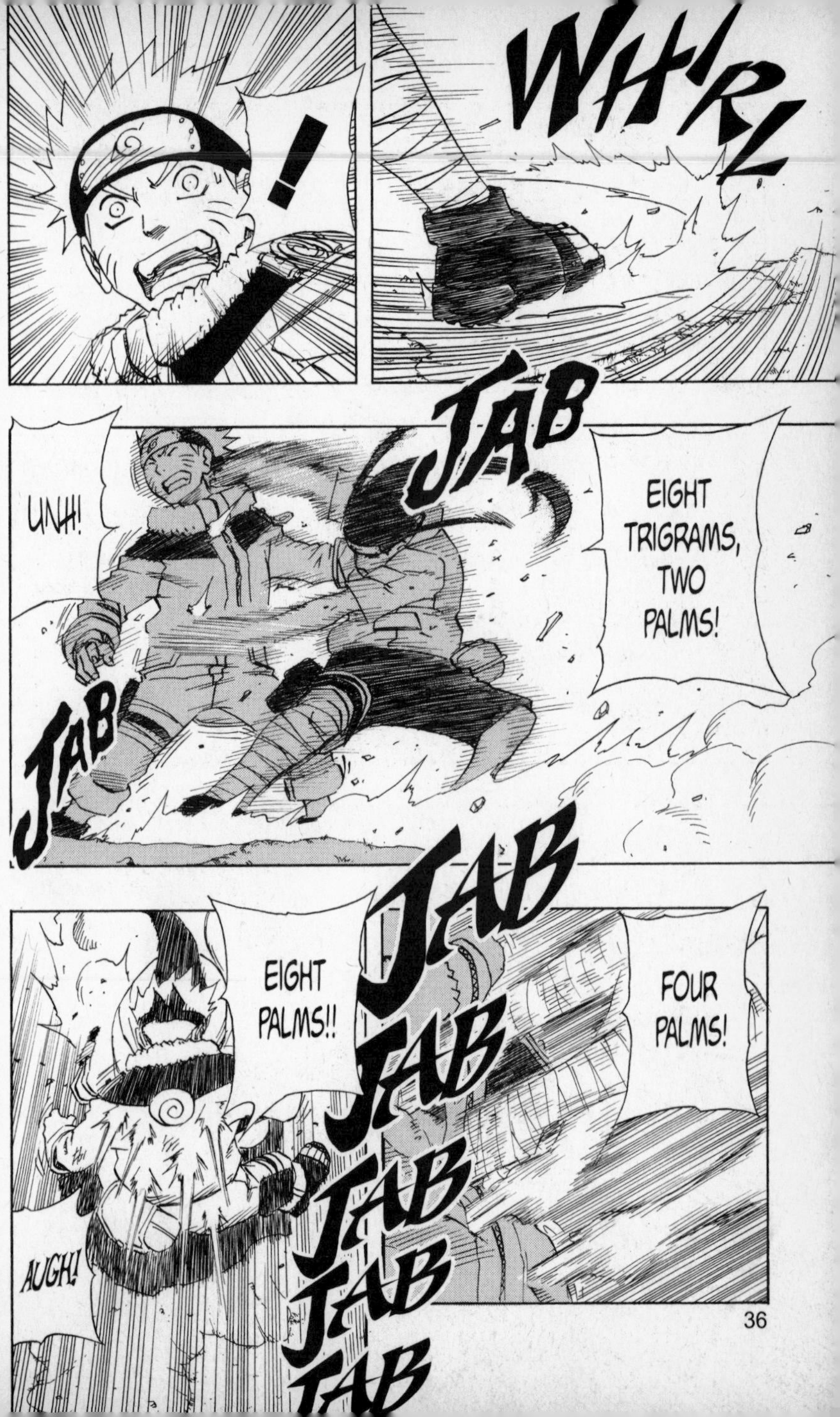
WHIRL
!
JAB
EIGHT TRIGRAMS, TWO PALMS!
UNH!
JAB
FOUR PALMS!
JAB
EIGHT PALMS!!
JAB
JAB
JAB
AUGH!

READ THIS WAY

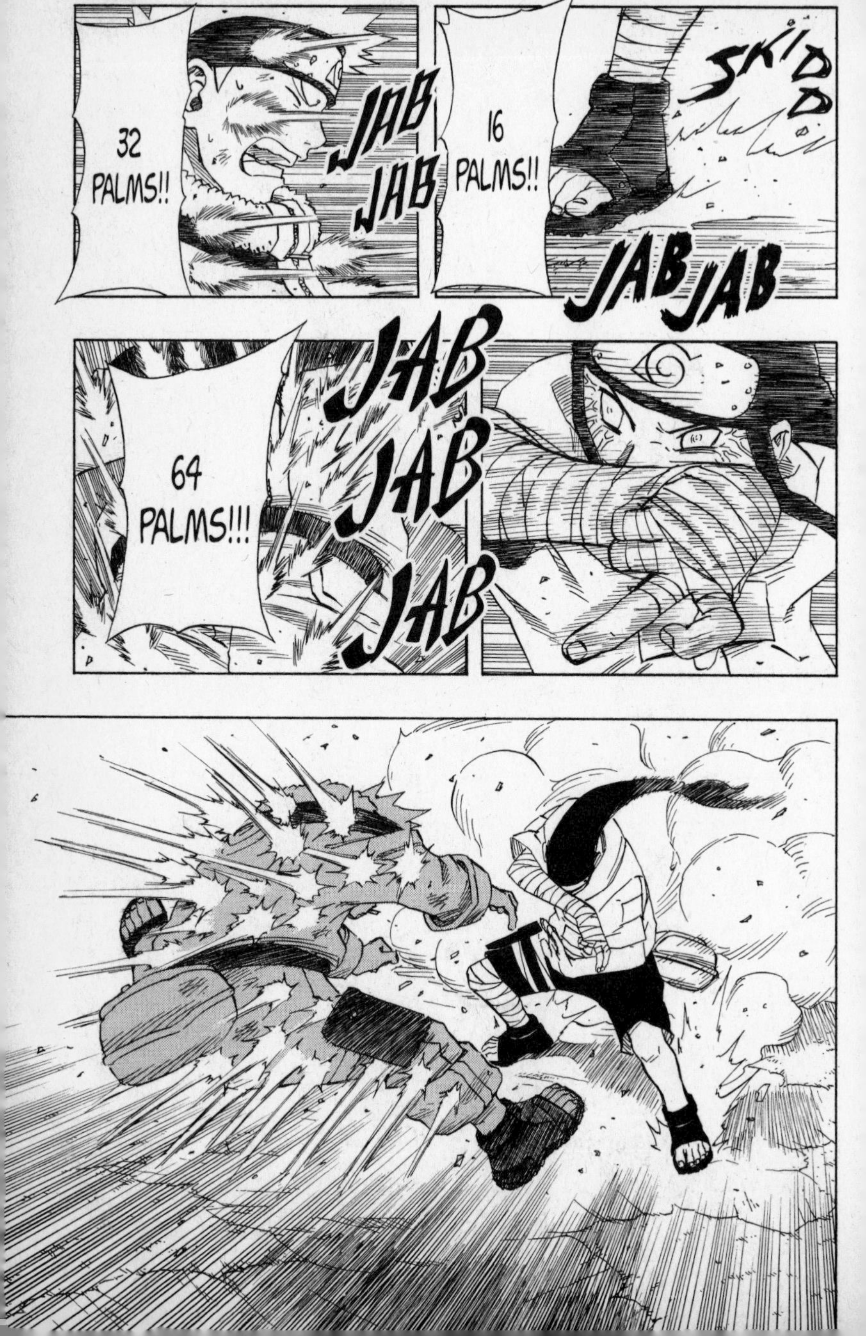
16 PALMS!!
SKIDD
JAB JAB
32 PALMS!!
JAB JAB
JAB JAB JAB
64 PALMS!!!

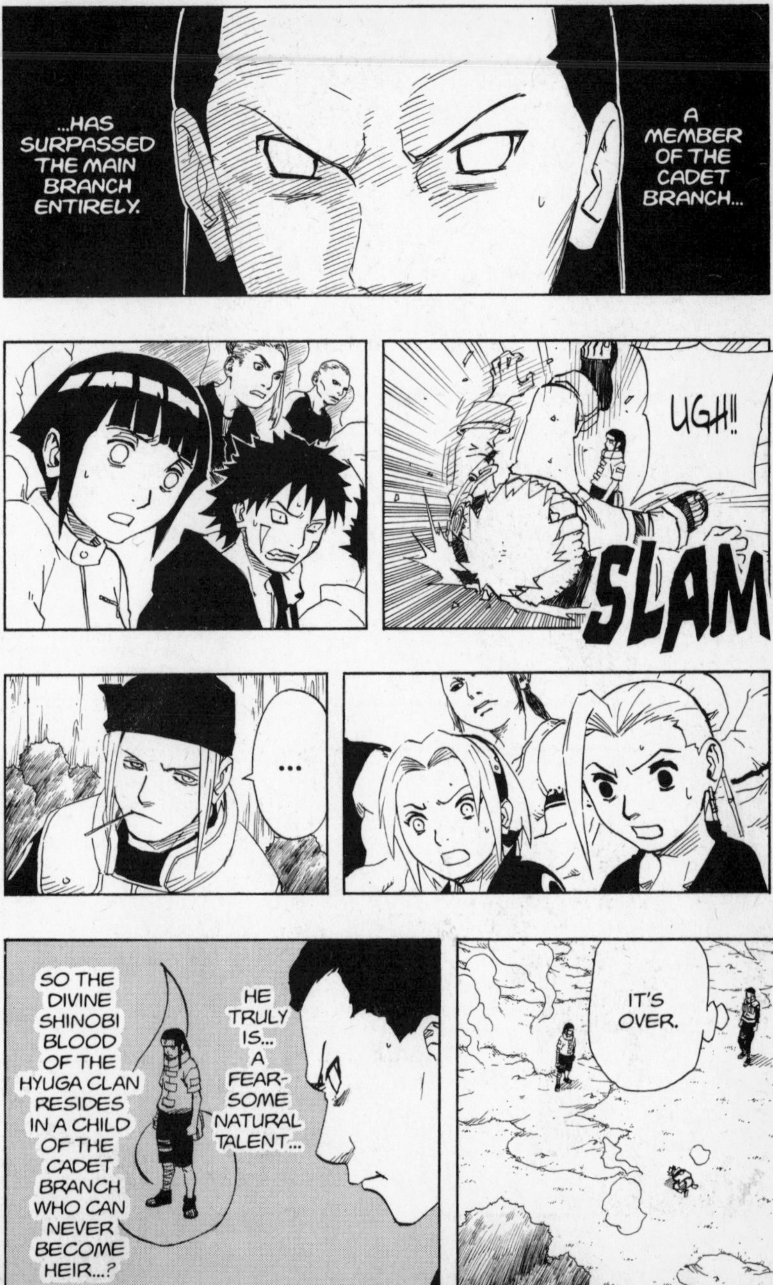
A MEMBER OF THE CADET BRANCH...
...HAS SURPASSED THE MAIN BRANCH ENTIRELY.
UGH!!
SLAM
...
IT'S OVER.
HE TRULY IS... A FEARSOME NATURAL TALENT...
SO THE DIVINE SHINOBI BLOOD OF THE HYUGA CLAN RESIDES IN A CHILD OF THE CADET BRANCH WHO CAN NEVER BECOME HEIR...?

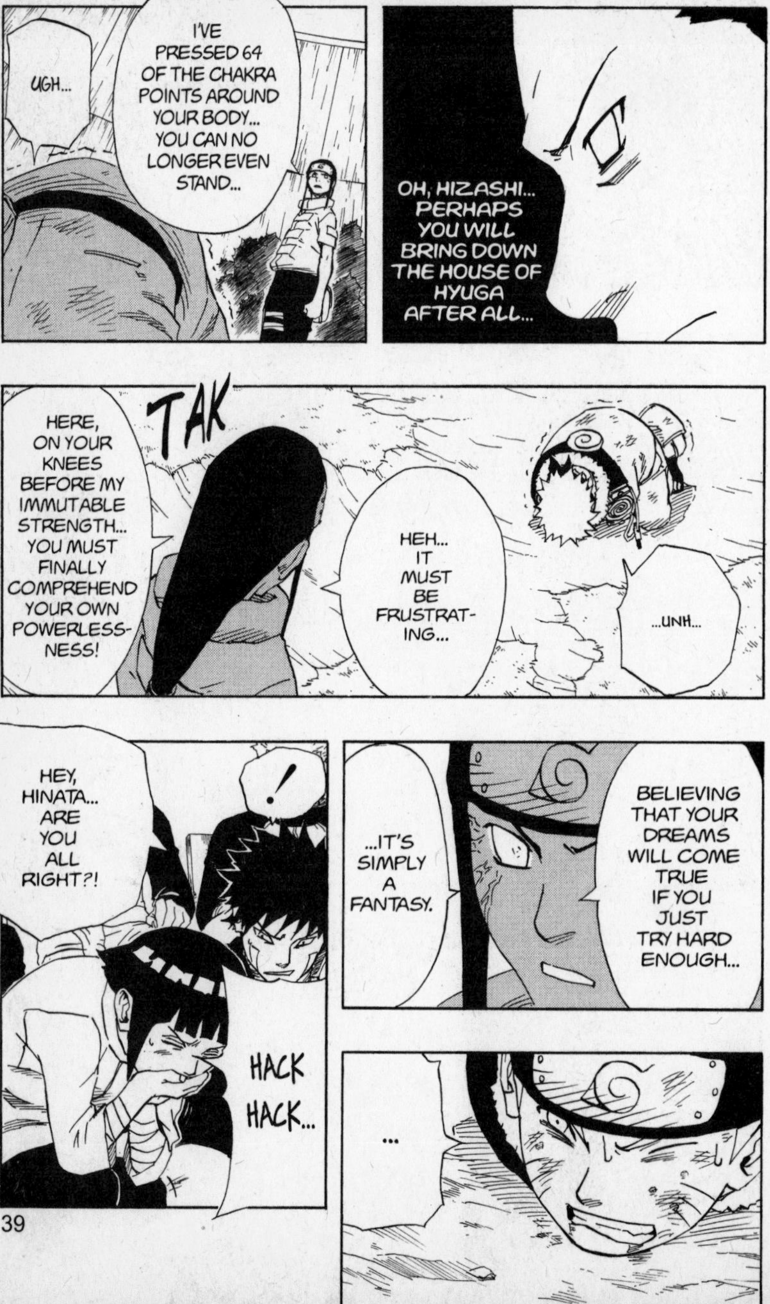
OH, HIZASHI... PERHAPS YOU WILL BRING DOWN THE HOUSE OF HYUGA AFTER ALL...
I'VE PRESSED 64 OF THE CHAKRA POINTS AROUND YOUR BODY... YOU CAN NO LONGER EVEN STAND...
UGH...
...UNH...
HEH... IT MUST BE FRUSTRATING...
TAK
HERE, ON YOUR KNEES BEFORE MY IMMUTABLE STRENGTH... YOU MUST FINALLY COMPREHEND YOUR OWN POWERLESSNESS!
BELIEVING THAT YOUR DREAMS WILL COME TRUE IF YOU JUST TRY HARD ENOUGH...
...IT'S SIMPLY A FANTASY.
...
!
HEY, HINATA... ARE YOU ALL RIGHT?!
HACK HACK...

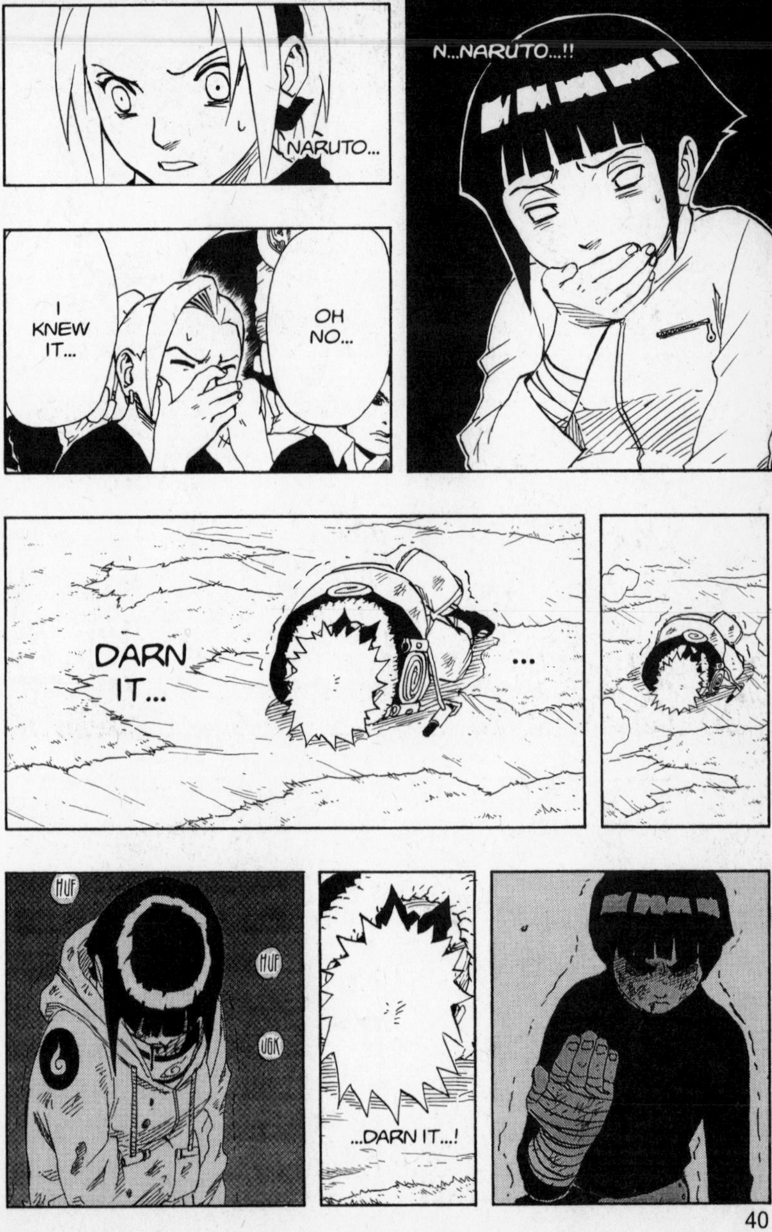

N...NARUTO...!!
NARUTO...
OH NO...
I KNEW IT...
...
DARN IT...
...DARN IT...!
HUF
HUF
UGK

READ THIS WAY

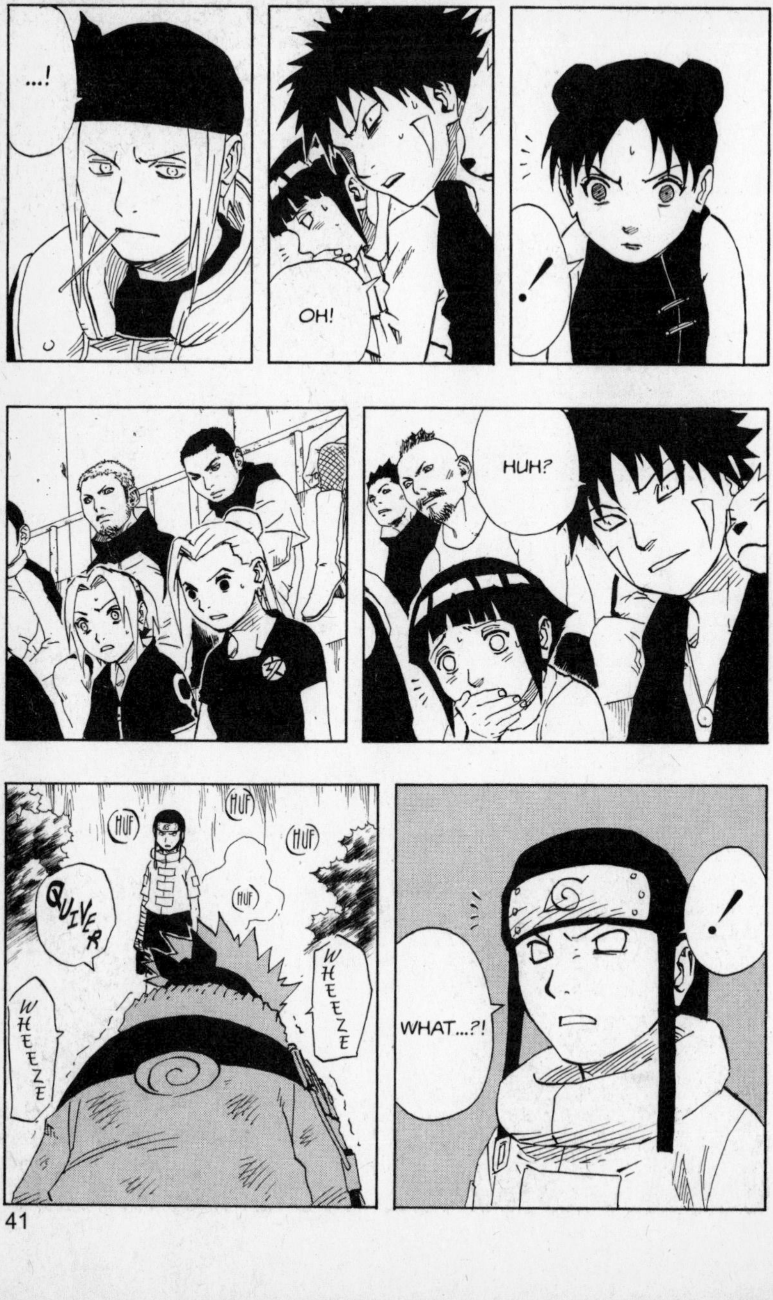
!
OH!
...!
HUH?
!
WHAT...?!
HUF
HUF
HUF
HUF
QUIVER
WHEEZE
WHEEZE

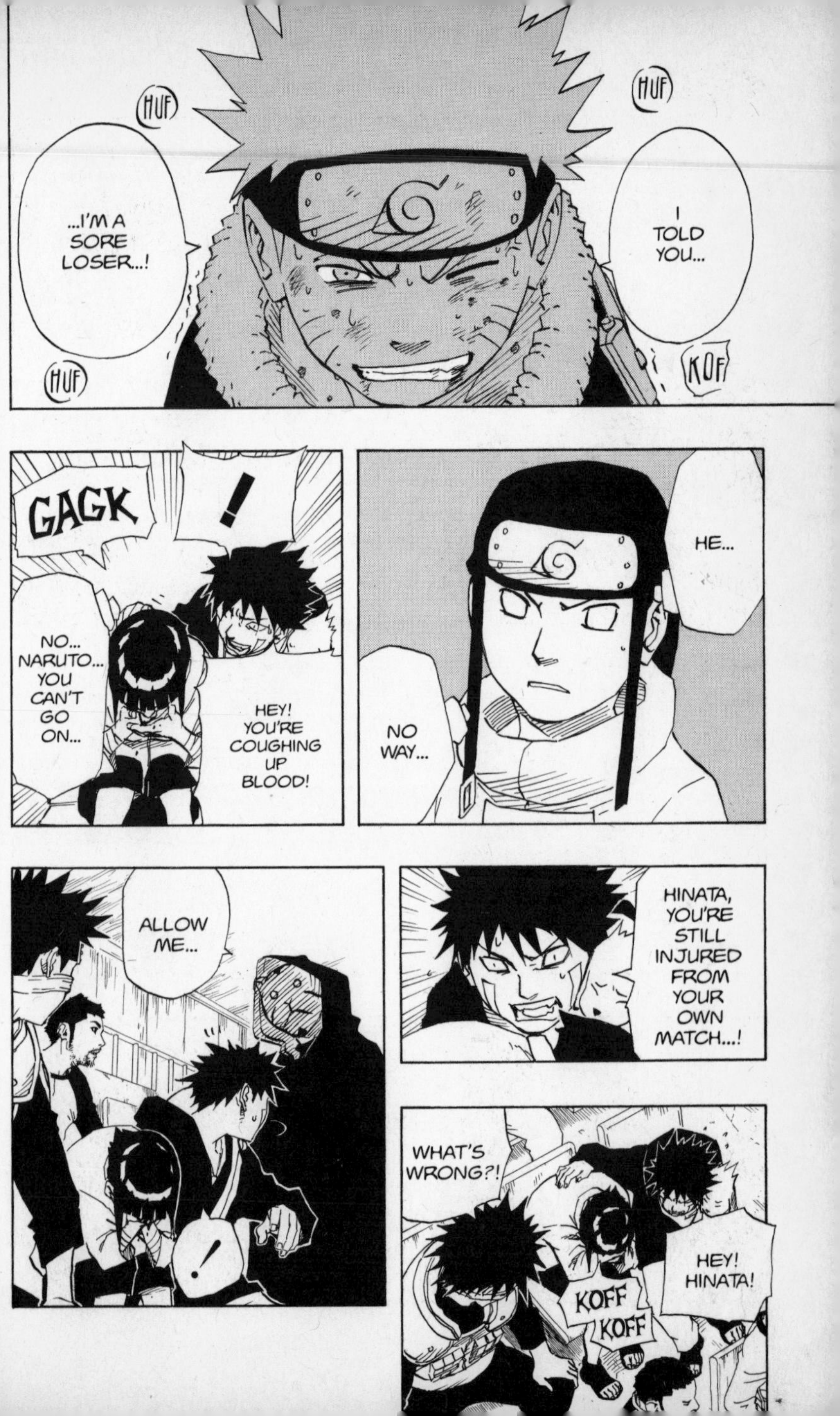
HUF
I TOLD YOU...
KOF
...I'M A SORE LOSER...!
HUF
HUF
HE...
NO WAY...
GAGK
!
HEY! YOU'RE COUGHING UP BLOOD!
NO... NARUTO... YOU CAN'T GO ON...
HINATA, YOU'RE STILL INJURED FROM YOUR OWN MATCH...!
HEY! HINATA!
WHAT'S WRONG?!
KOFF
KOFF
ALLOW ME...
!

READ THIS WAY

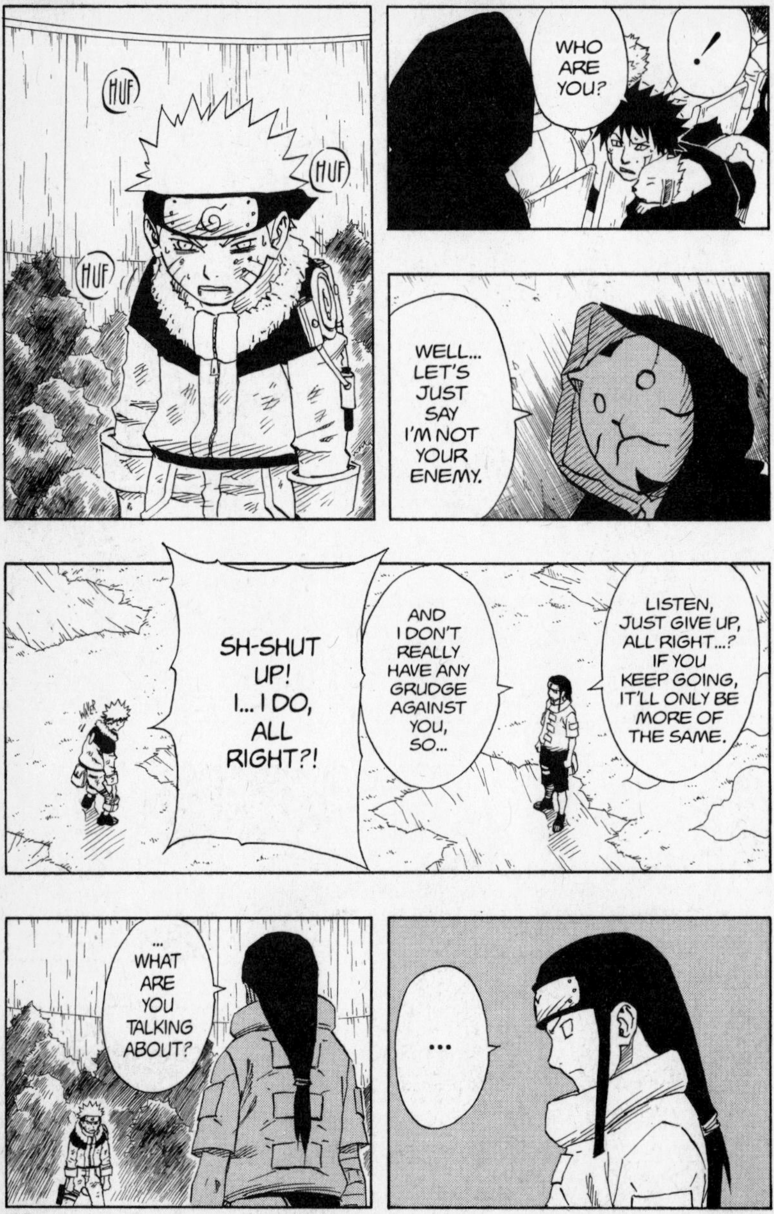
!
WHO ARE YOU?
WELL... LET'S JUST SAY I'M NOT YOUR ENEMY.
HUF
HUF
HUF
LISTEN, JUST GIVE UP, ALL RIGHT...? IF YOU KEEP GOING, IT'LL ONLY BE MORE OF THE SAME.
AND I DON'T REALLY HAVE ANY GRUDGE AGAINST YOU, SO...
SH-SHUT UP! I... I DO, ALL RIGHT?!
...
... WHAT ARE YOU TALKING ABOUT?

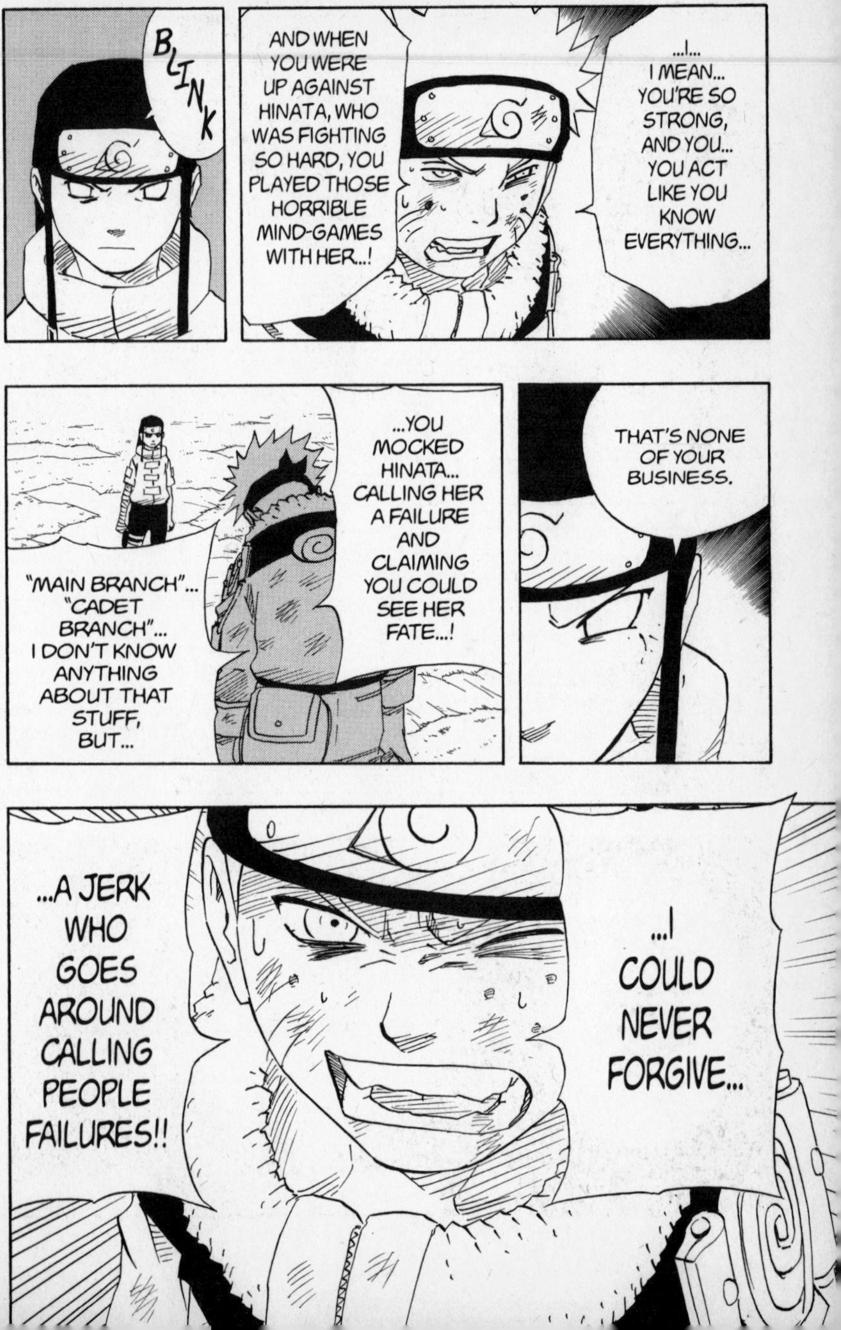
...I... I MEAN... YOU'RE SO STRONG, AND YOU... YOU ACT LIKE YOU KNOW EVERYTHING...
AND WHEN YOU WERE UP AGAINST HINATA, WHO WAS FIGHTING SO HARD, YOU PLAYED THOSE HORRIBLE MIND-GAMES WITH HER...!
BLINK
THAT'S NONE OF YOUR BUSINESS.
...YOU MOCKED HINATA... CALLING HER A FAILURE AND CLAIMING YOU COULD SEE HER FATE...!
"MAIN BRANCH"... "CADET BRANCH"... I DON'T KNOW ANYTHING ABOUT THAT STUFF, BUT...
...I COULD NEVER FORGIVE...
...A JERK WHO GOES AROUND CALLING PEOPLE FAILURES!!

READ THIS WAY

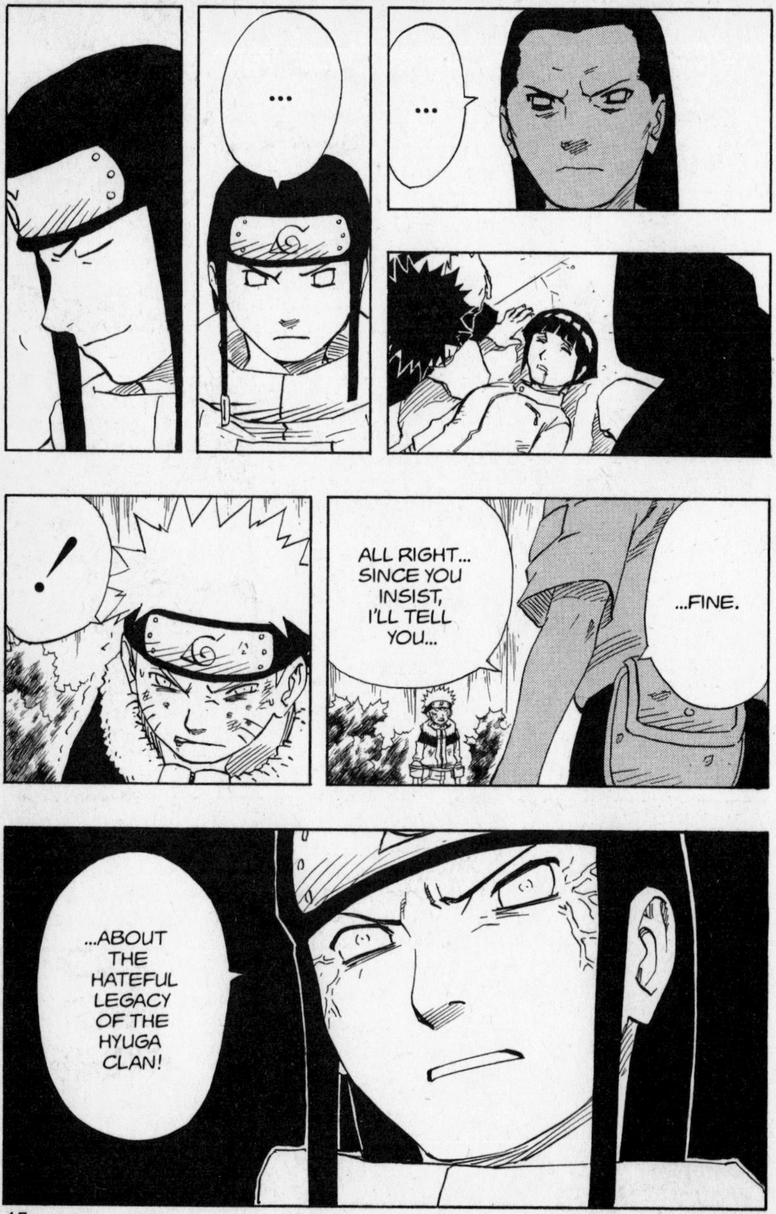
...
...
...FINE.
ALL RIGHT... SINCE YOU INSIST, I'LL TELL YOU...
!
...ABOUT THE HATEFUL LEGACY OF THE HYUGA CLAN!

HAPPY SECOND ANNIVERSARY!!

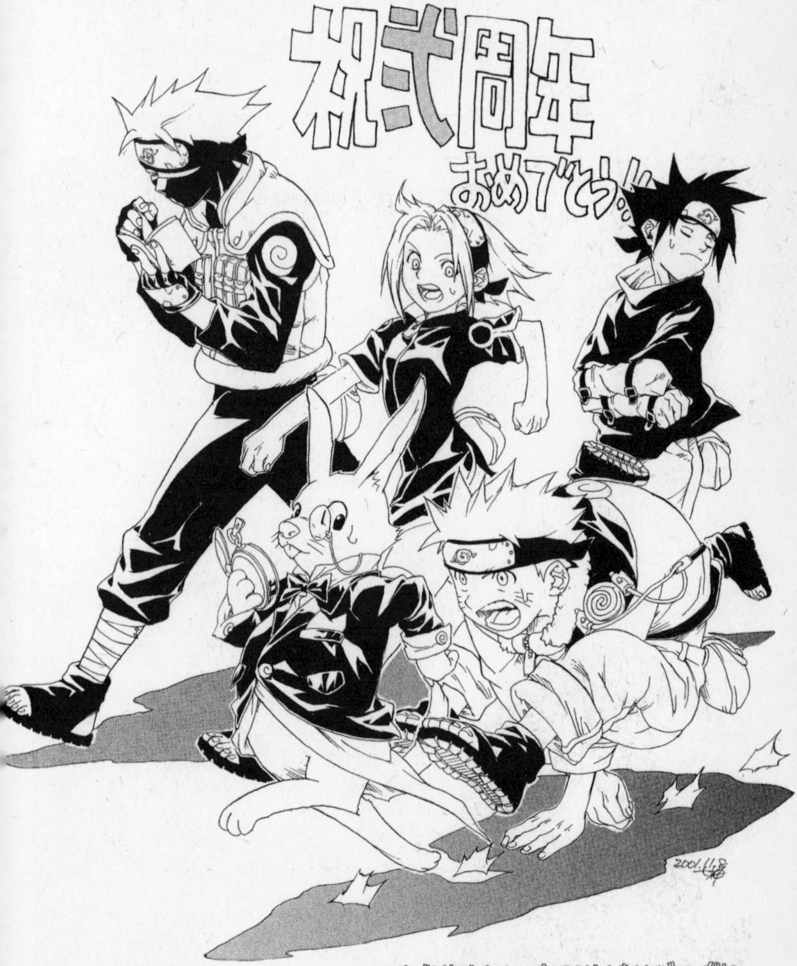
祝弐周年
おめでとう!!
2001.11.8

☆ いつまでもやる気まんまんのナルトのような岸本さんでいてください

高橋 一浩

PLEASE STAY FULL OF ENERGY, JUST LIKE NARUTO, FOREVER!

TAKAHASHI KAZUHIRO

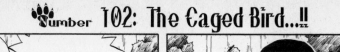

Number 102: The Caged Bird...!!

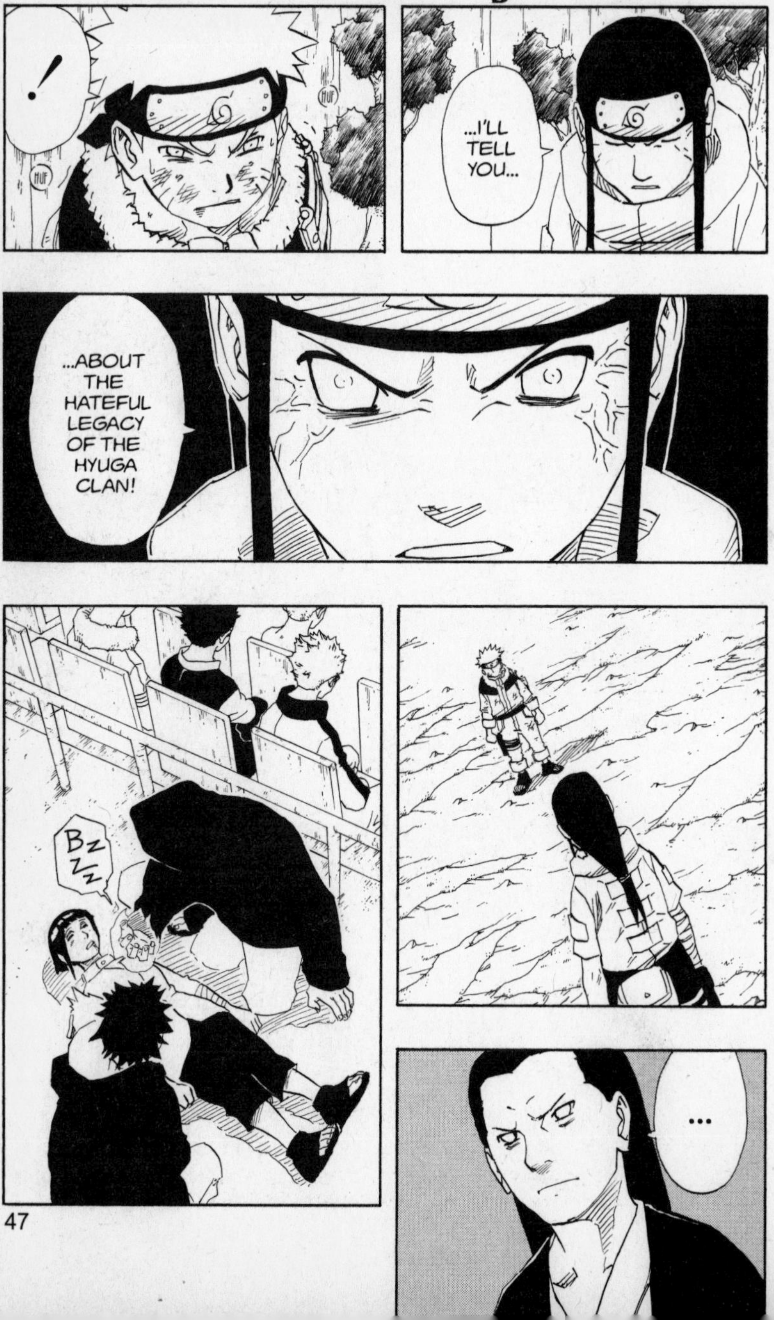
...I'LL TELL YOU...
!
HUF
HUF
...ABOUT THE HATEFUL LEGACY OF THE HYUGA CLAN!
...
BZZZ

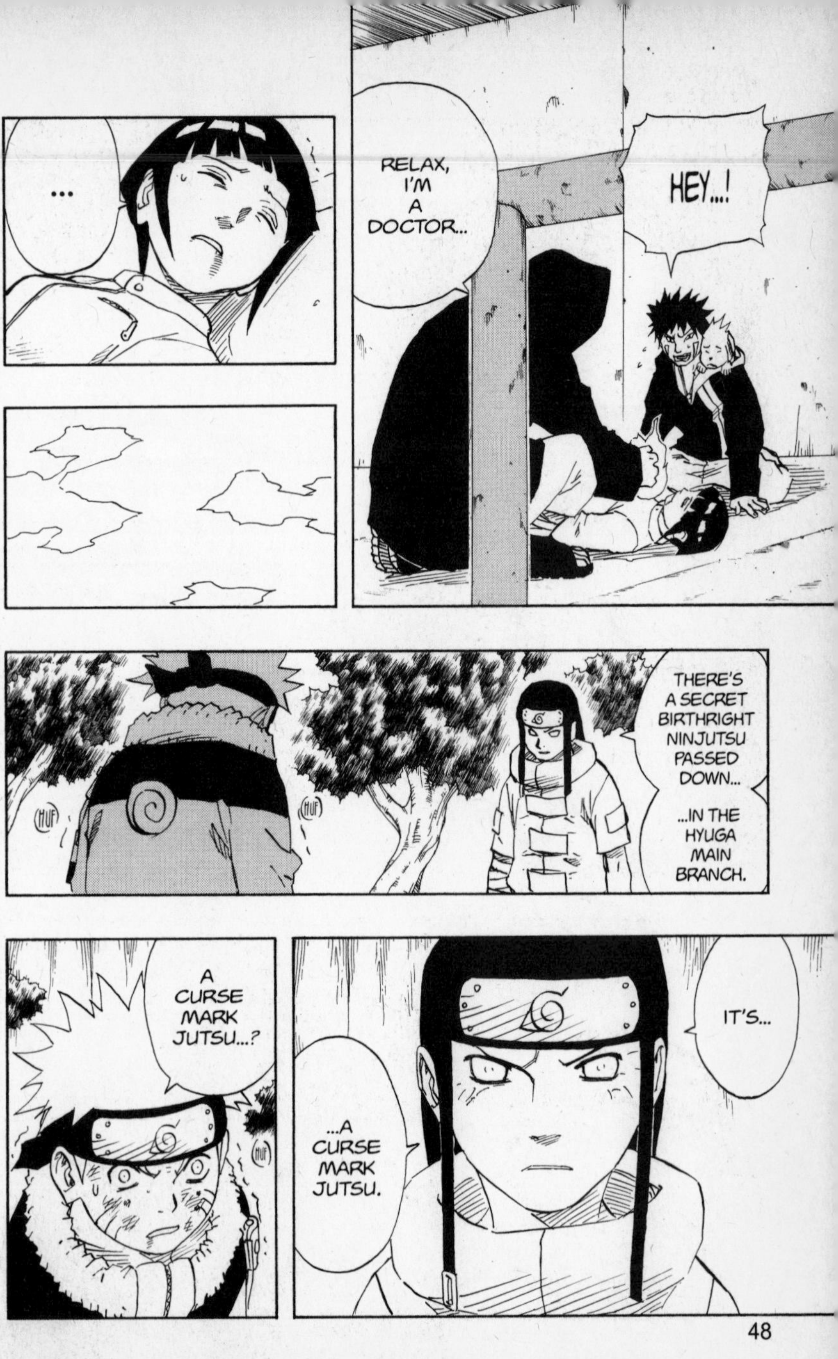
HEY...!
RELAX, I'M A DOCTOR...
...
THERE'S A SECRET BIRTHRIGHT NINJUTSU PASSED DOWN...
...IN THE HYUGA MAIN BRANCH.
HUF
HUF
IT'S...
...A CURSE MARK JUTSU.
A CURSE MARK JUTSU...?
HUF

READ THIS WAY

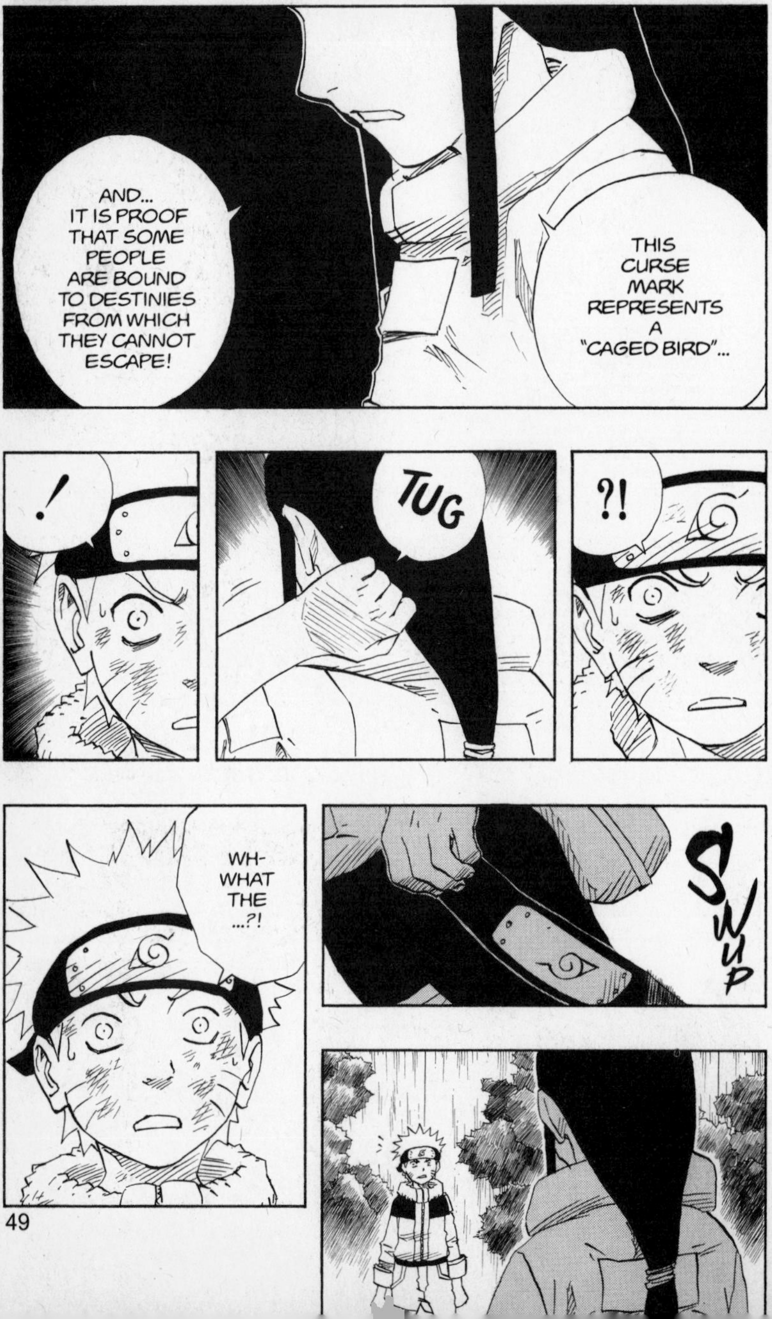

THIS CURSE MARK REPRESENTS A "CAGED BIRD"...
AND... IT IS PROOF THAT SOME PEOPLE ARE BOUND TO DESTINIES FROM WHICH THEY CANNOT ESCAPE!
?!
TUG
!
SWUP
WH- WHAT THE ...?!

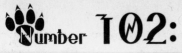

Number 102: The Caged Bird...!!

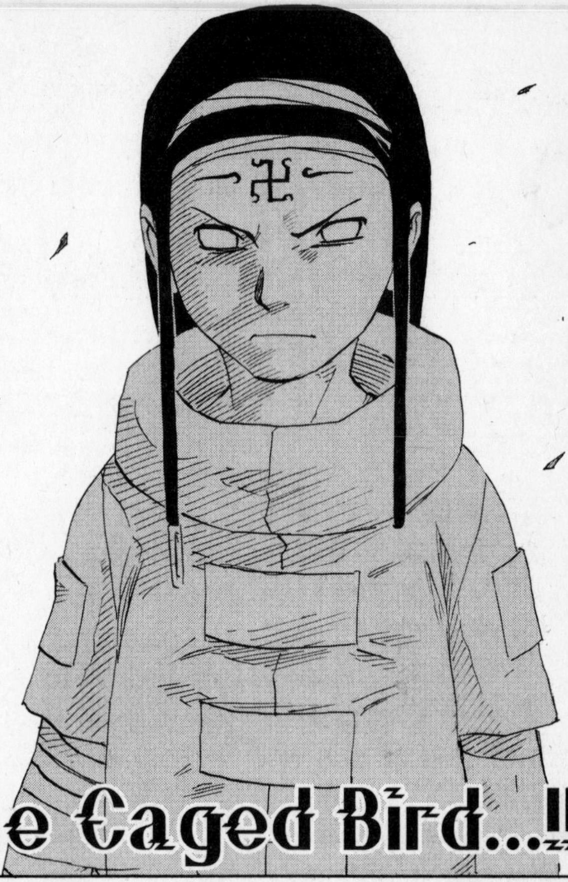

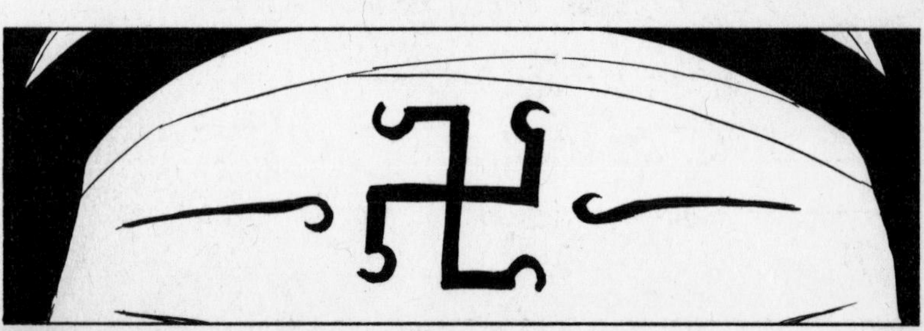

THE SYMBOL PICTURED ABOVE, CALLED A MANJI, IS TRADITIONAL IN BUDDHIST IMAGERY. --ED.

READ THIS WAY

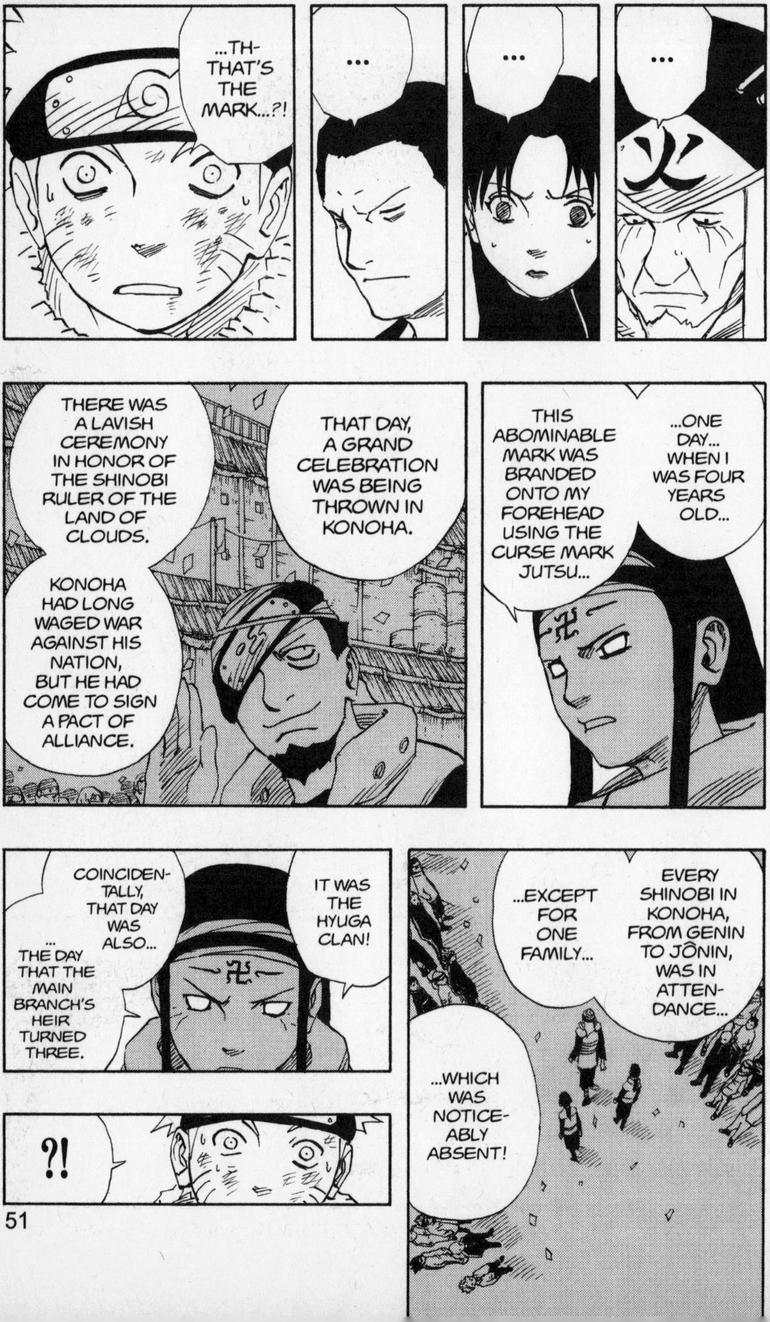
...
...
...
...TH-THAT'S THE MARK...?!
...ONE DAY... WHEN I WAS FOUR YEARS OLD...
THIS ABOMINABLE MARK WAS BRANDED ONTO MY FOREHEAD USING THE CURSE MARK JUTSU...
THAT DAY, A GRAND CELEBRATION WAS BEING THROWN IN KONOHA.
THERE WAS A LAVISH CEREMONY IN HONOR OF THE SHINOBI RULER OF THE LAND OF CLOUDS.
KONOHA HAD LONG WAGED WAR AGAINST HIS NATION, BUT HE HAD COME TO SIGN A PACT OF ALLIANCE.
EVERY SHINOBI IN KONOHA, FROM GENIN TO JÔNIN, WAS IN ATTENDANCE...
...EXCEPT FOR ONE FAMILY...
...WHICH WAS NOTICEABLY ABSENT!
IT WAS THE HYUGA CLAN!
COINCIDENTALLY, THAT DAY WAS ALSO...
...THE DAY THAT THE MAIN BRANCH'S HEIR TURNED THREE.
?!

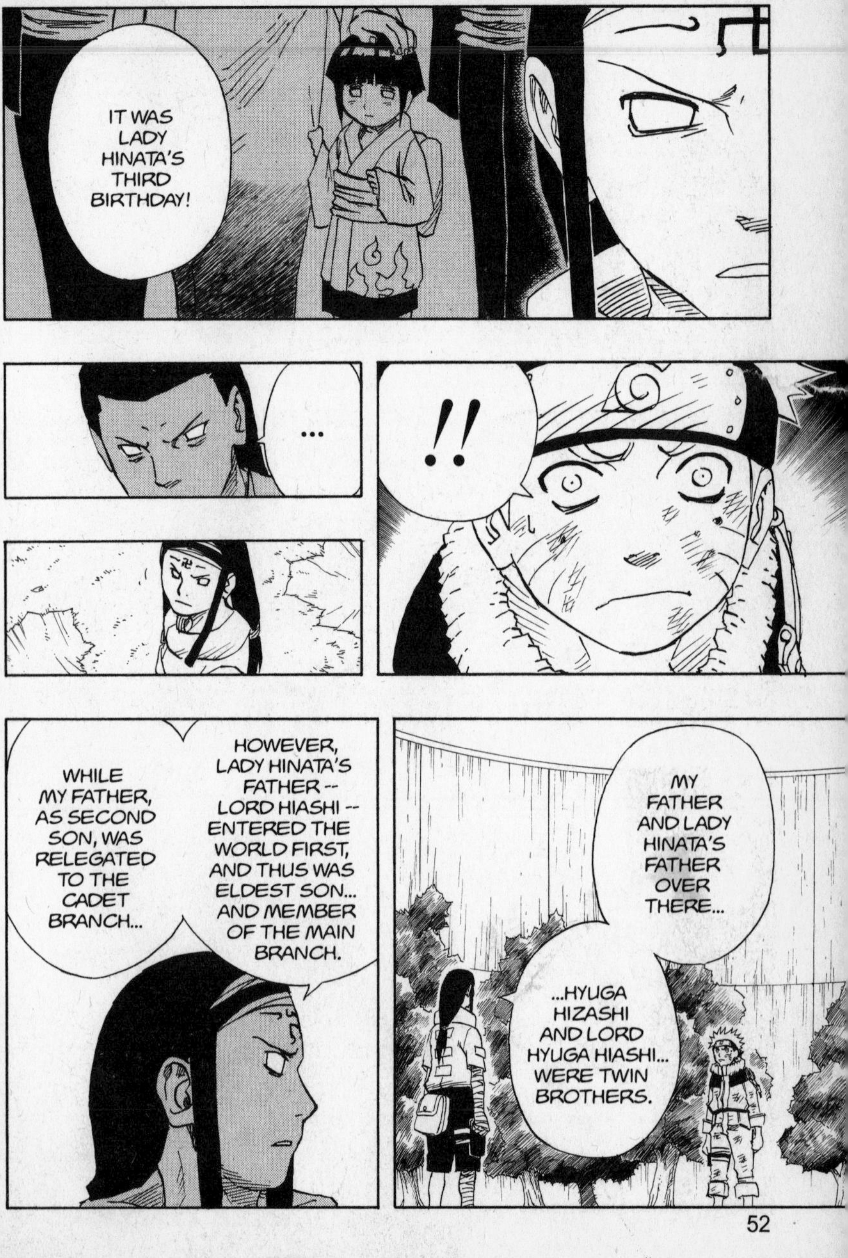
IT WAS LADY HINATA'S THIRD BIRTHDAY!
!!
...
MY FATHER AND LADY HINATA'S FATHER OVER THERE...
...HYUGA HIZASHI AND LORD HYUGA HIASHI... WERE TWIN BROTHERS.
WHILE MY FATHER, AS SECOND SON, WAS RELEGATED TO THE CADET BRANCH...
HOWEVER, LADY HINATA'S FATHER -- LORD HIASHI -- ENTERED THE WORLD FIRST, AND THUS WAS ELDEST SON... AND MEMBER OF THE MAIN BRANCH.

READ THIS WAY

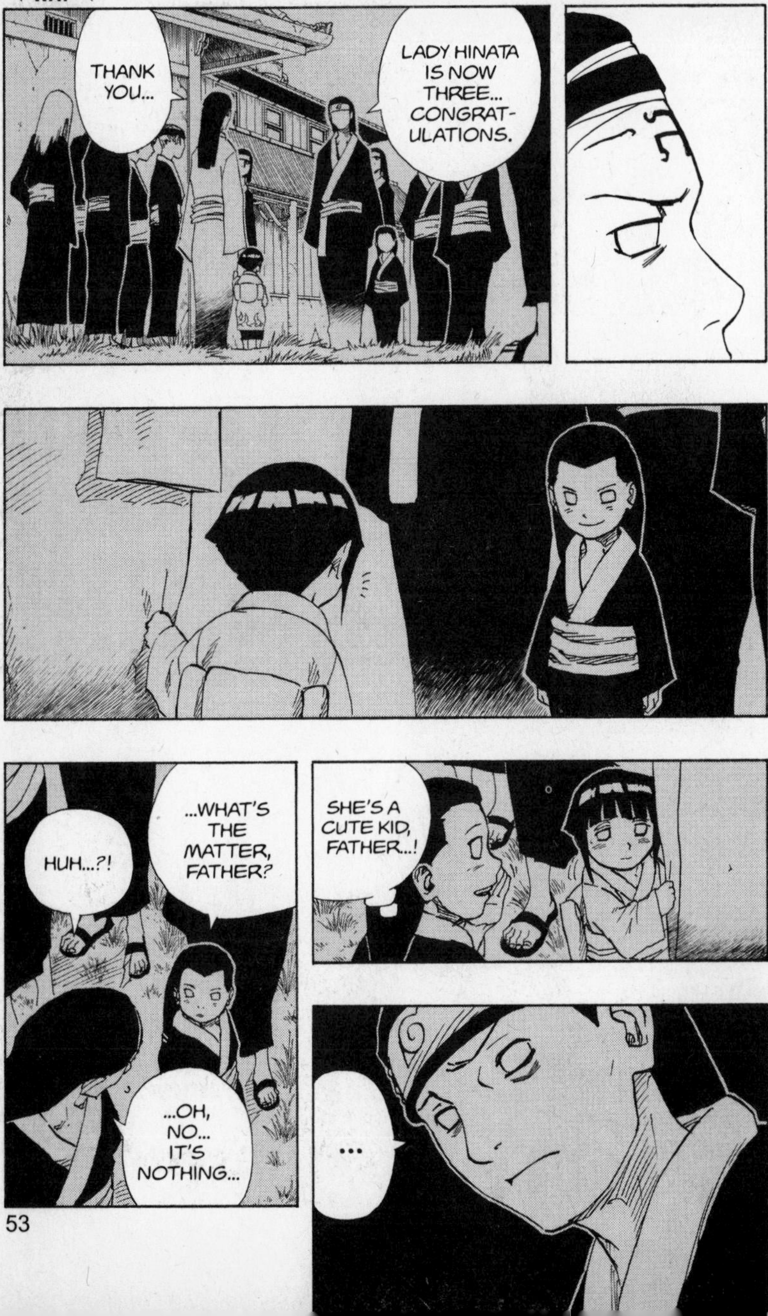
LADY HINATA IS NOW THREE... CONGRATULATIONS.
THANK YOU...
SHE'S A CUTE KID, FATHER...!
...
...WHAT'S THE MATTER, FATHER?
HUH...?!
...OH, NO... IT'S NOTHING...

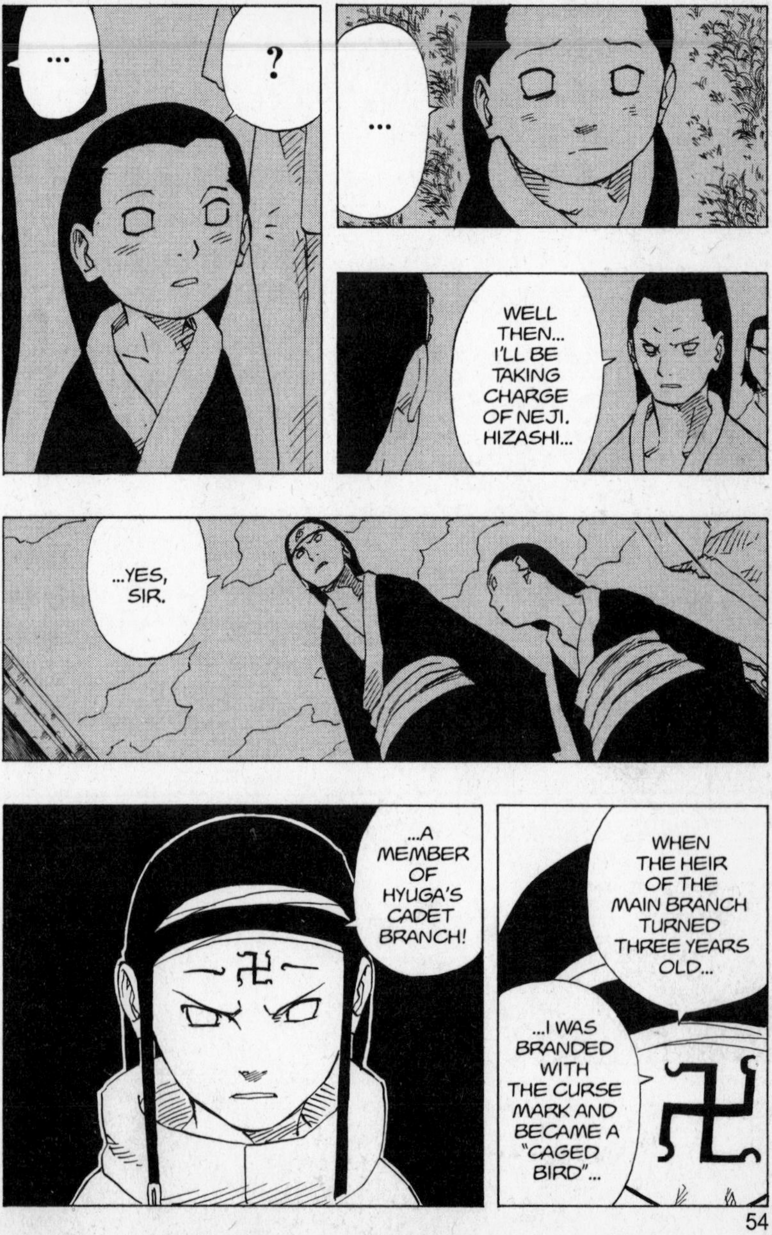
...
WELL THEN... I'LL BE TAKING CHARGE OF NEJI. HIZASHI...
?
...
...YES, SIR.
WHEN THE HEIR OF THE MAIN BRANCH TURNED THREE YEARS OLD...
...I WAS BRANDED WITH THE CURSE MARK AND BECAME A "CAGED BIRD"...
...A MEMBER OF HYUGA'S CADET BRANCH!

READ THIS WAY

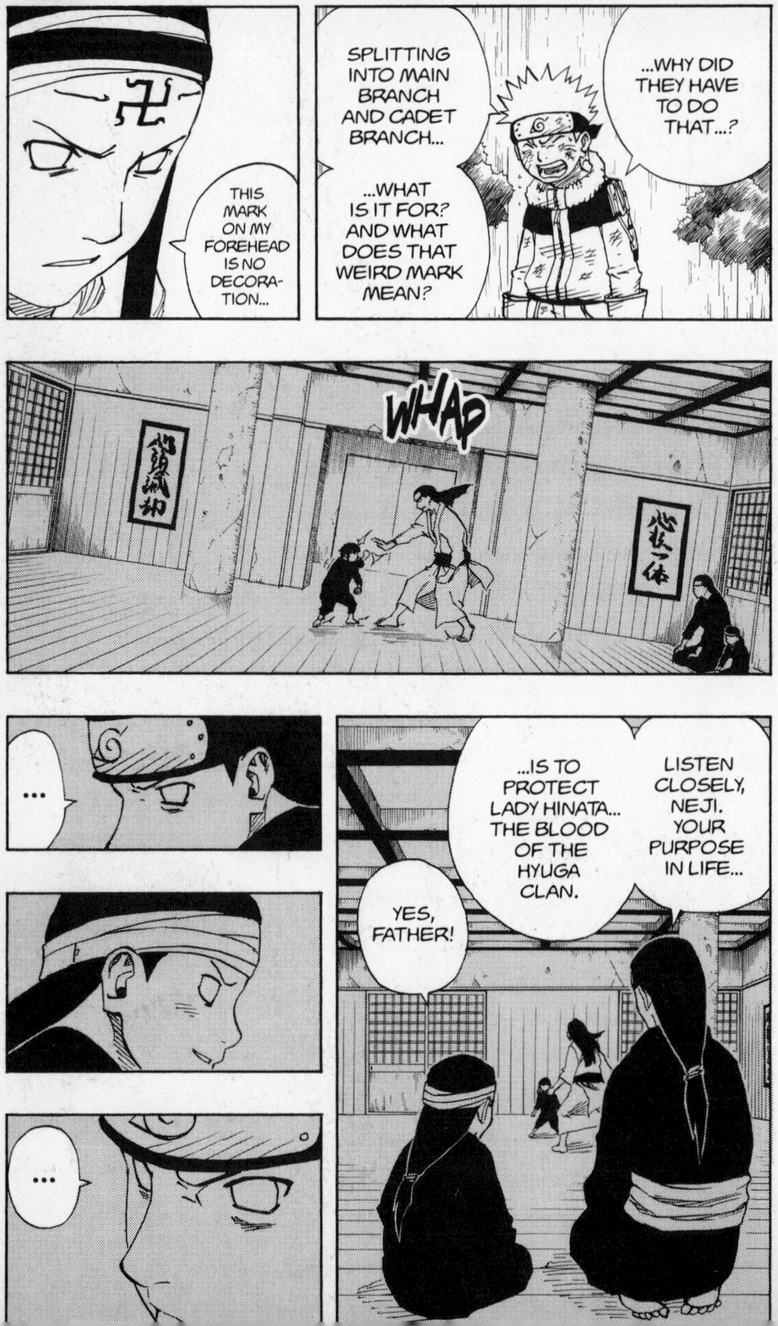
...WHY DID THEY HAVE TO DO THAT...?
SPLITTING INTO MAIN BRANCH AND CADET BRANCH...
...WHAT IS IT FOR? AND WHAT DOES THAT WEIRD MARK MEAN?
THIS MARK ON MY FOREHEAD IS NO DECORA-TION...
WHAP
LISTEN CLOSELY, NEJI. YOUR PURPOSE IN LIFE...
...IS TO PROTECT LADY HINATA... THE BLOOD OF THE HYUGA CLAN.
YES, FATHER!
...
...

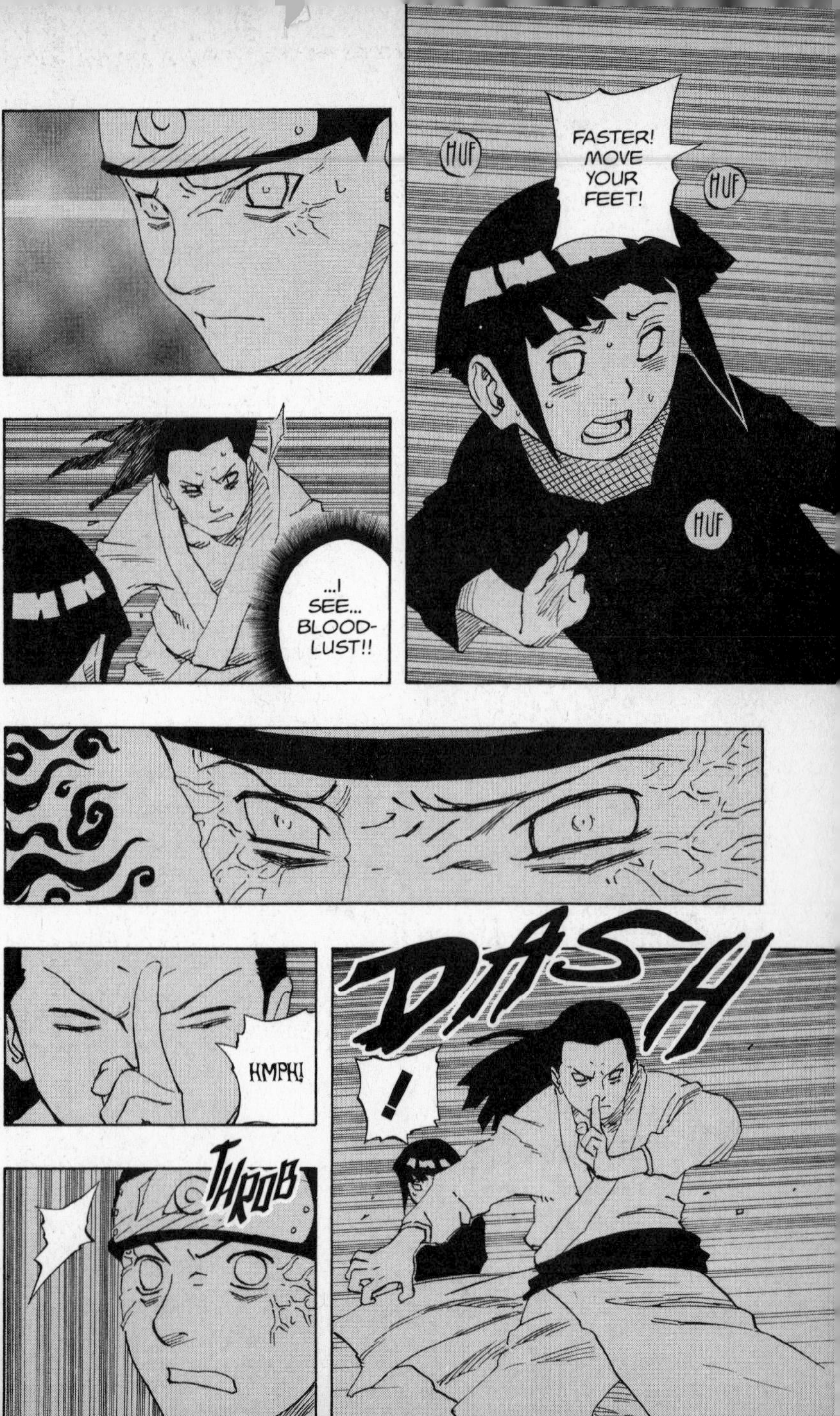
HUF
FASTER! MOVE YOUR FEET!
HUF
HUF
...I SEE... BLOOD-LUST!!
DASH
!
HMPH!
THROB

FATHER! WHAT'S WRONG?!

AAARGH!

!!

GAAH!!

FWUMP

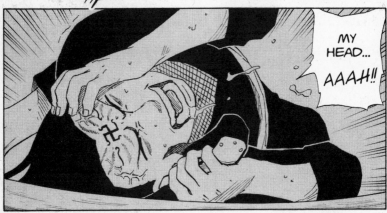

MY HEAD... AAAH!!

I WILL NOT TOLERATE THIS FOOLISH-NESS A SECOND TIME...

GO HOME NOW.

UGH... UNH...

FATHER!!

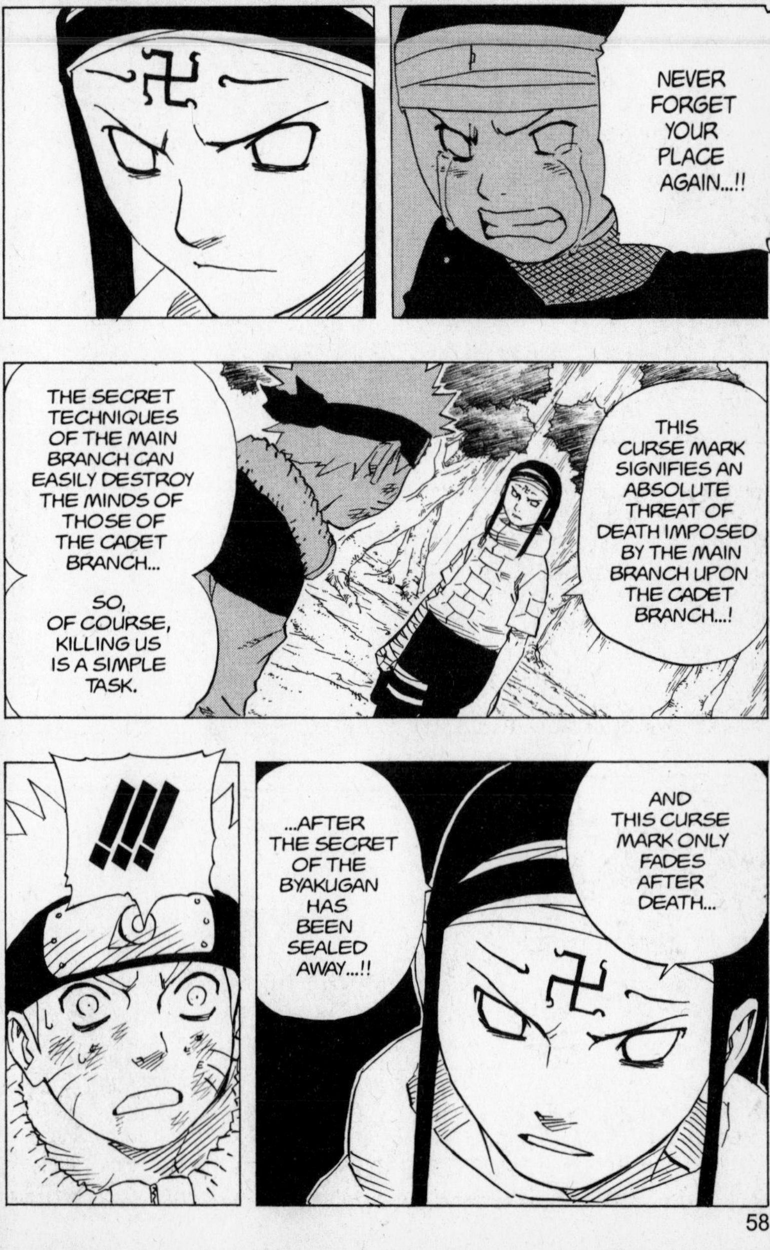
NEVER FORGET YOUR PLACE AGAIN...!!
THIS CURSE MARK SIGNIFIES AN ABSOLUTE THREAT OF DEATH IMPOSED BY THE MAIN BRANCH UPON THE CADET BRANCH...!
THE SECRET TECHNIQUES OF THE MAIN BRANCH CAN EASILY DESTROY THE MINDS OF THOSE OF THE CADET BRANCH...
SO, OF COURSE, KILLING US IS A SIMPLE TASK.
AND THIS CURSE MARK ONLY FADES AFTER DEATH...
...AFTER THE SECRET OF THE BYAKUGAN HAS BEEN SEALED AWAY...!!
!!!

READ THIS WAY

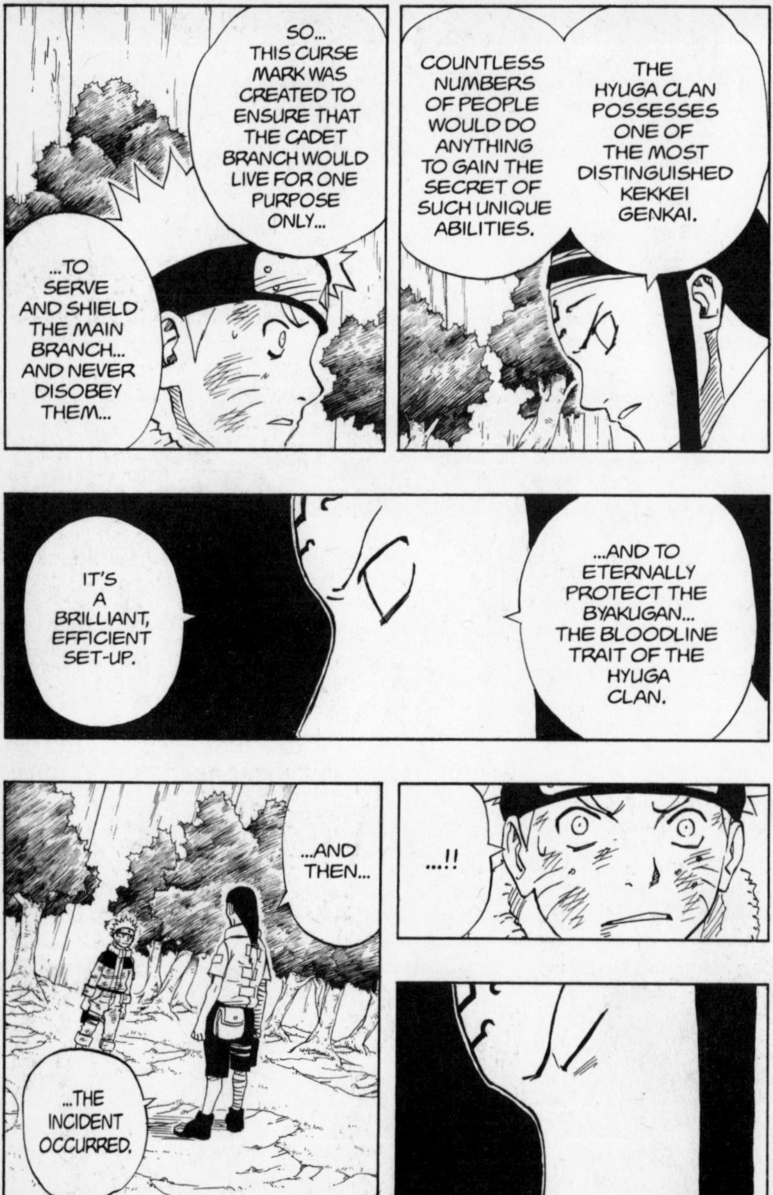
THE HYUGA CLAN POSSESSES ONE OF THE MOST DISTINGUISHED KEKKEI GENKAI.
COUNTLESS NUMBERS OF PEOPLE WOULD DO ANYTHING TO GAIN THE SECRET OF SUCH UNIQUE ABILITIES.
SO... THIS CURSE MARK WAS CREATED TO ENSURE THAT THE CADET BRANCH WOULD LIVE FOR ONE PURPOSE ONLY...
...TO SERVE AND SHIELD THE MAIN BRANCH... AND NEVER DISOBEY THEM...
...AND TO ETERNALLY PROTECT THE BYAKUGAN... THE BLOODLINE TRAIT OF THE HYUGA CLAN.
IT'S A BRILLIANT, EFFICIENT SET-UP.
...!!
...AND THEN...
...THE INCIDENT OCCURRED.

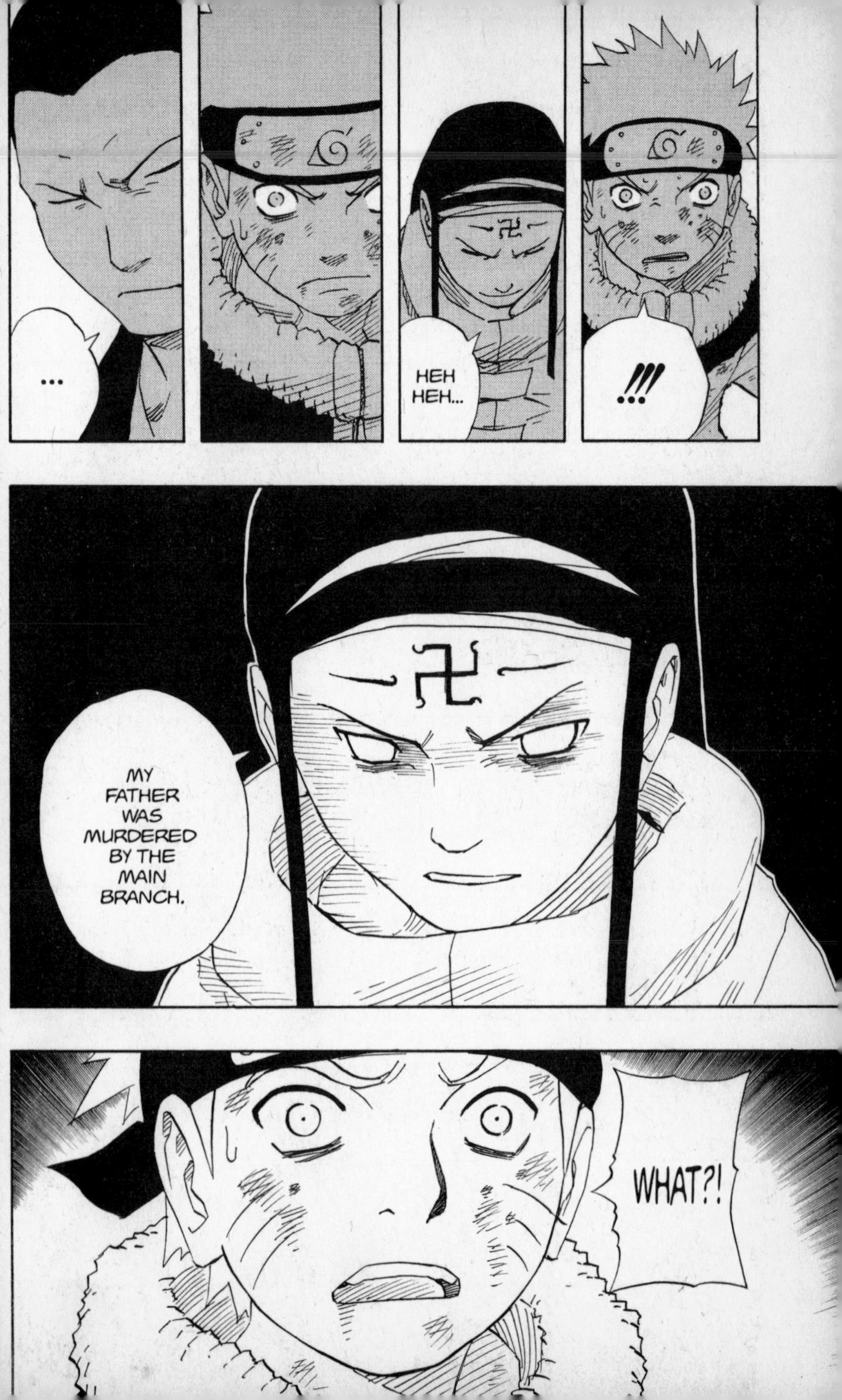
!!!
HEH HEH...
...
MY FATHER WAS MURDERED BY THE MAIN BRANCH.
WHAT?!

READ THIS WAY

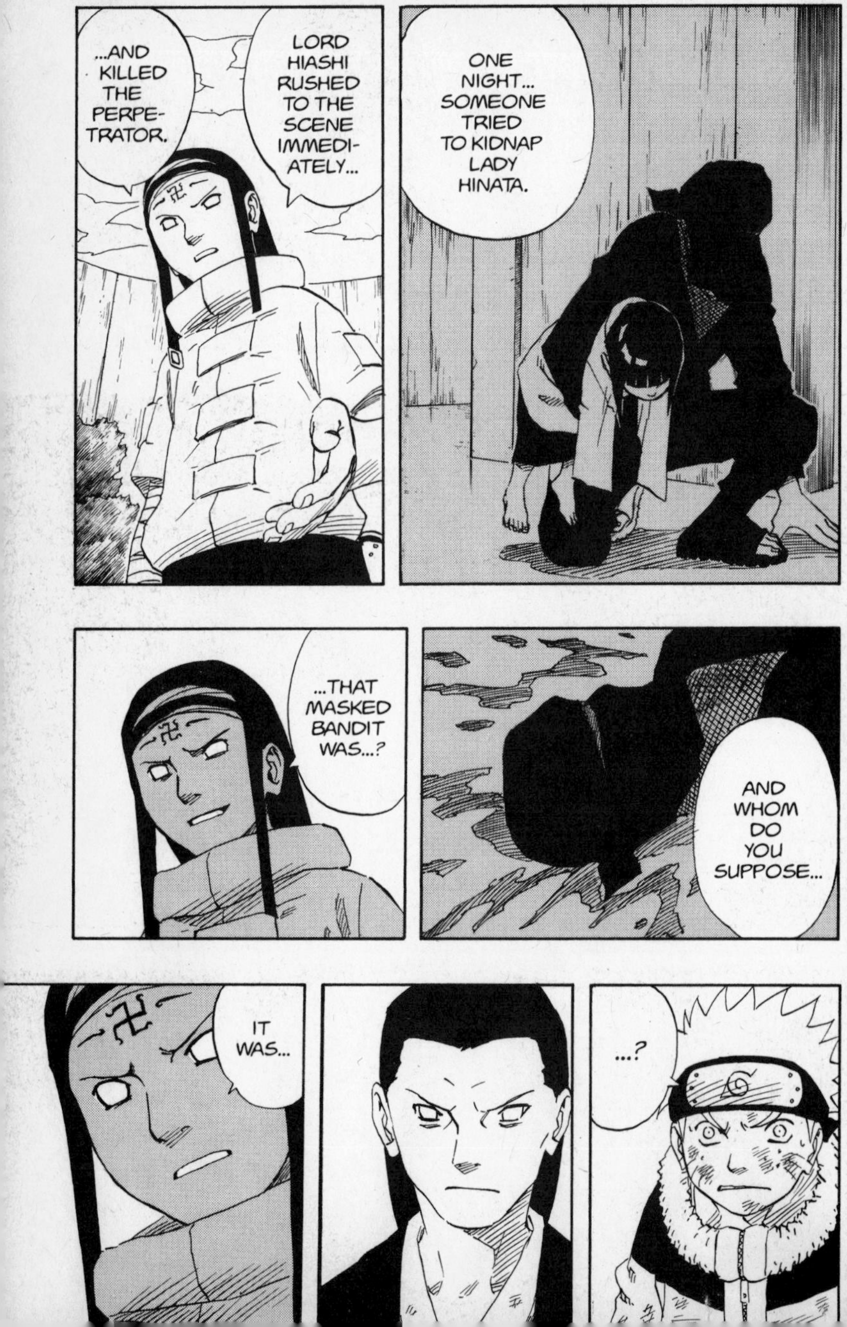
ONE NIGHT... SOMEONE TRIED TO KIDNAP LADY HINATA.
LORD HIASHI RUSHED TO THE SCENE IMMEDI-ATELY...
...AND KILLED THE PERPE-TRATOR.
AND WHOM DO YOU SUPPOSE...
...THAT MASKED BANDIT WAS...?
...?
IT WAS...

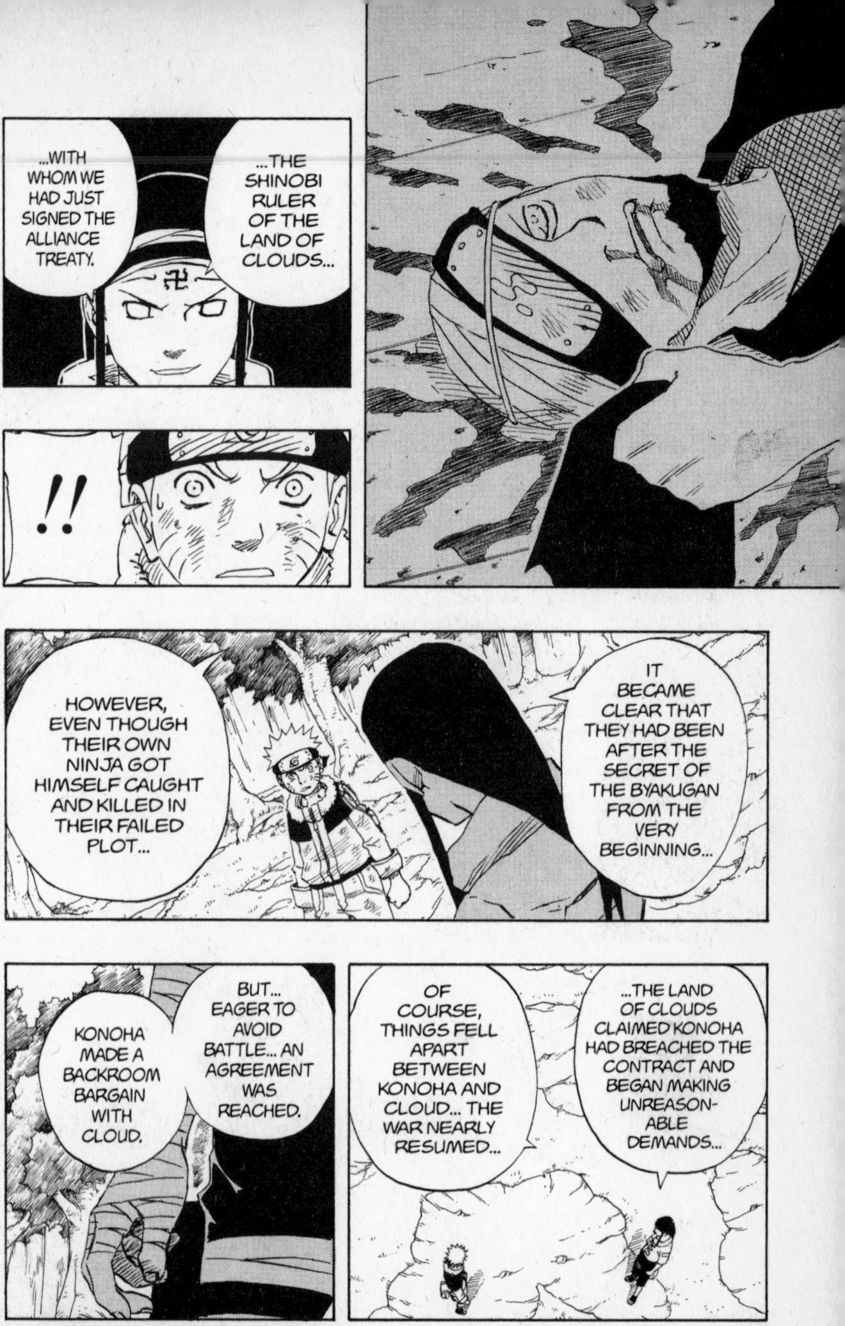
...THE SHINOBI RULER OF THE LAND OF CLOUDS...
...WITH WHOM WE HAD JUST SIGNED THE ALLIANCE TREATY.
!!
IT BECAME CLEAR THAT THEY HAD BEEN AFTER THE SECRET OF THE BYAKUGAN FROM THE VERY BEGINNING...
HOWEVER, EVEN THOUGH THEIR OWN NINJA GOT HIMSELF CAUGHT AND KILLED IN THEIR FAILED PLOT...
...THE LAND OF CLOUDS CLAIMED KONOHA HAD BREACHED THE CONTRACT AND BEGAN MAKING UNREASON-ABLE DEMANDS...
OF COURSE, THINGS FELL APART BETWEEN KONOHA AND CLOUD... THE WAR NEARLY RESUMED...
BUT... EAGER TO AVOID BATTLE... AN AGREEMENT WAS REACHED.
KONOHA MADE A BACKROOM BARGAIN WITH CLOUD.

READ THIS WAY

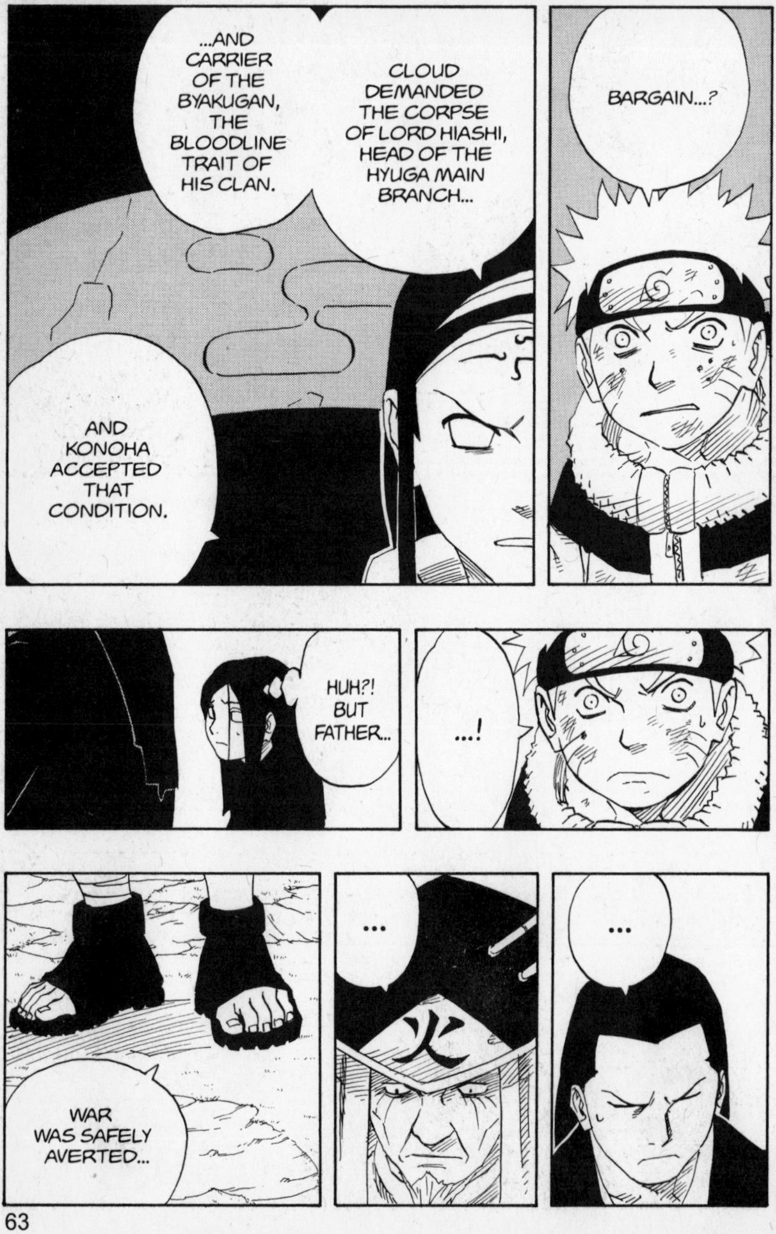
BARGAIN...?
CLOUD DEMANDED THE CORPSE OF LORD HIASHI, HEAD OF THE HYUGA MAIN BRANCH...
...AND CARRIER OF THE BYAKUGAN, THE BLOODLINE TRAIT OF HIS CLAN.
AND KONOHA ACCEPTED THAT CONDITION.
...!
HUH?! BUT FATHER...
...
...
WAR WAS SAFELY AVERTED...

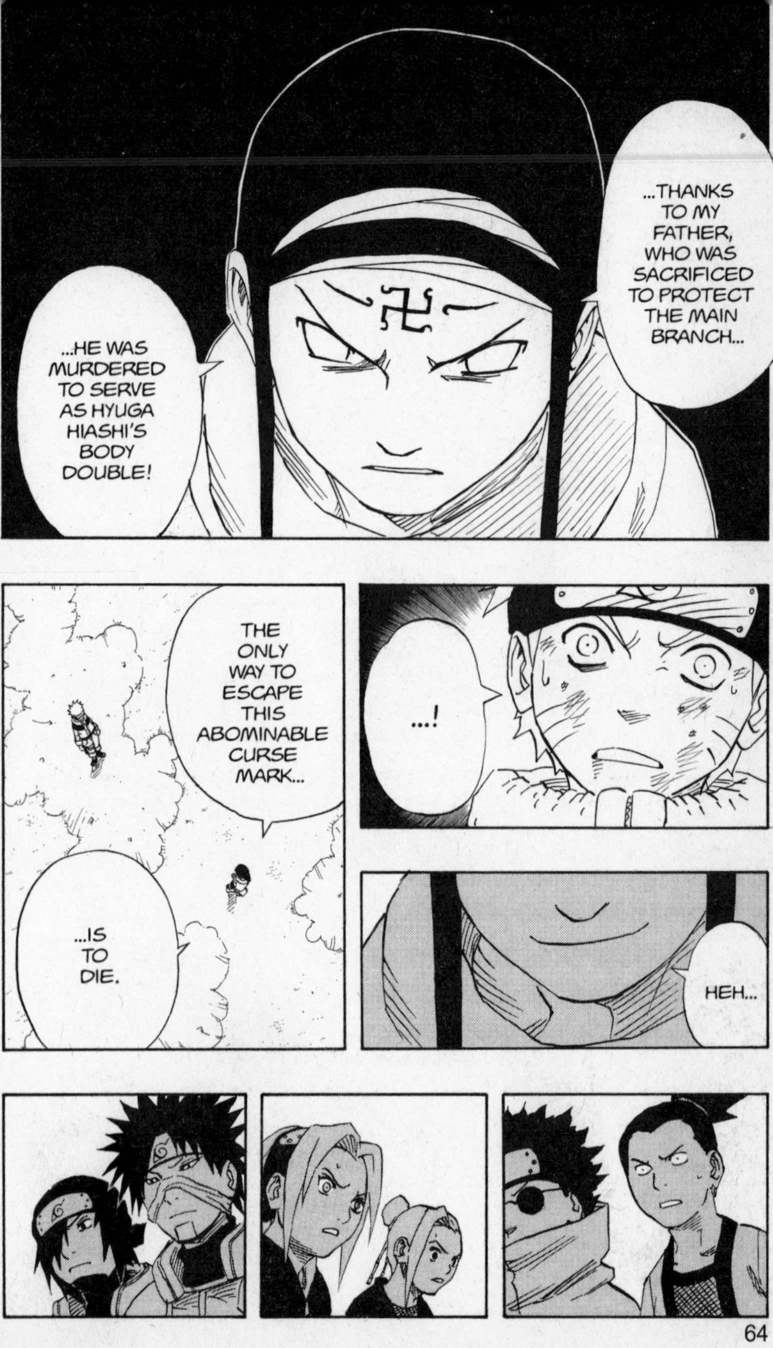
...THANKS TO MY FATHER, WHO WAS SACRIFICED TO PROTECT THE MAIN BRANCH...
...HE WAS MURDERED TO SERVE AS HYUGA HIASHI'S BODY DOUBLE!
THE ONLY WAY TO ESCAPE THIS ABOMINABLE CURSE MARK...
...!
...IS TO DIE.
HEH...

READ THIS WAY

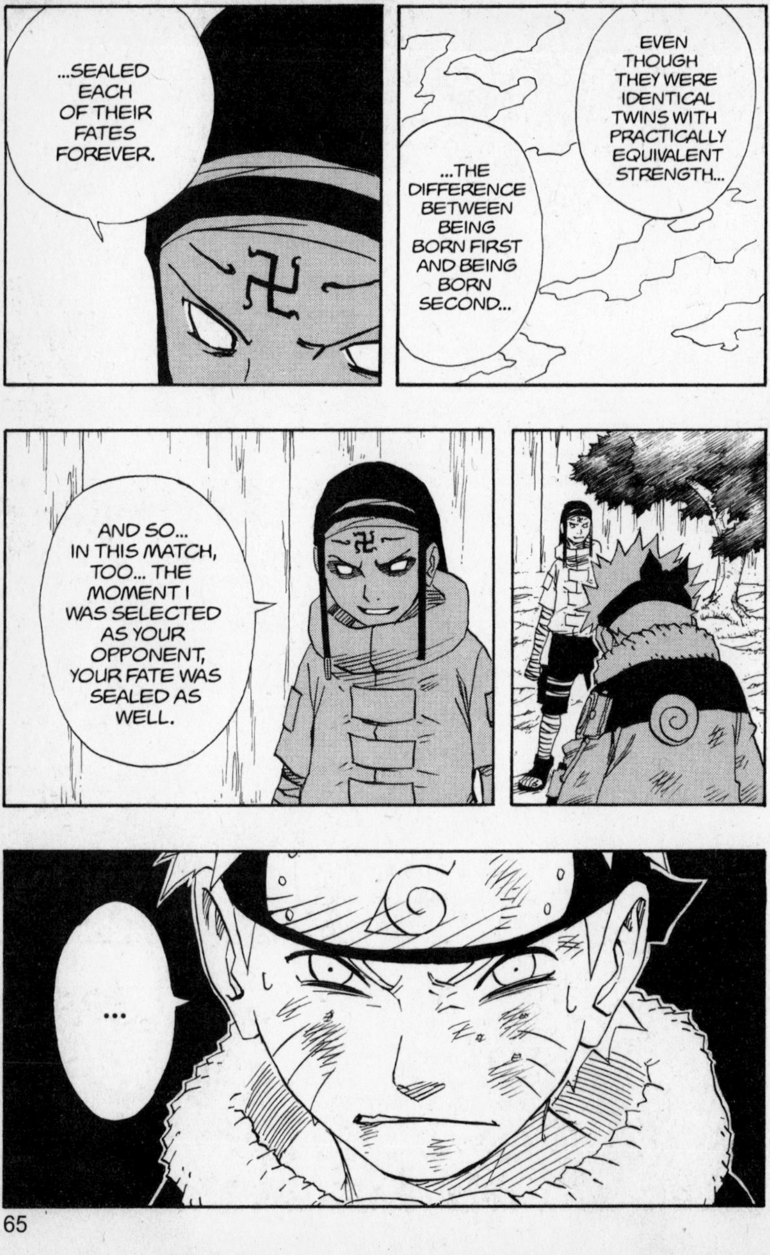
EVEN THOUGH THEY WERE IDENTICAL TWINS WITH PRACTICALLY EQUIVALENT STRENGTH...
...THE DIFFERENCE BETWEEN BEING BORN FIRST AND BEING BORN SECOND...
...SEALED EACH OF THEIR FATES FOREVER.
AND SO... IN THIS MATCH, TOO... THE MOMENT I WAS SELECTED AS YOUR OPPONENT, YOUR FATE WAS SEALED AS WELL.
...

Number 103: The Failure!!

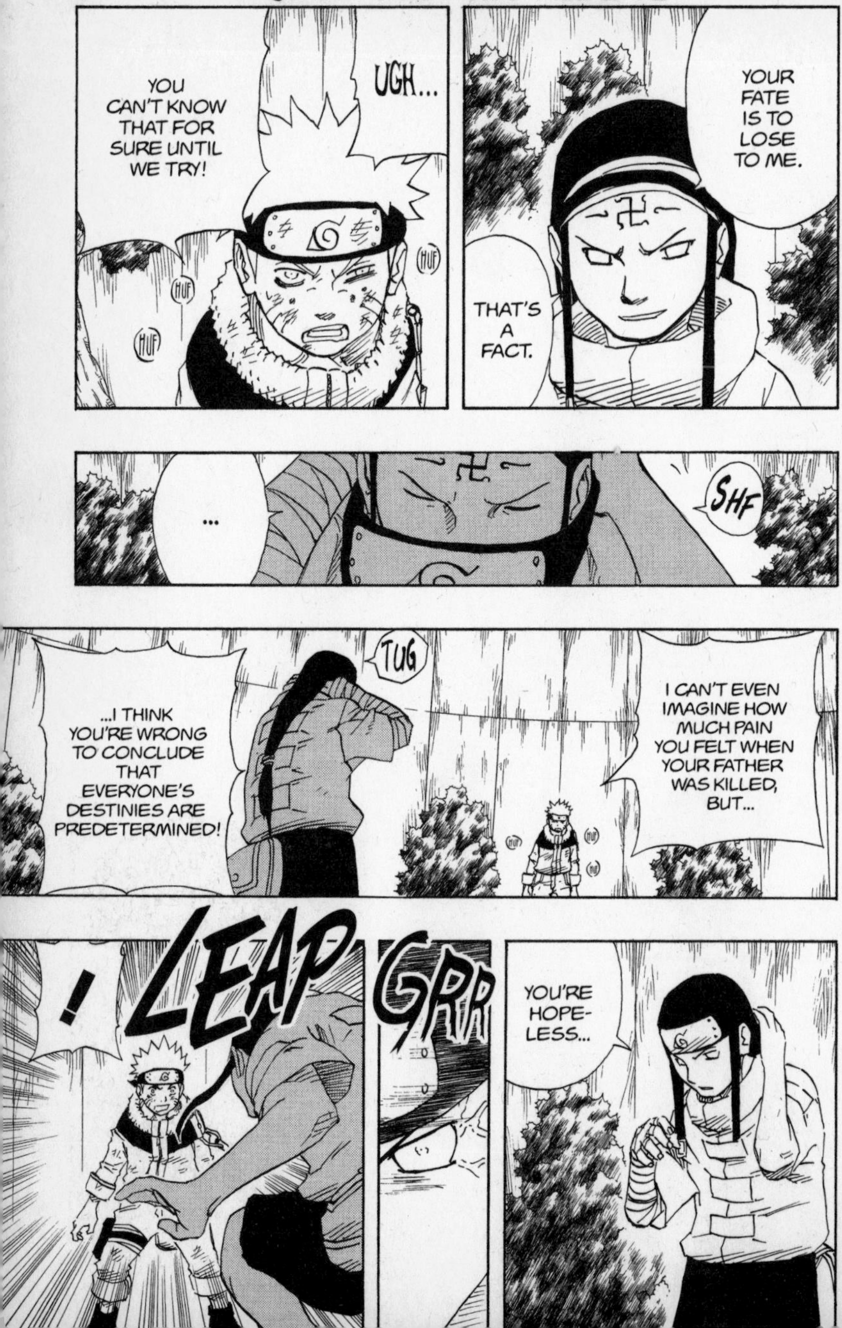
YOUR FATE IS TO LOSE TO ME.
THAT'S A FACT.
UGH...
YOU CAN'T KNOW THAT FOR SURE UNTIL WE TRY!
HUF
HUF
HUF
SHF
...
I CAN'T EVEN IMAGINE HOW MUCH PAIN YOU FELT WHEN YOUR FATHER WAS KILLED, BUT...
TUG
...I THINK YOU'RE WRONG TO CONCLUDE THAT EVERYONE'S DESTINIES ARE PREDETERMINED!
YOU'RE HOPE-LESS...
GRR
LEAP
!

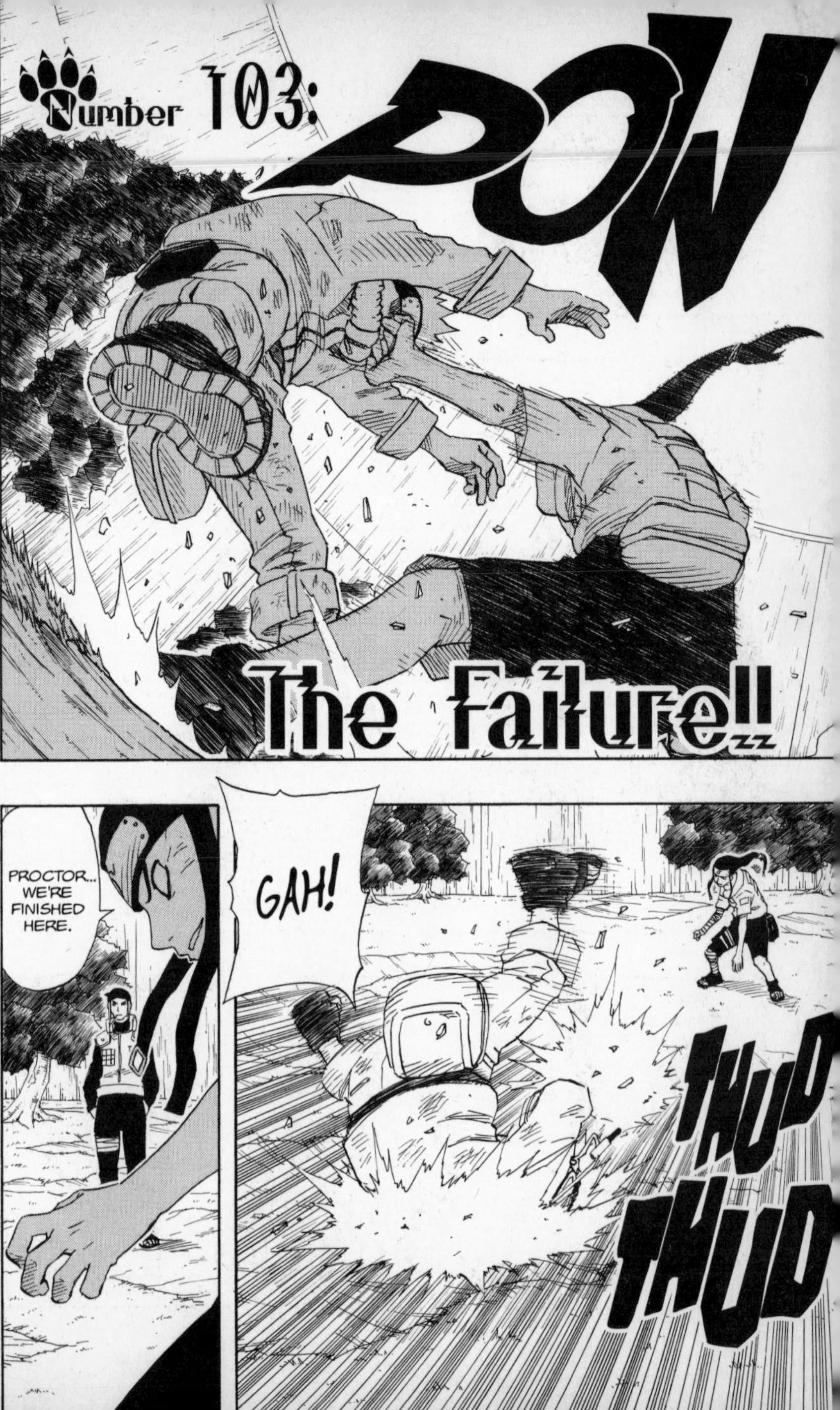
Number 103:
POW
The Failure!!
GAH!
THUD
THUD
PROCTOR... WE'RE FINISHED HERE.

READ THIS WAY

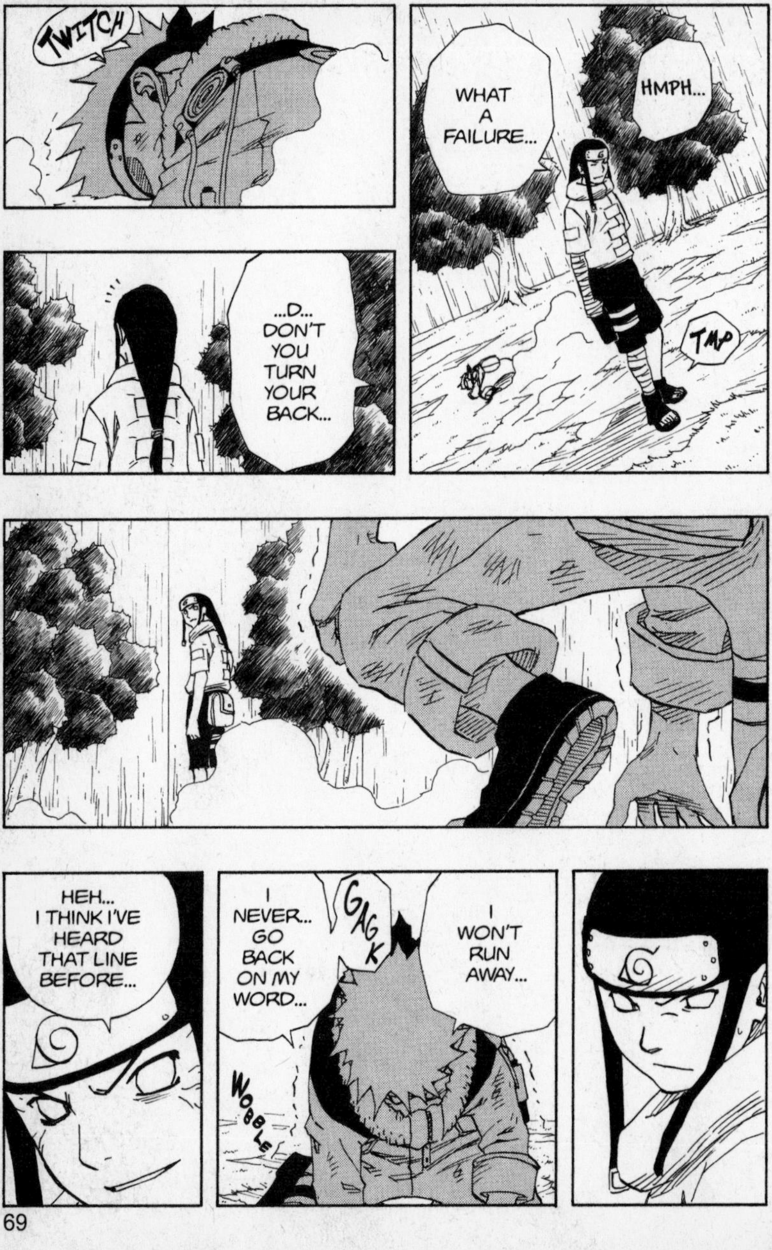
HMPH...
WHAT A FAILURE...
TMP
TWITCH
...D... DON'T YOU TURN YOUR BACK...
I WON'T RUN AWAY...
GAGK
I NEVER... GO BACK ON MY WORD...
WOBBLE
HEH... I THINK I'VE HEARD THAT LINE BEFORE...

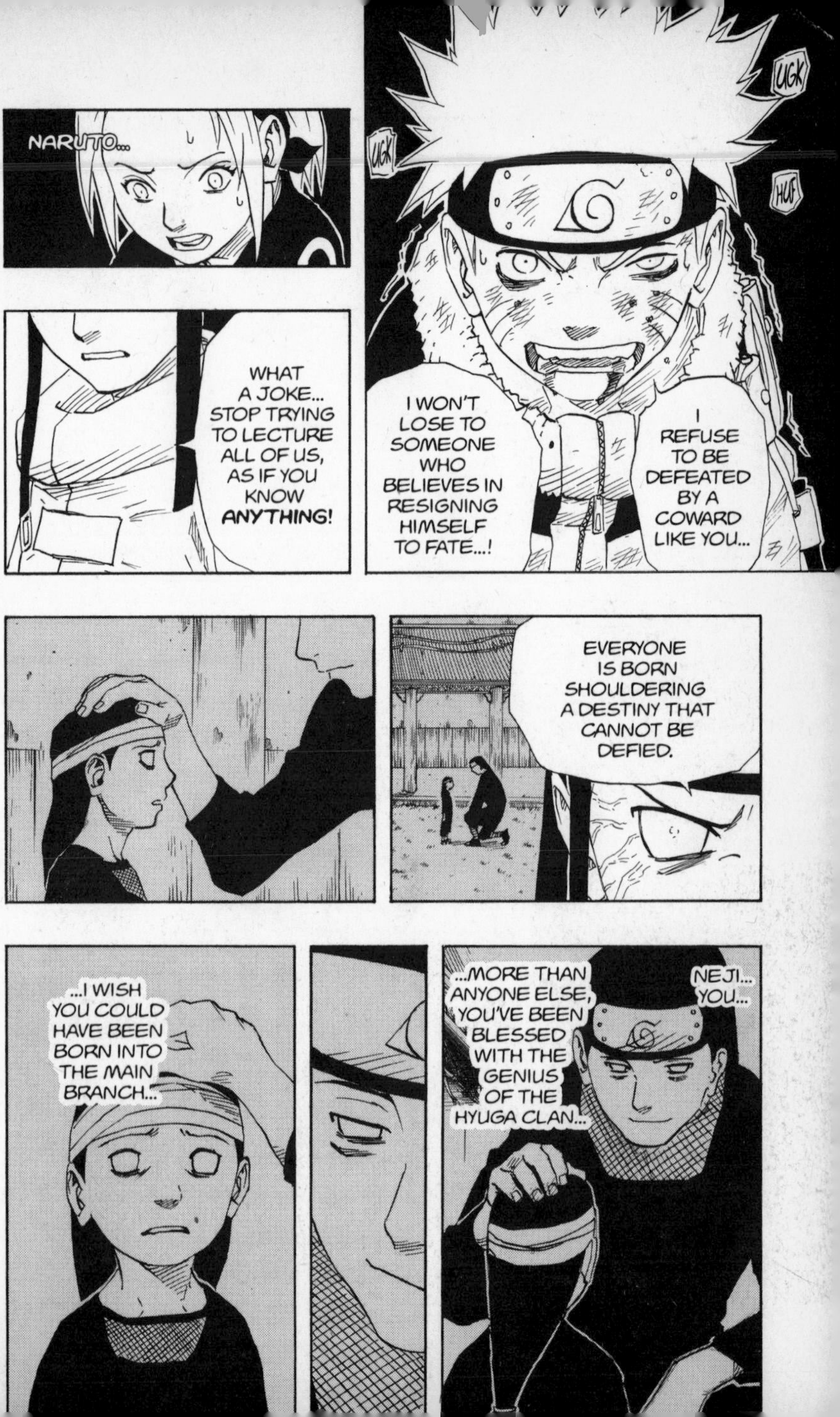
UGK
HUF
UGK
I REFUSE TO BE DEFEATED BY A COWARD LIKE YOU...
I WON'T LOSE TO SOMEONE WHO BELIEVES IN RESIGNING HIMSELF TO FATE...!
NARUTO...
WHAT A JOKE... STOP TRYING TO LECTURE ALL OF US, AS IF YOU KNOW **ANYTHING!**
EVERYONE IS BORN SHOULDERING A DESTINY THAT CANNOT BE DEFIED.
NEJI... YOU...
...MORE THAN ANYONE ELSE, YOU'VE BEEN BLESSED WITH THE GENIUS OF THE HYUGA CLAN...
...I WISH YOU COULD HAVE BEEN BORN INTO THE MAIN BRANCH...

HOW COULD YOU UNDERSTAND ANYTHING ABOUT MY FATE... ABOUT BEARING AN INDELIBLE, INESCAPABLE CURSE?!

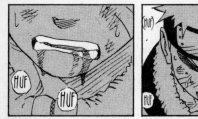

HUF
HUF
HUF

HUF
HUF

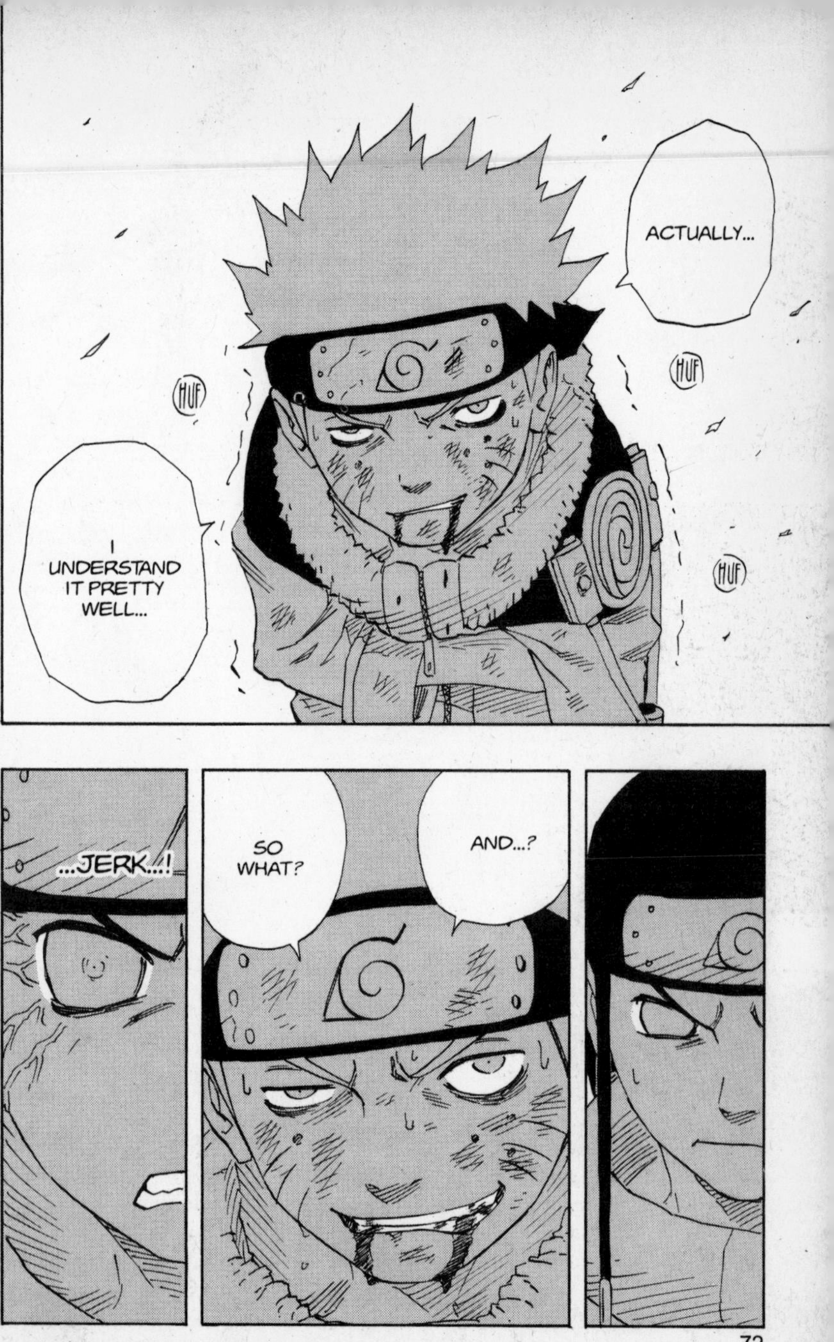
ACTUALLY...
HUF
HUF
HUF
I UNDERSTAND IT PRETTY WELL...
AND...?
SO WHAT?
...JERK...!

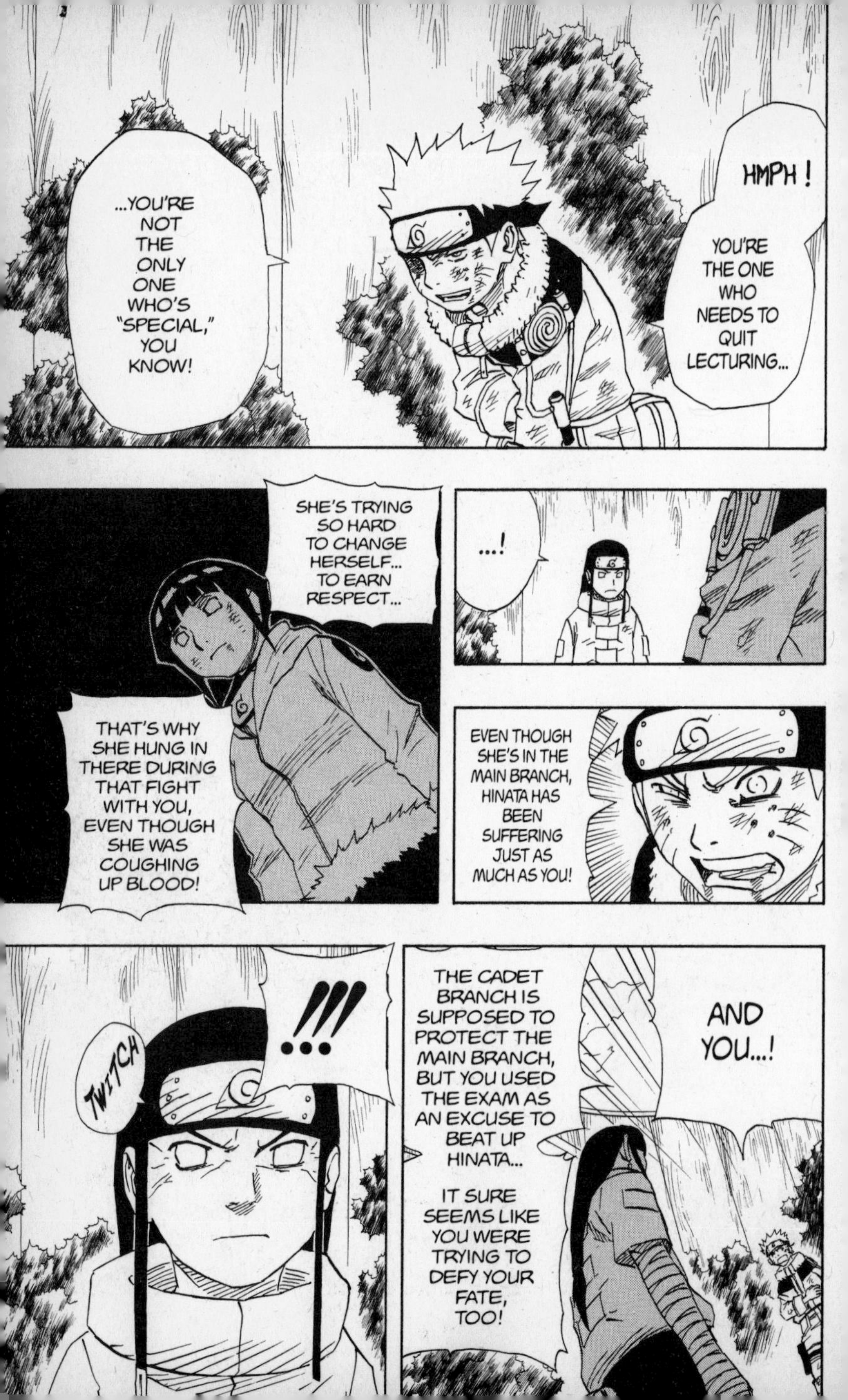
HMPH !
YOU'RE THE ONE WHO NEEDS TO QUIT LECTURING...
...YOU'RE NOT THE ONLY ONE WHO'S "SPECIAL," YOU KNOW!
...!
EVEN THOUGH SHE'S IN THE MAIN BRANCH, HINATA HAS BEEN SUFFERING JUST AS MUCH AS YOU!
SHE'S TRYING SO HARD TO CHANGE HERSELF... TO EARN RESPECT...
THAT'S WHY SHE HUNG IN THERE DURING THAT FIGHT WITH YOU, EVEN THOUGH SHE WAS COUGHING UP BLOOD!
AND YOU...!
THE CADET BRANCH IS SUPPOSED TO PROTECT THE MAIN BRANCH, BUT YOU USED THE EXAM AS AN EXCUSE TO BEAT UP HINATA...
IT SURE SEEMS LIKE YOU WERE TRYING TO DEFY YOUR FATE, TOO!
...!!!
TWITCH

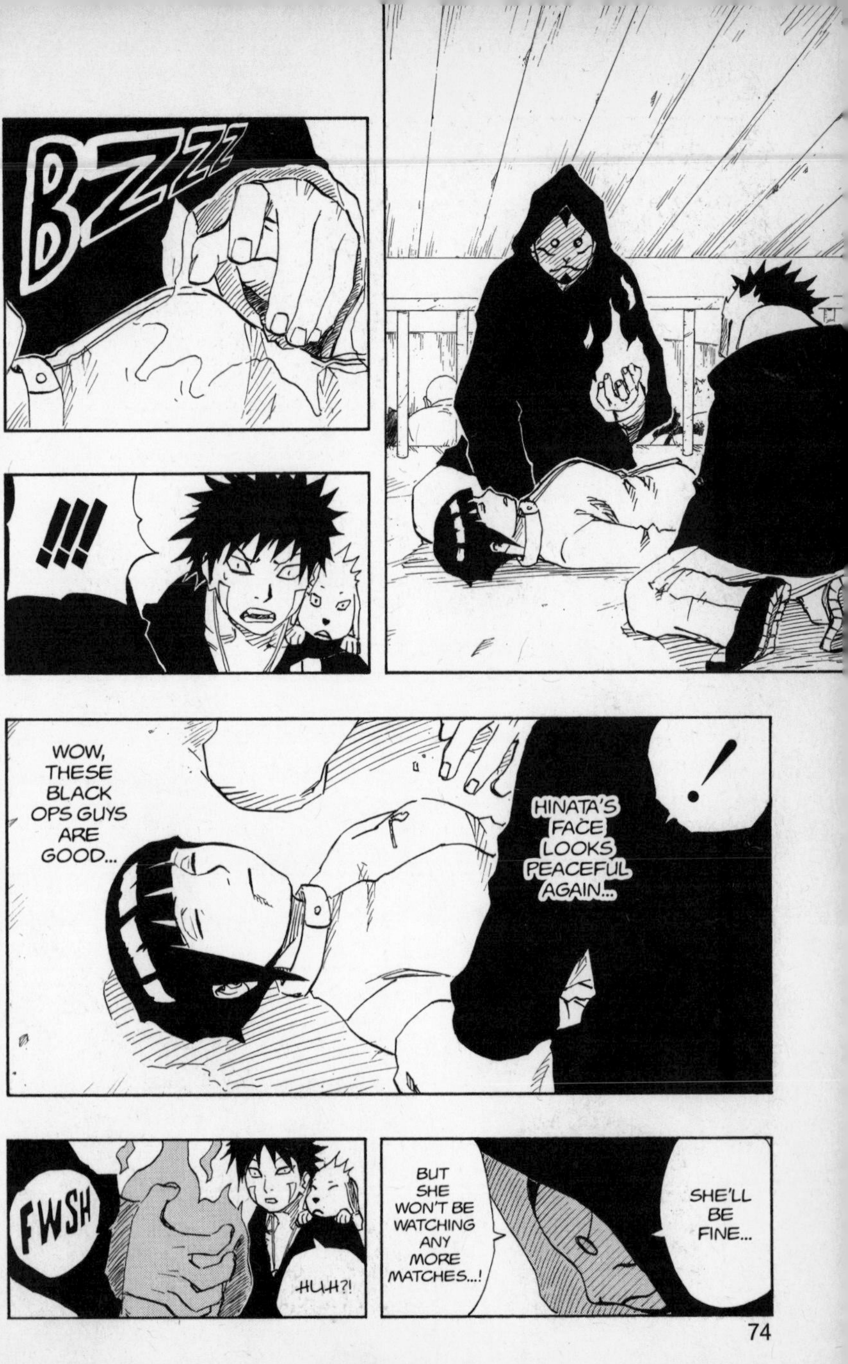
BZZZ
!!!
!
HINATA'S FACE LOOKS PEACEFUL AGAIN...
WOW, THESE BLACK OPS GUYS ARE GOOD...
SHE'LL BE FINE...
BUT SHE WON'T BE WATCHING ANY MORE MATCHES...!
FWSH
HUH?!

READ THIS WAY

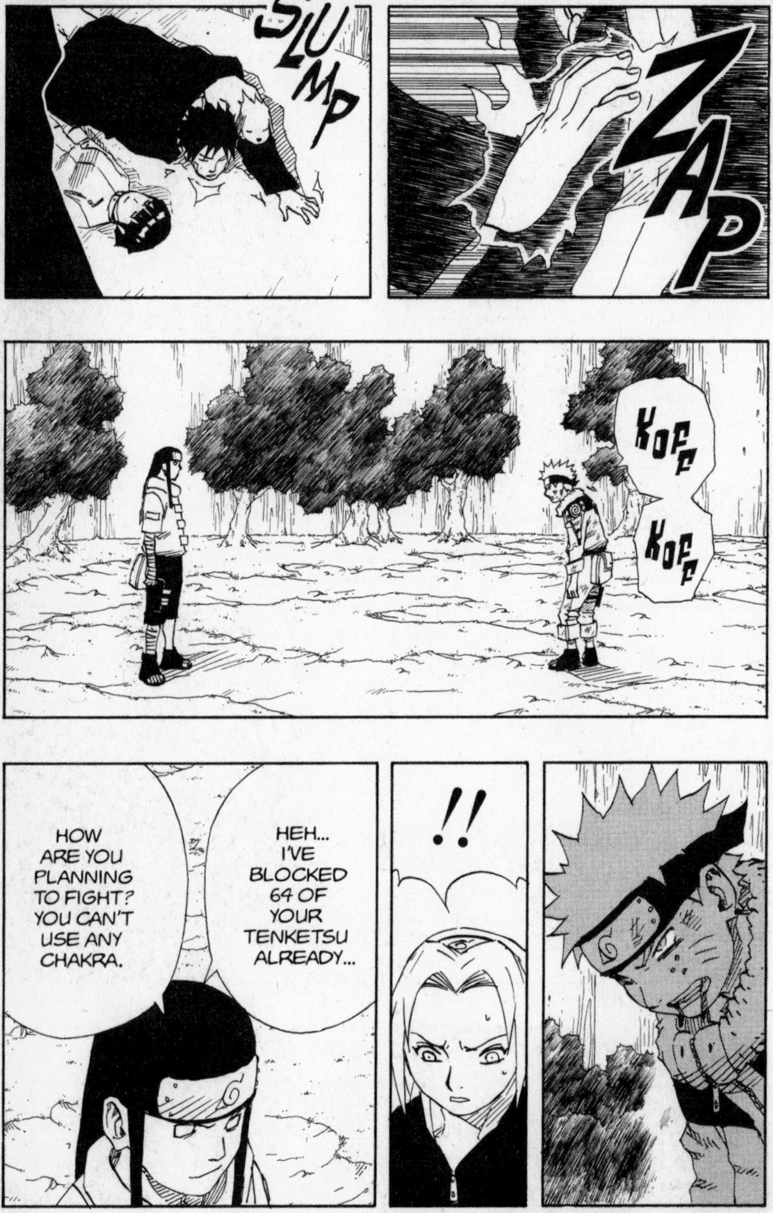
ZAP
SLUMP
KOFF KOFF
!!
HEH... I'VE BLOCKED 64 OF YOUR TENKETSU ALREADY...
HOW ARE YOU PLANNING TO FIGHT? YOU CAN'T USE ANY CHAKRA.

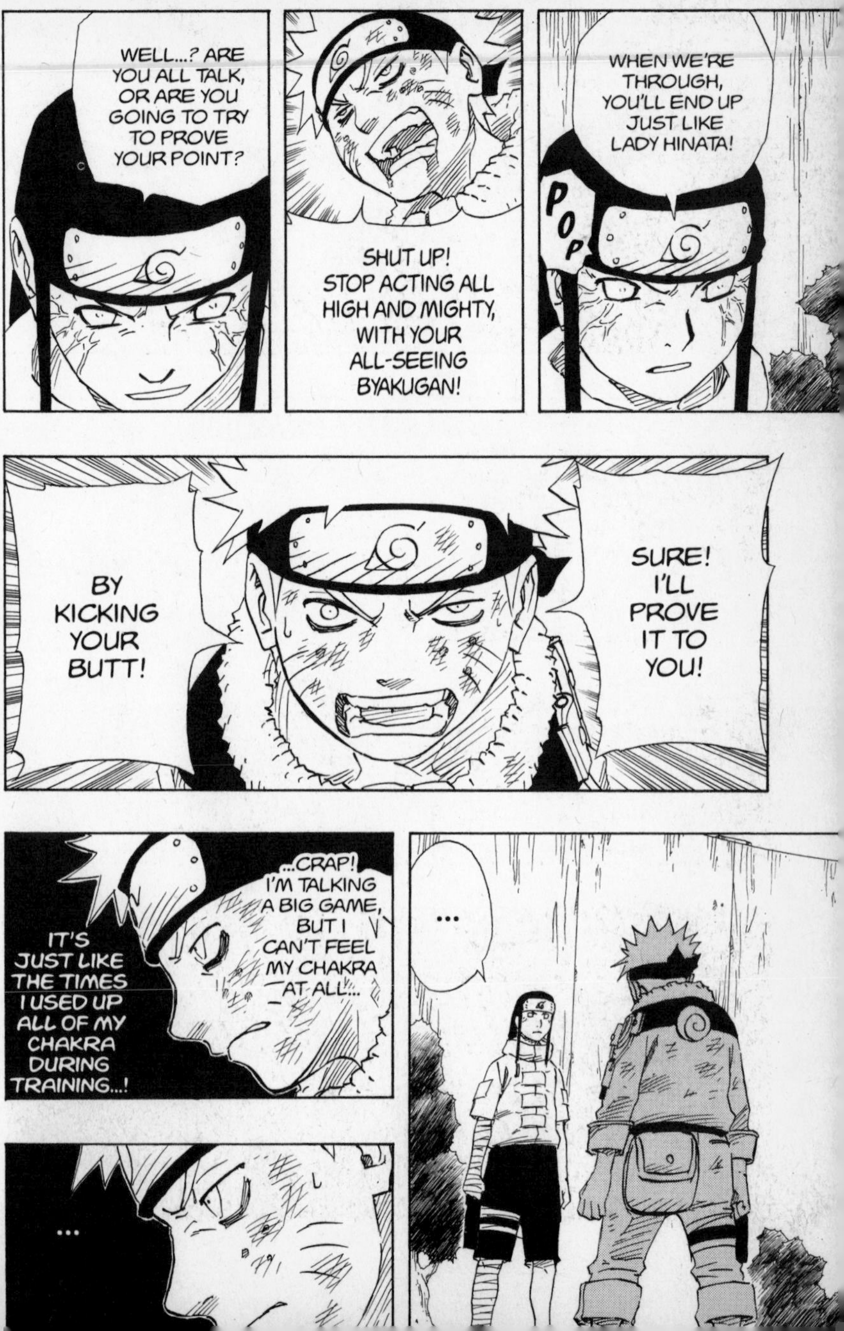
WHEN WE'RE THROUGH, YOU'LL END UP JUST LIKE LADY HINATA!
POP
SHUT UP! STOP ACTING ALL HIGH AND MIGHTY, WITH YOUR ALL-SEEING BYAKUGAN!
WELL...? ARE YOU ALL TALK, OR ARE YOU GOING TO TRY TO PROVE YOUR POINT?
SURE! I'LL PROVE IT TO YOU!
BY KICKING YOUR BUTT!
...
...CRAP! I'M TALKING A BIG GAME, BUT I CAN'T FEEL MY CHAKRA AT ALL...
IT'S JUST LIKE THE TIMES I USED UP ALL OF MY CHAKRA DURING TRAINING...!
...

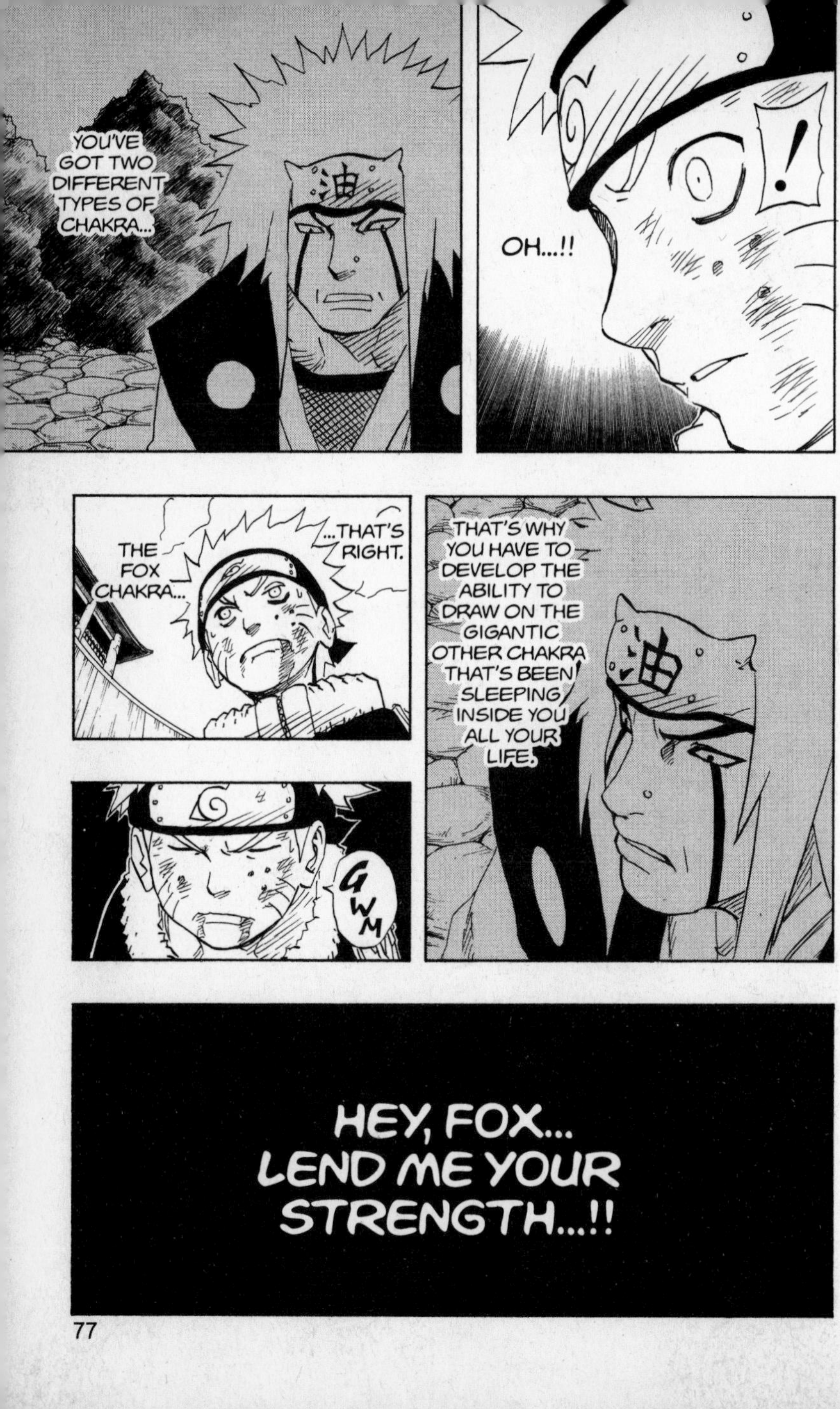
!
OH...!!
YOU'VE GOT TWO DIFFERENT TYPES OF CHAKRA...
THAT'S WHY YOU HAVE TO DEVELOP THE ABILITY TO DRAW ON THE GIGANTIC OTHER CHAKRA THAT'S BEEN SLEEPING INSIDE YOU ALL YOUR LIFE.
...THAT'S RIGHT.
THE FOX CHAKRA...
GWM
HEY, FOX... LEND ME YOUR STRENGTH...!!

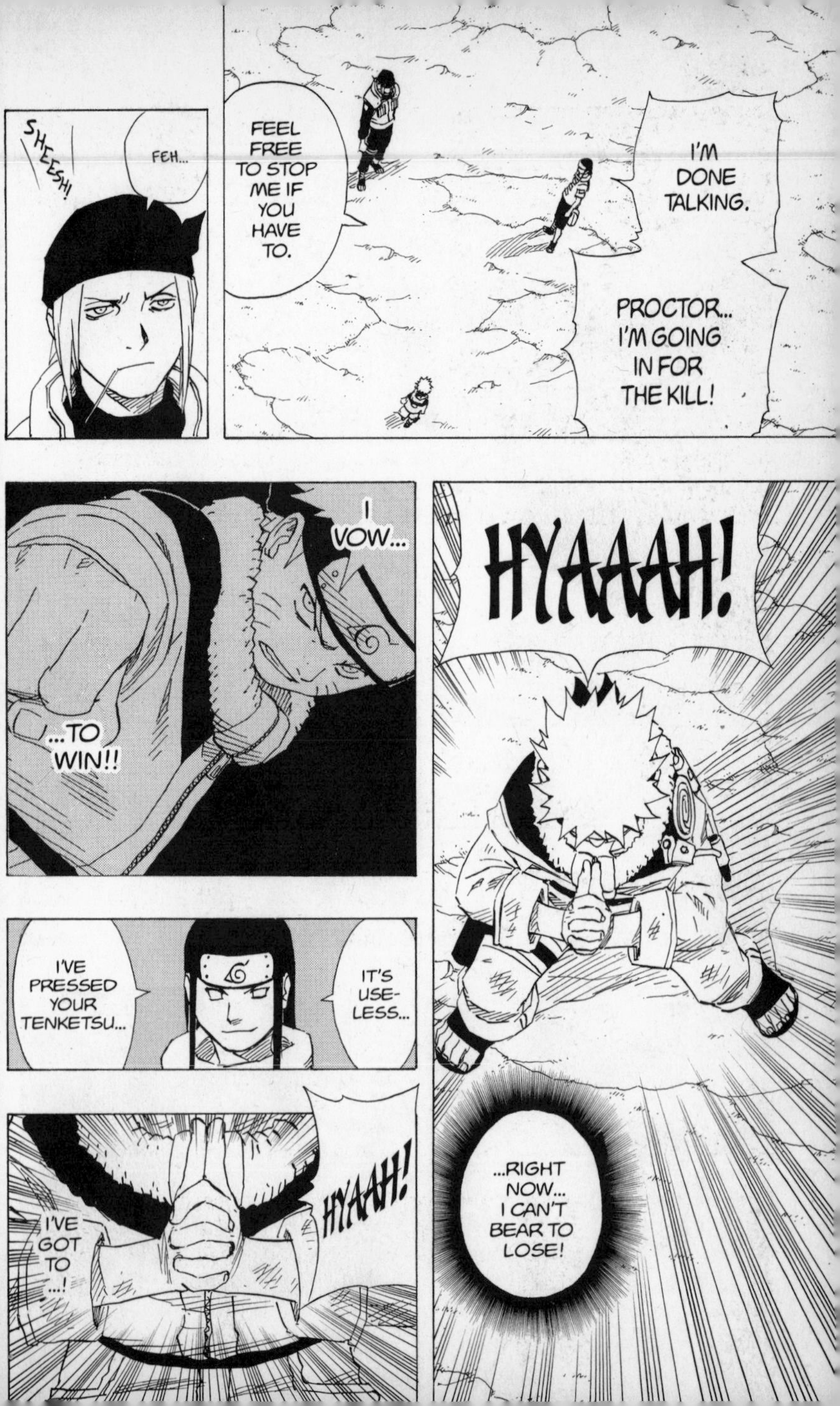
I'M DONE TALKING.
PROCTOR... I'M GOING IN FOR THE KILL!
FEEL FREE TO STOP ME IF YOU HAVE TO.
SHEESH!
FEH...
HYAAAH!
...RIGHT NOW... I CAN'T BEAR TO LOSE!
I VOW...
...TO WIN!!
IT'S USE-LESS...
I'VE PRESSED YOUR TENKETSU...
HYAAH!
I'VE GOT TO ...!

READ THIS WAY

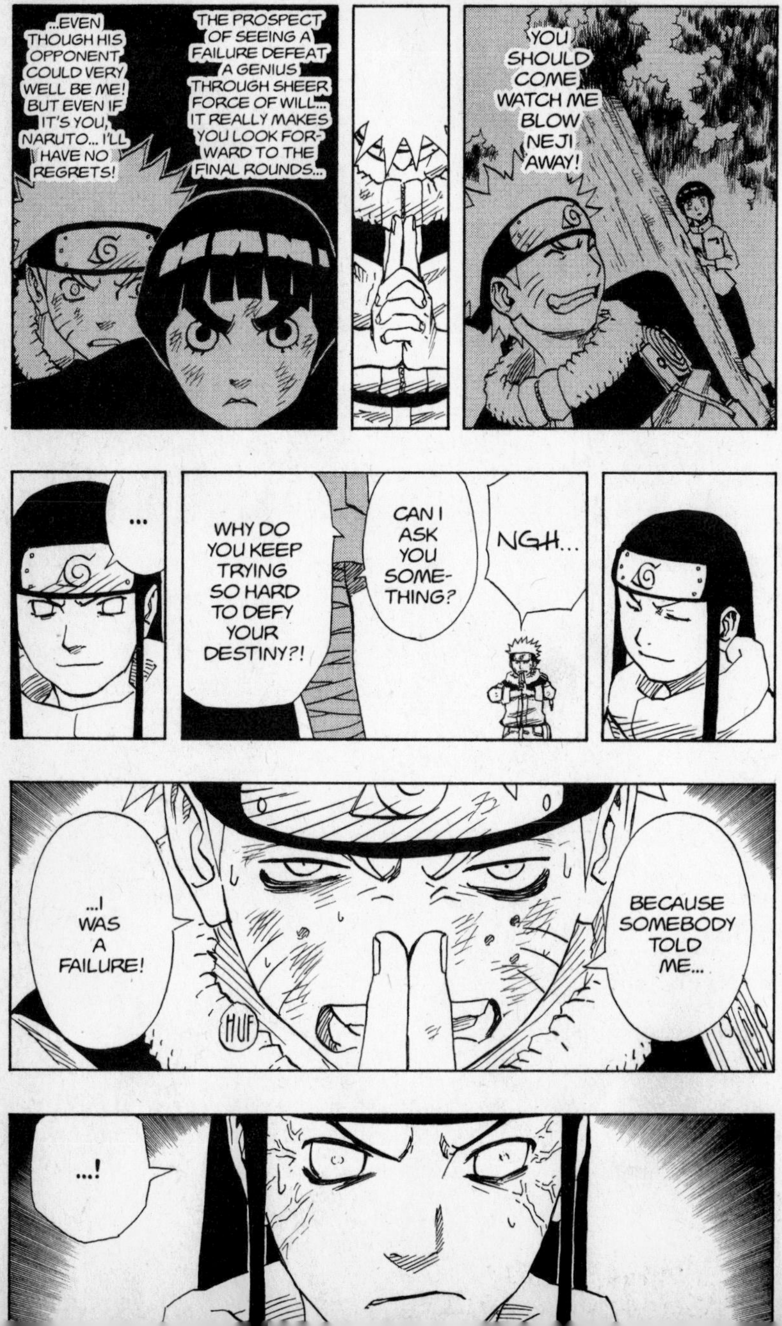
YOU SHOULD COME WATCH ME BLOW NEJI AWAY!
THE PROSPECT OF SEEING A FAILURE DEFEAT A GENIUS THROUGH SHEER FORCE OF WILL... IT REALLY MAKES YOU LOOK FORWARD TO THE FINAL ROUNDS...
...EVEN THOUGH HIS OPPONENT COULD VERY WELL BE ME! BUT EVEN IF IT'S YOU, NARUTO... I'LL HAVE NO REGRETS!
NGH...
CAN I ASK YOU SOMETHING?
WHY DO YOU KEEP TRYING SO HARD TO DEFY YOUR DESTINY?!
...
BECAUSE SOMEBODY TOLD ME...
...I WAS A FAILURE!
HUF
...!

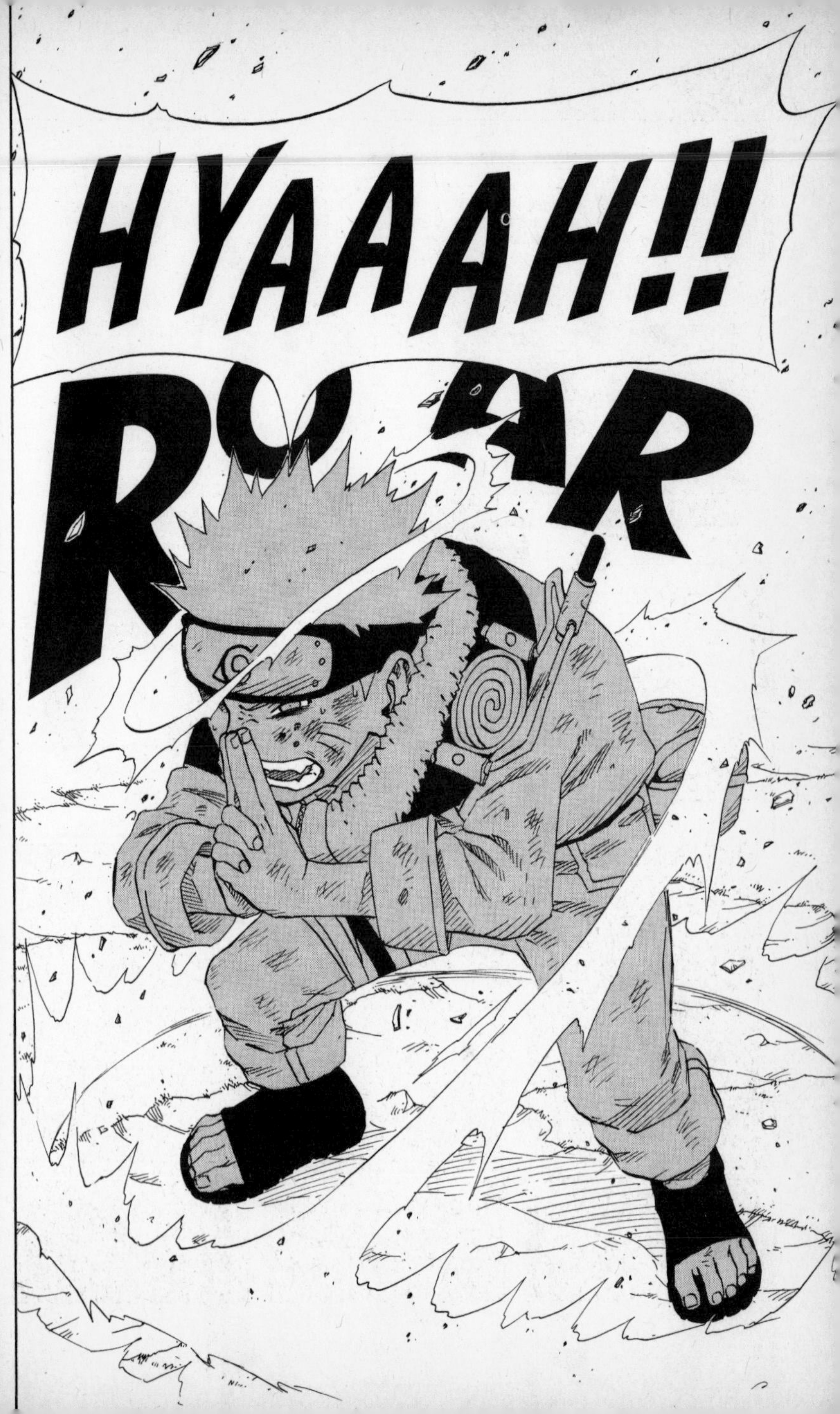
HYAAAH!!
ROAR

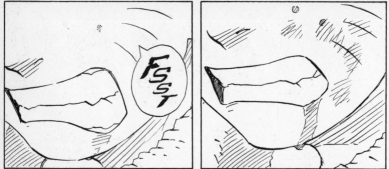

HIS CHAKRA IS OOZING OUT... WHAT'S GOING ON...?

...IMPOSSIBLE!

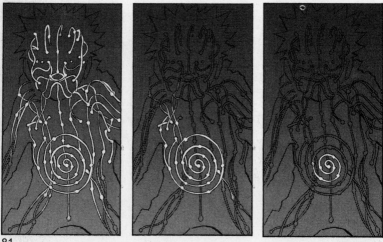

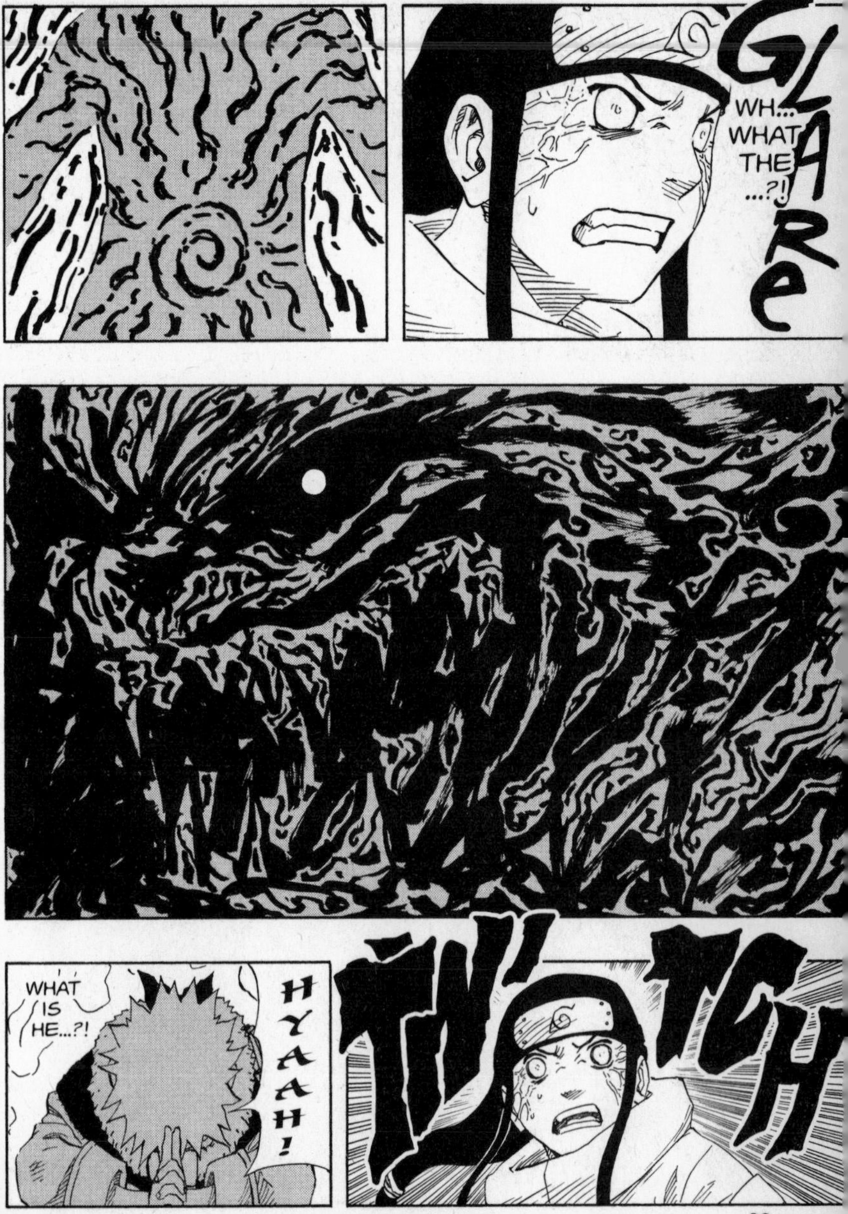
GLARE
WH... WHAT THE ...?!
THTCH
WHAT IS HE...?!
HYAAAH!

READ THIS WAY

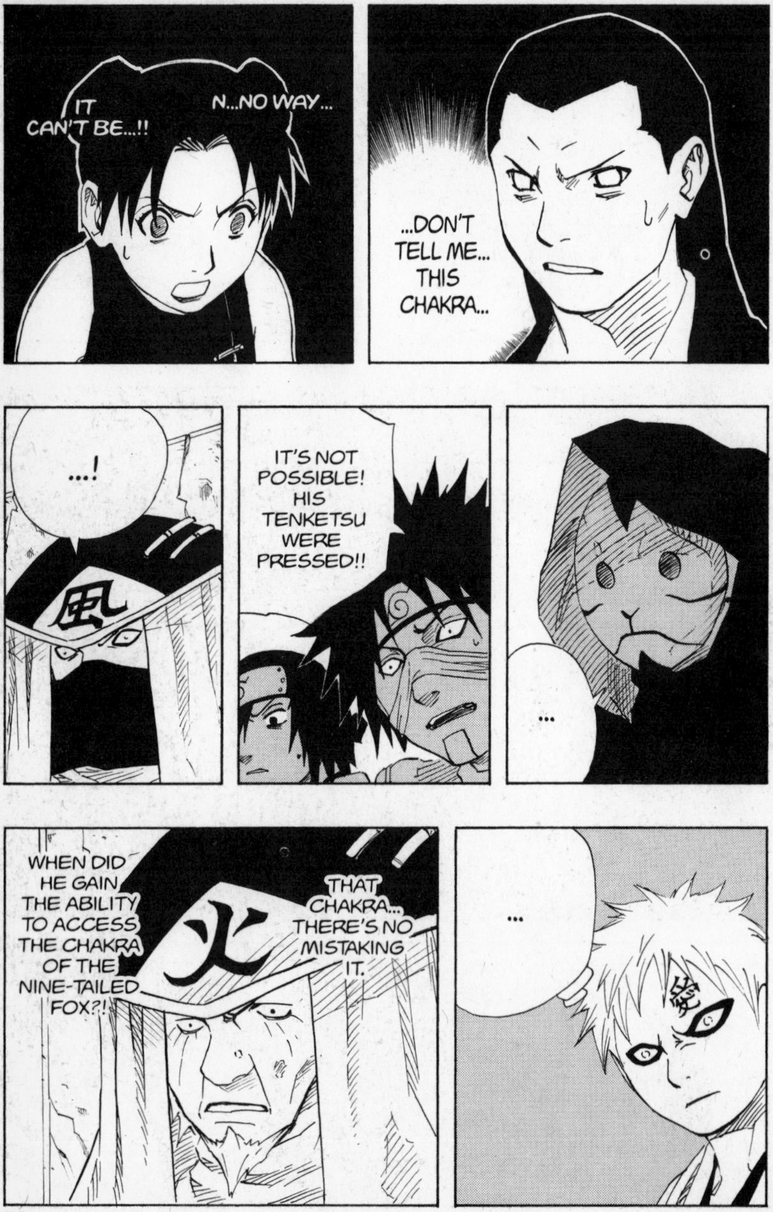
...DON'T TELL ME... THIS CHAKRA...
N...NO WAY...
IT CAN'T BE...!!
...
IT'S NOT POSSIBLE! HIS TENKETSU WERE PRESSED!!
...!
...
THAT CHAKRA... THERE'S NO MISTAKING IT.
WHEN DID HE GAIN THE ABILITY TO ACCESS THE CHAKRA OF THE NINE-TAILED FOX?!

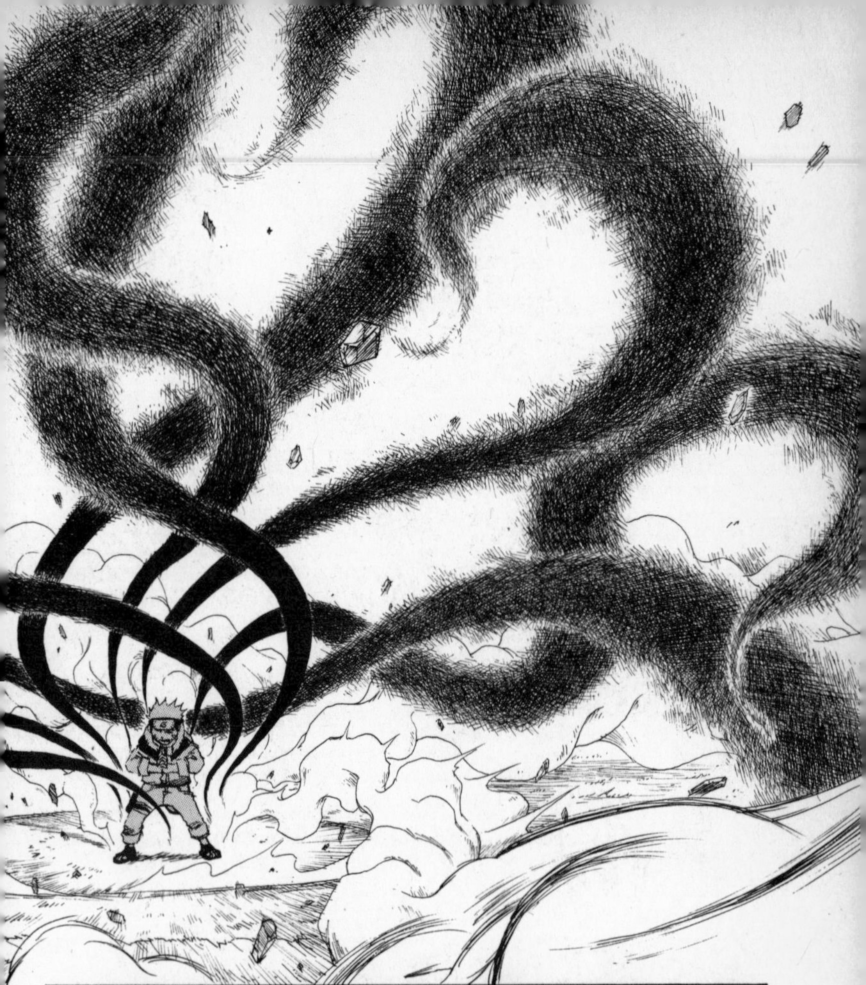

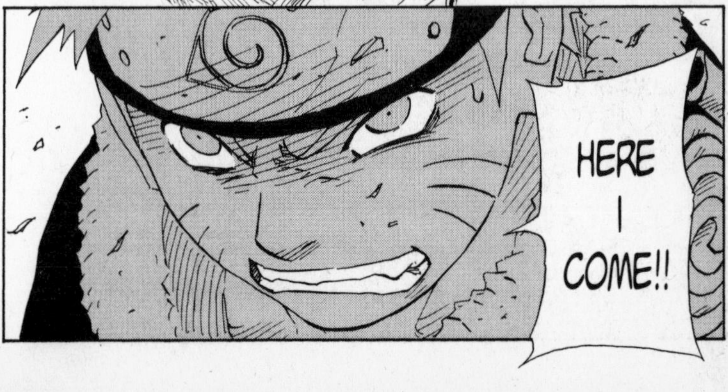
HERE I COME!!

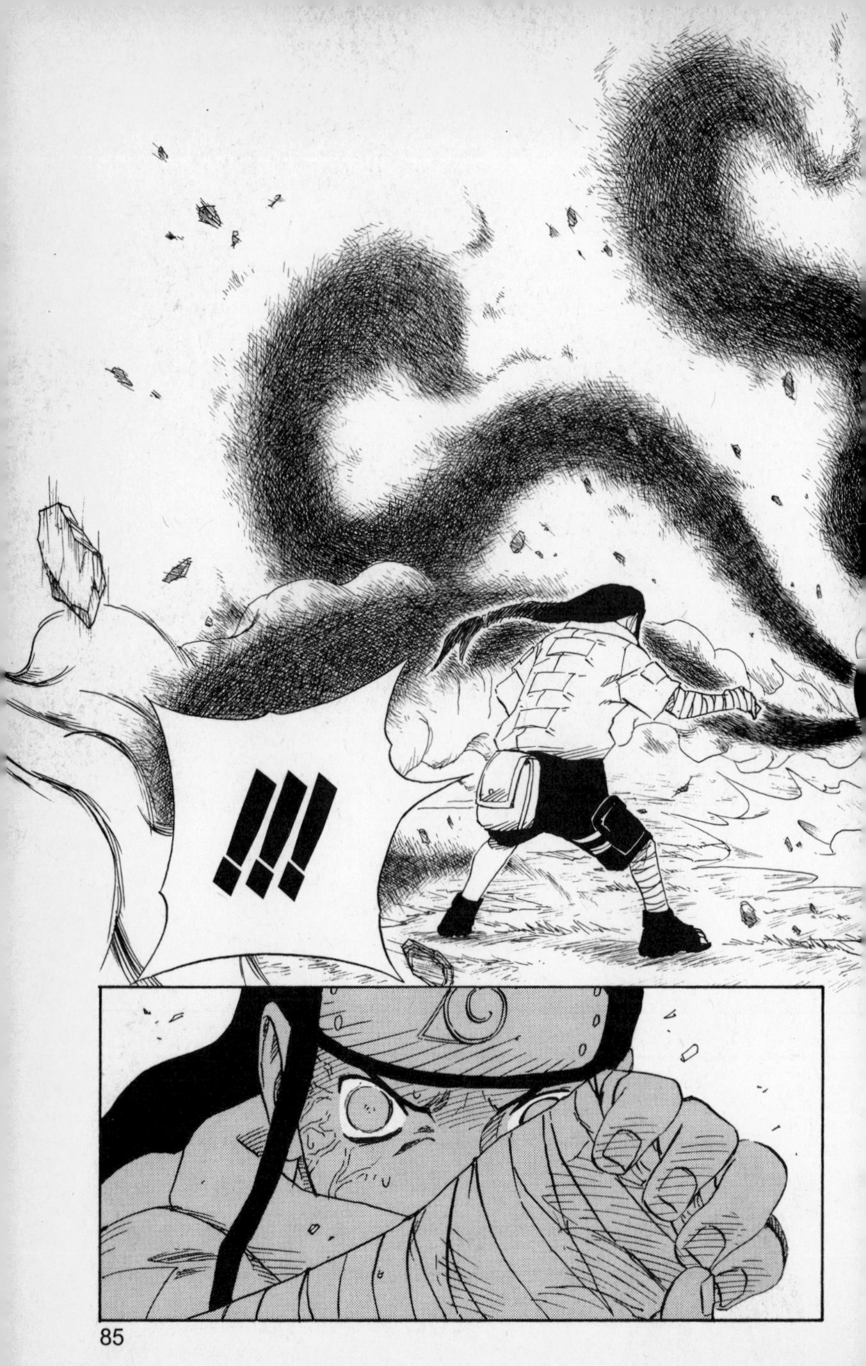
!!!

SECOND ANNIVERSARY CELEBRATION!

祝 二周年

2001.11.8
加治佐 修
KAZISA OSAMU

I CAN'T BELIEVE IT'S ALREADY BEEN TWO YEARS!
I HOPE YOU CAN ALWAYS KEEP DRAWING WITH
THE AMAZING ENERGY YOU HAVE NOW!

はやいもんで もう2年ですね。
これからも 今と変わらぬテンションで描きまくって下さい。

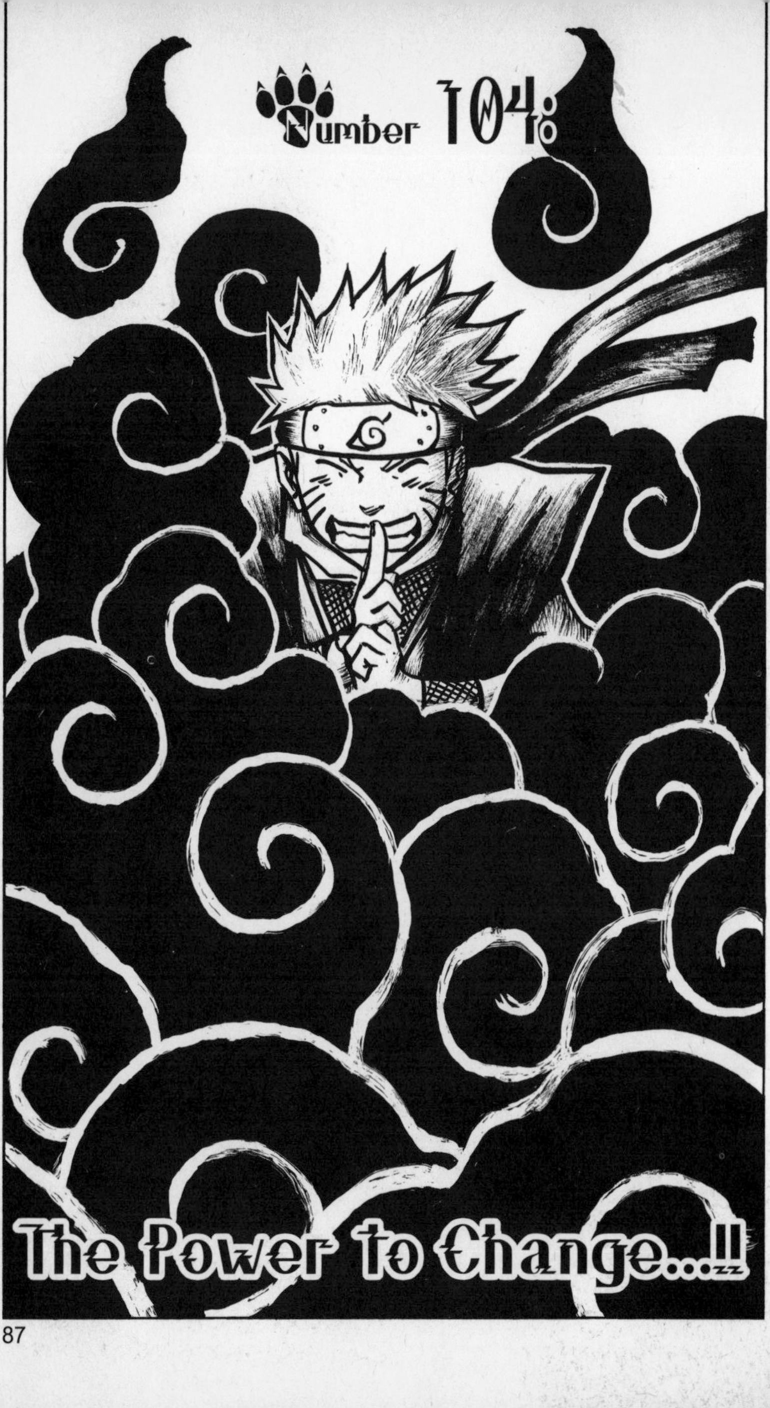
Number 104:
The Power to Change...!!

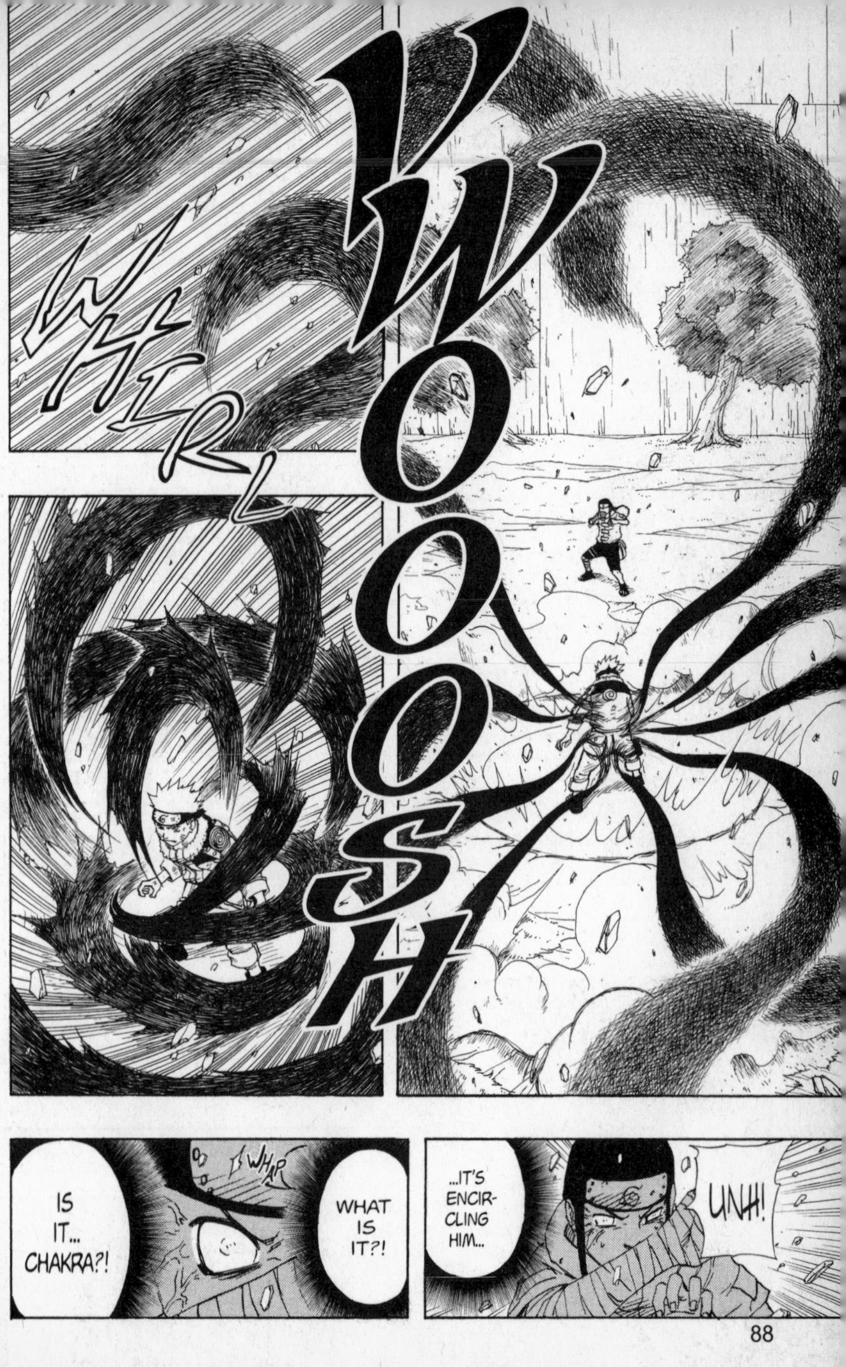
WOOOOSH
WHIRL
UNH!
...IT'S ENCIRCLING HIM...
WHAP
WHAT IS IT?!
IS IT... CHAKRA?!

READ THIS WAY

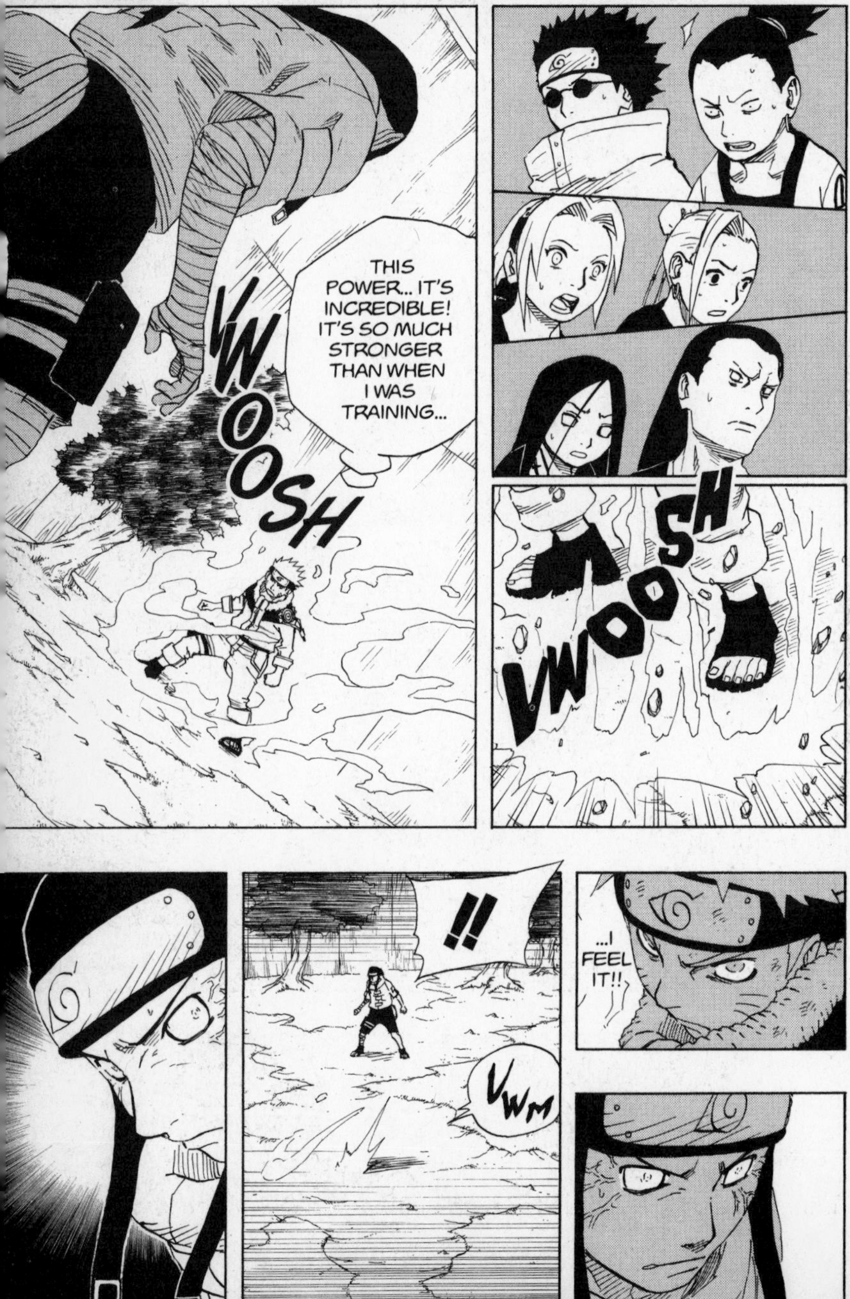
VWOOSH
THIS POWER... IT'S INCREDIBLE! IT'S SO MUCH STRONGER THAN WHEN I WAS TRAINING...
VWOOSH
...I FEEL IT!!
!!
VWM

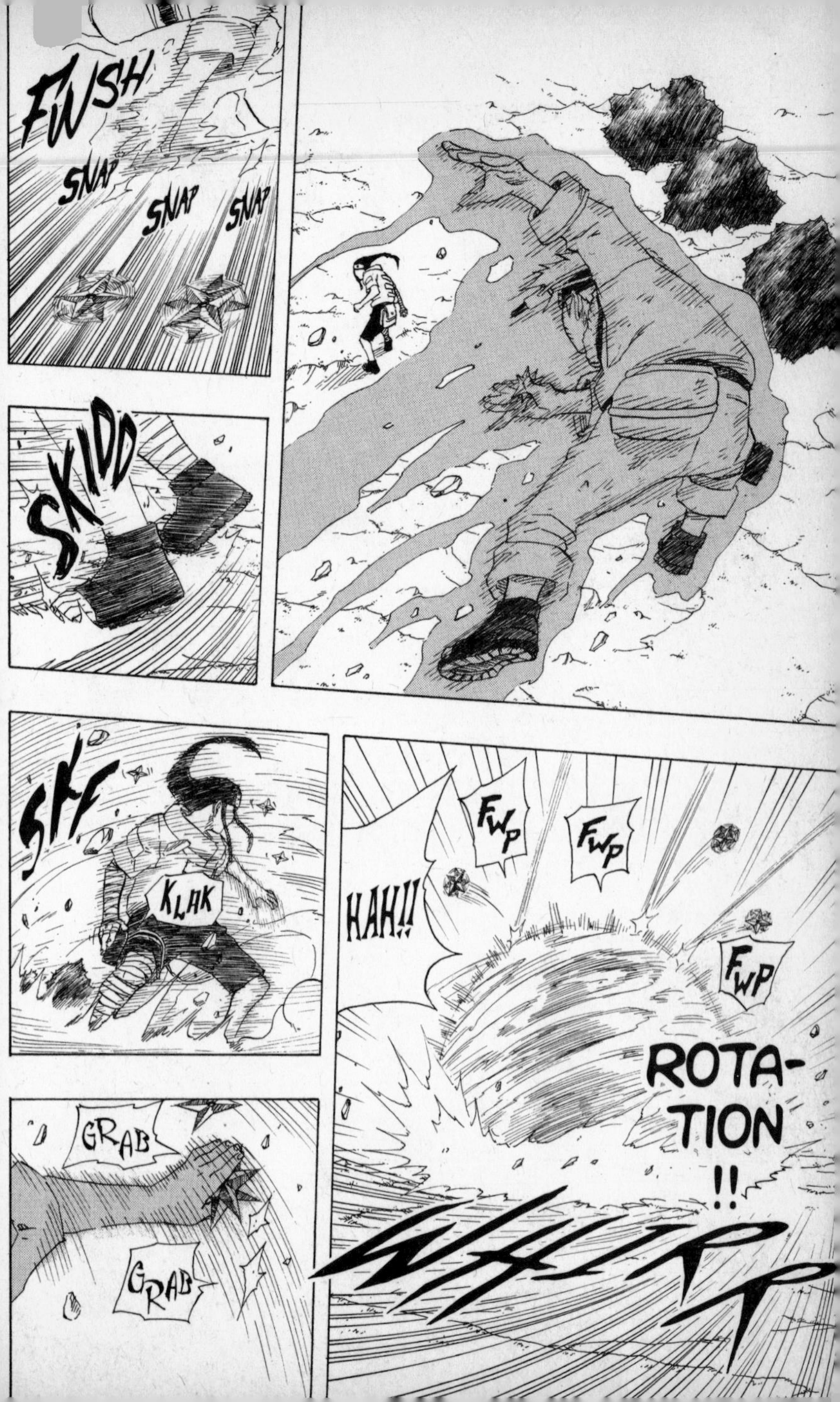
FWSH
SNAP
SNAP
SNAP
SKIDD
FWP
FWP
HAH!!
FWP
ROTATION!!
WHIRR
SKF
KLAK
GRAB
GRAB

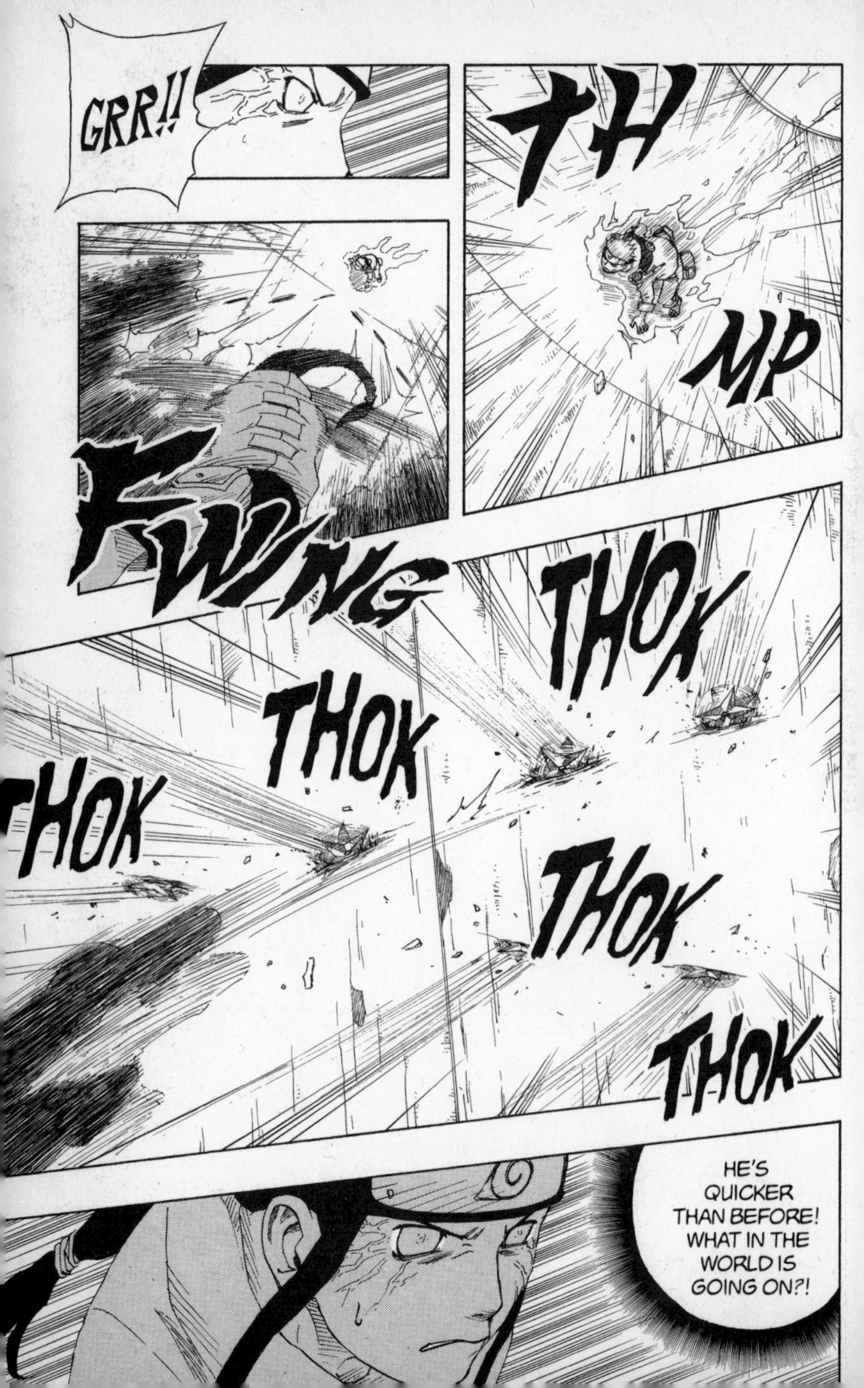
TH
MP
GRR!!
FWING
THOK
THOK
THOK
THOK
THOK
HE'S QUICKER THAN BEFORE! WHAT IN THE WORLD IS GOING ON?!

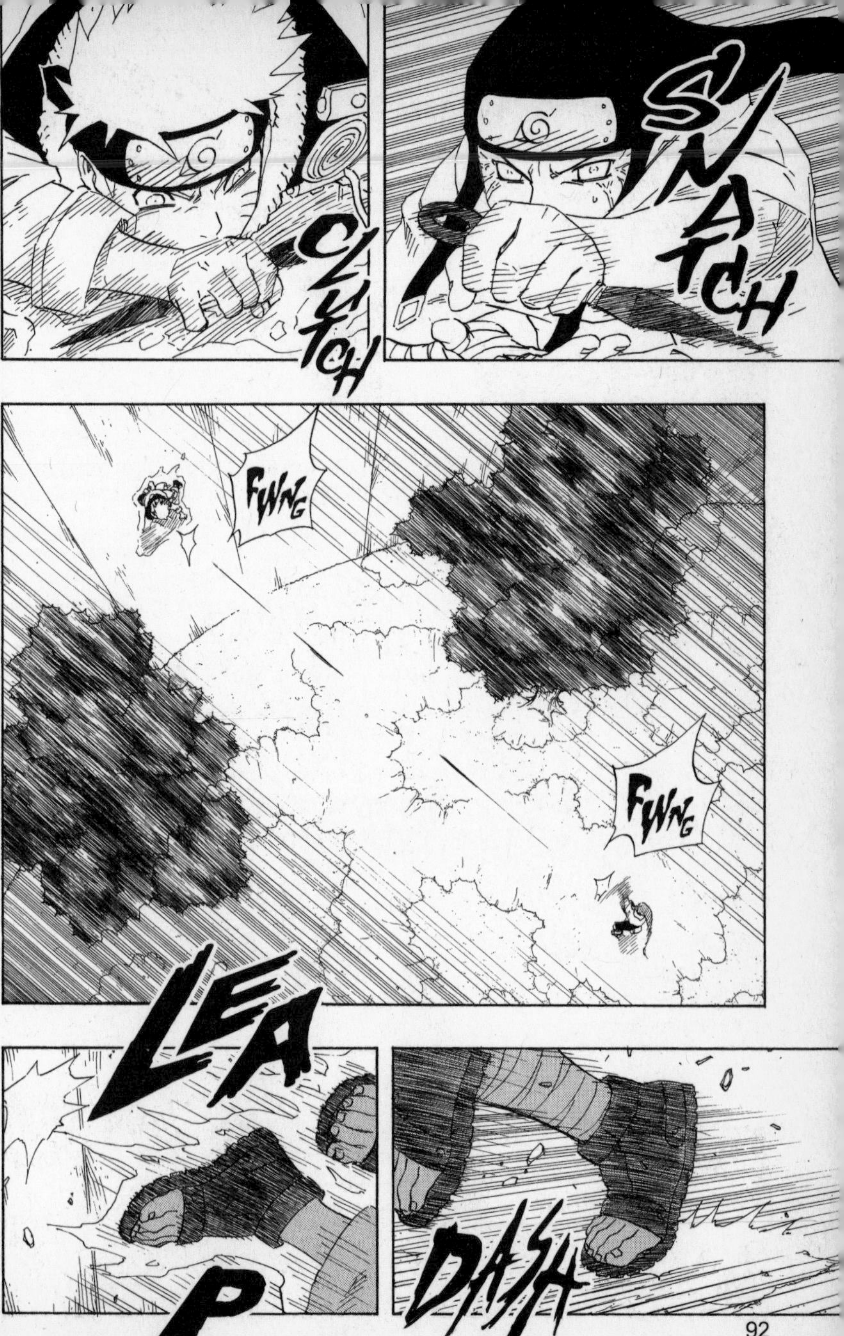
SNATCH
CLUTCH
FWNG
FWNG
DASH
LEAP

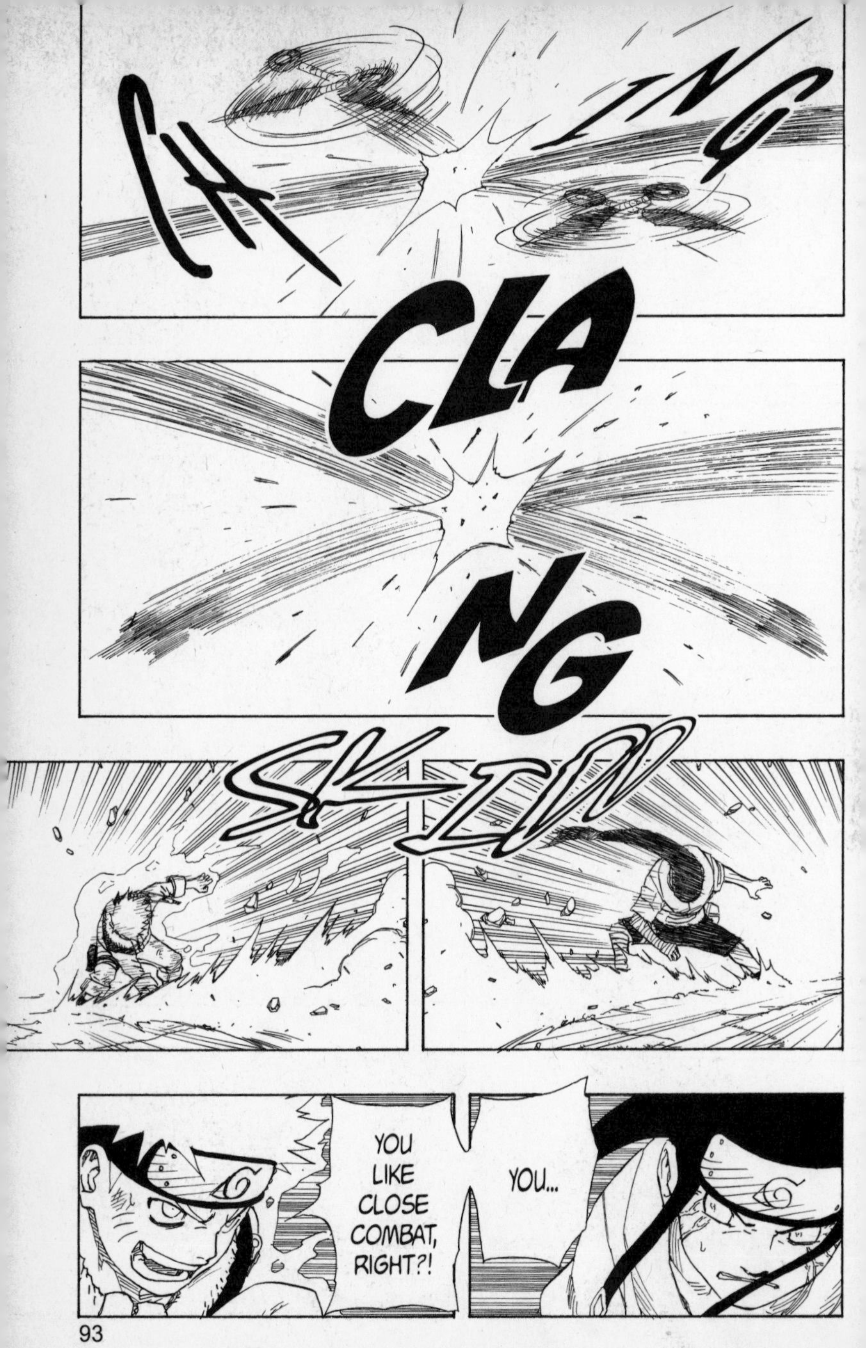
CHING
CLANG
YOU...
YOU LIKE CLOSE COMBAT, RIGHT?!

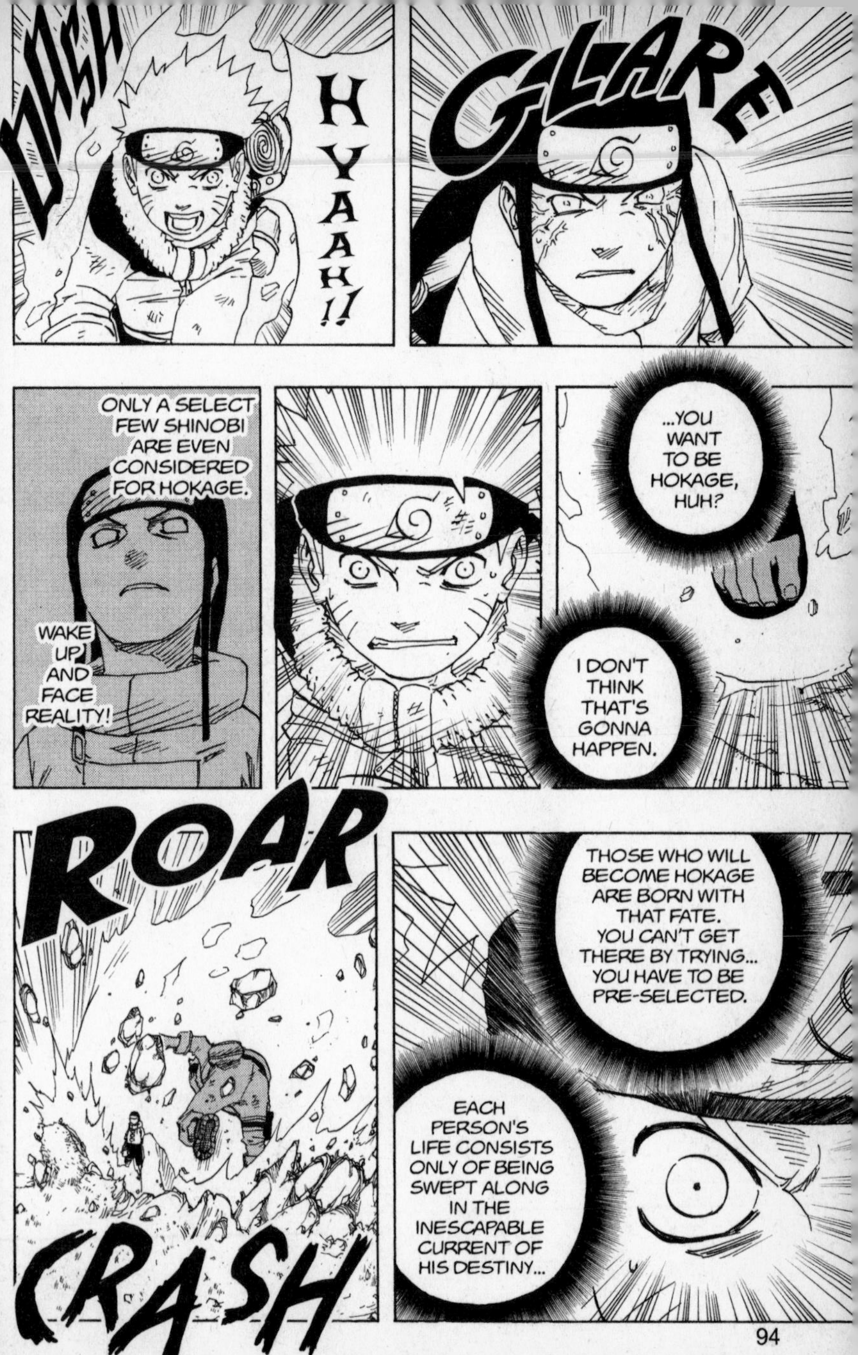
GLARE
DASH
HYAAH!!
...YOU WANT TO BE HOKAGE, HUH?
I DON'T THINK THAT'S GONNA HAPPEN.
ONLY A SELECT FEW SHINOBI ARE EVEN CONSIDERED FOR HOKAGE.
WAKE UP AND FACE REALITY!
THOSE WHO WILL BECOME HOKAGE ARE BORN WITH THAT FATE. YOU CAN'T GET THERE BY TRYING... YOU HAVE TO BE PRE-SELECTED.
EACH PERSON'S LIFE CONSISTS ONLY OF BEING SWEPT ALONG IN THE INESCAPABLE CURRENT OF HIS DESTINY...
ROAR
CRASH

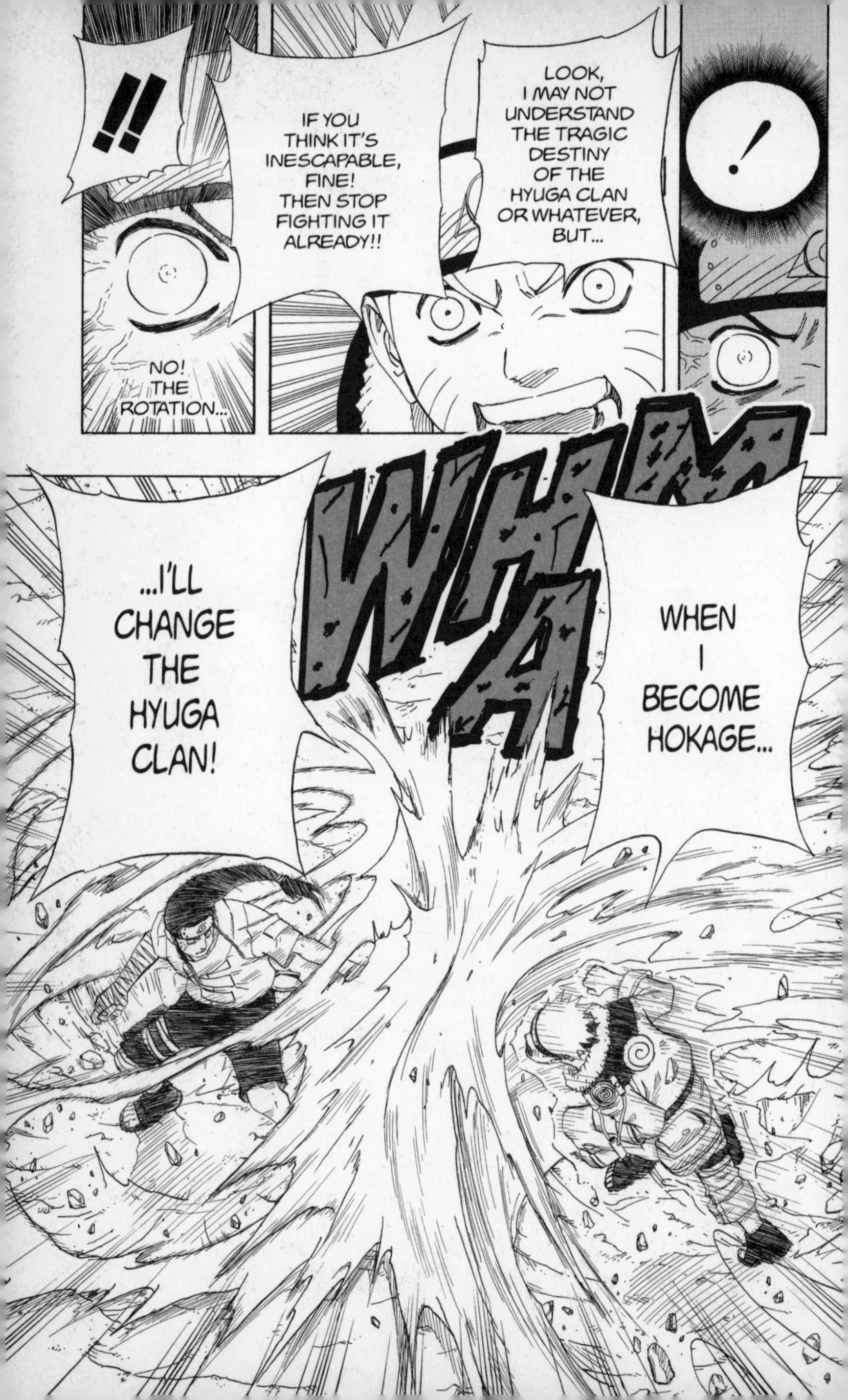
!
LOOK, I MAY NOT UNDERSTAND THE TRAGIC DESTINY OF THE HYUGA CLAN OR WHATEVER, BUT...
IF YOU THINK IT'S INESCAPABLE, FINE! THEN STOP FIGHTING IT ALREADY!!
!!
NO! THE ROTATION...
WHEN I BECOME HOKAGE...
WHAM
...I'LL CHANGE THE HYUGA CLAN!

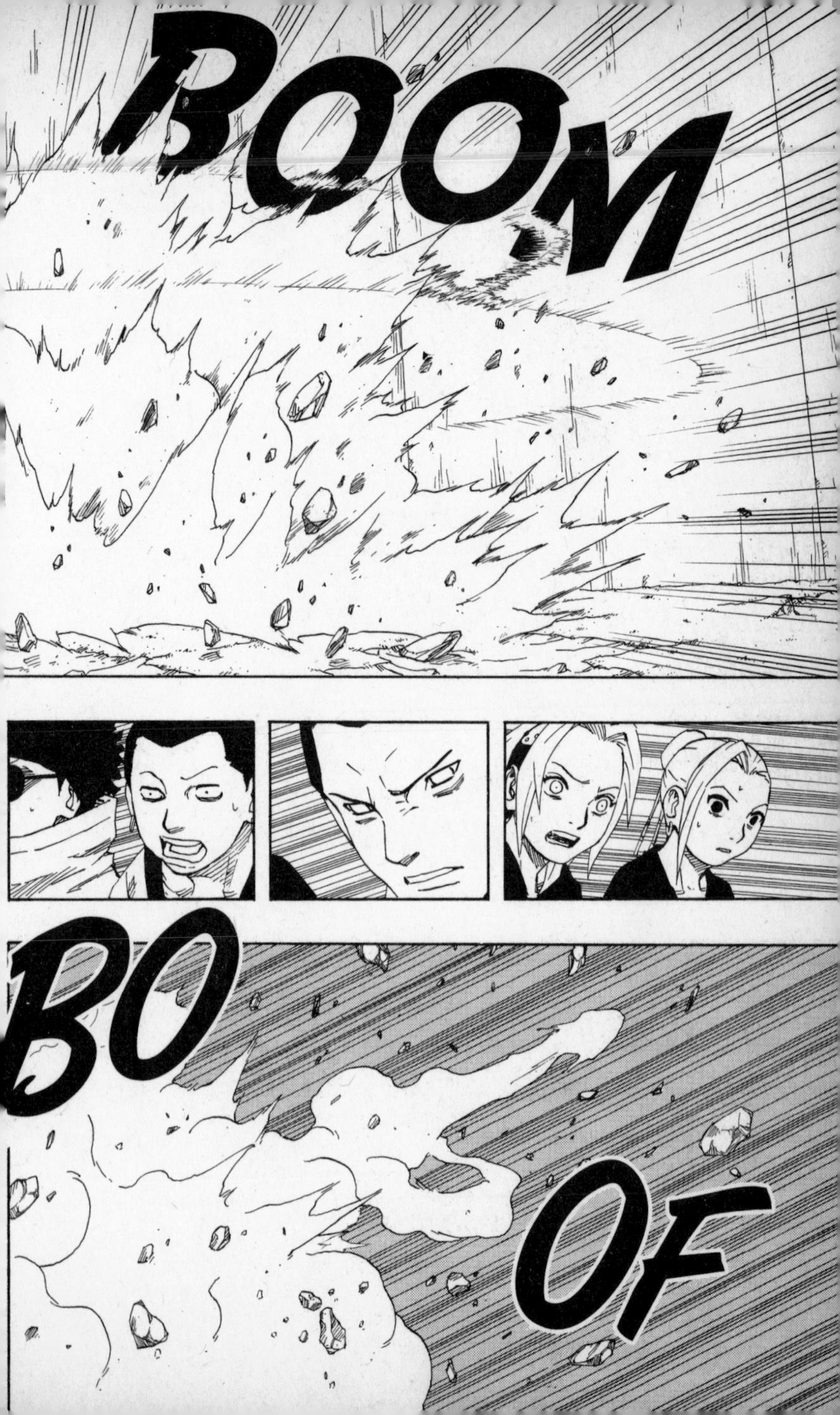
BOOM
BO
OF

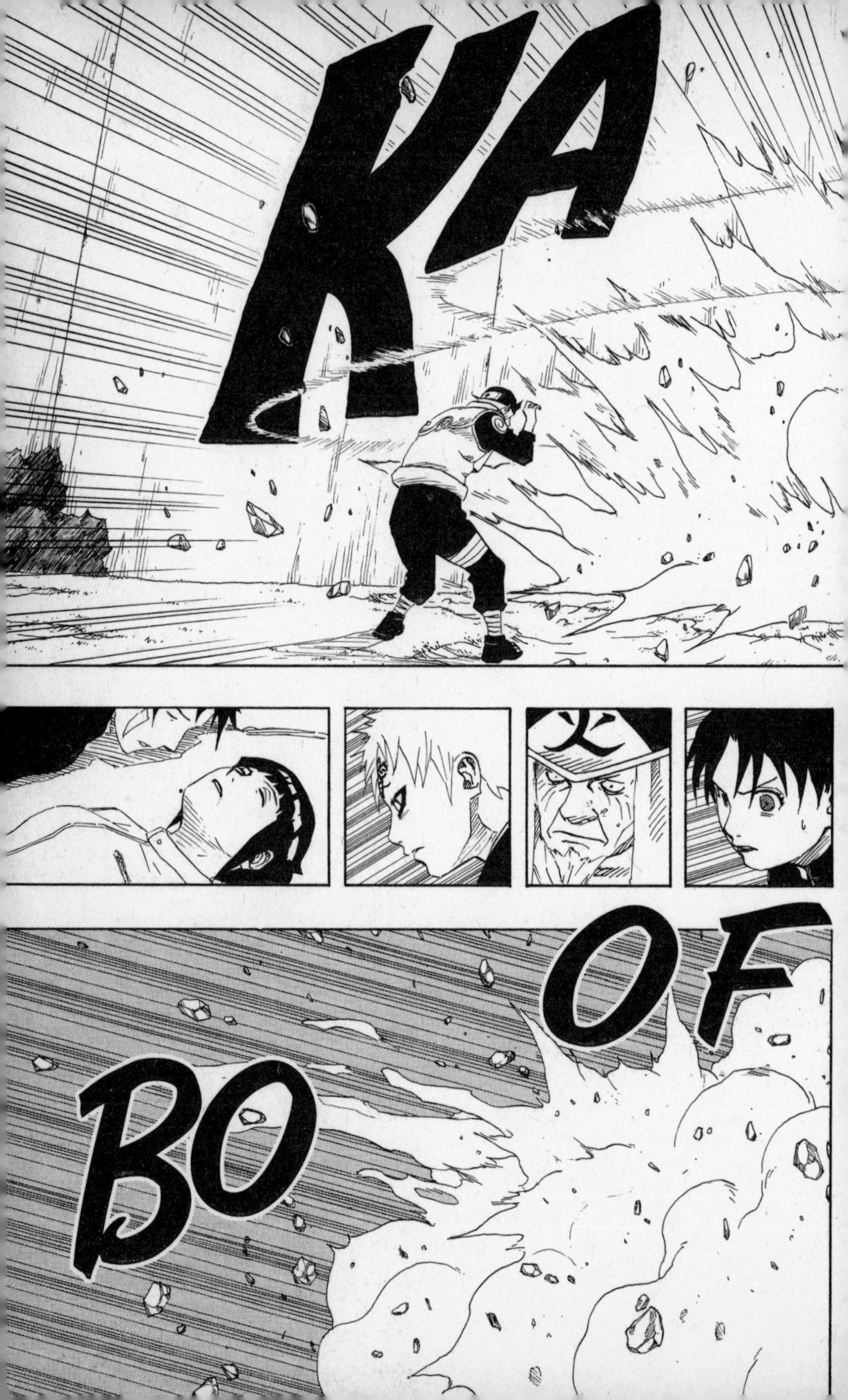
KA
BOOF

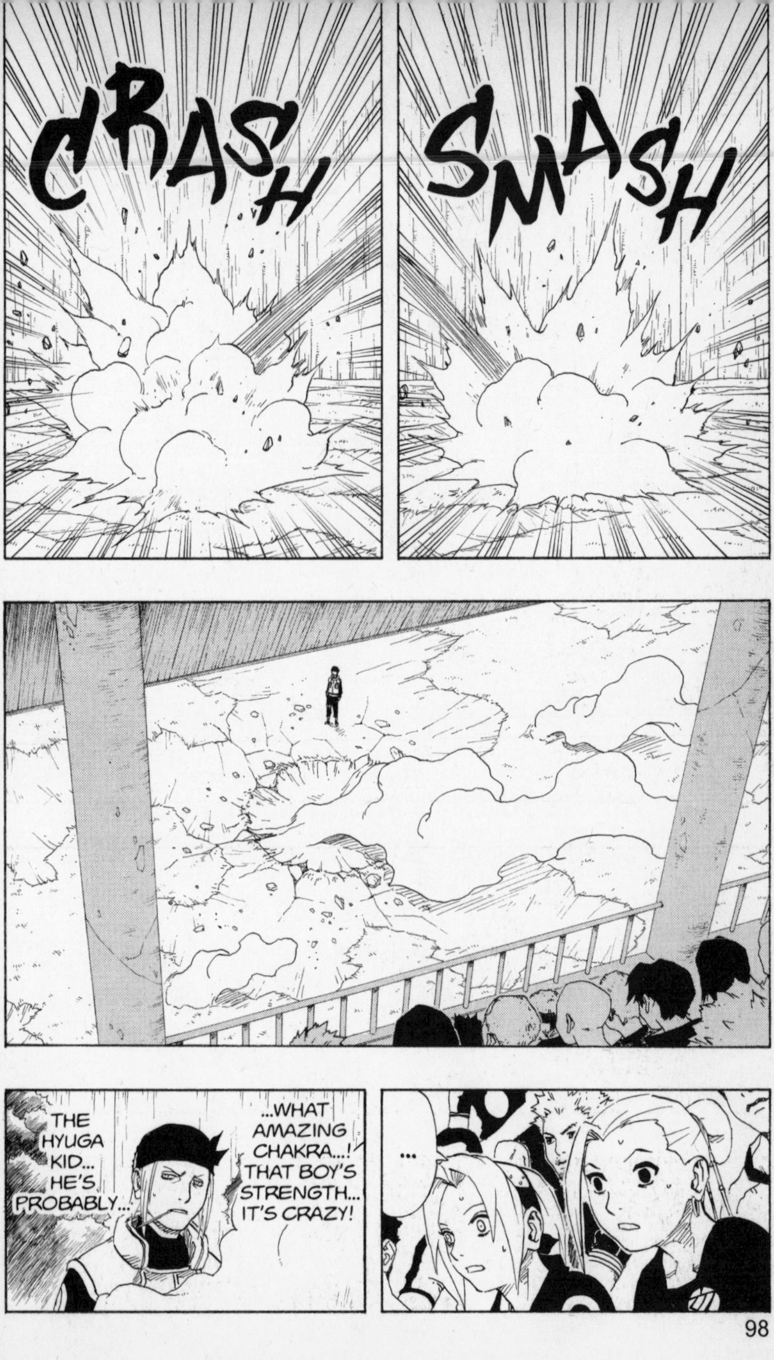
SMASH
CRASH
...
...WHAT AMAZING CHAKRA...! THAT BOY'S STRENGTH... IT'S CRAZY!
THE HYUGA KID... HE'S PROBABLY...

READ THIS WAY

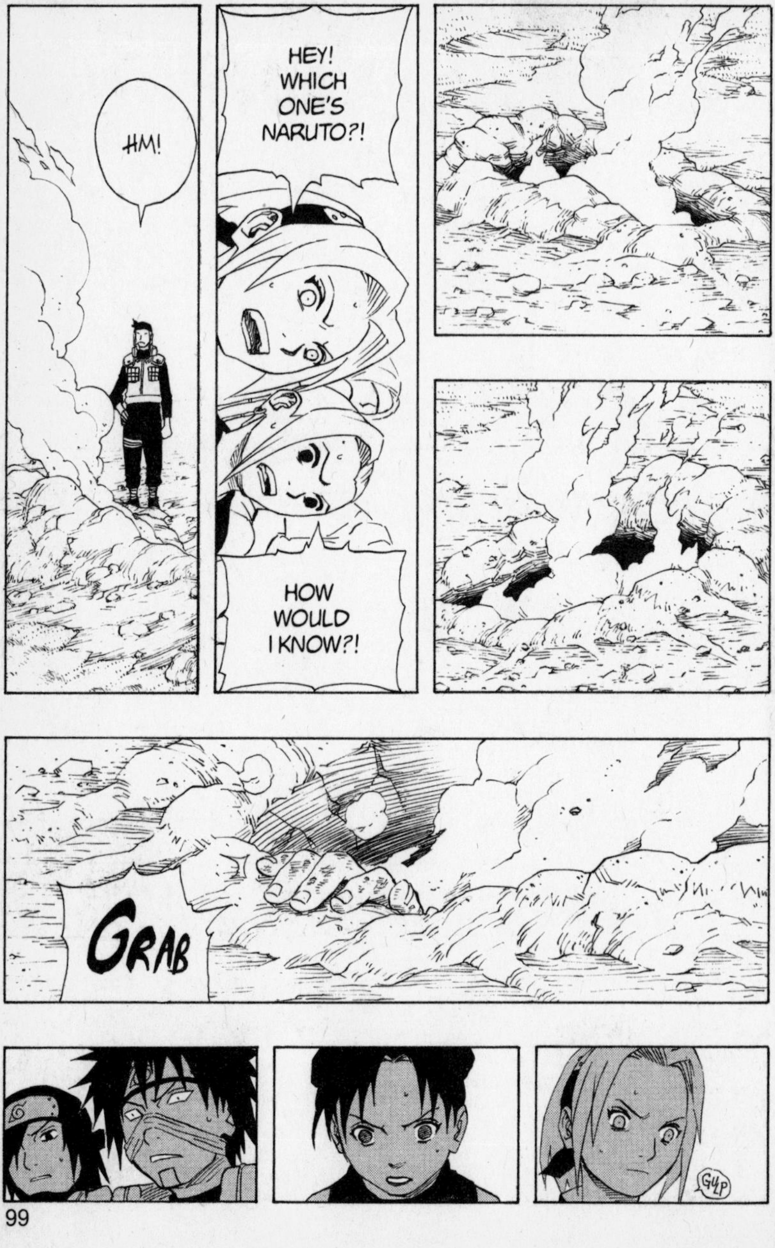

HEY! WHICH ONE'S NARUTO?!
HOW WOULD I KNOW?!
HM!
GRAB
GULP

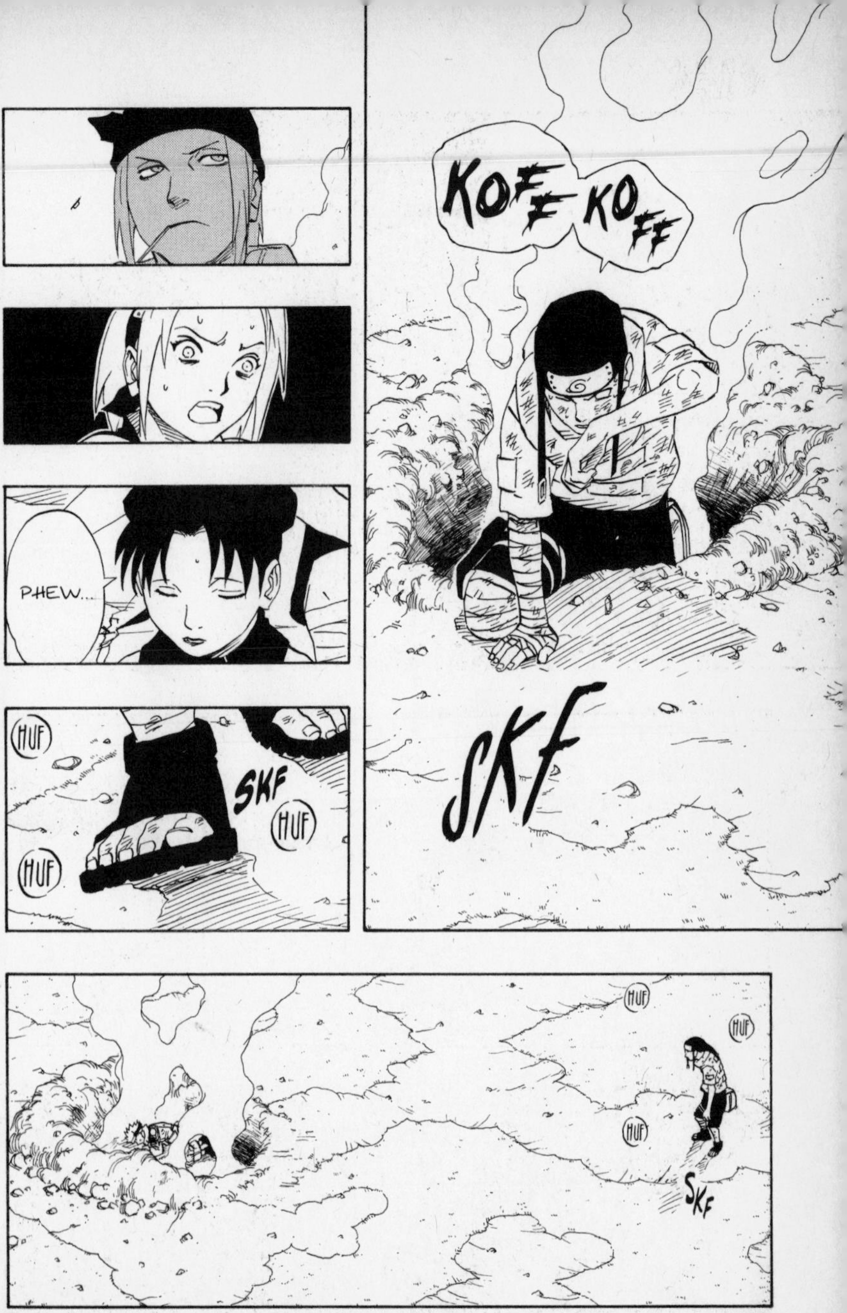
KOFF KOFF
SKF
PHEW...
HUF
SKF
HUF
HUF
HUF
HUF
HUF
SKF

READ THIS WAY

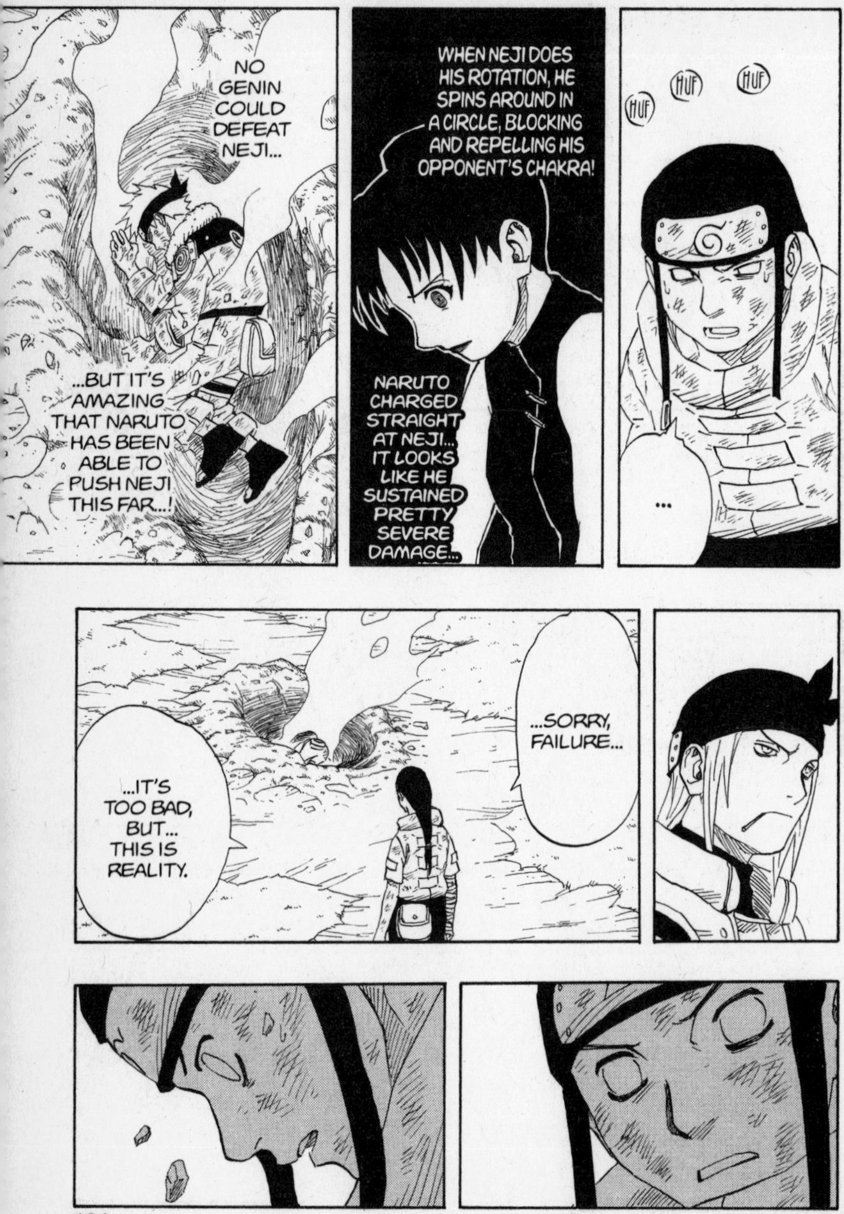

HUF
HUF
HUF
...
WHEN NEJI DOES HIS ROTATION, HE SPINS AROUND IN A CIRCLE, BLOCKING AND REPELLING HIS OPPONENT'S CHAKRA!
NARUTO CHARGED STRAIGHT AT NEJI... IT LOOKS LIKE HE SUSTAINED PRETTY SEVERE DAMAGE...
NO GENIN COULD DEFEAT NEJI...
...BUT IT'S AMAZING THAT NARUTO HAS BEEN ABLE TO PUSH NEJI THIS FAR...!
...SORRY, FAILURE...
...IT'S TOO BAD, BUT... THIS IS REALITY.

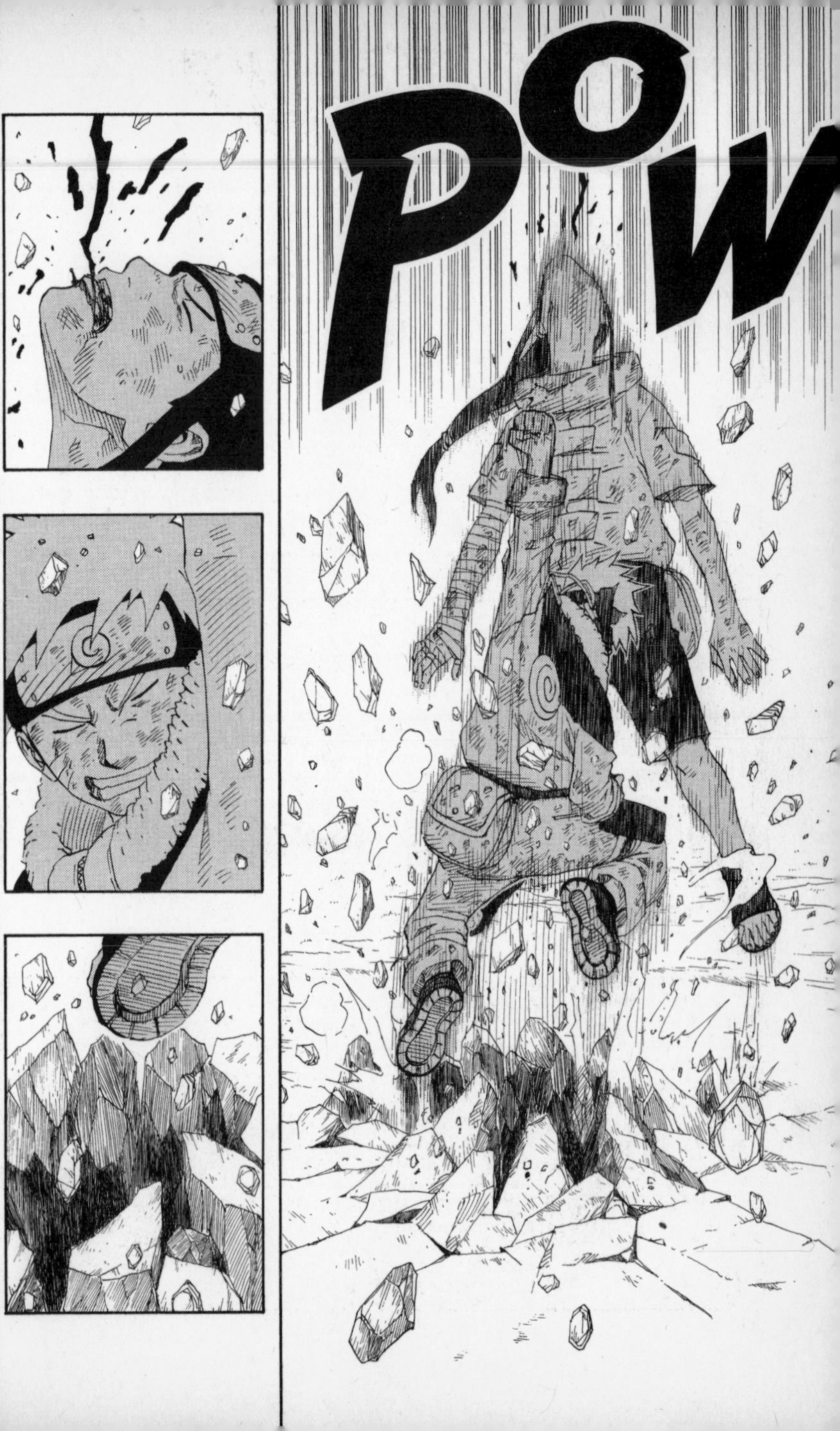
POW

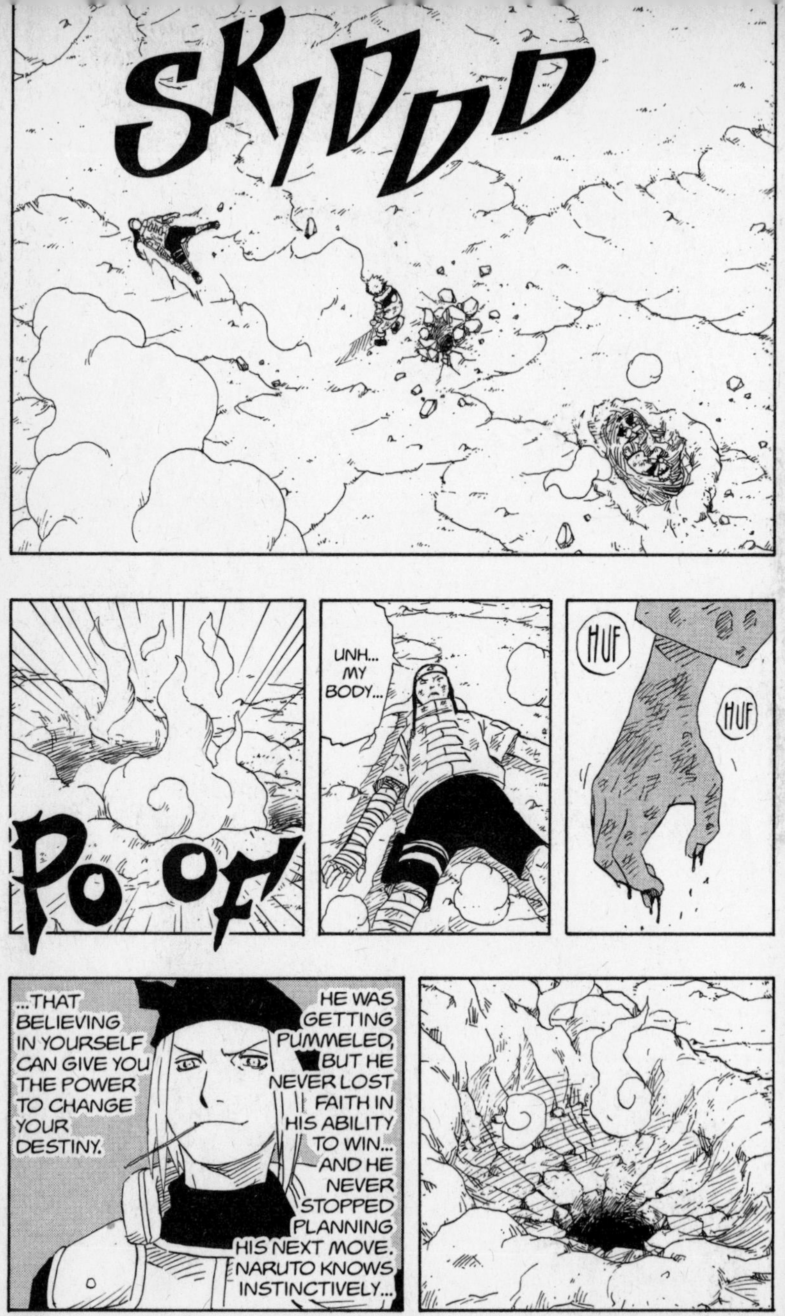
SKIDDD
HUF
HUF
UNH... MY BODY...
POOF
HE WAS GETTING PUMMELED, BUT HE NEVER LOST FAITH IN HIS ABILITY TO WIN... AND HE NEVER STOPPED PLANNING HIS NEXT MOVE. NARUTO KNOWS INSTINCTIVELY...
...THAT BELIEVING IN YOURSELF CAN GIVE YOU THE POWER TO CHANGE YOUR DESTINY.

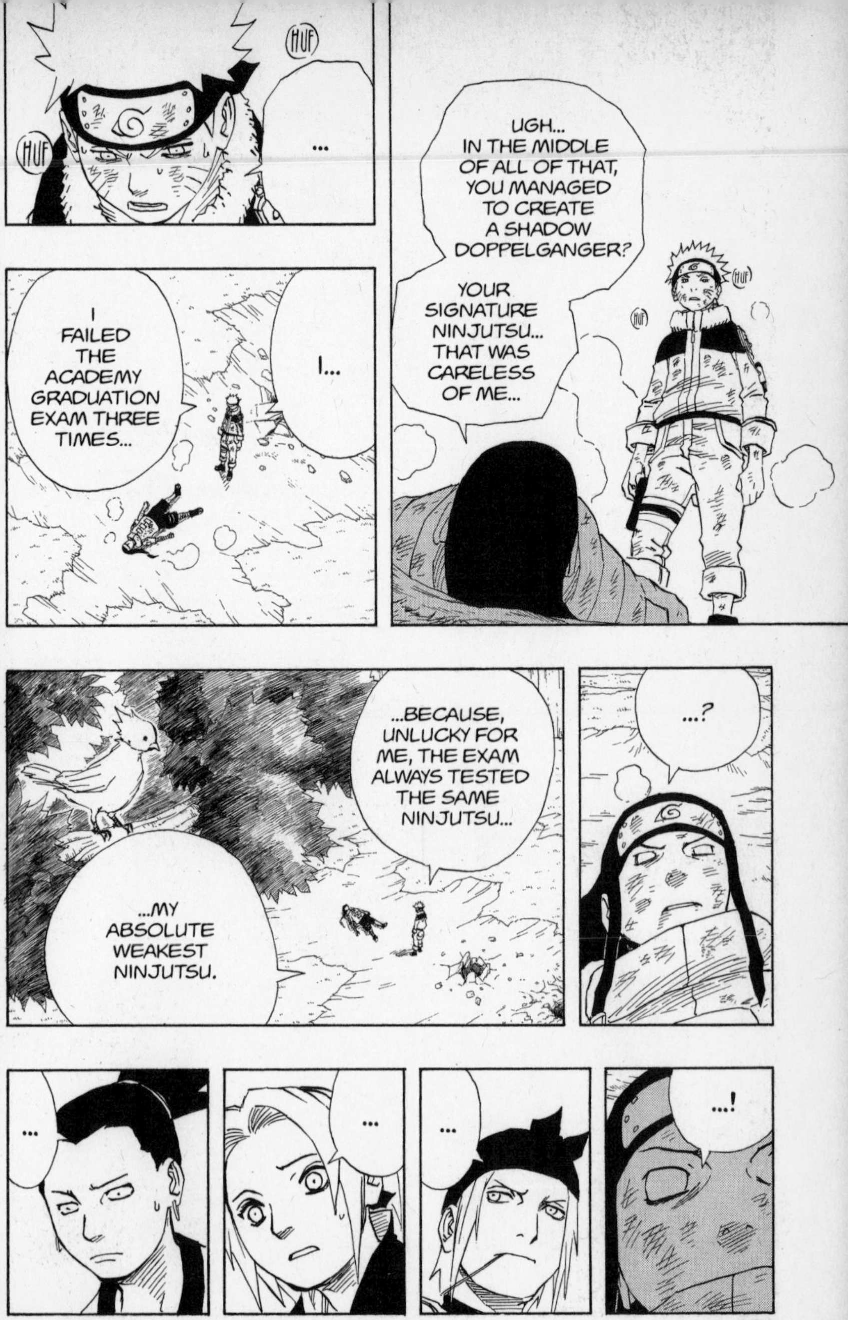
UGH... IN THE MIDDLE OF ALL OF THAT, YOU MANAGED TO CREATE A SHADOW DOPPELGANGER?
YOUR SIGNATURE NINJUTSU... THAT WAS CARELESS OF ME...
HUF
HUF
HUF
...
HUF
I...
I FAILED THE ACADEMY GRADUATION EXAM THREE TIMES...
...?
...BECAUSE, UNLUCKY FOR ME, THE EXAM ALWAYS TESTED THE SAME NINJUTSU...
...MY ABSOLUTE WEAKEST NINJUTSU.
...!
...
...
...

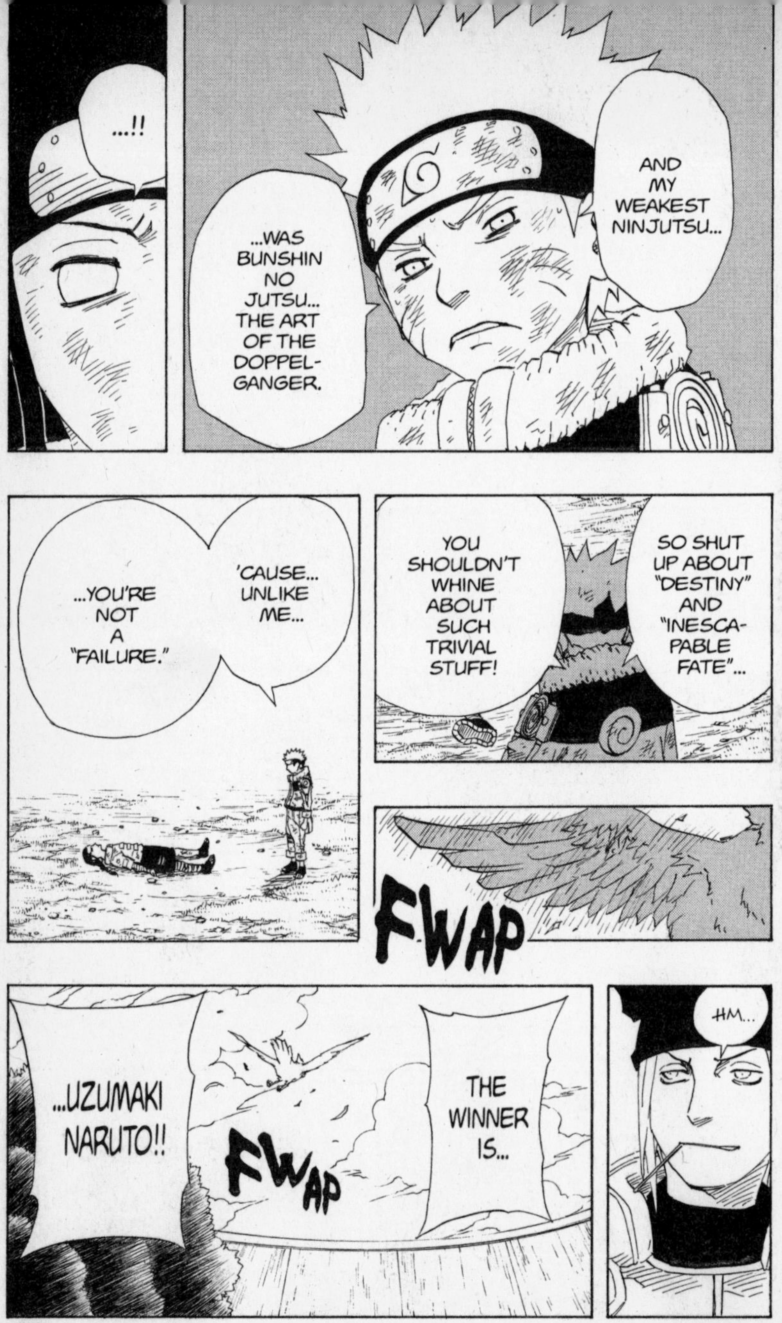
AND MY WEAKEST NINJUTSU...
...WAS BUNSHIN NO JUTSU... THE ART OF THE DOPPEL-GANGER.
...!!
SO SHUT UP ABOUT "DESTINY" AND "INESCA-PABLE FATE"...
YOU SHOULDN'T WHINE ABOUT SUCH TRIVIAL STUFF!
FWAP
'CAUSE... UNLIKE ME...
...YOU'RE NOT A "FAILURE."
HM...
THE WINNER IS...
FWAP
...UZUMAKI NARUTO!!

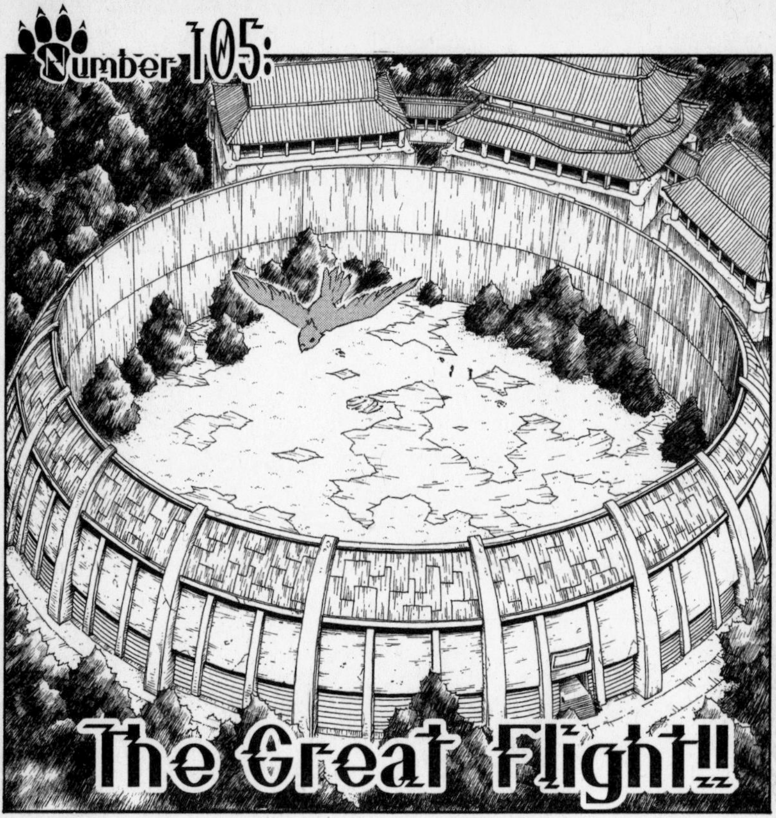
Number 105:
The Great Flight!!

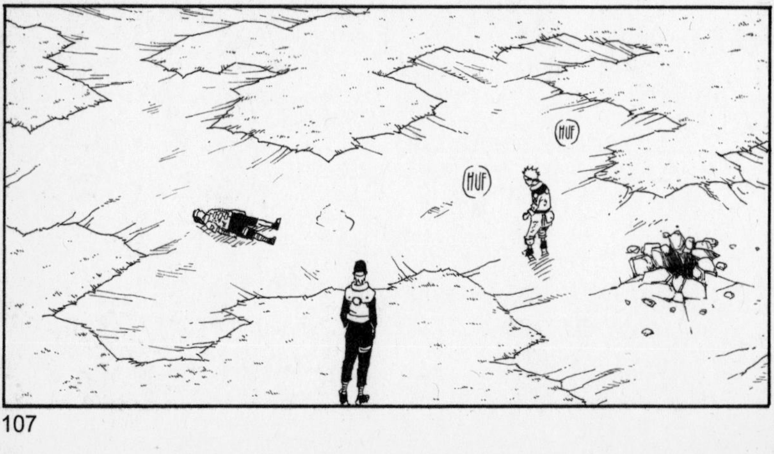
HUF
HUF

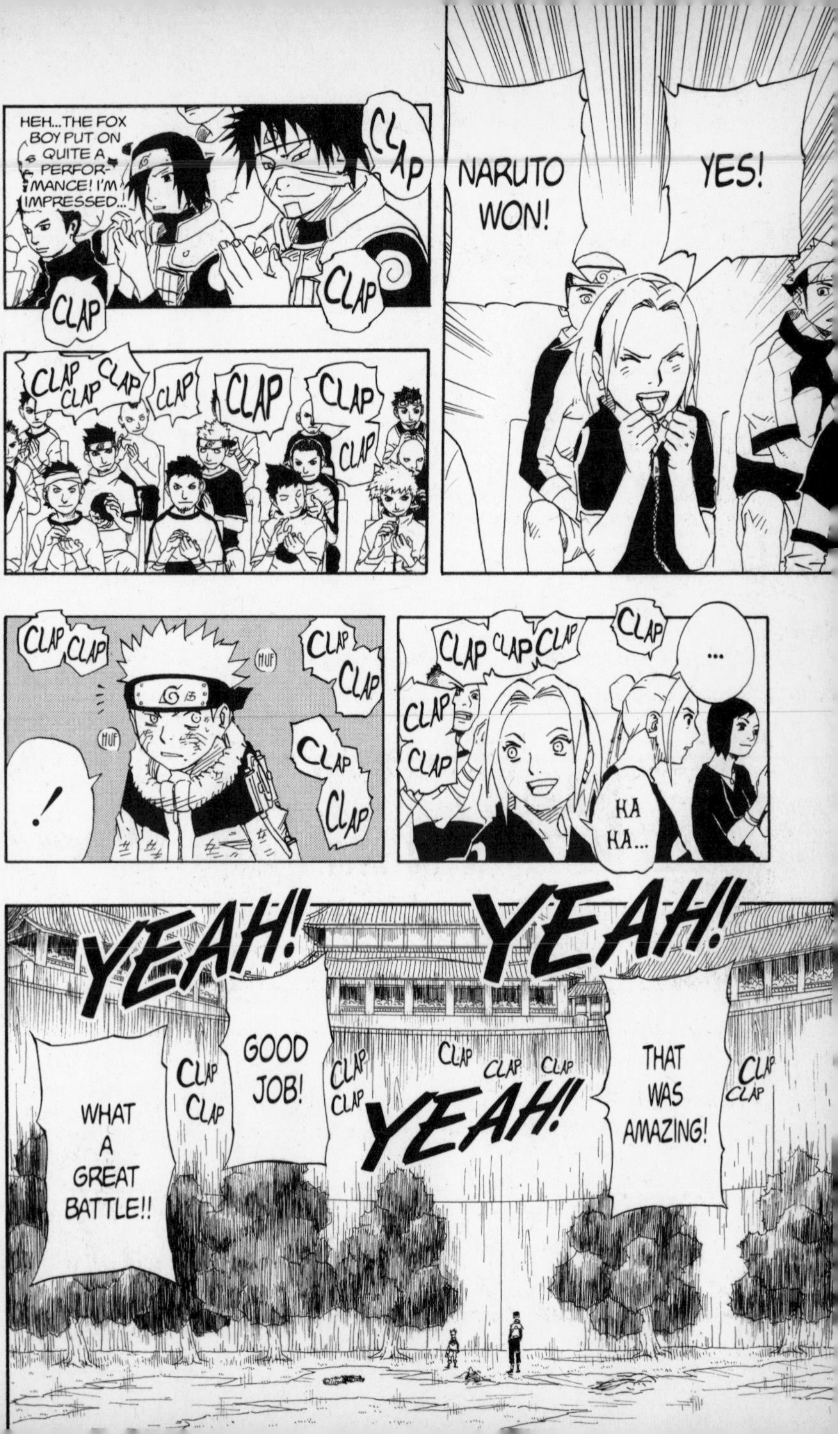
YES!
NARUTO WON!
CLAP
HEH...THE FOX BOY PUT ON QUITE A PERFORMANCE! I'M IMPRESSED...!
CLAP
CLAP
CLAP
CLAP
CLAP
CLAP
CLAP CLAP CLAP
...
CLAP
CLAP CLAP CLAP
CLAP
CLAP
HA HA...
CLAP
CLAP
CLAP
CLAP
HUF
CLAP CLAP
HUF
!
YEAH!
YEAH!
CLAP
CLAP
THAT WAS AMAZING!
CLAP CLAP CLAP
YEAH!
CLAP
CLAP
GOOD JOB!
CLAP
CLAP
WHAT A GREAT BATTLE!!

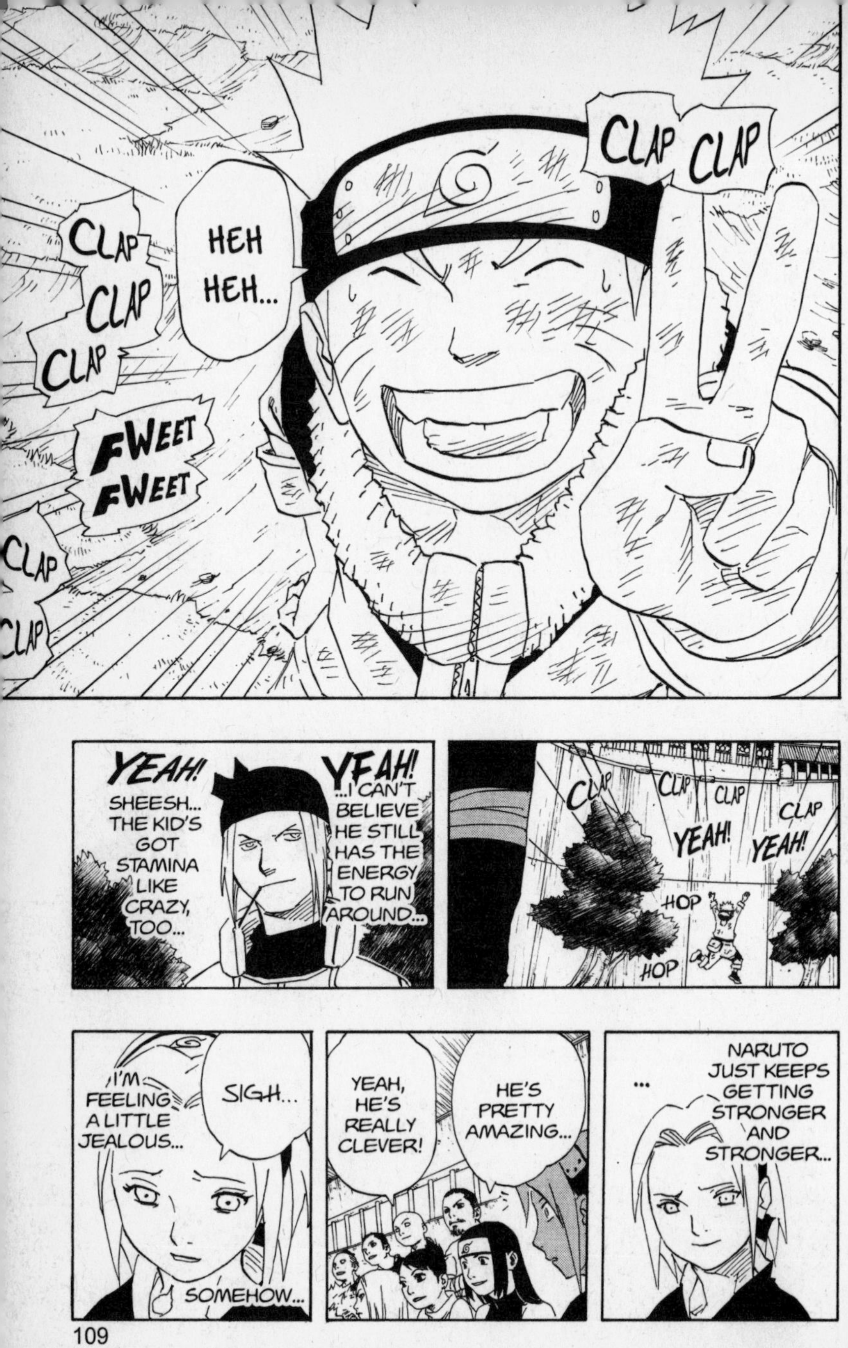

CLAP CLAP
HEH HEH...
CLAP CLAP CLAP
FWEET FWEET
CLAP CLAP
CLAP
CLAP
CLAP
CLAP
YEAH!
YEAH!
HOP
HOP
YEAH!
...I CAN'T BELIEVE HE STILL HAS THE ENERGY TO RUN AROUND...
YEAH!
SHEESH... THE KID'S GOT STAMINA LIKE CRAZY, TOO...
NARUTO JUST KEEPS GETTING STRONGER AND STRONGER...
...
HE'S PRETTY AMAZING...
YEAH, HE'S REALLY CLEVER!
SIGH...
I'M FEELING A LITTLE JEALOUS...
SOMEHOW...

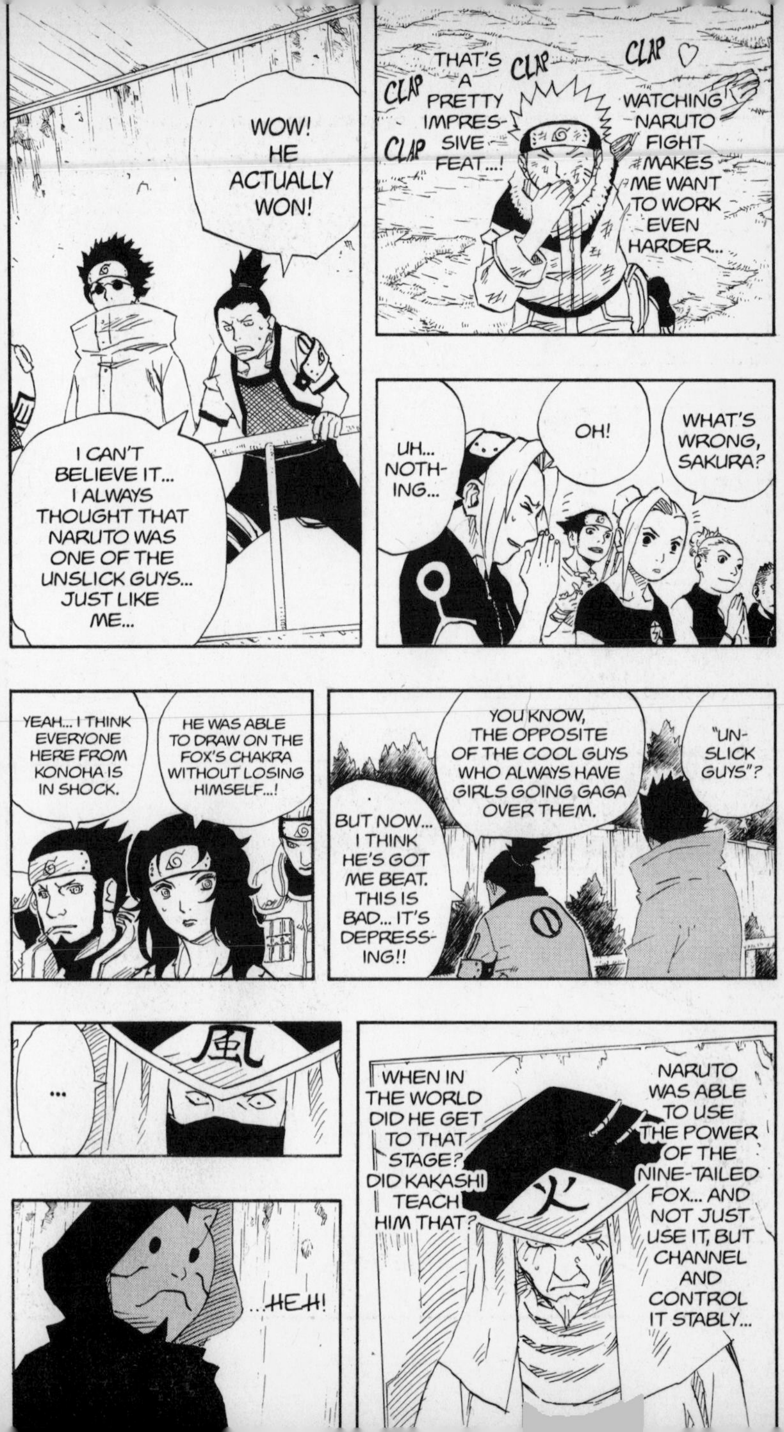
CLAP ♡
WATCHING NARUTO FIGHT MAKES ME WANT TO WORK EVEN HARDER...
CLAP
THAT'S A PRETTY IMPRES-SIVE FEAT...!
CLAP
CLAP
WHAT'S WRONG, SAKURA?
OH!
UH... NOTH-ING...
WOW! HE ACTUALLY WON!
I CAN'T BELIEVE IT... I ALWAYS THOUGHT THAT NARUTO WAS ONE OF THE UNSLICK GUYS... JUST LIKE ME...
"UN-SLICK GUYS"?
YOU KNOW, THE OPPOSITE OF THE COOL GUYS WHO ALWAYS HAVE GIRLS GOING GAGA OVER THEM.
BUT NOW... I THINK HE'S GOT ME BEAT. THIS IS BAD... IT'S DEPRESS-ING!!
HE WAS ABLE TO DRAW ON THE FOX'S CHAKRA WITHOUT LOSING HIMSELF...!
YEAH... I THINK EVERYONE HERE FROM KONOHA IS IN SHOCK.
NARUTO WAS ABLE TO USE THE POWER OF THE NINE-TAILED FOX... AND NOT JUST USE IT, BUT CHANNEL AND CONTROL IT STABLY...
WHEN IN THE WORLD DID HE GET TO THAT STAGE? DID KAKASHI TEACH HIM THAT?
...
...HEH!

READ THIS WAY

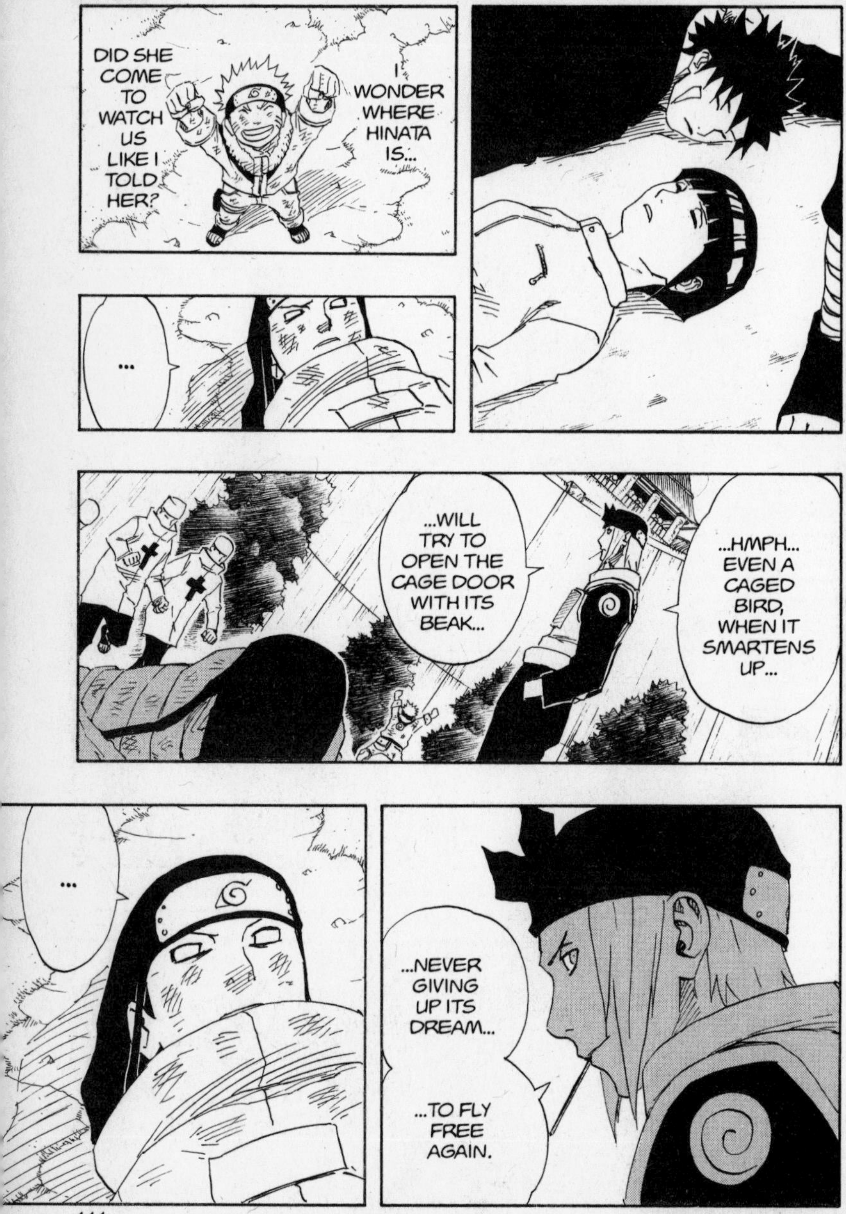
I WONDER WHERE HINATA IS...
DID SHE COME TO WATCH US LIKE I TOLD HER?
...
...HMPH... EVEN A CAGED BIRD, WHEN IT SMARTENS UP...
...WILL TRY TO OPEN THE CAGE DOOR WITH ITS BEAK...
...NEVER GIVING UP ITS DREAM...
...TO FLY FREE AGAIN.
...

BUT THIS TIME, YOU GOT BEAT.

FATHER...

...

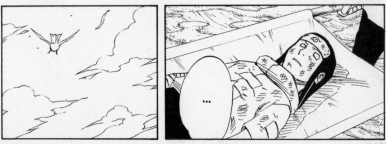

...

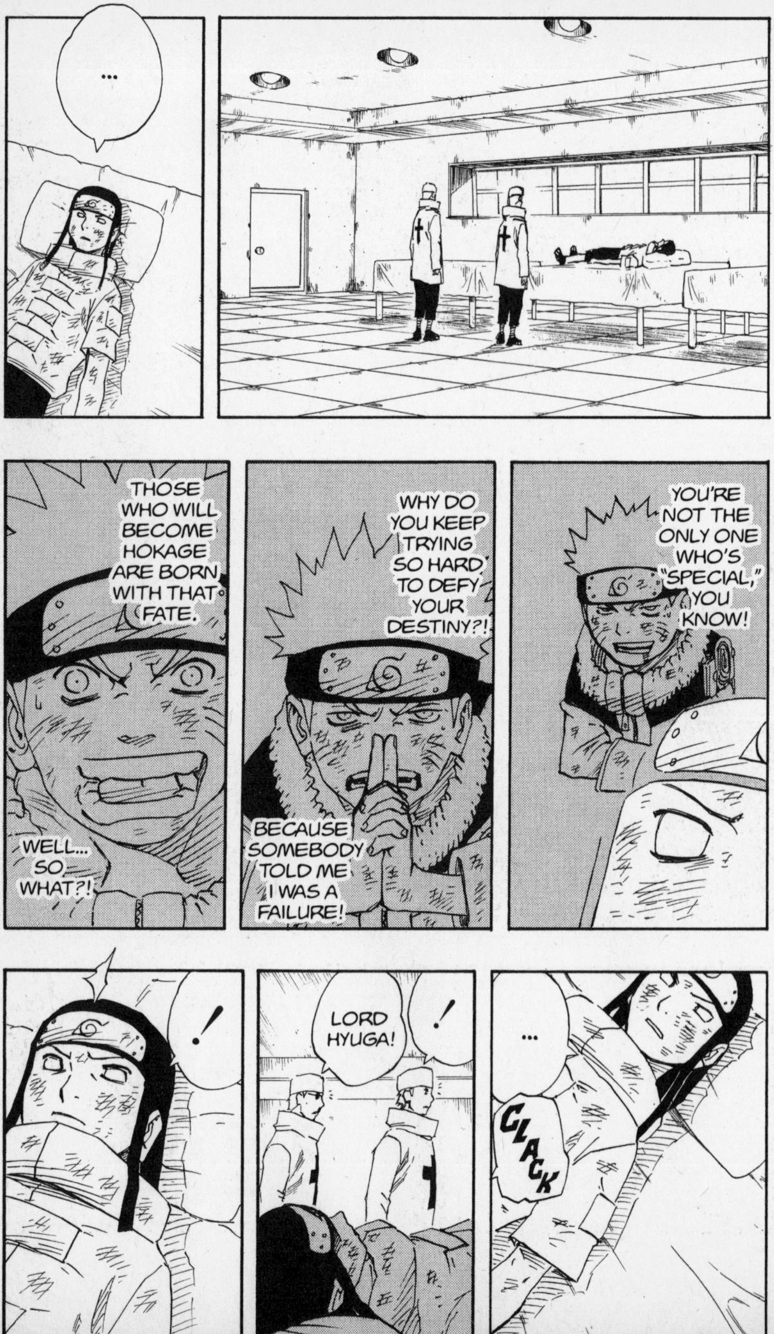
...
THOSE WHO WILL BECOME HOKAGE ARE BORN WITH THAT FATE.
WELL... SO WHAT?!
WHY DO YOU KEEP TRYING SO HARD TO DEFY YOUR DESTINY?!
BECAUSE SOMEBODY TOLD ME I WAS A FAILURE!
YOU'RE NOT THE ONLY ONE WHO'S "SPECIAL," YOU KNOW!
!
LORD HYUGA!
!
...
CLACK

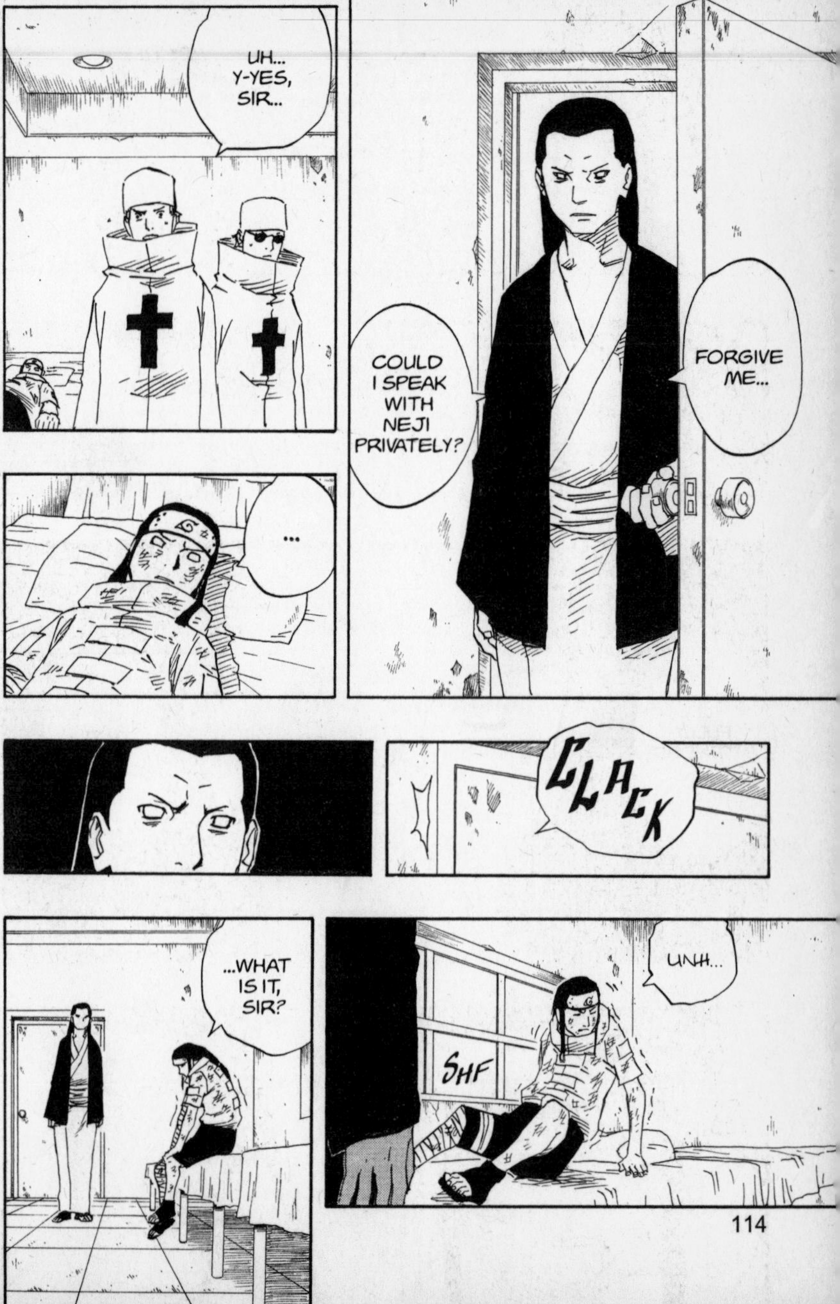
FORGIVE ME...
COULD I SPEAK WITH NEJI PRIVATELY?
UH... Y-YES, SIR...
...
CLACK
UNH...
SHF
...WHAT IS IT, SIR?

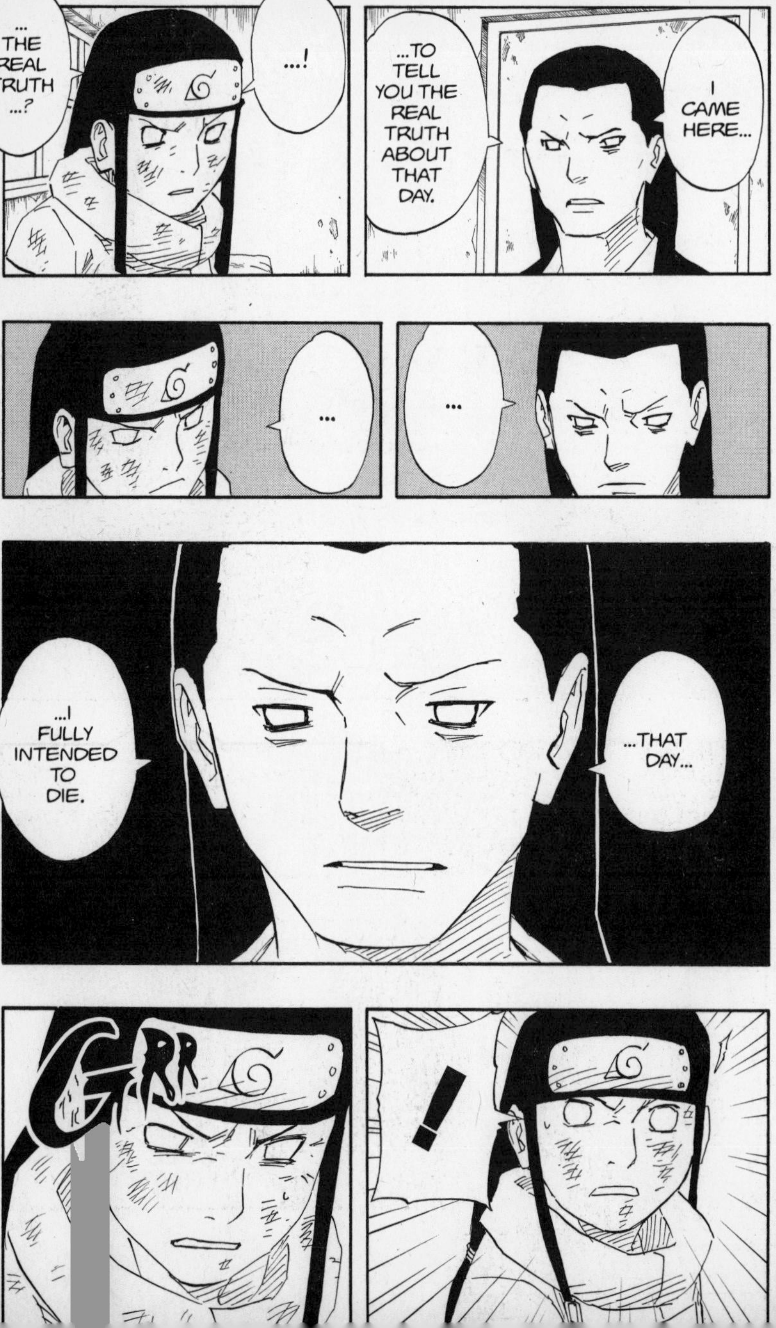
I CAME HERE...
...TO TELL YOU THE REAL TRUTH ABOUT THAT DAY.
...!
... THE REAL TRUTH ...?
...
...
...THAT DAY...
...I FULLY INTENDED TO DIE.
!
GRR

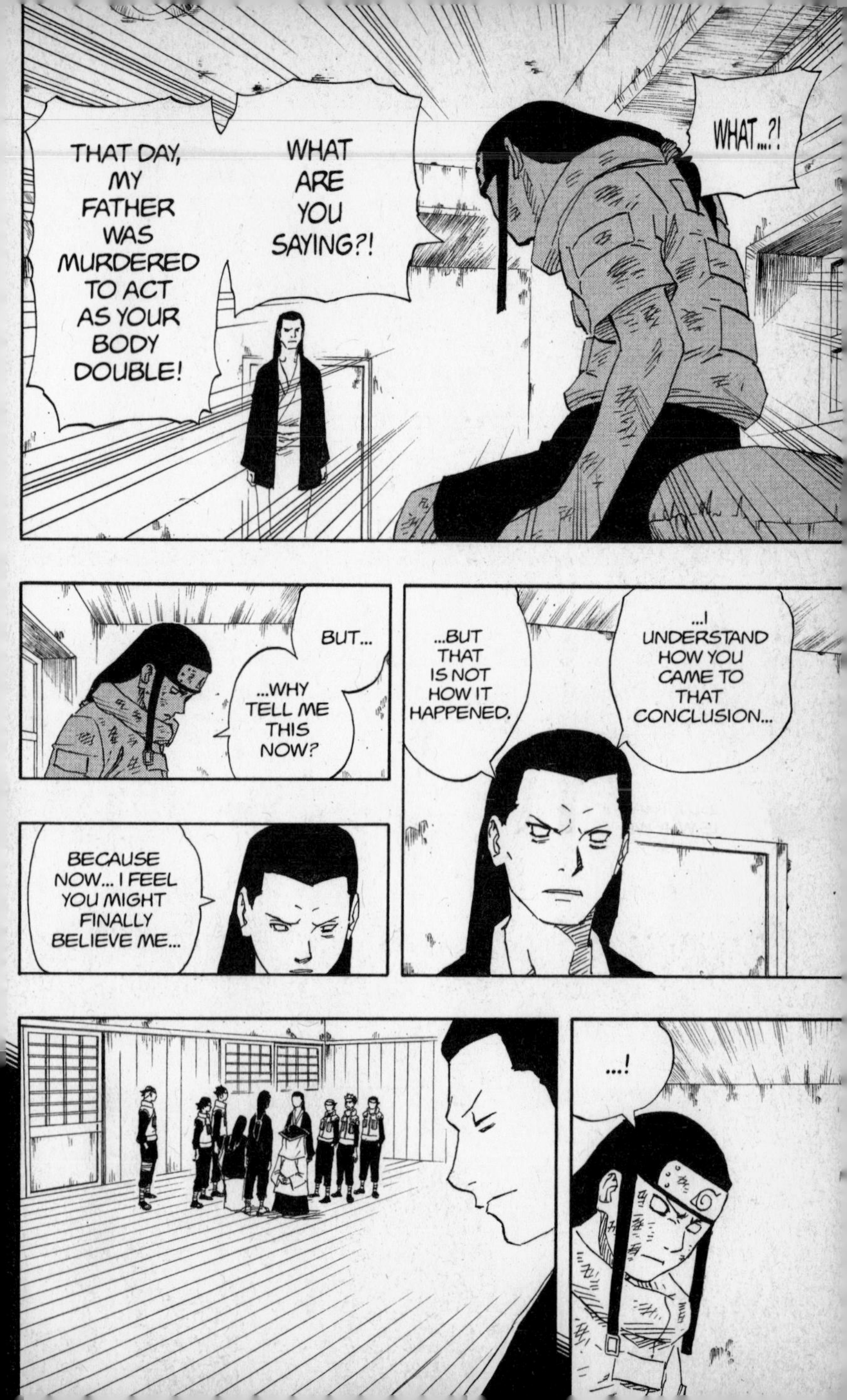
WHAT...?!
WHAT ARE YOU SAYING?!
THAT DAY, MY FATHER WAS MURDERED TO ACT AS YOUR BODY DOUBLE!
...I UNDERSTAND HOW YOU CAME TO THAT CONCLUSION...
...BUT THAT IS NOT HOW IT HAPPENED.
BUT...
...WHY TELL ME THIS NOW?
BECAUSE NOW... I FEEL YOU MIGHT FINALLY BELIEVE ME...
...!

READ THIS WAY

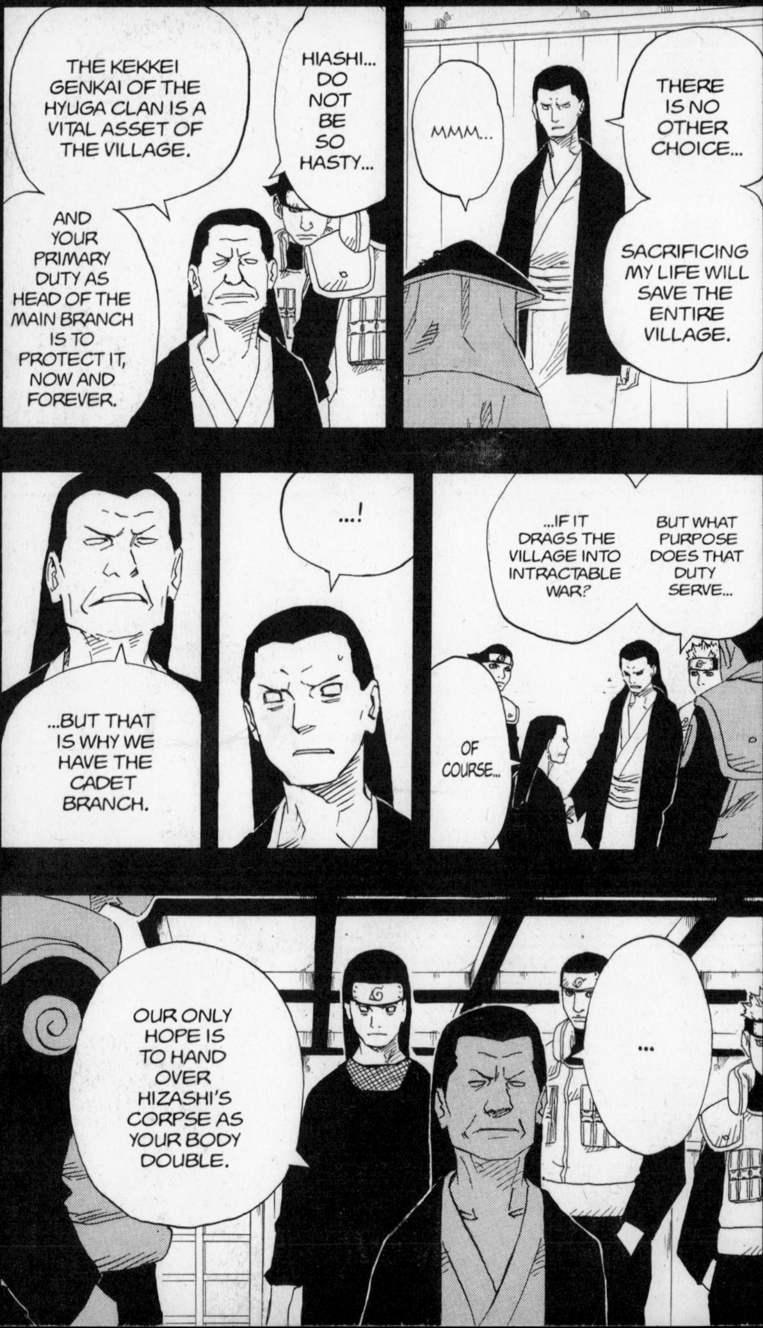
THERE IS NO OTHER CHOICE...
MMM...
SACRIFICING MY LIFE WILL SAVE THE ENTIRE VILLAGE.
HIASHI... DO NOT BE SO HASTY...
THE KEKKEI GENKAI OF THE HYUGA CLAN IS A VITAL ASSET OF THE VILLAGE.
AND YOUR PRIMARY DUTY AS HEAD OF THE MAIN BRANCH IS TO PROTECT IT, NOW AND FOREVER.
BUT WHAT PURPOSE DOES THAT DUTY SERVE...
...IF IT DRAGS THE VILLAGE INTO INTRACTABLE WAR?
OF COURSE...
...!
...BUT THAT IS WHY WE HAVE THE CADET BRANCH.
...
OUR ONLY HOPE IS TO HAND OVER HIZASHI'S CORPSE AS YOUR BODY DOUBLE.

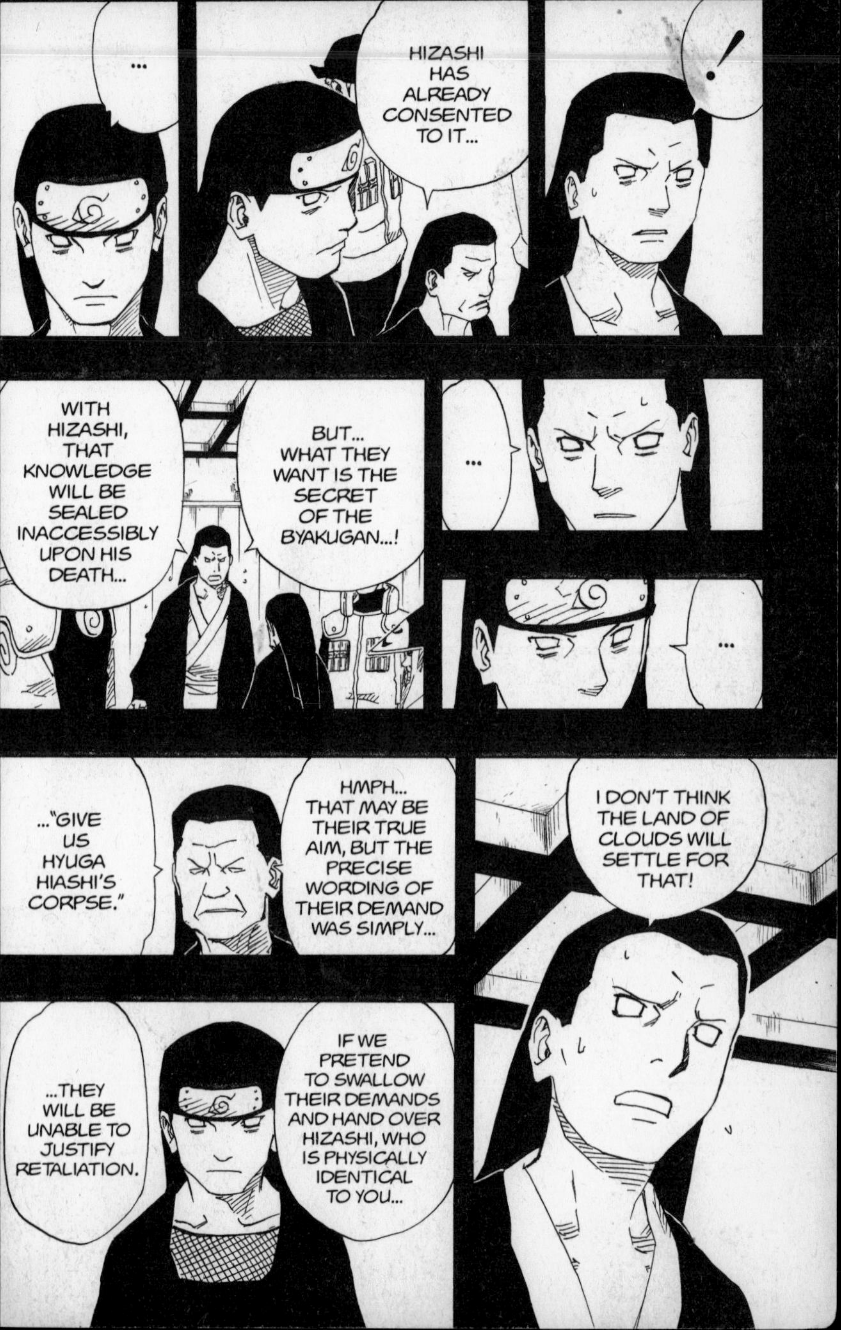
!
HIZASHI HAS ALREADY CONSENTED TO IT...
...
...
...
BUT... WHAT THEY WANT IS THE SECRET OF THE BYAKUGAN...!
WITH HIZASHI, THAT KNOWLEDGE WILL BE SEALED INACCESSIBLY UPON HIS DEATH...
I DON'T THINK THE LAND OF CLOUDS WILL SETTLE FOR THAT!
HMPH... THAT MAY BE THEIR TRUE AIM, BUT THE PRECISE WORDING OF THEIR DEMAND WAS SIMPLY...
..."GIVE US HYUGA HIASHI'S CORPSE."
IF WE PRETEND TO SWALLOW THEIR DEMANDS AND HAND OVER HIZASHI, WHO IS PHYSICALLY IDENTICAL TO YOU...
...THEY WILL BE UNABLE TO JUSTIFY RETALIATION.

READ THIS WAY

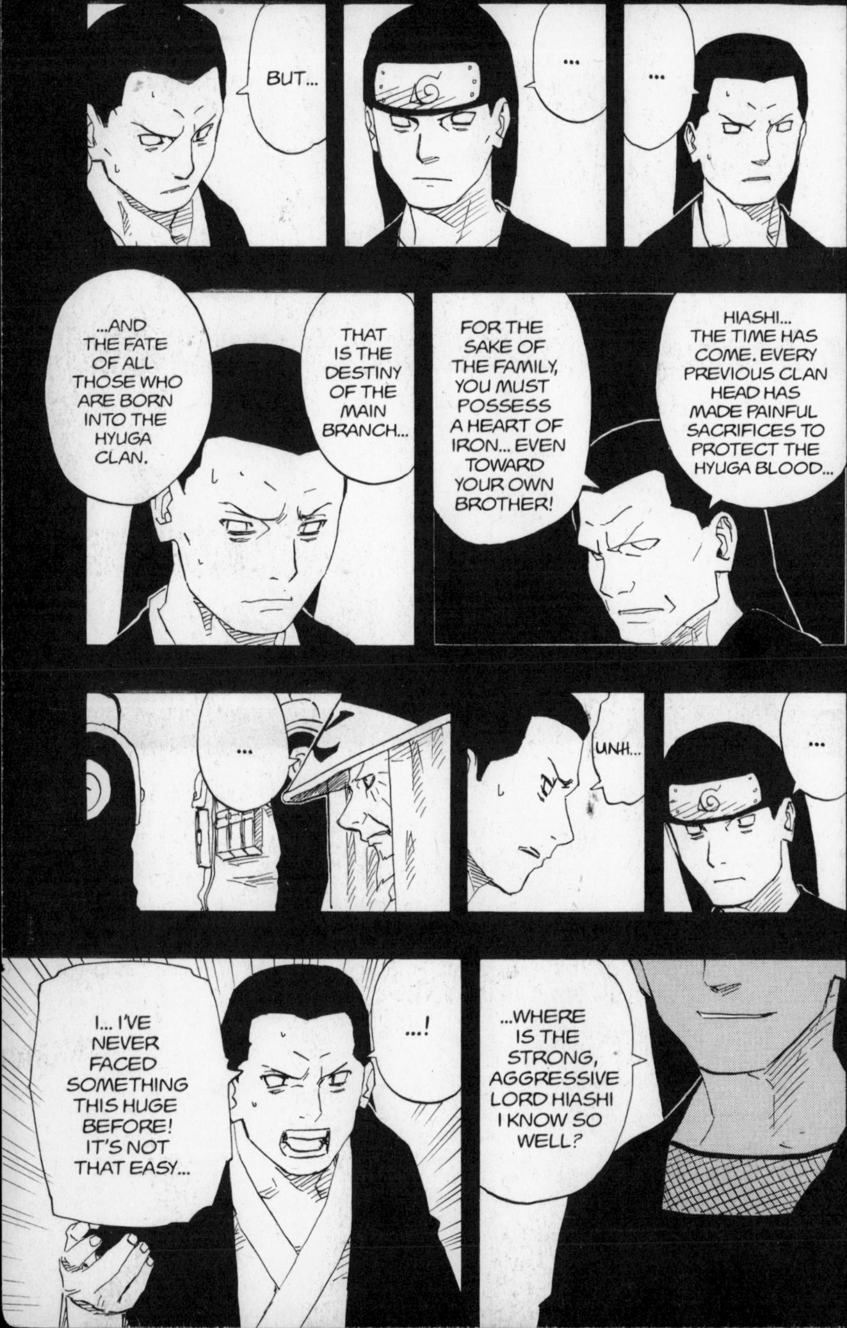
...
...
BUT...
HIASHI... THE TIME HAS COME. EVERY PREVIOUS CLAN HEAD HAS MADE PAINFUL SACRIFICES TO PROTECT THE HYUGA BLOOD...
FOR THE SAKE OF THE FAMILY, YOU MUST POSSESS A HEART OF IRON... EVEN TOWARD YOUR OWN BROTHER!
THAT IS THE DESTINY OF THE MAIN BRANCH...
...AND THE FATE OF ALL THOSE WHO ARE BORN INTO THE HYUGA CLAN.
...
UNH...
...
...WHERE IS THE STRONG, AGGRESSIVE LORD HIASHI I KNOW SO WELL?
...!
I... I'VE NEVER FACED SOMETHING THIS HUGE BEFORE! IT'S NOT THAT EASY...

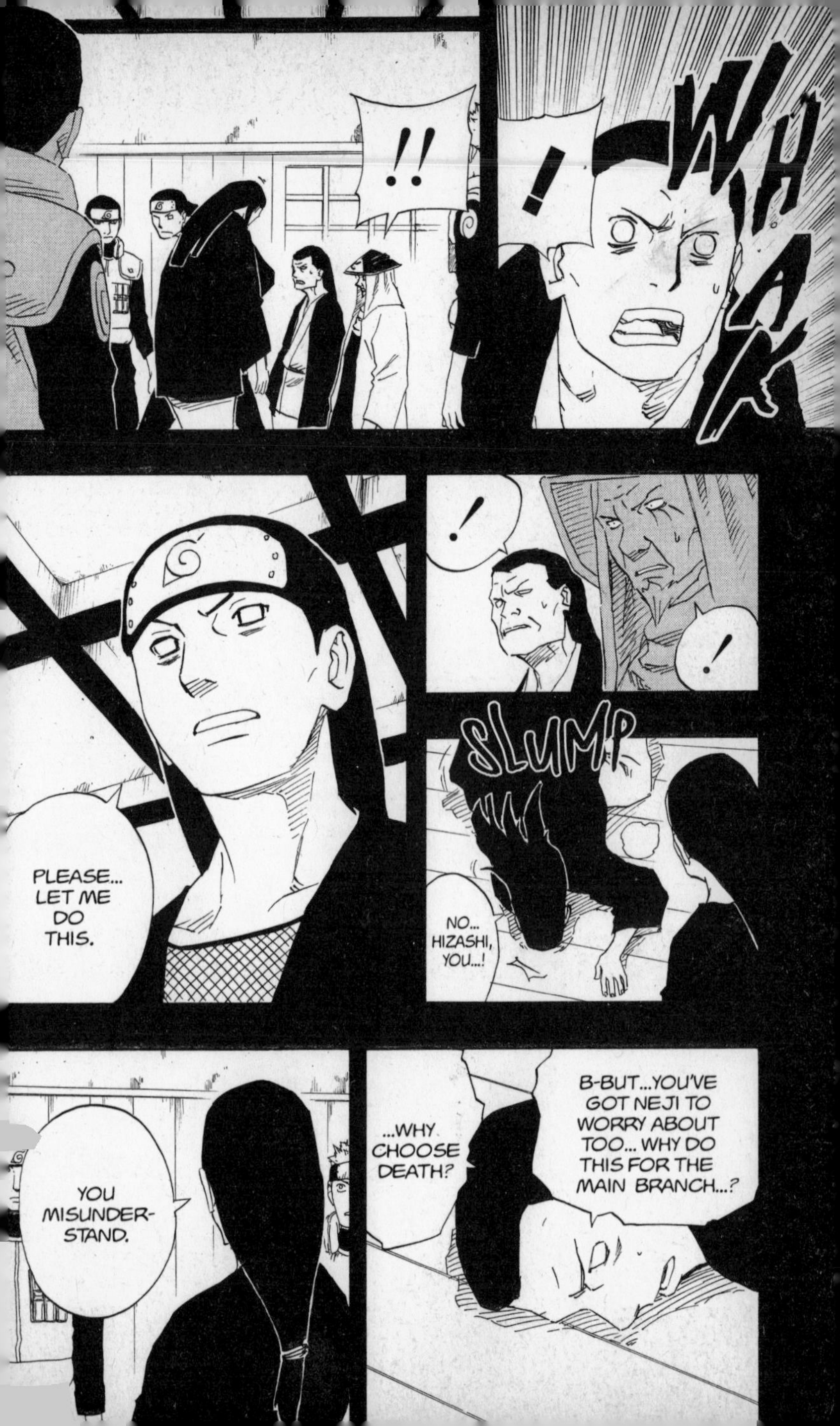
!
WHAK
!!
!
!
SLUMP
NO... HIZASHI, YOU...!
PLEASE... LET ME DO THIS.
B-BUT...YOU'VE GOT NEJI TO WORRY ABOUT TOO... WHY DO THIS FOR THE MAIN BRANCH...?
...WHY CHOOSE DEATH?
YOU MISUNDERSTAND.

READ THIS WAY

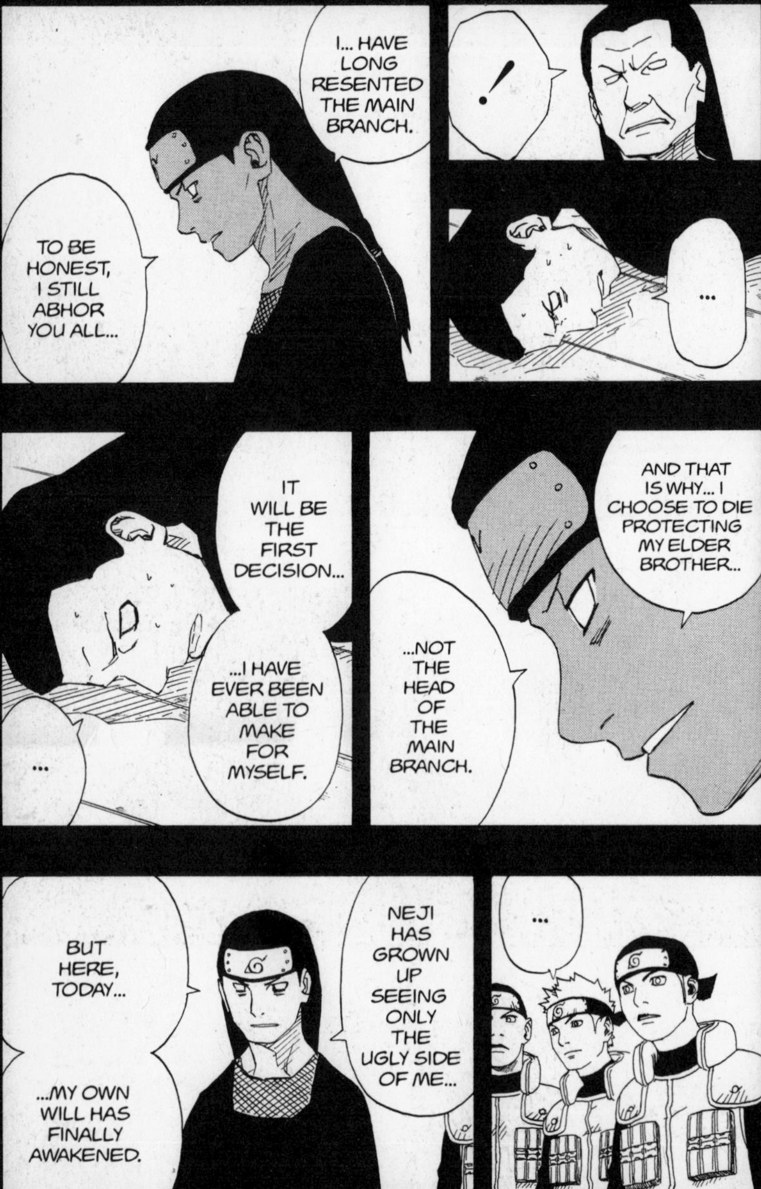
!
...
I... HAVE LONG RESENTED THE MAIN BRANCH.
TO BE HONEST, I STILL ABHOR YOU ALL...
AND THAT IS WHY... I CHOOSE TO DIE PROTECTING MY ELDER BROTHER...
...NOT THE HEAD OF THE MAIN BRANCH.
IT WILL BE THE FIRST DECISION...
...I HAVE EVER BEEN ABLE TO MAKE FOR MYSELF.
...
...
NEJI HAS GROWN UP SEEING ONLY THE UGLY SIDE OF ME...
BUT HERE, TODAY...
...MY OWN WILL HAS FINALLY AWAKENED.

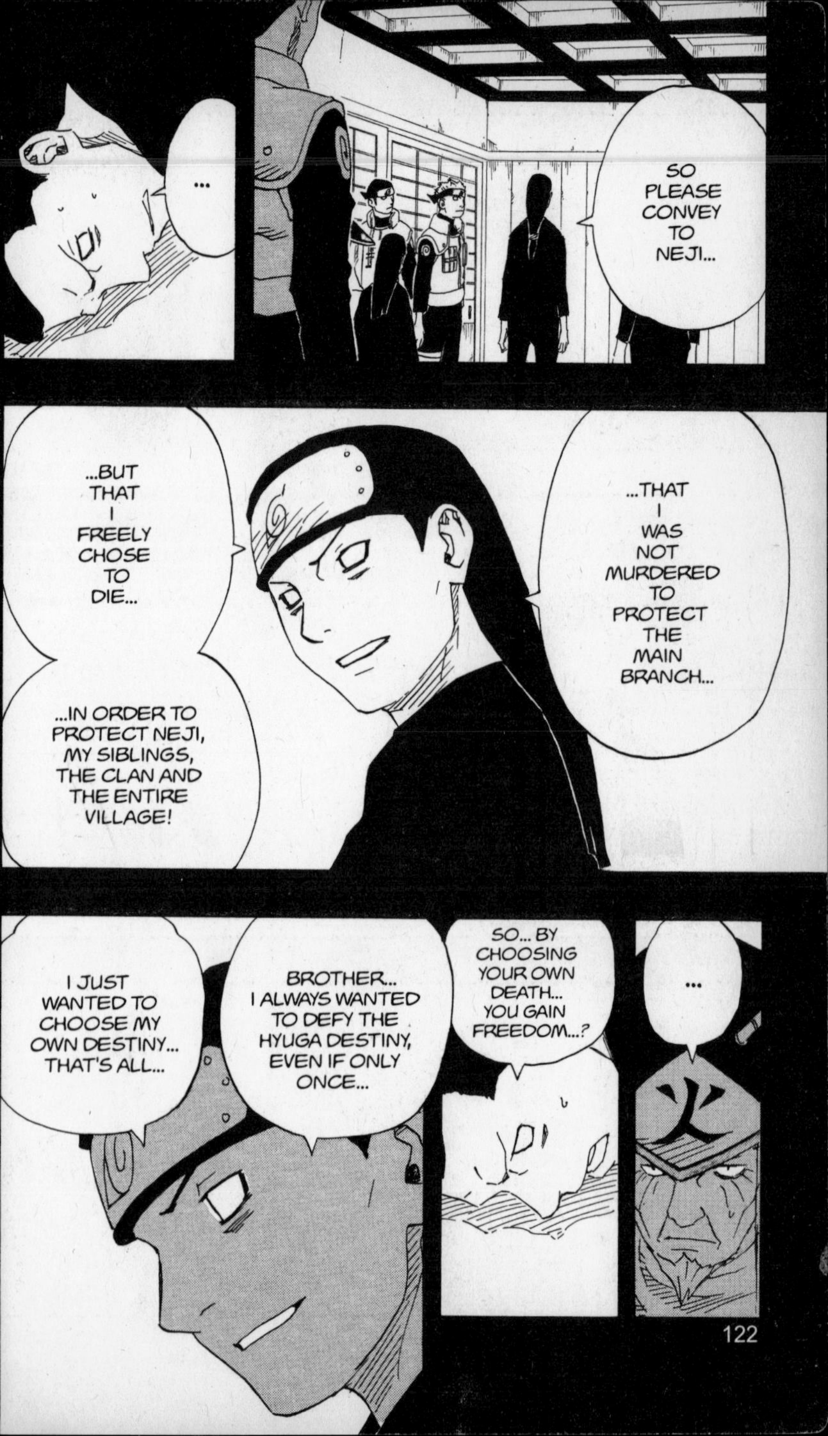
SO PLEASE CONVEY TO NEJI...
...
...THAT I WAS NOT MURDERED TO PROTECT THE MAIN BRANCH...
...BUT THAT I FREELY CHOSE TO DIE...
...IN ORDER TO PROTECT NEJI, MY SIBLINGS, THE CLAN AND THE ENTIRE VILLAGE!
...
SO... BY CHOOSING YOUR OWN DEATH... YOU GAIN FREEDOM...?
BROTHER... I ALWAYS WANTED TO DEFY THE HYUGA DESTINY, EVEN IF ONLY ONCE...
I JUST WANTED TO CHOOSE MY OWN DESTINY... THAT'S ALL...

READ THIS WAY

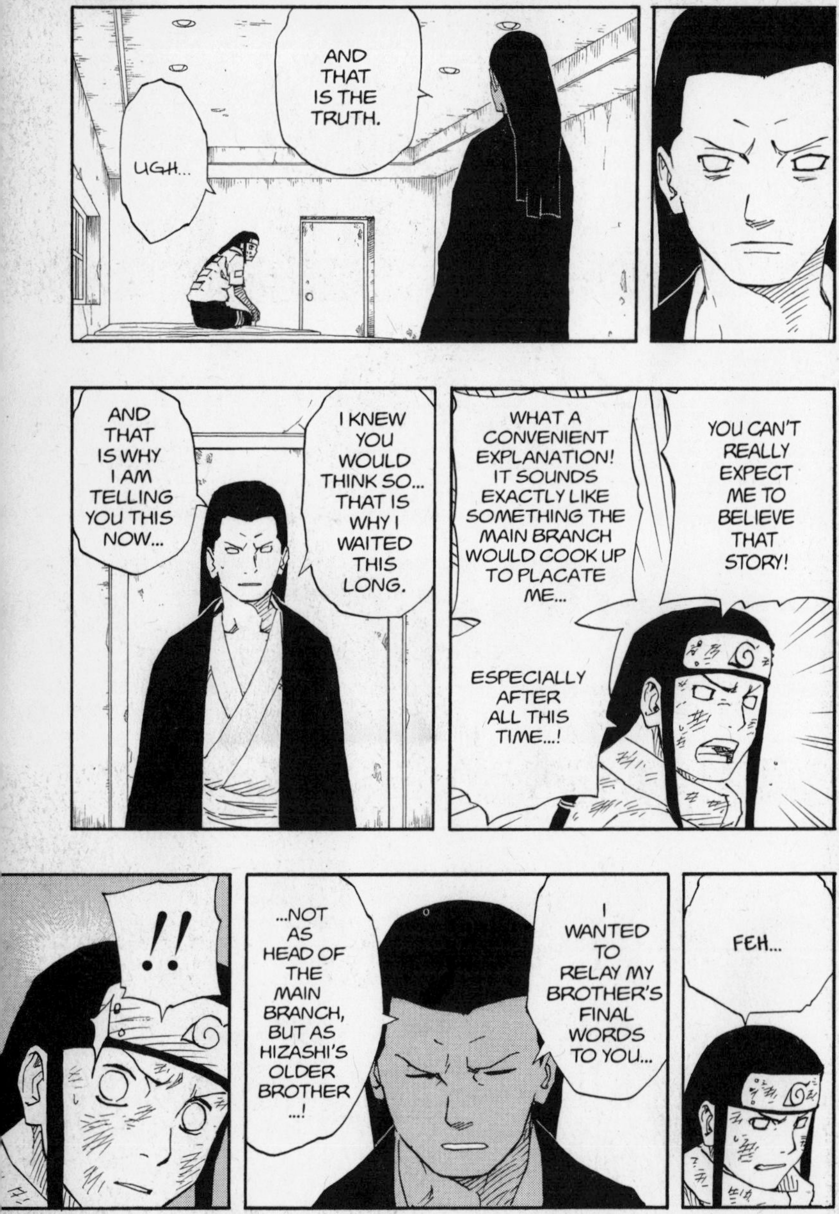
AND THAT IS THE TRUTH.
UGH...
YOU CAN'T REALLY EXPECT ME TO BELIEVE THAT STORY!
WHAT A CONVENIENT EXPLANATION! IT SOUNDS EXACTLY LIKE SOMETHING THE MAIN BRANCH WOULD COOK UP TO PLACATE ME...
ESPECIALLY AFTER ALL THIS TIME...!
I KNEW YOU WOULD THINK SO... THAT IS WHY I WAITED THIS LONG.
AND THAT IS WHY I AM TELLING YOU THIS NOW...
FEH...
I WANTED TO RELAY MY BROTHER'S FINAL WORDS TO YOU...
...NOT AS HEAD OF THE MAIN BRANCH, BUT AS HIZASHI'S OLDER BROTHER...!
!!

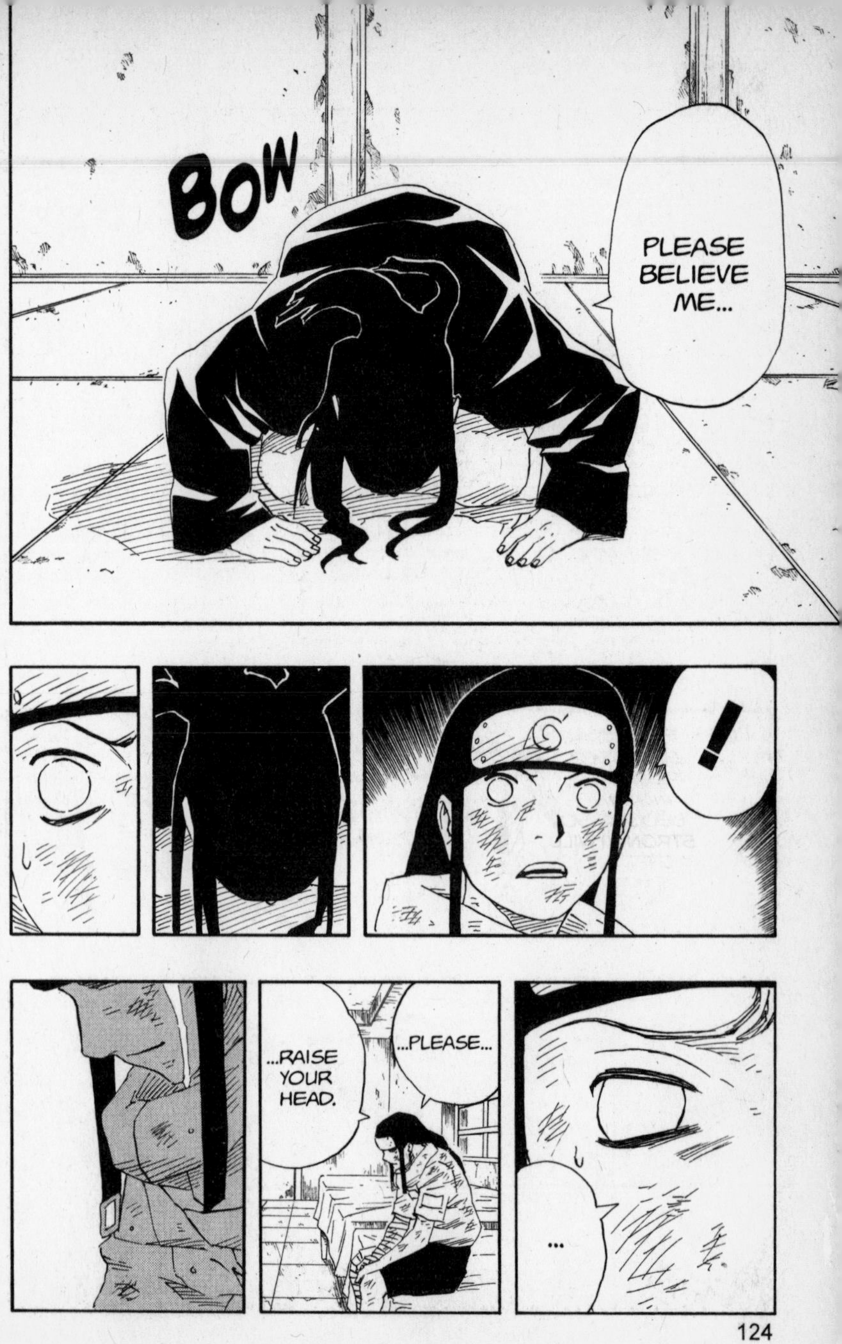
PLEASE BELIEVE ME...
BOW
!
...
...PLEASE...
...RAISE YOUR HEAD.

READ THIS WAY

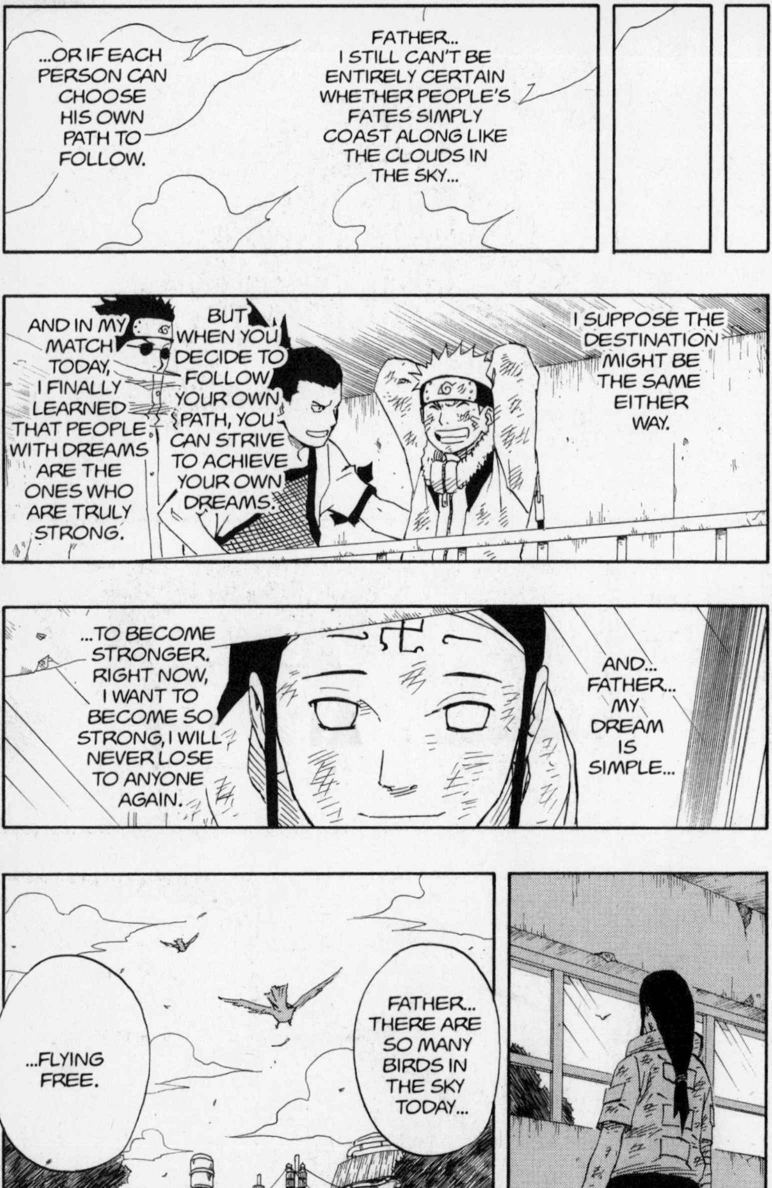

FATHER... I STILL CAN'T BE ENTIRELY CERTAIN WHETHER PEOPLE'S FATES SIMPLY COAST ALONG LIKE THE CLOUDS IN THE SKY...
...OR IF EACH PERSON CAN CHOOSE HIS OWN PATH TO FOLLOW.
I SUPPOSE THE DESTINATION MIGHT BE THE SAME EITHER WAY.
BUT WHEN YOU DECIDE TO FOLLOW YOUR OWN PATH, YOU CAN STRIVE TO ACHIEVE YOUR OWN DREAMS.
AND IN MY MATCH TODAY, I FINALLY LEARNED THAT PEOPLE WITH DREAMS ARE THE ONES WHO ARE TRULY STRONG.
AND... FATHER... MY DREAM IS SIMPLE...
...TO BECOME STRONGER. RIGHT NOW, I WANT TO BECOME SO STRONG, I WILL NEVER LOSE TO ANYONE AGAIN.
FATHER... THERE ARE SO MANY BIRDS IN THE SKY TODAY...
...FLYING FREE.

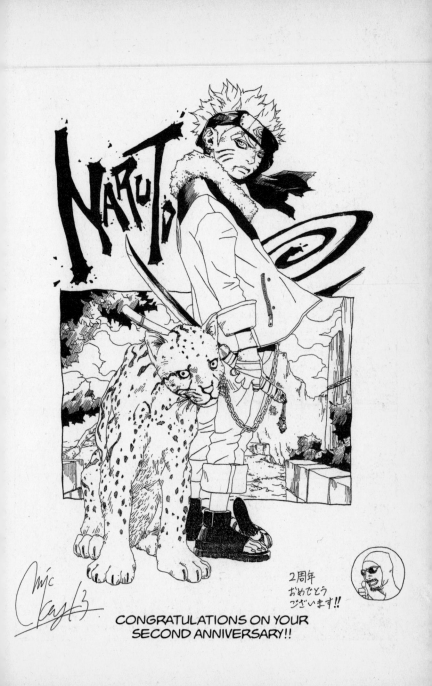

2周年
おめでとう
ございます!!

CONGRATULATIONS ON YOUR
SECOND ANNIVERSARY!!

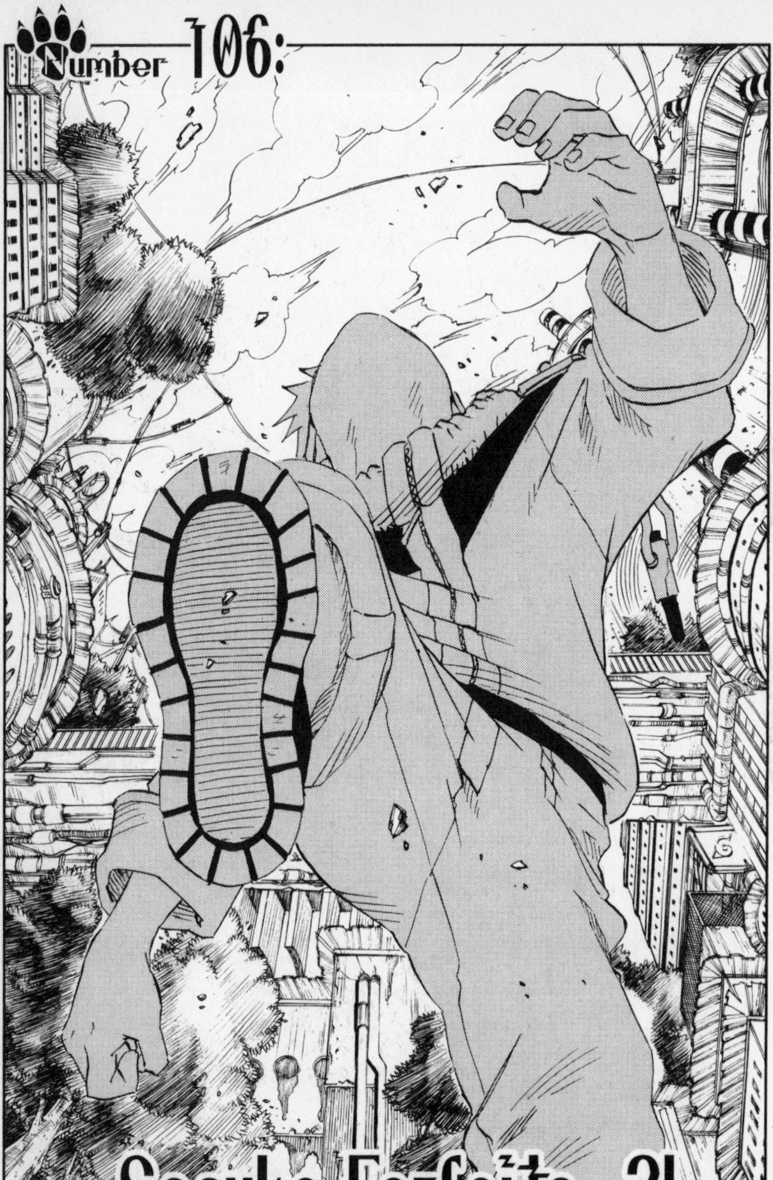
Number 106:
Sasuke Forfeits...?!

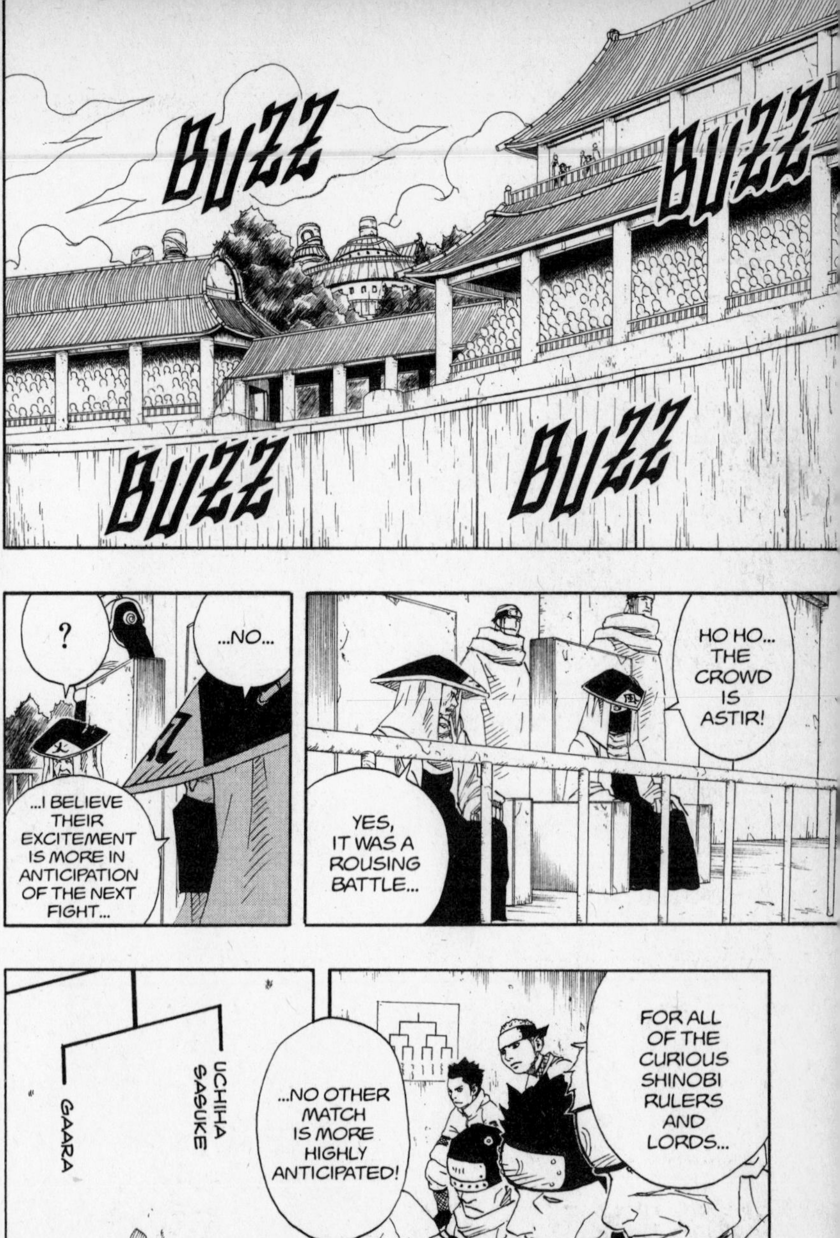
BUZZ
BUZZ
BUZZ
BUZZ
HO HO... THE CROWD IS ASTIR!
YES, IT WAS A ROUSING BATTLE...
...NO...
?
...I BELIEVE THEIR EXCITEMENT IS MORE IN ANTICIPATION OF THE NEXT FIGHT...
FOR ALL OF THE CURIOUS SHINOBI RULERS AND LORDS...
...NO OTHER MATCH IS MORE HIGHLY ANTICIPATED!
UCHIHA SASUKE
GAARA

READ THIS WAY

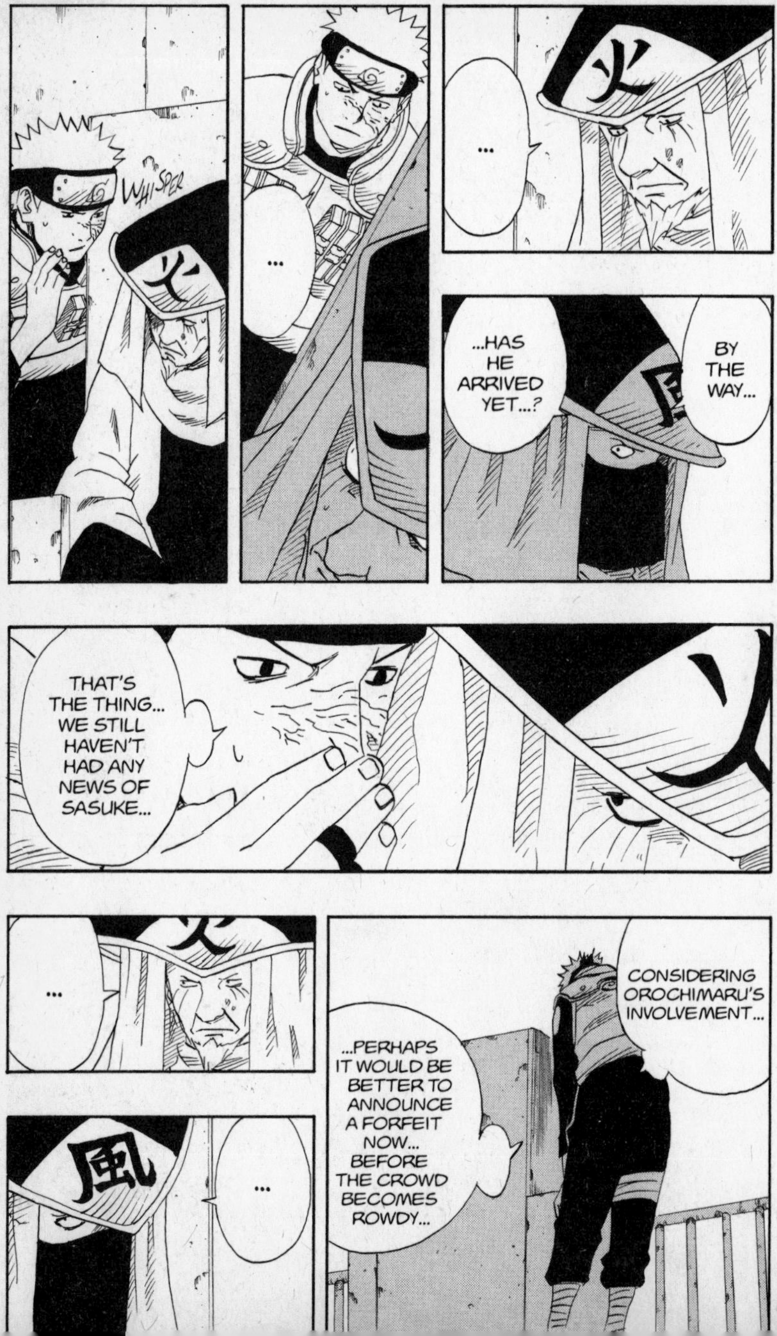
...
BY THE WAY...
...HAS HE ARRIVED YET...?
...
WHISPER
THAT'S THE THING... WE STILL HAVEN'T HAD ANY NEWS OF SASUKE...
CONSIDERING OROCHIMARU'S INVOLVEMENT...
...PERHAPS IT WOULD BE BETTER TO ANNOUNCE A FORFEIT NOW... BEFORE THE CROWD BECOMES ROWDY...
...
...

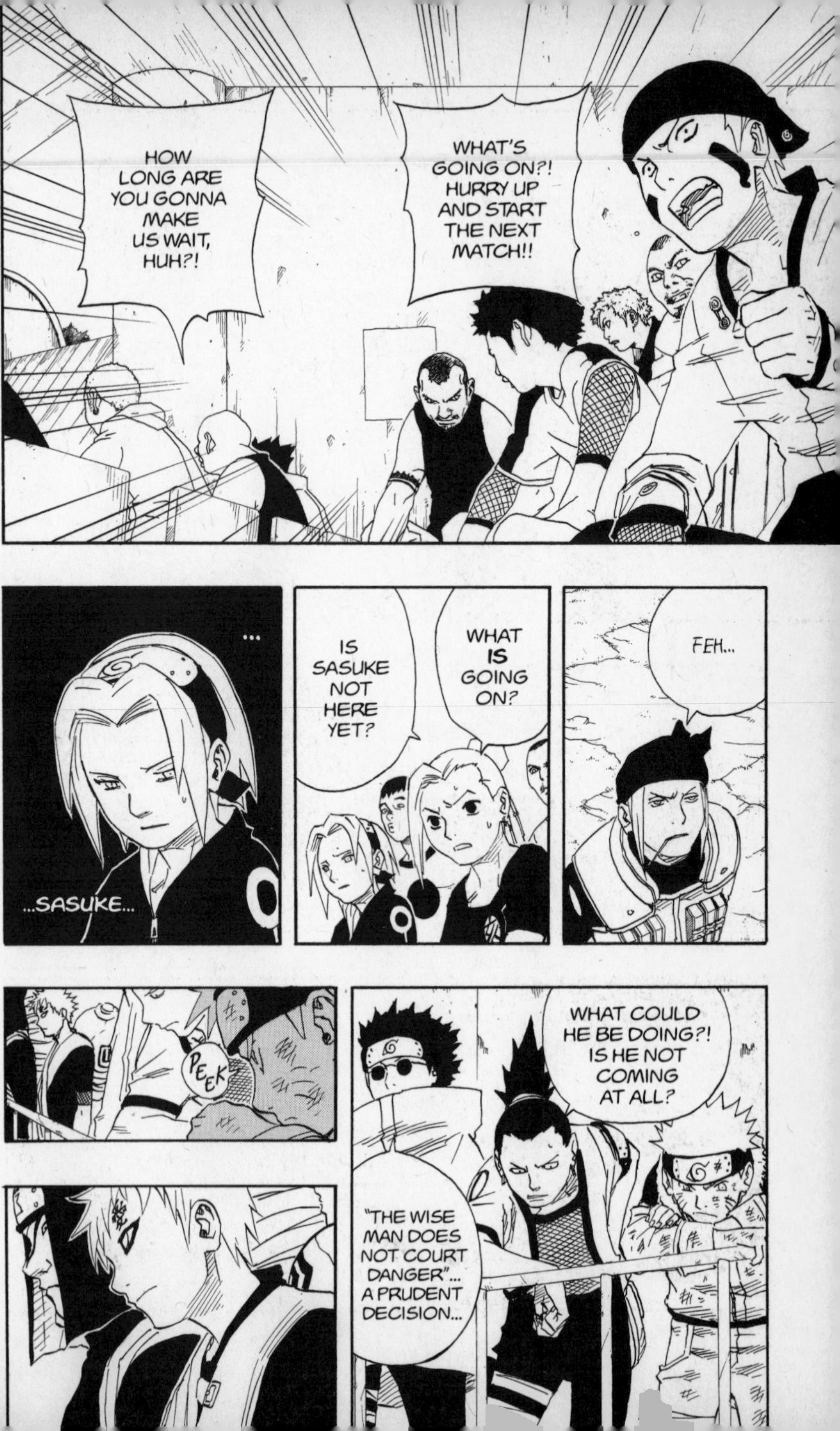
WHAT'S GOING ON?! HURRY UP AND START THE NEXT MATCH!!
HOW LONG ARE YOU GONNA MAKE US WAIT, HUH?!
FEH...
WHAT IS GOING ON?
IS SASUKE NOT HERE YET?
...
...SASUKE...
WHAT COULD HE BE DOING?! IS HE NOT COMING AT ALL?
"THE WISE MAN DOES NOT COURT DANGER"... A PRUDENT DECISION...
PEEK

READ THIS WAY

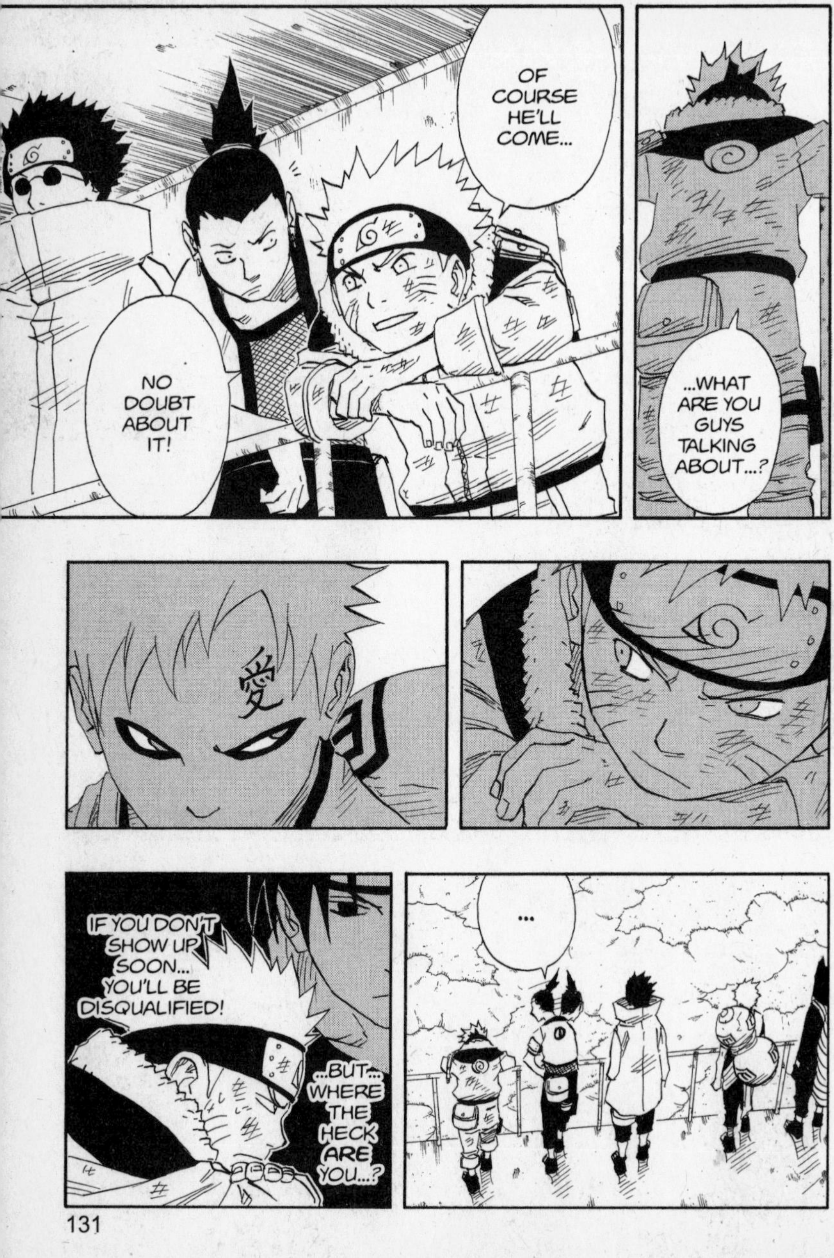
...WHAT ARE YOU GUYS TALKING ABOUT...?
OF COURSE HE'LL COME...
NO DOUBT ABOUT IT!
...
IF YOU DON'T SHOW UP SOON... YOU'LL BE DISQUALIFIED!
...BUT... WHERE THE HECK ARE YOU...?

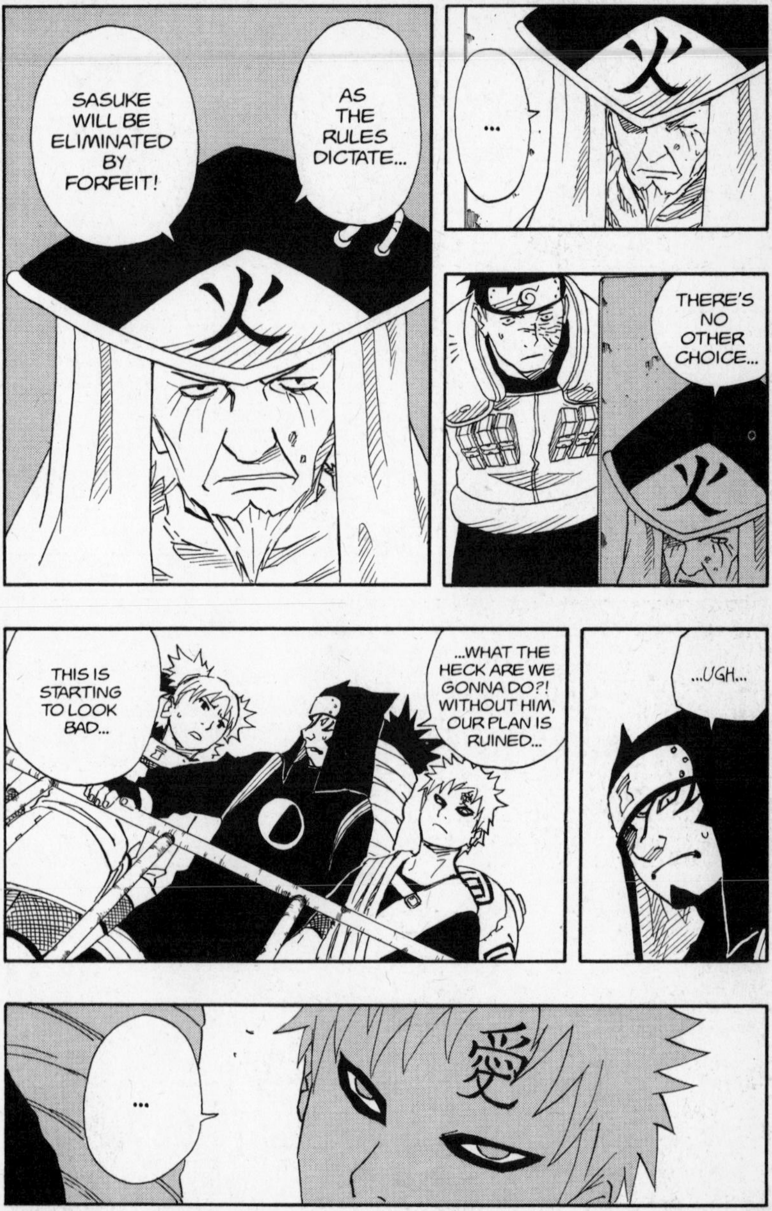
...
THERE'S NO OTHER CHOICE...
AS THE RULES DICTATE...
SASUKE WILL BE ELIMINATED BY FORFEIT!
...UGH...
...WHAT THE HECK ARE WE GONNA DO?! WITHOUT HIM, OUR PLAN IS RUINED...
THIS IS STARTING TO LOOK BAD...
...

READ THIS WAY

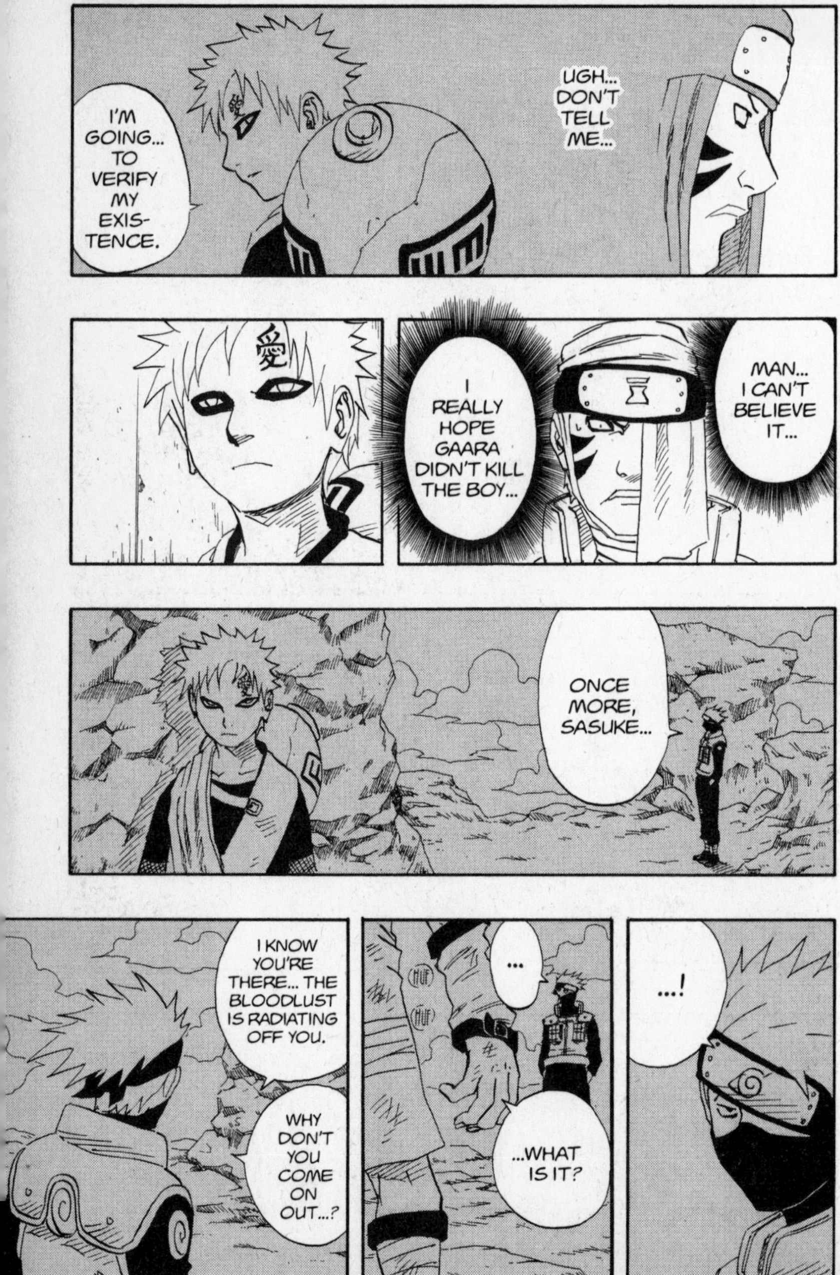
UGH... DON'T TELL ME...
I'M GOING... TO VERIFY MY EXISTENCE.
MAN... I CAN'T BELIEVE IT...
I REALLY HOPE GAARA DIDN'T KILL THE BOY...
ONCE MORE, SASUKE...
...!
...
HUF
HUF
...WHAT IS IT?
I KNOW YOU'RE THERE... THE BLOODLUST IS RADIATING OFF YOU.
WHY DON'T YOU COME ON OUT...?

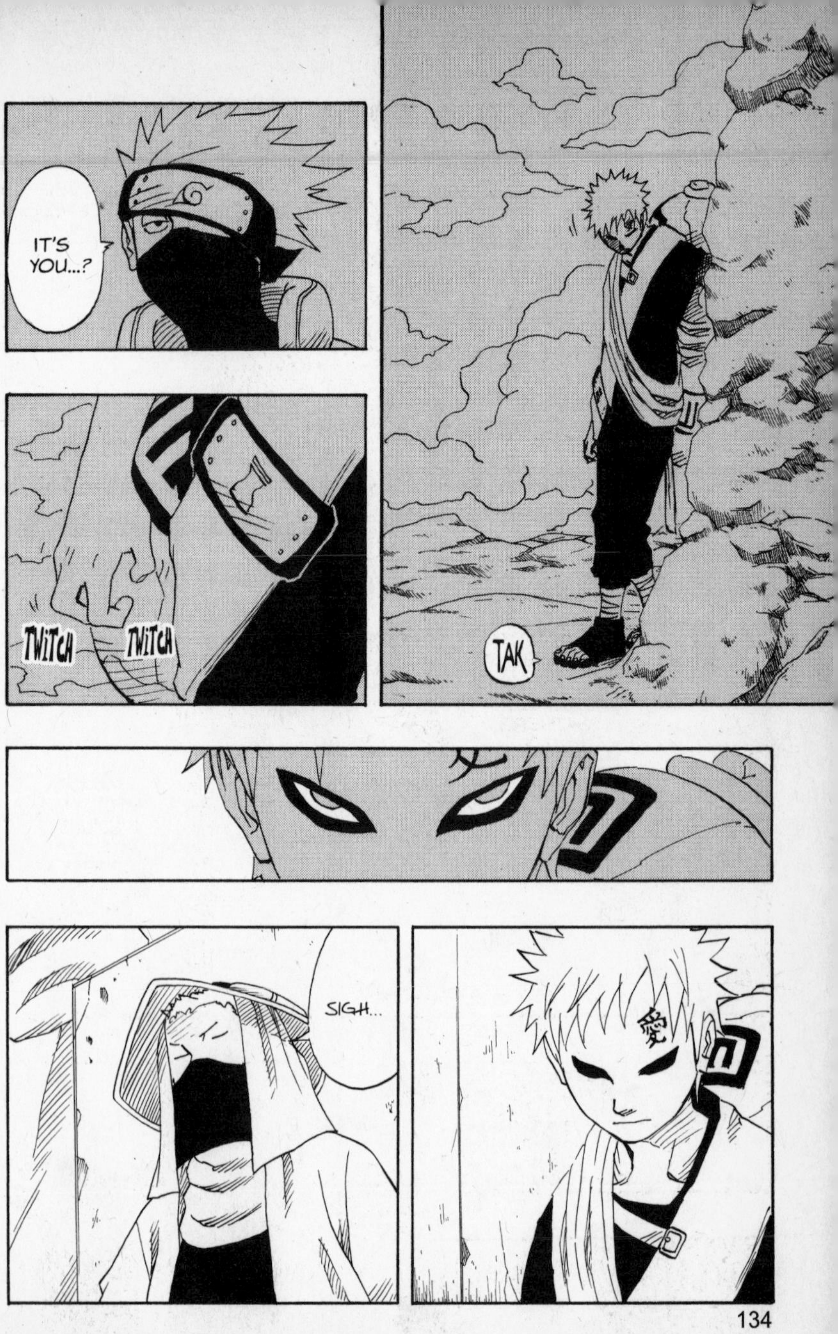
TAK
IT'S YOU...?
TWITCH
TWITCH
SIGH...

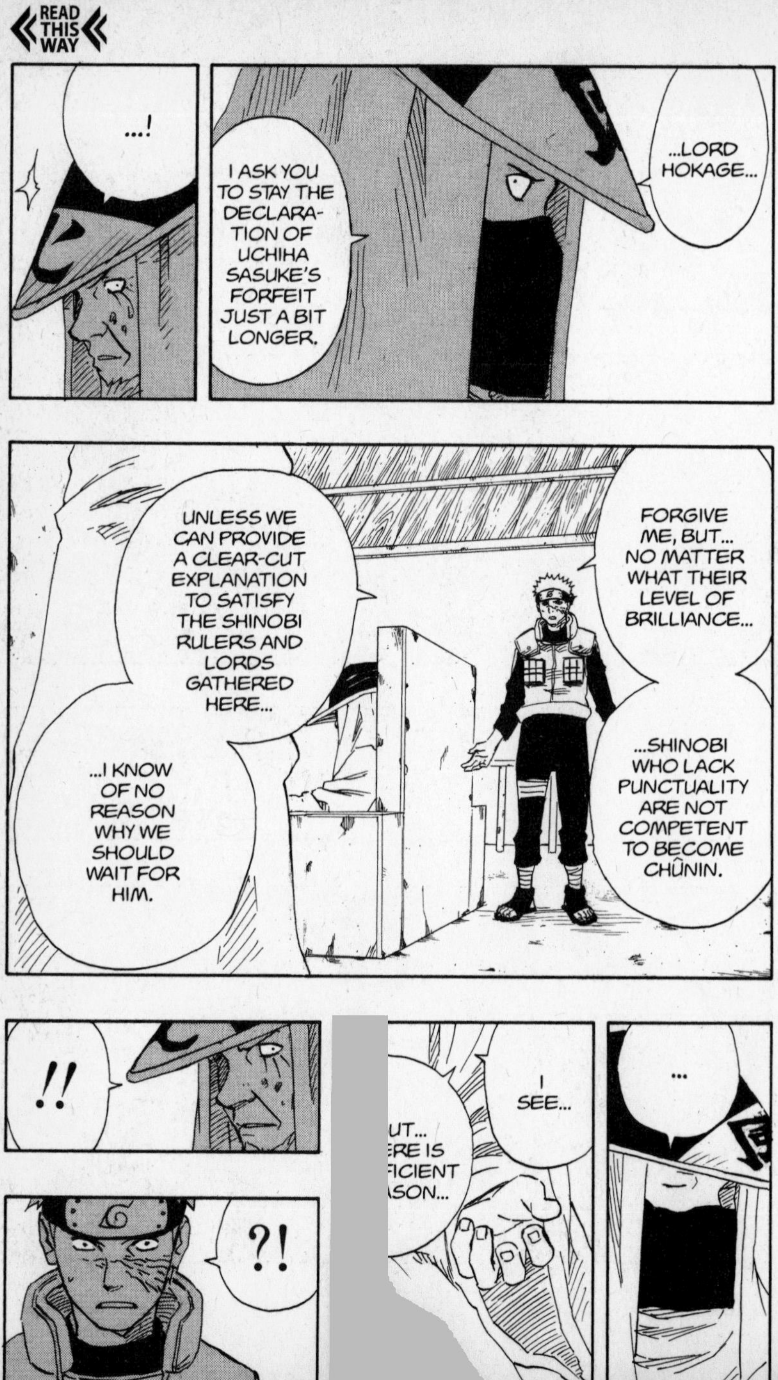
READ THIS WAY
...LORD HOKAGE...
I ASK YOU TO STAY THE DECLARATION OF UCHIHA SASUKE'S FORFEIT JUST A BIT LONGER.
...!
FORGIVE ME, BUT... NO MATTER WHAT THEIR LEVEL OF BRILLIANCE...
...SHINOBI WHO LACK PUNCTUALITY ARE NOT COMPETENT TO BECOME CHÛNIN.
UNLESS WE CAN PROVIDE A CLEAR-CUT EXPLANATION TO SATISFY THE SHINOBI RULERS AND LORDS GATHERED HERE...
...I KNOW OF NO REASON WHY WE SHOULD WAIT FOR HIM.
...
I SEE...
UT... ERE IS FICIENT ASON...
!!
?!

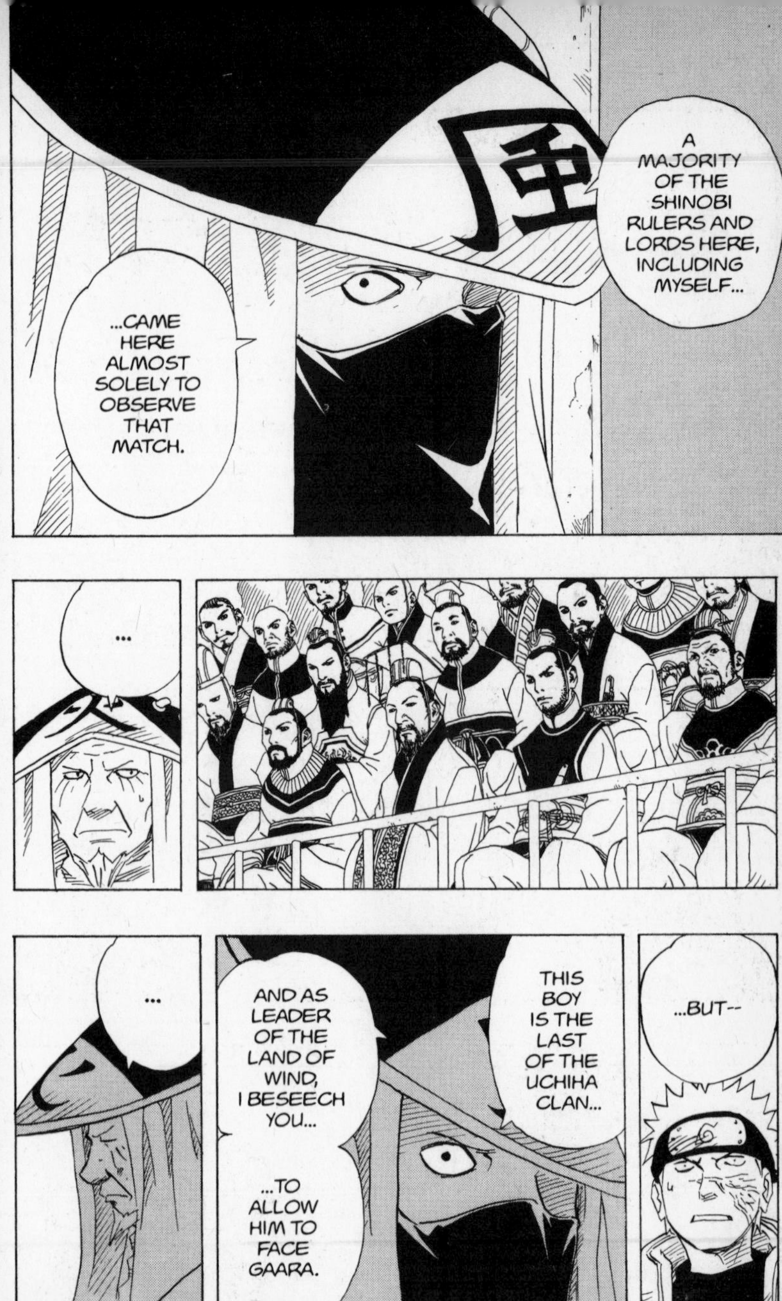
A MAJORITY OF THE SHINOBI RULERS AND LORDS HERE, INCLUDING MYSELF...
...CAME HERE ALMOST SOLELY TO OBSERVE THAT MATCH.
...
...BUT--
THIS BOY IS THE LAST OF THE UCHIHA CLAN...
AND AS LEADER OF THE LAND OF WIND, I BESEECH YOU...
...TO ALLOW HIM TO FACE GAARA.
...

READ THIS WAY

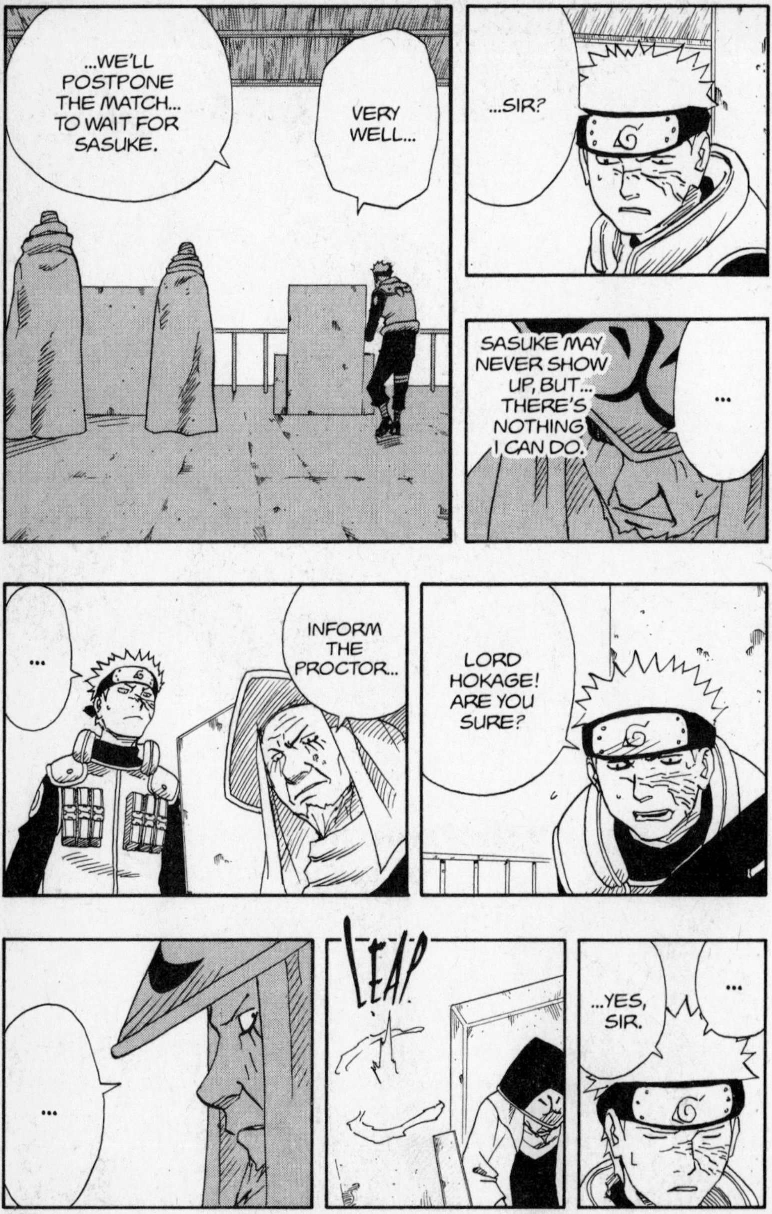
...SIR?
...
SASUKE MAY NEVER SHOW UP, BUT... THERE'S NOTHING I CAN DO.
VERY WELL...
...WE'LL POSTPONE THE MATCH... TO WAIT FOR SASUKE.
LORD HOKAGE! ARE YOU SURE?
INFORM THE PROCTOR...
...
...
...YES, SIR.
LEAP
...

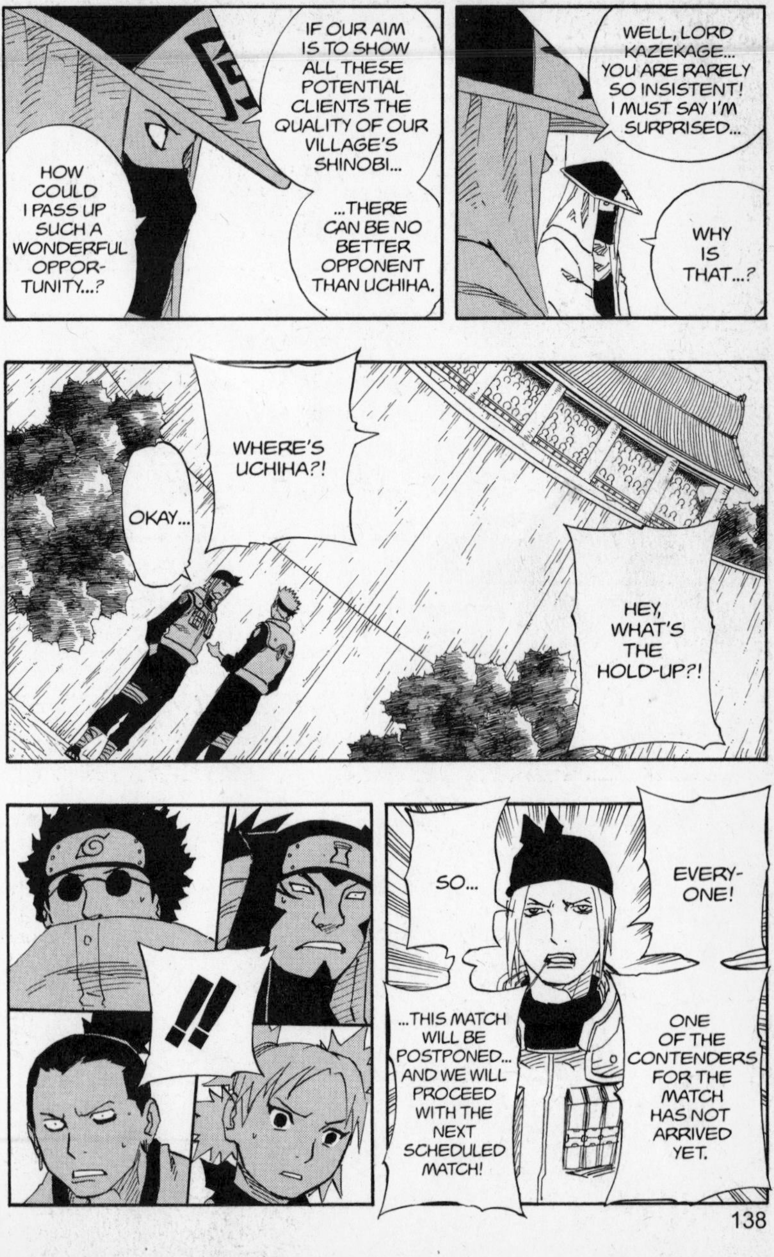
WELL, LORD KAZEKAGE... YOU ARE RARELY SO INSISTENT! I MUST SAY I'M SURPRISED...
WHY IS THAT...?
IF OUR AIM IS TO SHOW ALL THESE POTENTIAL CLIENTS THE QUALITY OF OUR VILLAGE'S SHINOBI...
...THERE CAN BE NO BETTER OPPONENT THAN UCHIHA.
HOW COULD I PASS UP SUCH A WONDERFUL OPPOR-TUNITY...?
HEY, WHAT'S THE HOLD-UP?!
WHERE'S UCHIHA?!
OKAY...
EVERY-ONE!
SO...
ONE OF THE CONTENDERS FOR THE MATCH HAS NOT ARRIVED YET.
...THIS MATCH WILL BE POSTPONED... AND WE WILL PROCEED WITH THE NEXT SCHEDULED MATCH!
!!

READ THIS WAY

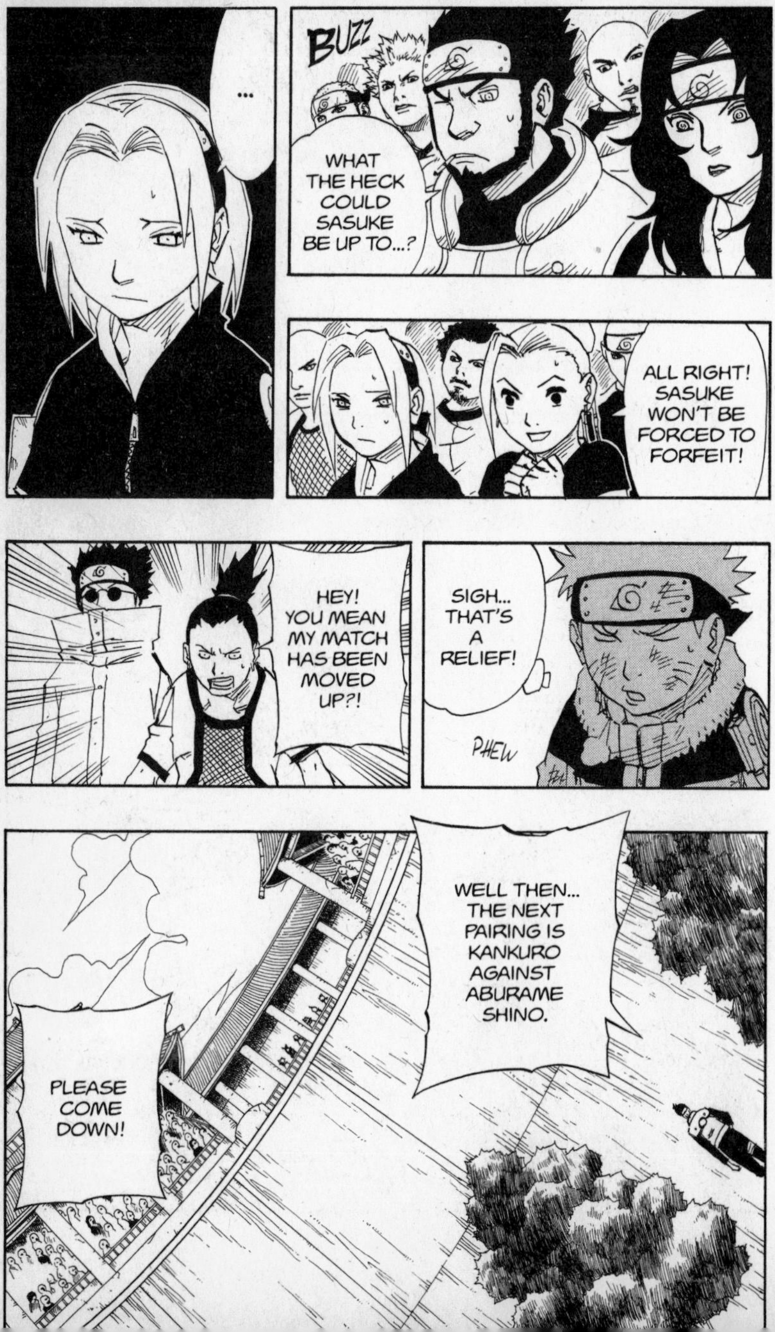

BUZZ
WHAT THE HECK COULD SASUKE BE UP TO...?
ALL RIGHT! SASUKE WON'T BE FORCED TO FORFEIT!
...
SIGH... THAT'S A RELIEF!
PHEW
HEY! YOU MEAN MY MATCH HAS BEEN MOVED UP?!
WELL THEN... THE NEXT PAIRING IS KANKURO AGAINST ABURAME SHINO.
PLEASE COME DOWN!

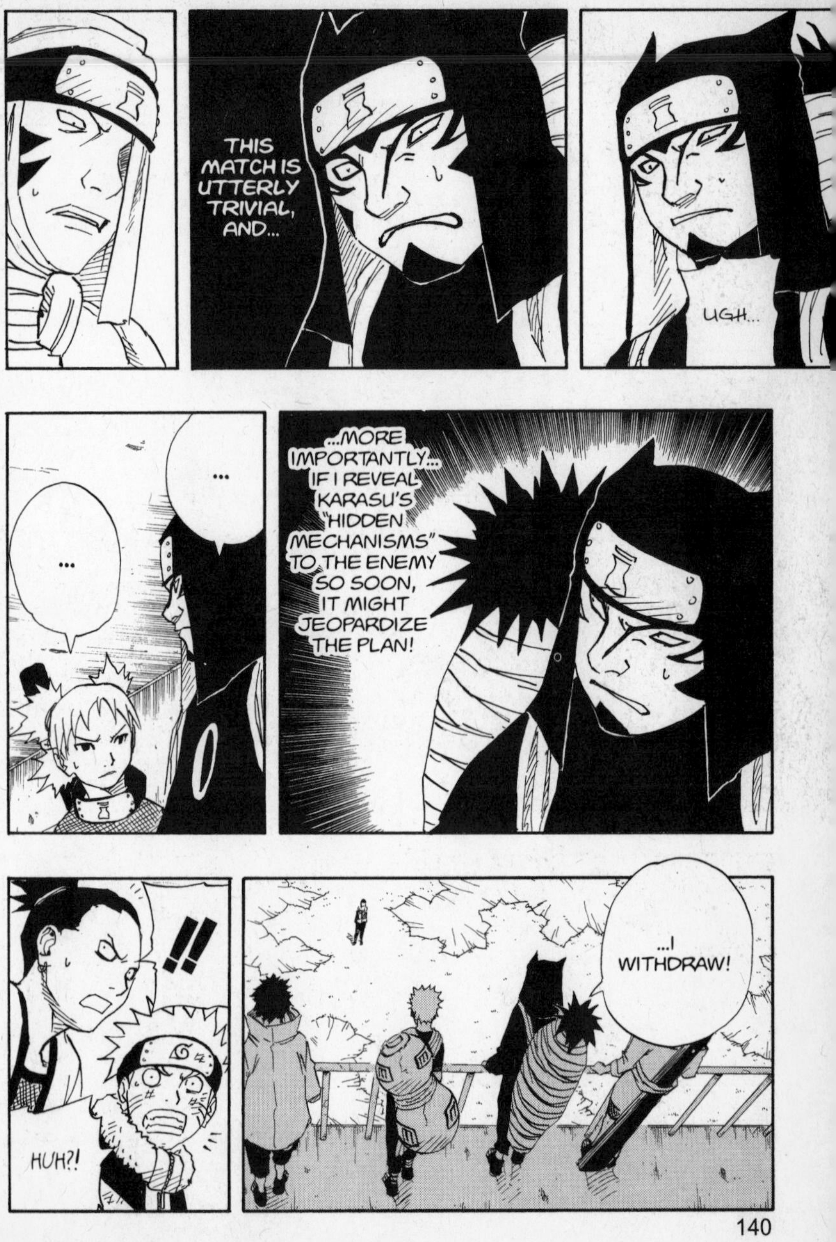
UGH...
THIS MATCH IS UTTERLY TRIVIAL, AND...
...MORE IMPORTANTLY... IF I REVEAL KARASU'S "HIDDEN MECHANISMS" TO THE ENEMY SO SOON, IT MIGHT JEOPARDIZE THE PLAN!
...
...
...I WITHDRAW!
!!
HUH?!

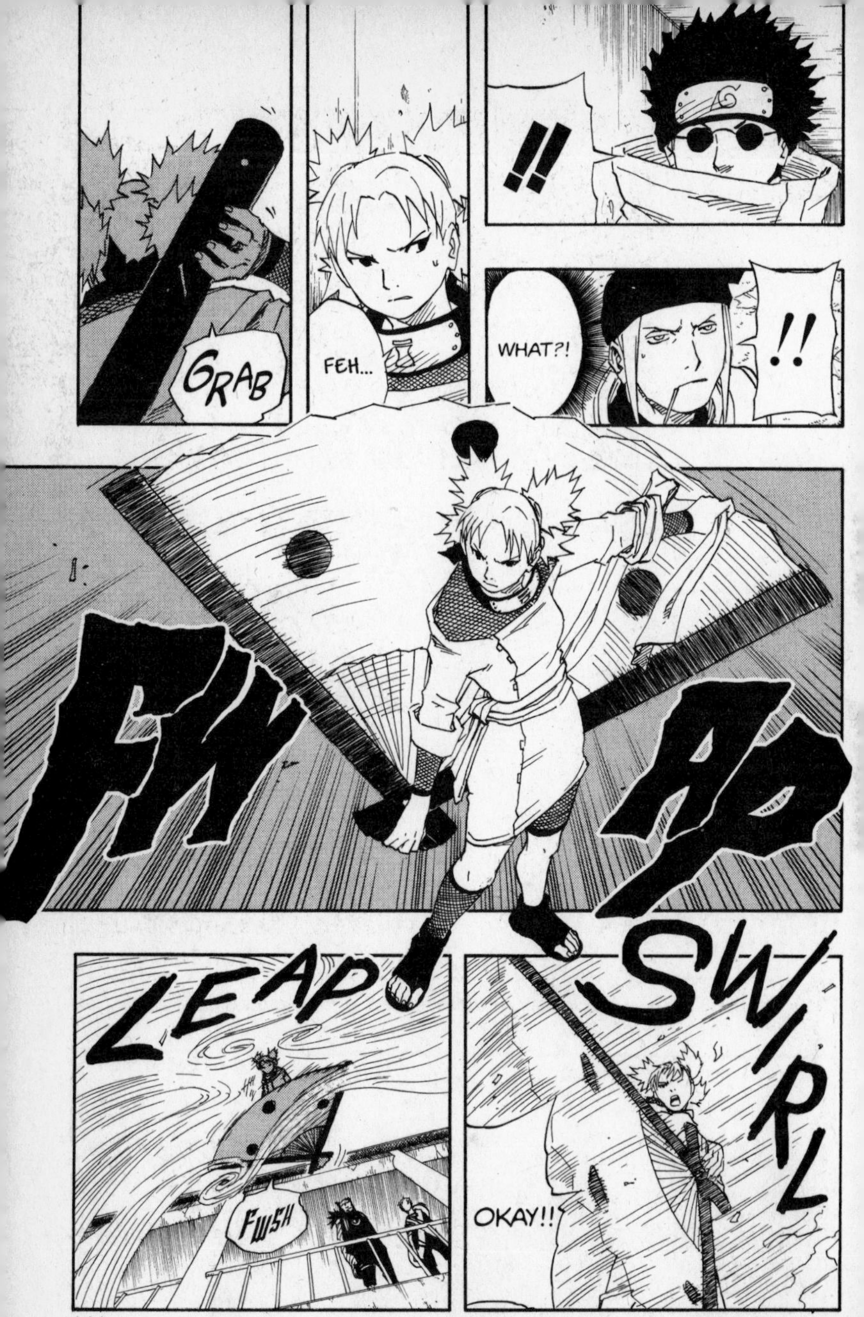
!!
!!
WHAT?!
FEH...
GRAB
FWAP
SWIRL
OKAY!!
LEAP
FWSH

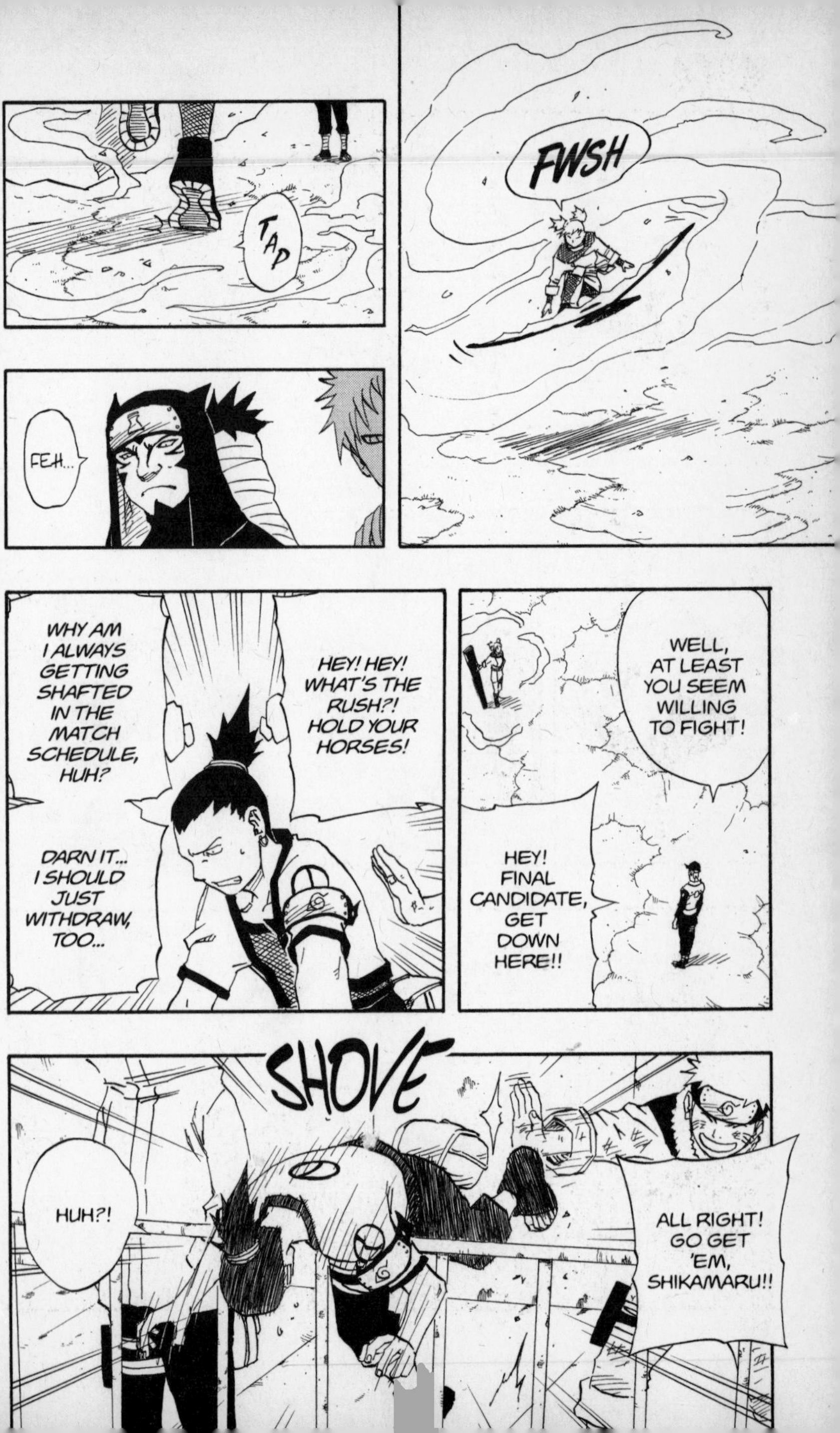
FWSH
TAP
FEH...
WELL, AT LEAST YOU SEEM WILLING TO FIGHT!
HEY! FINAL CANDIDATE, GET DOWN HERE!!
HEY! HEY! WHAT'S THE RUSH?! HOLD YOUR HORSES!
WHY AM I ALWAYS GETTING SHAFTED IN THE MATCH SCHEDULE, HUH?
DARN IT... I SHOULD JUST WITHDRAW, TOO...
SHOVE
ALL RIGHT! GO GET 'EM, SHIKAMARU!!
HUH?!

READ THIS WAY

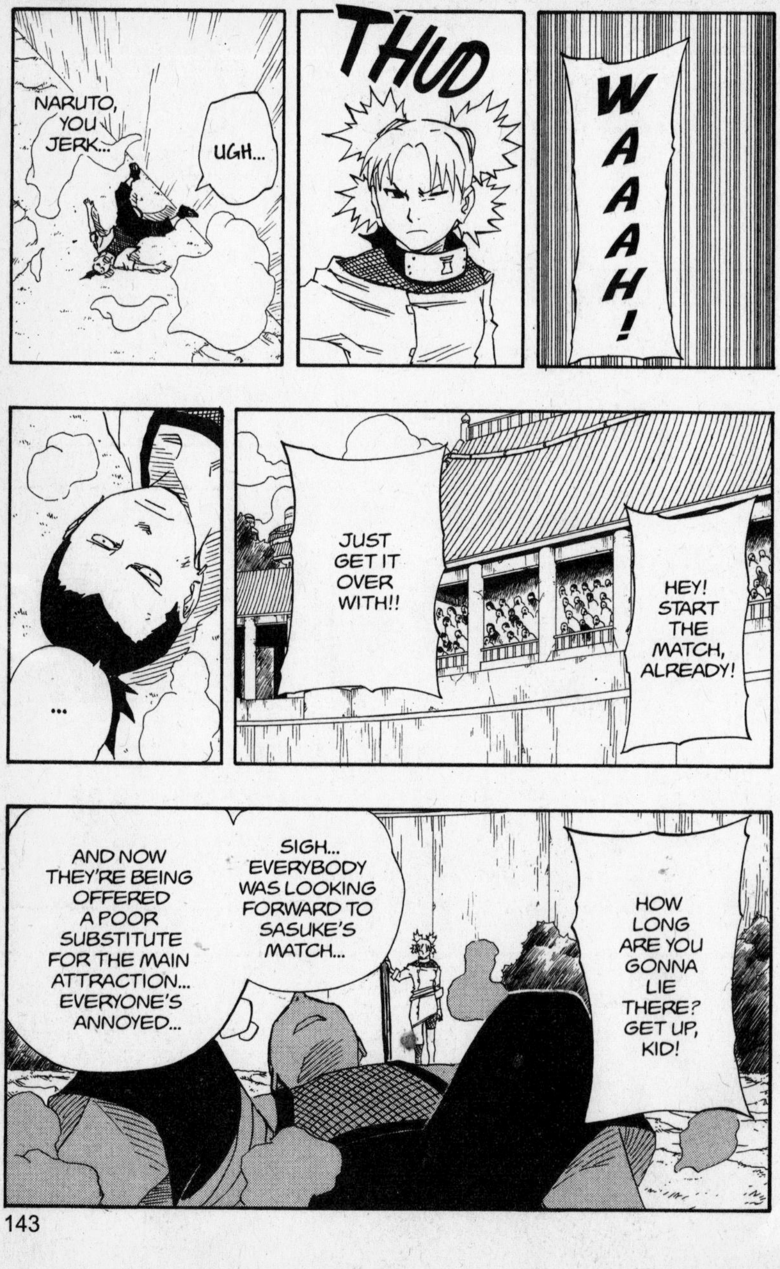
WAAAAH!
THUD
UGH...
NARUTO, YOU JERK...
HEY! START THE MATCH, ALREADY!
JUST GET IT OVER WITH!!
...
HOW LONG ARE YOU GONNA LIE THERE? GET UP, KID!
SIGH... EVERYBODY WAS LOOKING FORWARD TO SASUKE'S MATCH...
AND NOW THEY'RE BEING OFFERED A POOR SUBSTITUTE FOR THE MAIN ATTRACTION... EVERYONE'S ANNOYED...

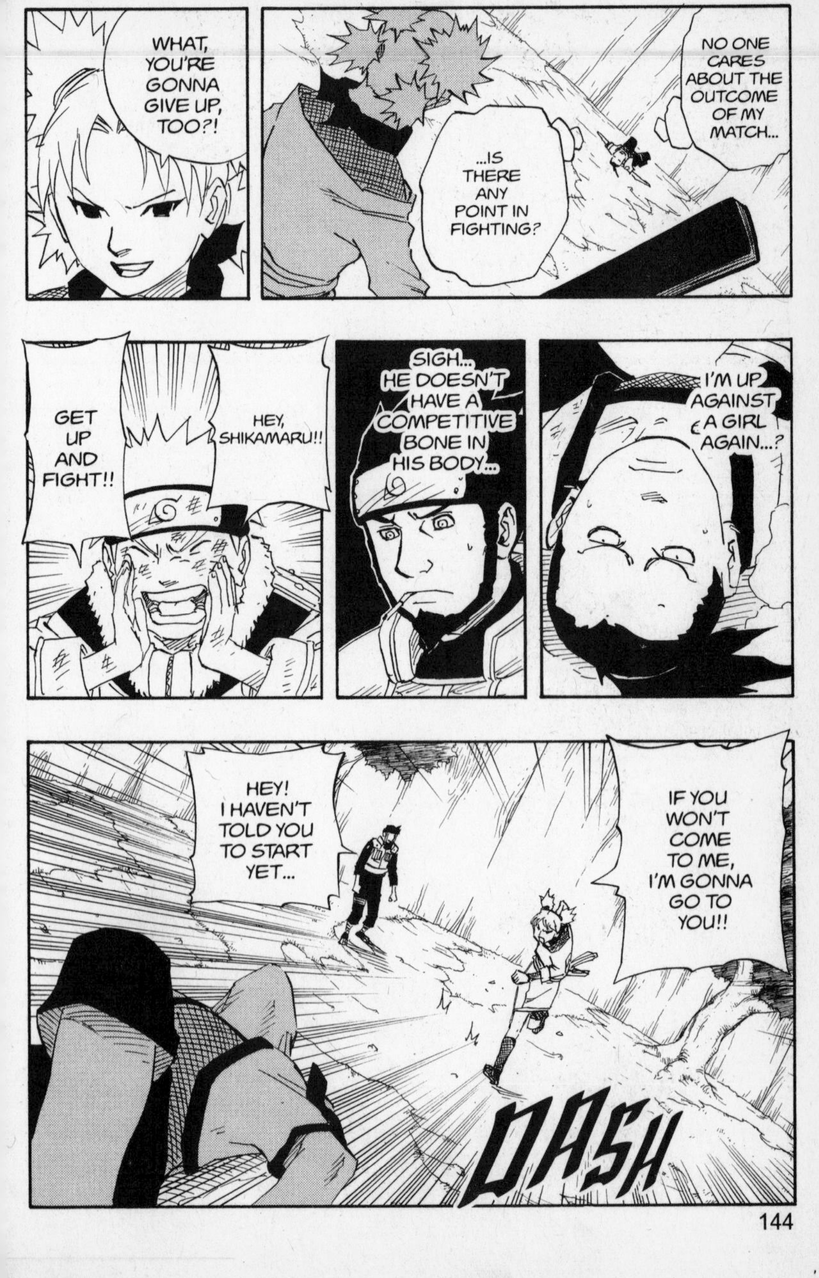
NO ONE CARES ABOUT THE OUTCOME OF MY MATCH...
...IS THERE ANY POINT IN FIGHTING?
WHAT, YOU'RE GONNA GIVE UP, TOO?!
I'M UP AGAINST A GIRL AGAIN...?
SIGH... HE DOESN'T HAVE A COMPETITIVE BONE IN HIS BODY...
HEY, SHIKAMARU!!
GET UP AND FIGHT!!
IF YOU WON'T COME TO ME, I'M GONNA GO TO YOU!!
HEY! I HAVEN'T TOLD YOU TO START YET...
DASH

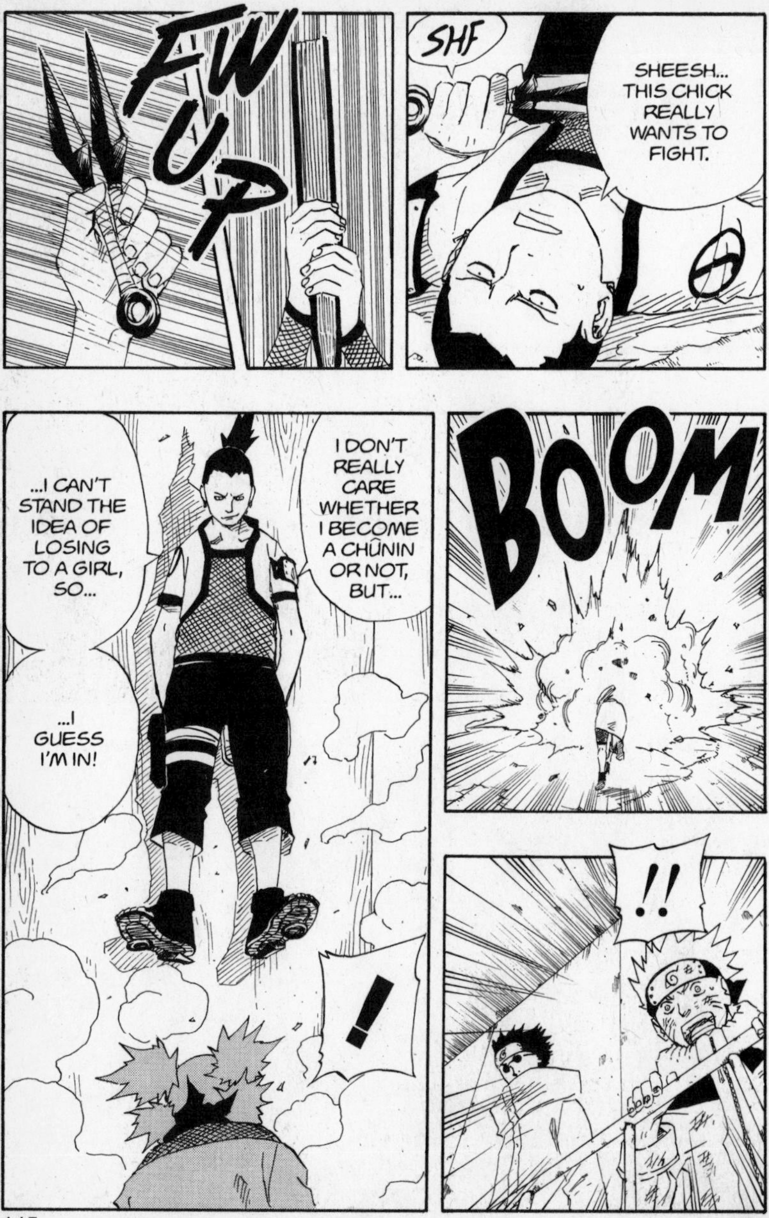
SHF
SHEESH... THIS CHICK REALLY WANTS TO FIGHT.
FWUP
BOOM
!!
I DON'T REALLY CARE WHETHER I BECOME A CHŪNIN OR NOT, BUT...
...I CAN'T STAND THE IDEA OF LOSING TO A GIRL, SO...
...I GUESS I'M IN!
!

THE RESULTS OF THE SECOND CHARACTER POPULARITY SURVEY!!

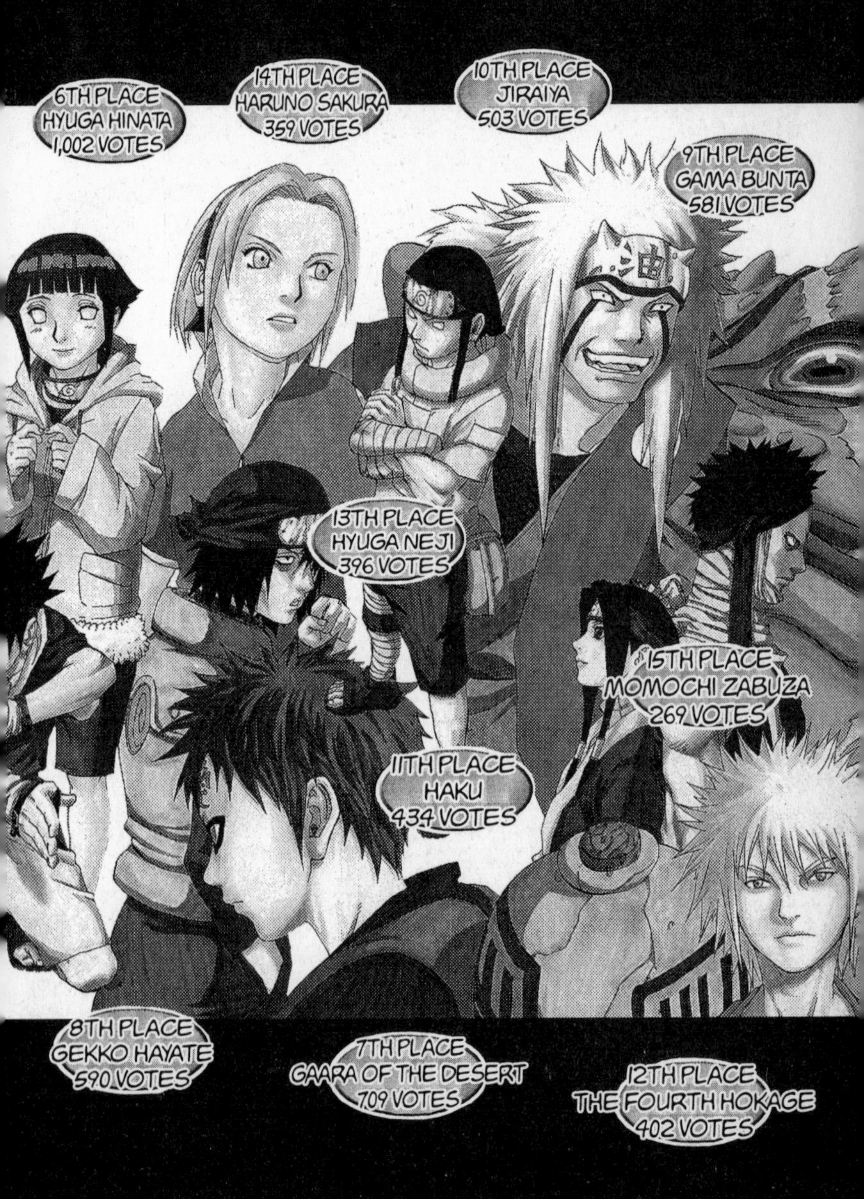
9TH PLACE GAMA BUNTA 581 VOTES
10TH PLACE JIRAIYA 503 VOTES
14TH PLACE HARUNO SAKURA 359 VOTES
6TH PLACE HYUGA HINATA 1,002 VOTES
15TH PLACE MOMOCHI ZABUZA 269 VOTES
13TH PLACE HYUGA NEJI 396 VOTES
11TH PLACE HAKU 434 VOTES
12TH PLACE THE FOURTH HOKAGE 402 VOTES
7TH PLACE GAARA OF THE DESERT 709 VOTES
8TH PLACE GEKKO HAYATE 590 VOTES

SECOND ANNIVERSARY CELEBRATION!

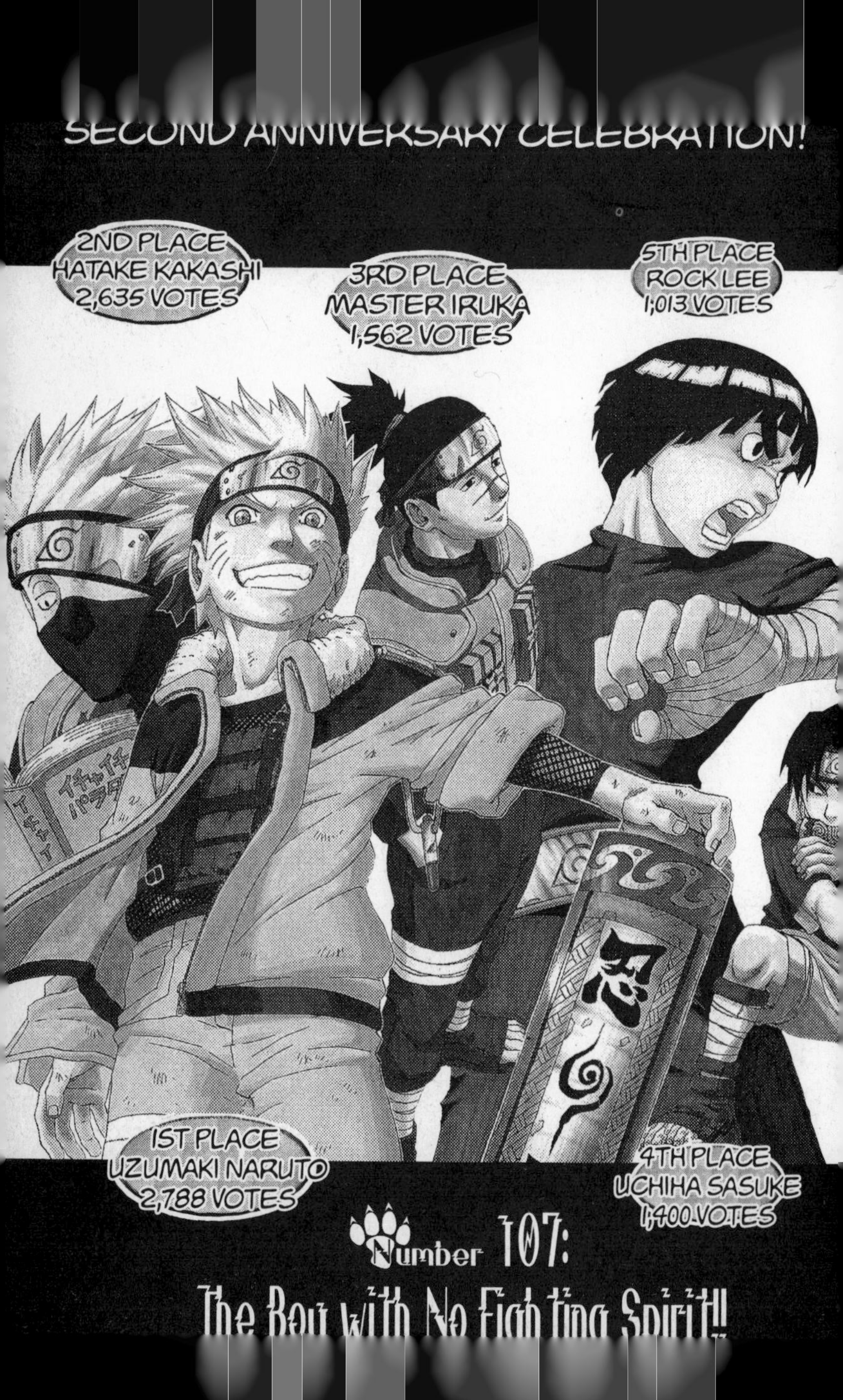
2ND PLACE HATAKE KAKASHI 2,635 VOTES
3RD PLACE MASTER IRUKA 1,562 VOTES
5TH PLACE ROCK LEE 1,013 VOTES
1ST PLACE UZUMAKI NARUTO 2,788 VOTES
4TH PLACE UCHIHA SASUKE 1,400 VOTES

Number 107: The Boy with No Fighting Spirit!!

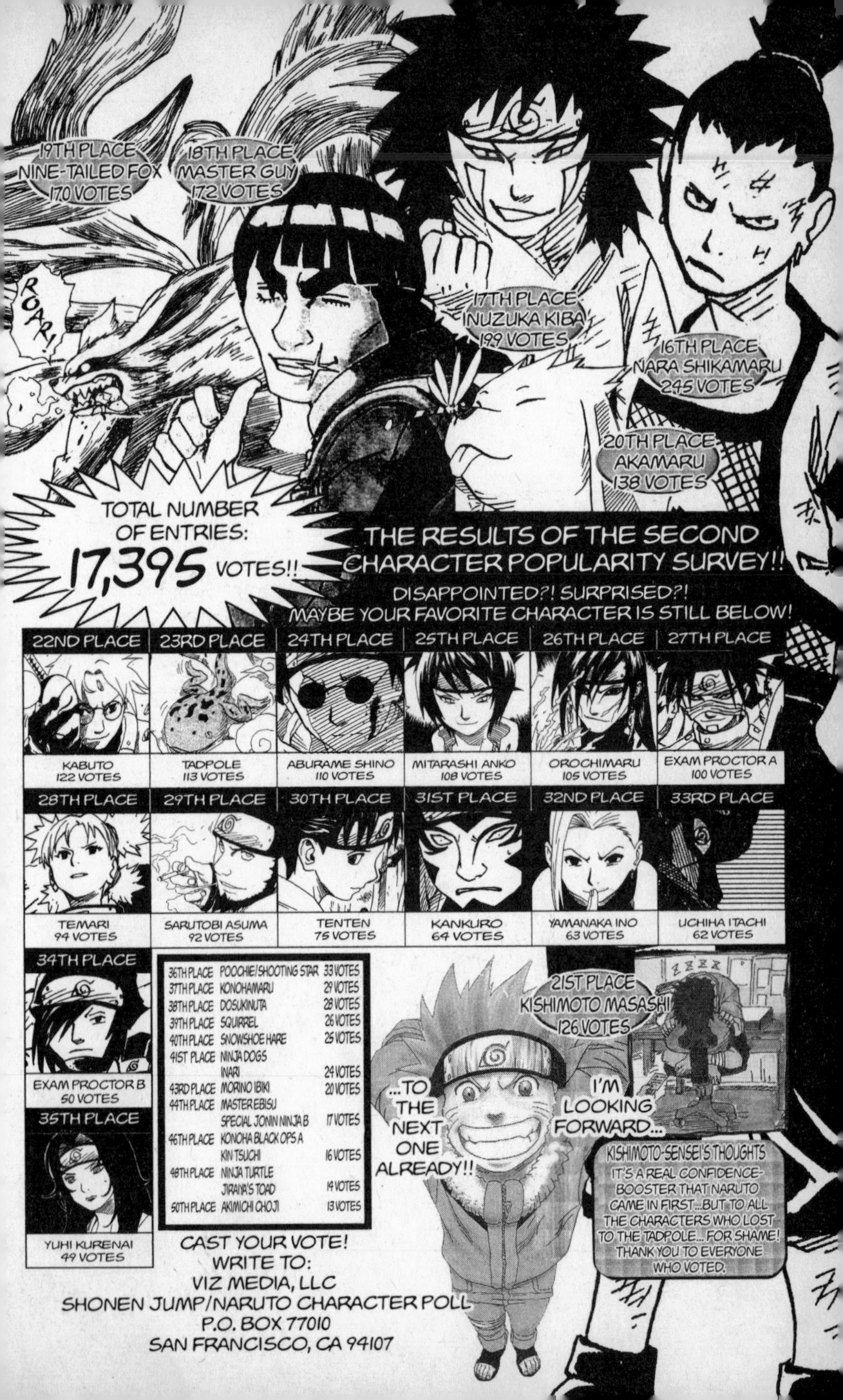
19TH PLACE NINE-TAILED FOX 170 VOTES
18TH PLACE MASTER GUY 172 VOTES
ROAR!
17TH PLACE INUZUKA KIBA 199 VOTES
16TH PLACE NARA SHIKAMARU 245 VOTES
20TH PLACE AKAMARU 138 VOTES
TOTAL NUMBER OF ENTRIES: 17,395 VOTES!!
THE RESULTS OF THE SECOND CHARACTER POPULARITY SURVEY!!
DISAPPOINTED?! SURPRISED?! MAYBE YOUR FAVORITE CHARACTER IS STILL BELOW!
22ND PLACE KABUTO 122 VOTES
23RD PLACE TADPOLE 113 VOTES
24TH PLACE ABURAME SHINO 110 VOTES
25TH PLACE MITARASHI ANKO 108 VOTES
26TH PLACE OROCHIMARU 105 VOTES
27TH PLACE EXAM PROCTOR A 100 VOTES
28TH PLACE TEMARI 94 VOTES
29TH PLACE SARUTOBI ASUMA 92 VOTES
30TH PLACE TENTEN 75 VOTES
31ST PLACE KANKURO 64 VOTES
32ND PLACE YAMANAKA INO 63 VOTES
33RD PLACE UCHIHA ITACHI 62 VOTES
34TH PLACE EXAM PROCTOR B 50 VOTES
35TH PLACE YUHI KURENAI 49 VOTES
36TH PLACE POOCHIE/SHOOTING STAR 33 VOTES
37TH PLACE KONOHAMARU 29 VOTES
38TH PLACE DOSUKINUTA 28 VOTES
39TH PLACE SQUIRREL 26 VOTES
40TH PLACE SNOWSHOE HARE 25 VOTES
41ST PLACE NINJA DOGS
INARI 24 VOTES
43RD PLACE MORINO IBIKI 20 VOTES
44TH PLACE MASTER EBISU
SPECIAL JONIN NINJA B 17 VOTES
46TH PLACE KONOHA BLACK OPS A
KIN TSUCHI 16 VOTES
48TH PLACE NINJA TURTLE
JIRAIYA'S TOAD 14 VOTES
50TH PLACE AKIMICHI CHOJI 13 VOTES
21ST PLACE KISHIMOTO MASASHI 126 VOTES
ZZZZ
I'M LOOKING FORWARD...
...TO THE NEXT ONE ALREADY!!
KISHIMOTO-SENSEI'S THOUGHTS
IT'S A REAL CONFIDENCE-BOOSTER THAT NARUTO CAME IN FIRST...BUT TO ALL THE CHARACTERS WHO LOST TO THE TADPOLE... FOR SHAME! THANK YOU TO EVERYONE WHO VOTED.
CAST YOUR VOTE!
WRITE TO:
VIZ MEDIA, LLC
SHONEN JUMP/NARUTO CHARACTER POLL
P.O. BOX 77010
SAN FRANCISCO, CA 94107

READ THIS WAY

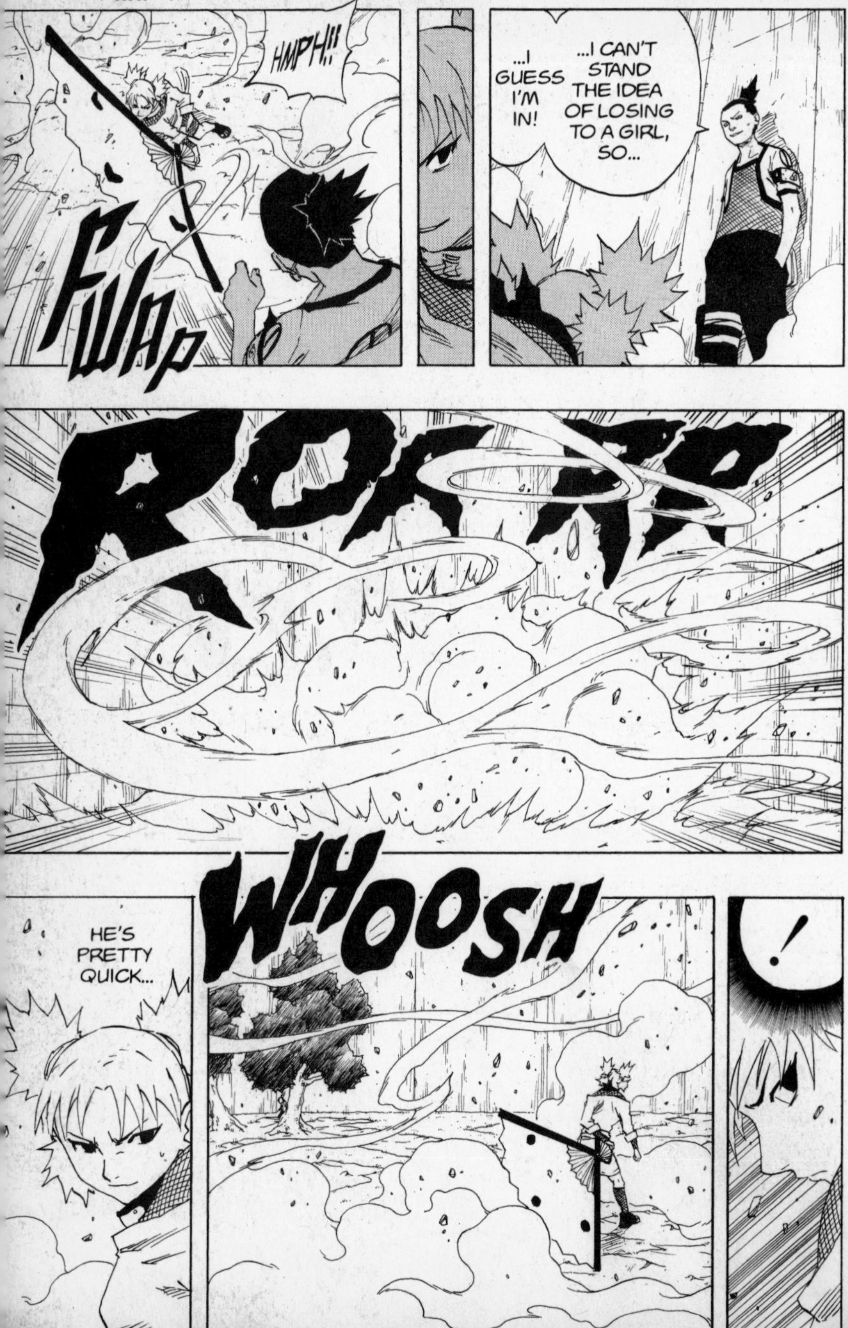
...I CAN'T STAND THE IDEA OF LOSING TO A GIRL, SO...
...I GUESS I'M IN!
HMPH!!
FWAP
ROAR
!
WHOOSH
HE'S PRETTY QUICK...

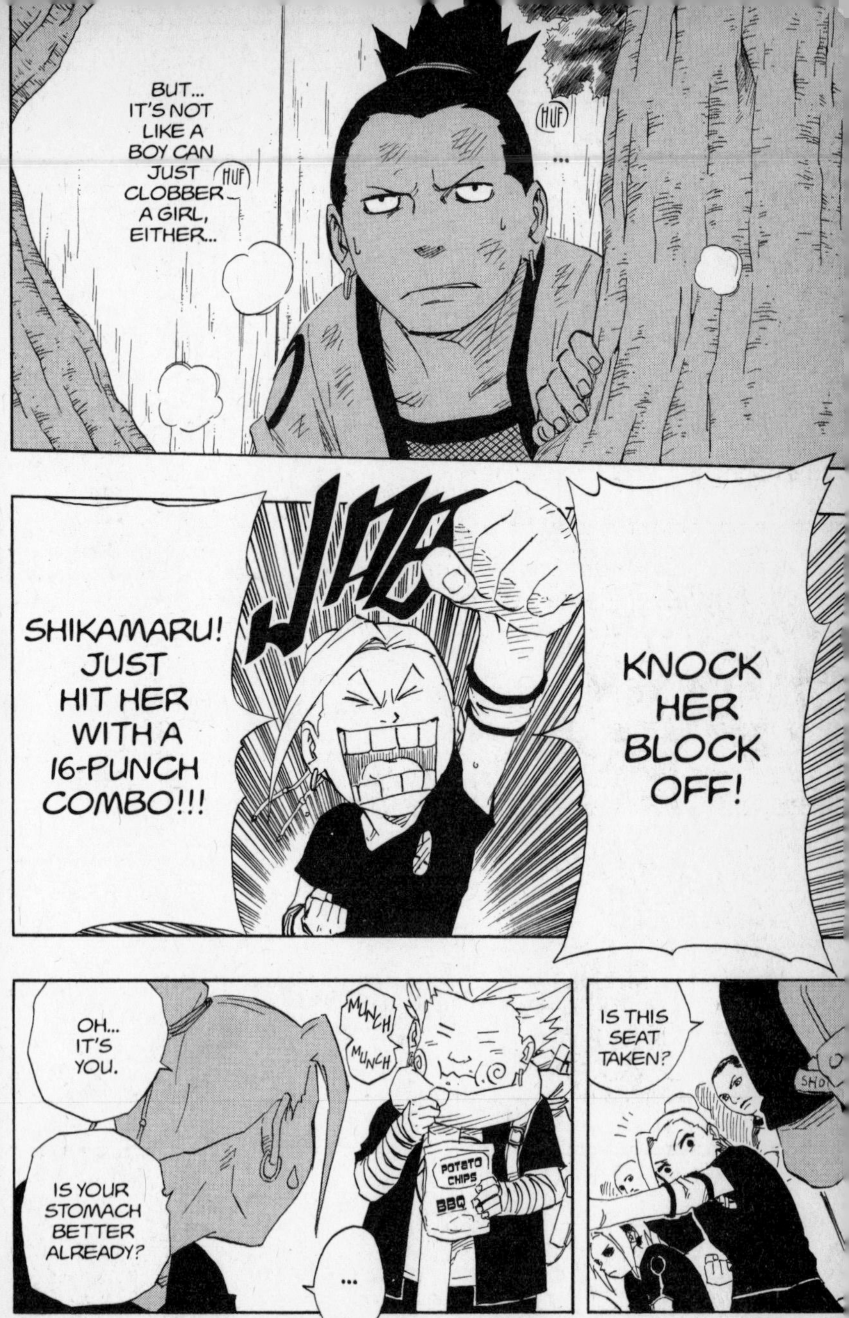
BUT... IT'S NOT LIKE A BOY CAN JUST CLOBBER A GIRL, EITHER...
HUF
HUF
...
KNOCK HER BLOCK OFF!
JAB
SHIKAMARU! JUST HIT HER WITH A 16-PUNCH COMBO!!!
IS THIS SEAT TAKEN?
MUNCH
MUNCH
POTATO CHIPS
BBQ
...
OH... IT'S YOU.
IS YOUR STOMACH BETTER ALREADY?

READ THIS WAY

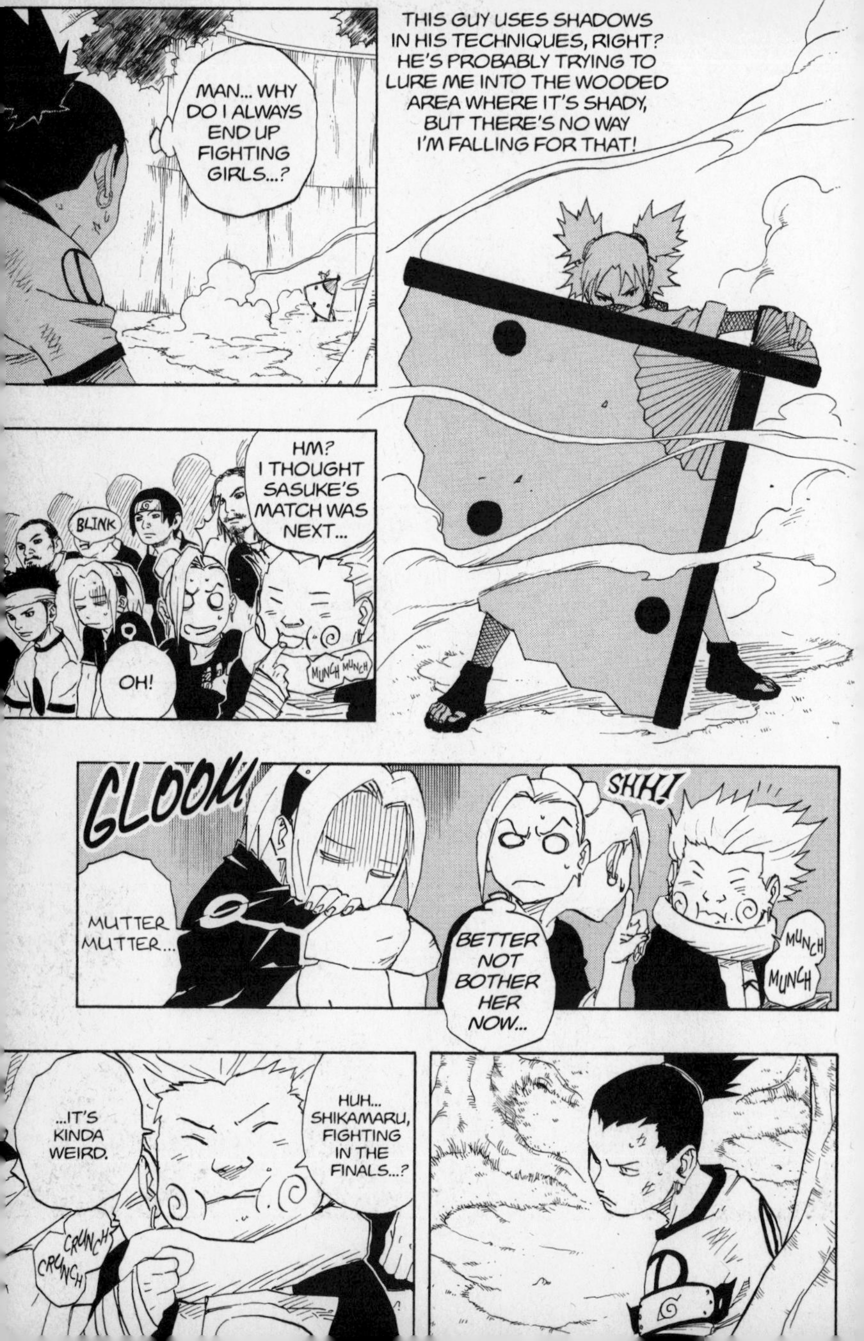
THIS GUY USES SHADOWS IN HIS TECHNIQUES, RIGHT? HE'S PROBABLY TRYING TO LURE ME INTO THE WOODED AREA WHERE IT'S SHADY, BUT THERE'S NO WAY I'M FALLING FOR THAT!
MAN... WHY DO I ALWAYS END UP FIGHTING GIRLS...?
HM? I THOUGHT SASUKE'S MATCH WAS NEXT...
MUNCH MUNCH
BLINK
OH!
SHH!
BETTER NOT BOTHER HER NOW...
MUNCH
MUNCH
GLOOM
MUTTER MUTTER...
HUH... SHIKAMARU, FIGHTING IN THE FINALS...?
...IT'S KINDA WEIRD.
CRUNCH
CRUNCH

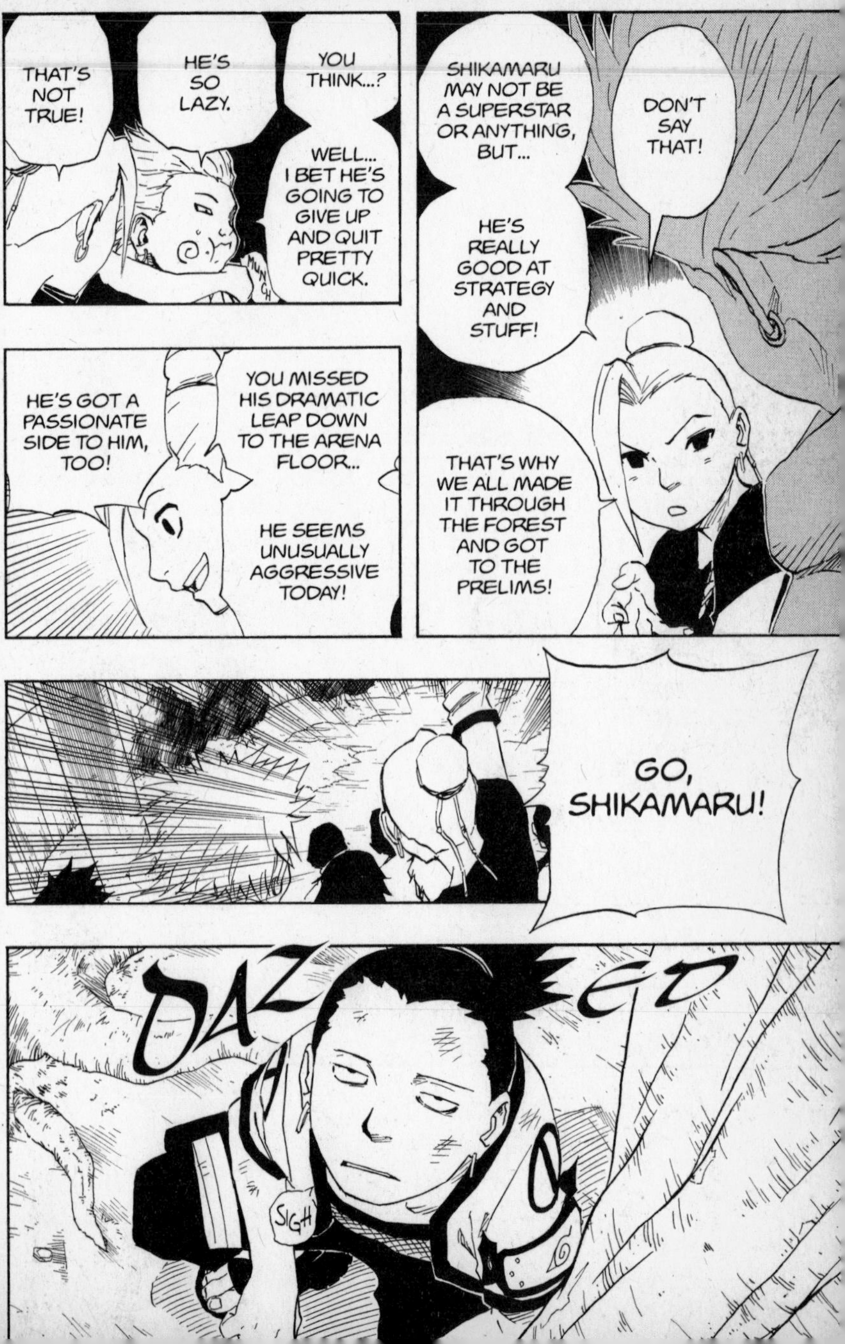
DON'T SAY THAT!
SHIKAMARU MAY NOT BE A SUPERSTAR OR ANYTHING, BUT...
HE'S REALLY GOOD AT STRATEGY AND STUFF!
THAT'S WHY WE ALL MADE IT THROUGH THE FOREST AND GOT TO THE PRELIMS!
YOU THINK...?
WELL... I BET HE'S GOING TO GIVE UP AND QUIT PRETTY QUICK.
MUNCH
HE'S SO LAZY.
THAT'S NOT TRUE!
YOU MISSED HIS DRAMATIC LEAP DOWN TO THE ARENA FLOOR...
HE SEEMS UNUSUALLY AGGRESSIVE TODAY!
HE'S GOT A PASSIONATE SIDE TO HIM, TOO!
GO, SHIKAMARU!
DAZED
SIGH

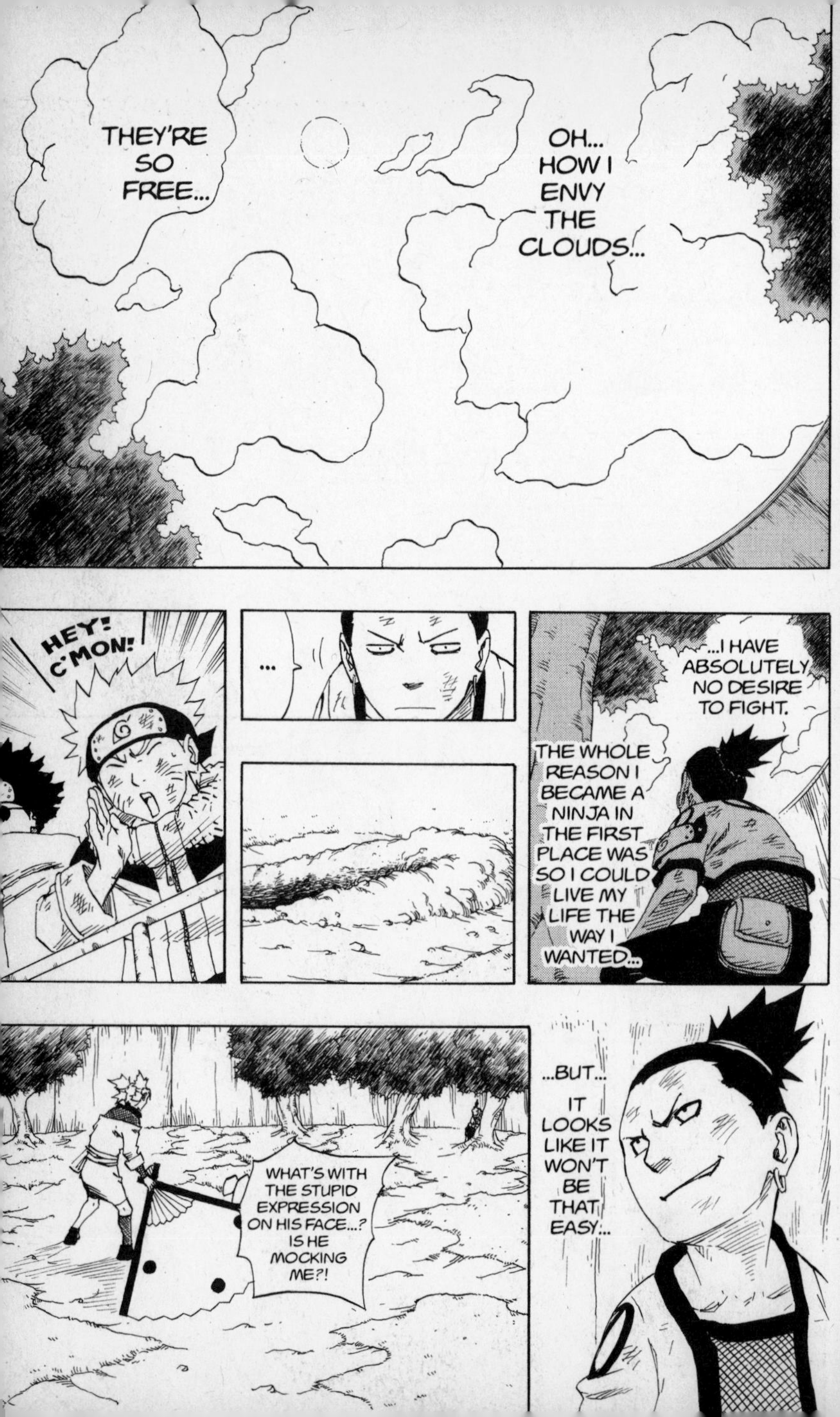
OH... HOW I ENVY THE CLOUDS...
THEY'RE SO FREE...
...I HAVE ABSOLUTELY NO DESIRE TO FIGHT.
THE WHOLE REASON I BECAME A NINJA IN THE FIRST PLACE WAS SO I COULD LIVE MY LIFE THE WAY I WANTED...
...
HEY! C'MON!
...BUT...
IT LOOKS LIKE IT WON'T BE THAT EASY...
WHAT'S WITH THE STUPID EXPRESSION ON HIS FACE...? IS HE MOCKING ME?!

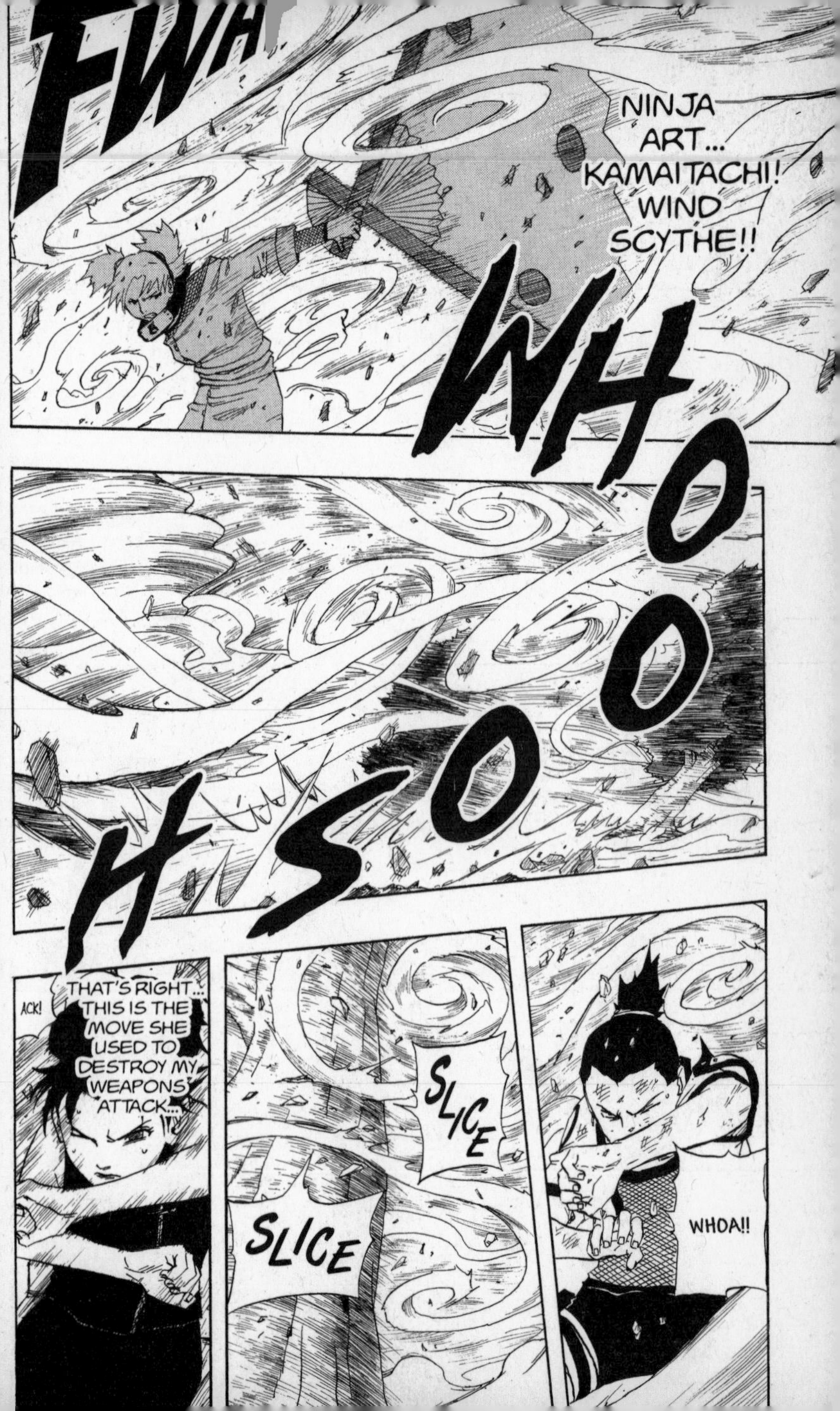
FWA
NINJA ART... KAMAITACHI! WIND SCYTHE!!
WHOOOOSH
WHOA!!
SLICE
SLICE
ACK!
THAT'S RIGHT... THIS IS THE MOVE SHE USED TO DESTROY MY WEAPONS ATTACK...

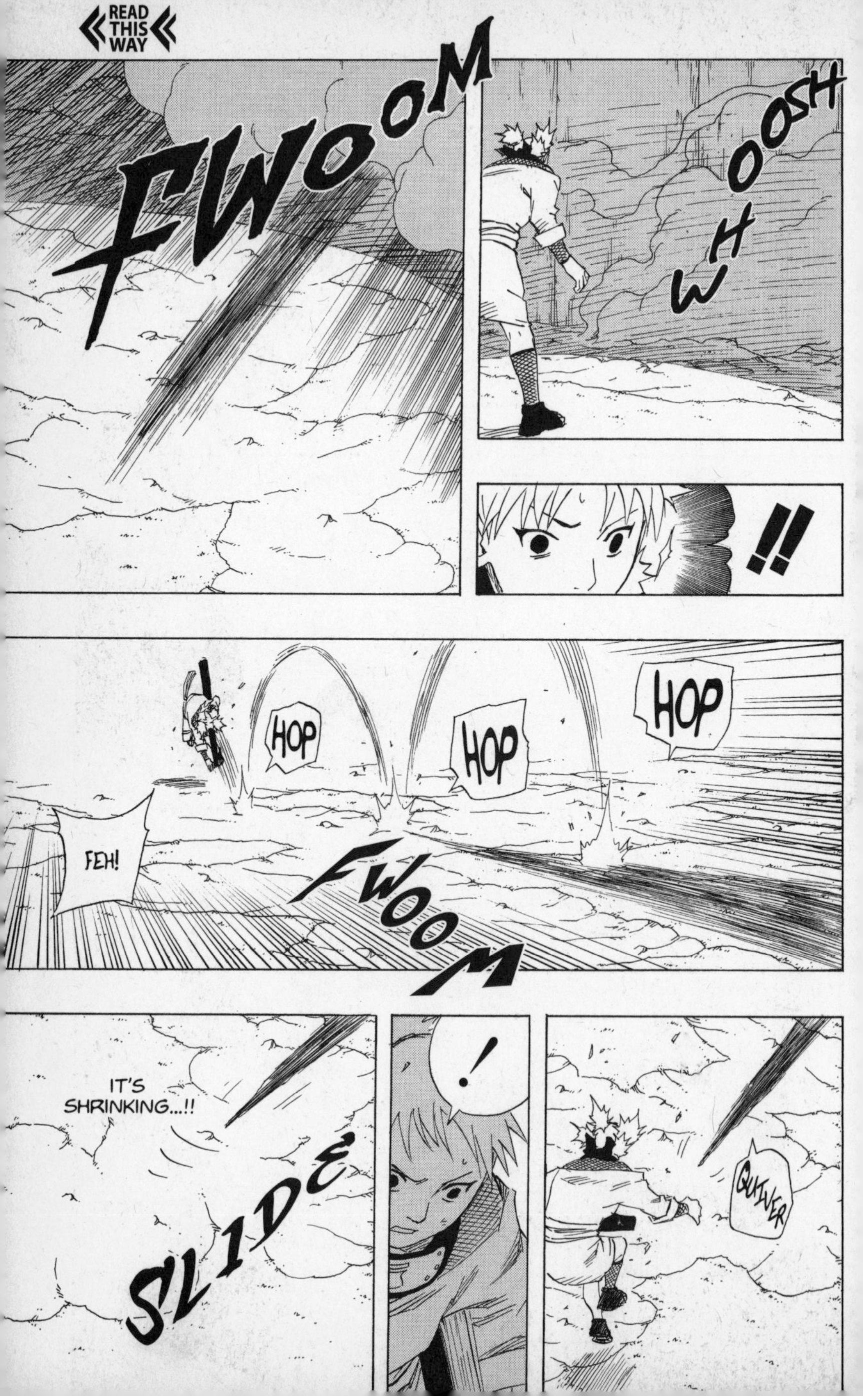
READ THIS WAY
WHOOSH
FWOOM
!!
HOP
HOP
HOP
FEH!
FWOOM
QUIVER
!
SLIDE
IT'S SHRINKING...!!

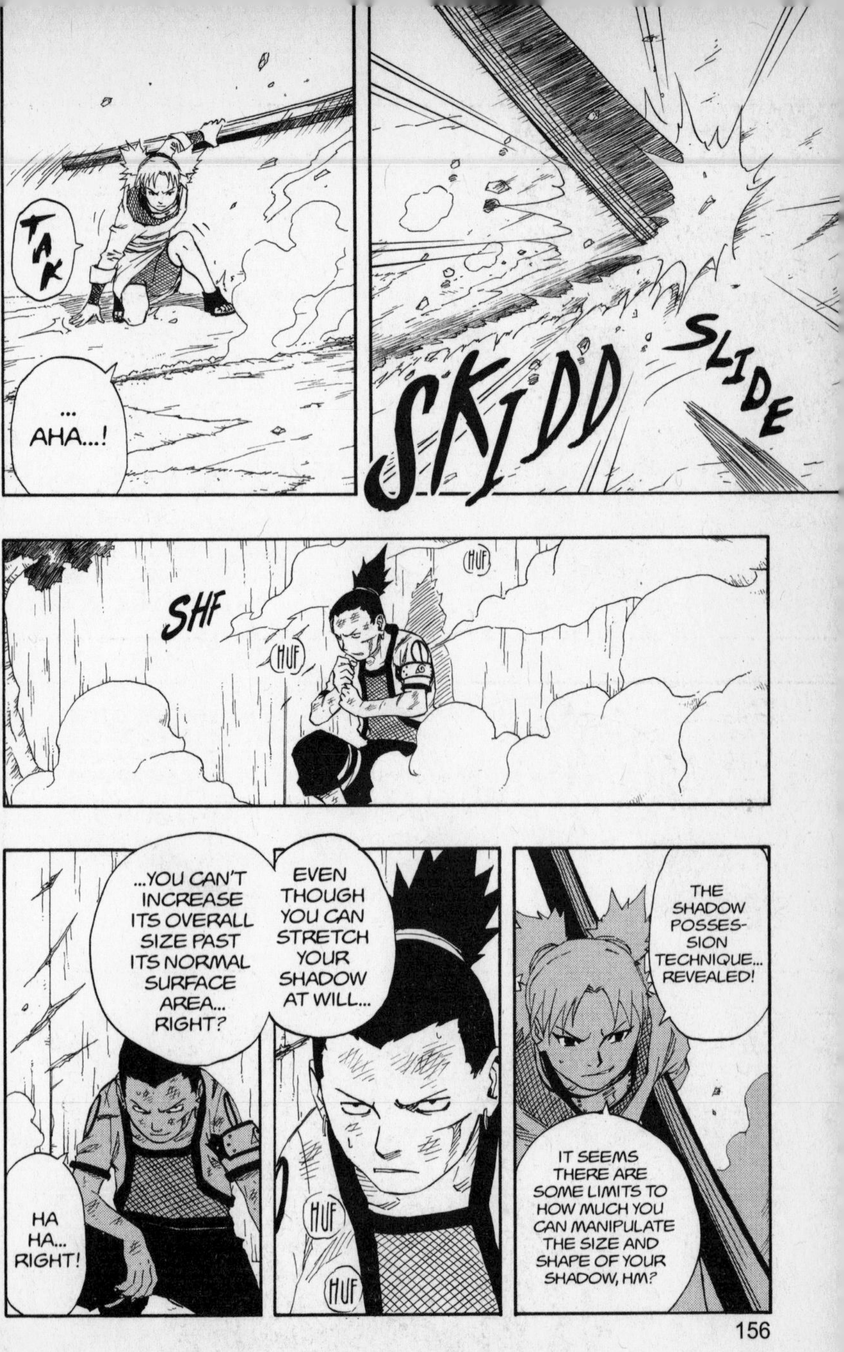
SKIDD
SLIDE
TAK
... AHA...!
SHF
HUF
HUF
THE SHADOW POSSES-SION TECHNIQUE... REVEALED!
IT SEEMS THERE ARE SOME LIMITS TO HOW MUCH YOU CAN MANIPULATE THE SIZE AND SHAPE OF YOUR SHADOW, HM?
EVEN THOUGH YOU CAN STRETCH YOUR SHADOW AT WILL...
HUF
HUF
...YOU CAN'T INCREASE ITS OVERALL SIZE PAST ITS NORMAL SURFACE AREA... RIGHT?
HA HA... RIGHT!

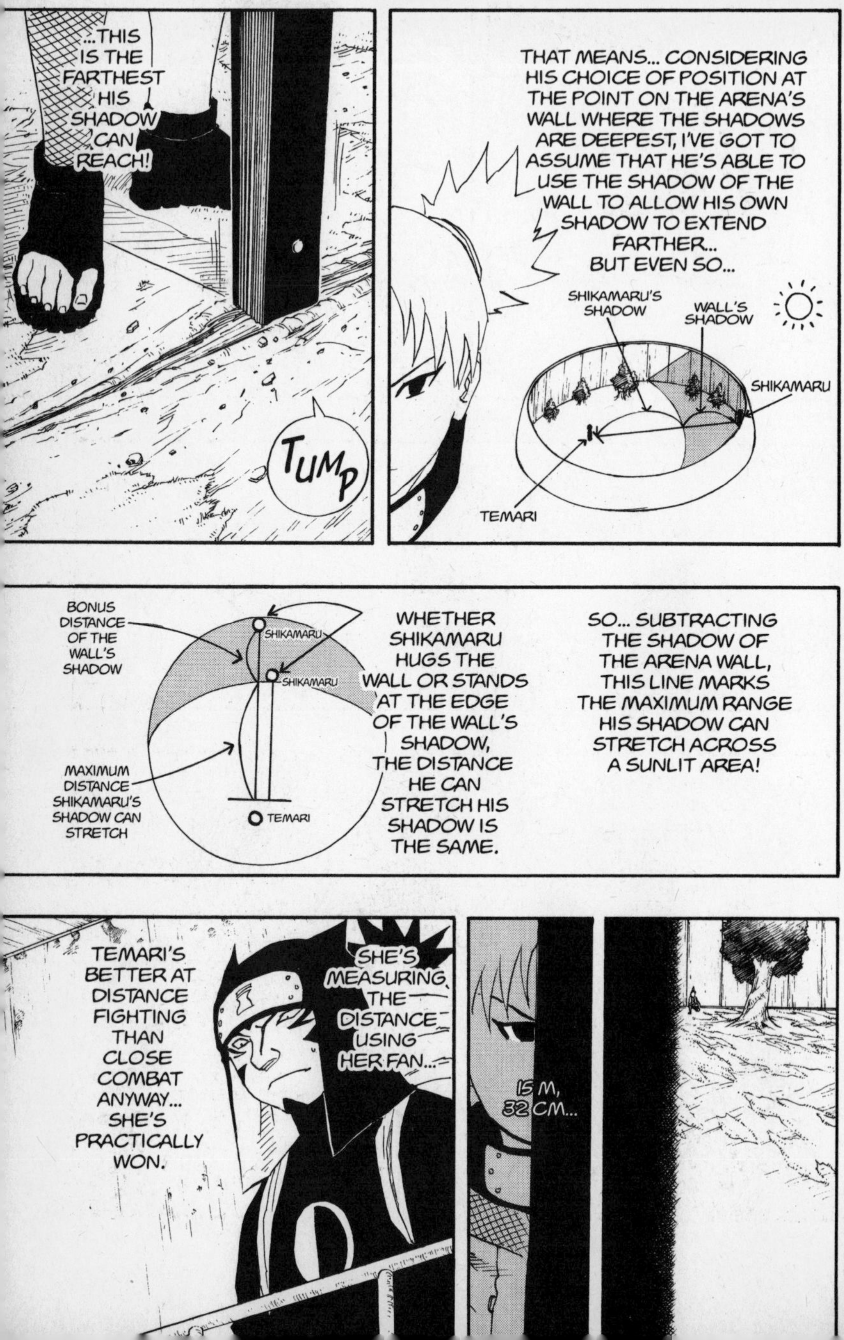
THAT MEANS... CONSIDERING HIS CHOICE OF POSITION AT THE POINT ON THE ARENA'S WALL WHERE THE SHADOWS ARE DEEPEST, I'VE GOT TO ASSUME THAT HE'S ABLE TO USE THE SHADOW OF THE WALL TO ALLOW HIS OWN SHADOW TO EXTEND FARTHER... BUT EVEN SO...
WALL'S SHADOW
SHIKAMARU'S SHADOW
SHIKAMARU
TEMARI
...THIS IS THE FARTHEST HIS SHADOW CAN REACH!
TUMP
SO... SUBTRACTING THE SHADOW OF THE ARENA WALL, THIS LINE MARKS THE MAXIMUM RANGE HIS SHADOW CAN STRETCH ACROSS A SUNLIT AREA!
WHETHER SHIKAMARU HUGS THE WALL OR STANDS AT THE EDGE OF THE WALL'S SHADOW, THE DISTANCE HE CAN STRETCH HIS SHADOW IS THE SAME.
BONUS DISTANCE OF THE WALL'S SHADOW
SHIKAMARU
SHIKAMARU
MAXIMUM DISTANCE SHIKAMARU'S SHADOW CAN STRETCH
TEMARI
15 M, 32 CM...
SHE'S MEASURING THE DISTANCE USING HER FAN...
TEMARI'S BETTER AT DISTANCE FIGHTING THAN CLOSE COMBAT ANYWAY... SHE'S PRACTICALLY WON.

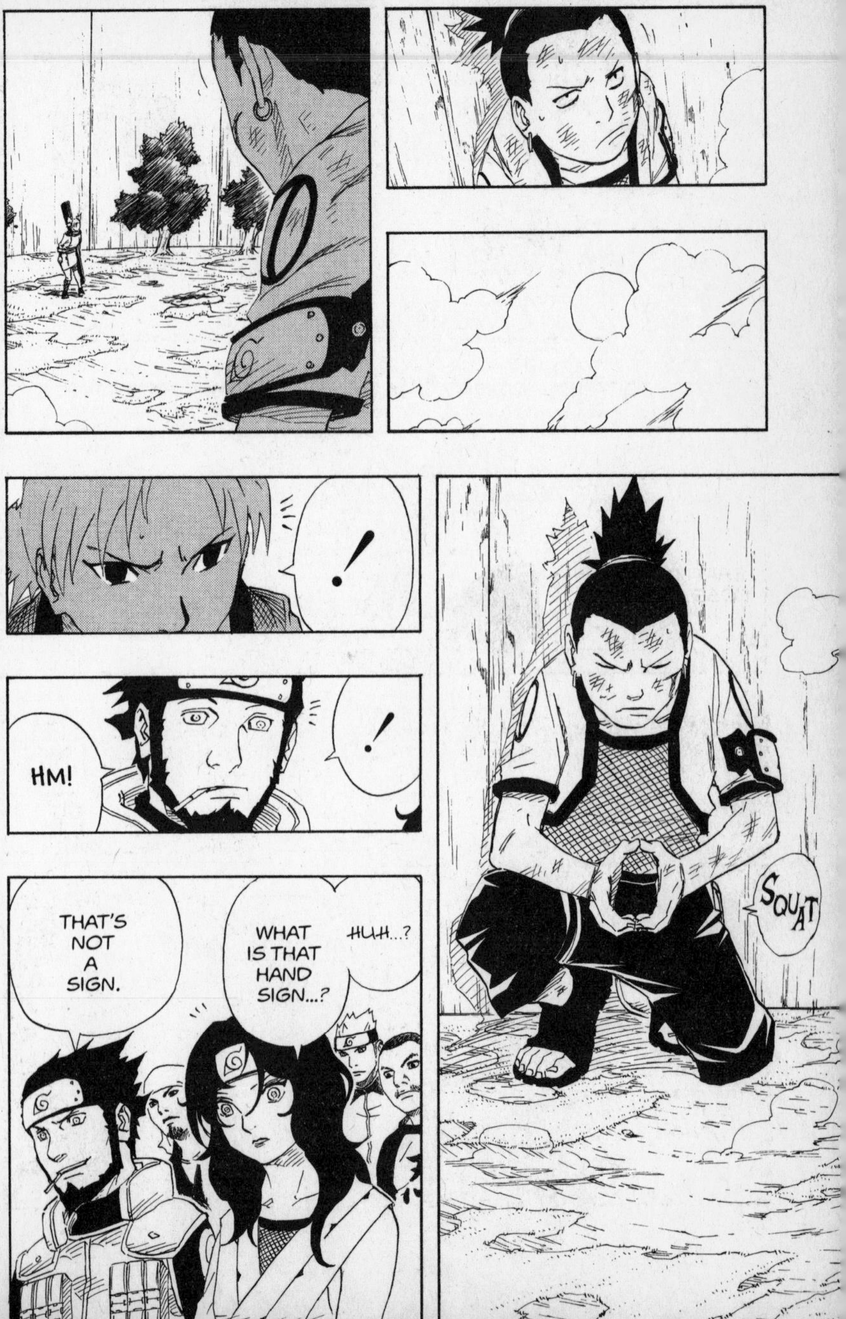
SQUAT
!
!
HM!
HUH...?
WHAT IS THAT HAND SIGN...?
THAT'S NOT A SIGN.

READ THIS WAY

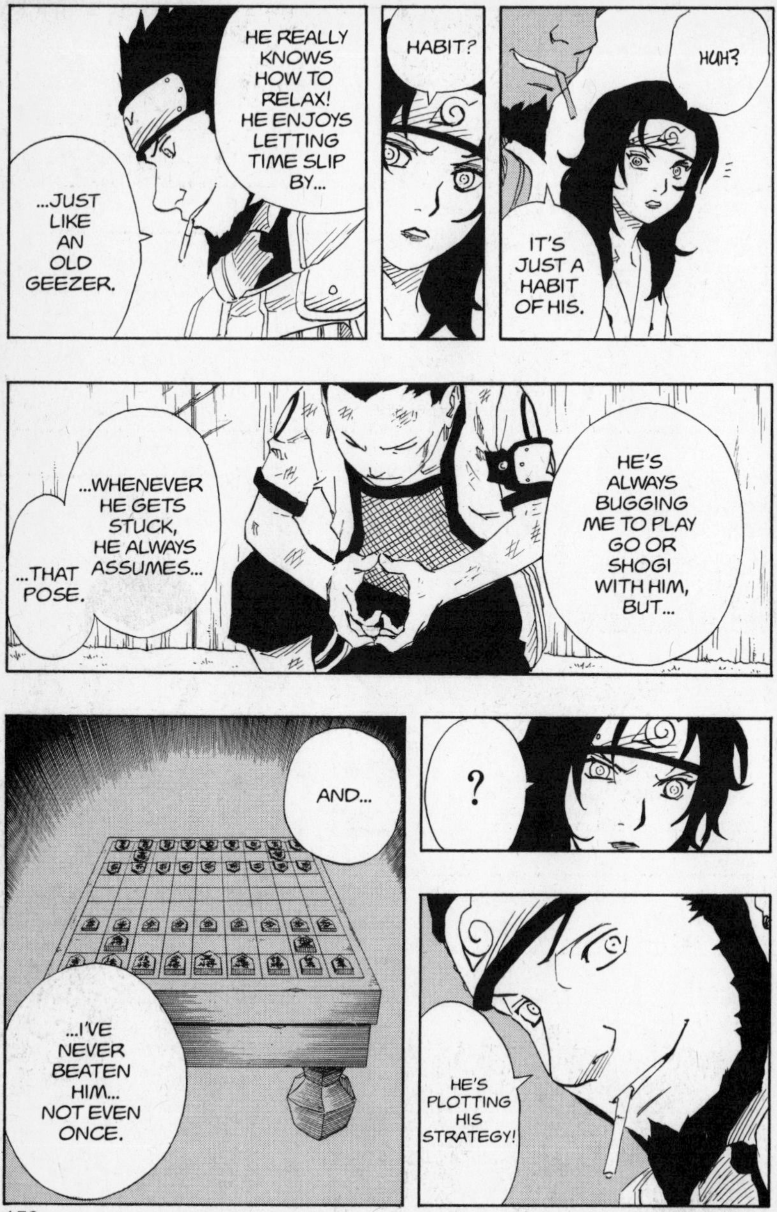
HUH?
IT'S JUST A HABIT OF HIS.
HABIT?
HE REALLY KNOWS HOW TO RELAX! HE ENJOYS LETTING TIME SLIP BY...
...JUST LIKE AN OLD GEEZER.
HE'S ALWAYS BUGGING ME TO PLAY GO OR SHOGI WITH HIM, BUT...
...WHENEVER HE GETS STUCK, HE ALWAYS ASSUMES...
...THAT POSE.
?
HE'S PLOTTING HIS STRATEGY!
AND...
...I'VE NEVER BEATEN HIM... NOT EVEN ONCE.

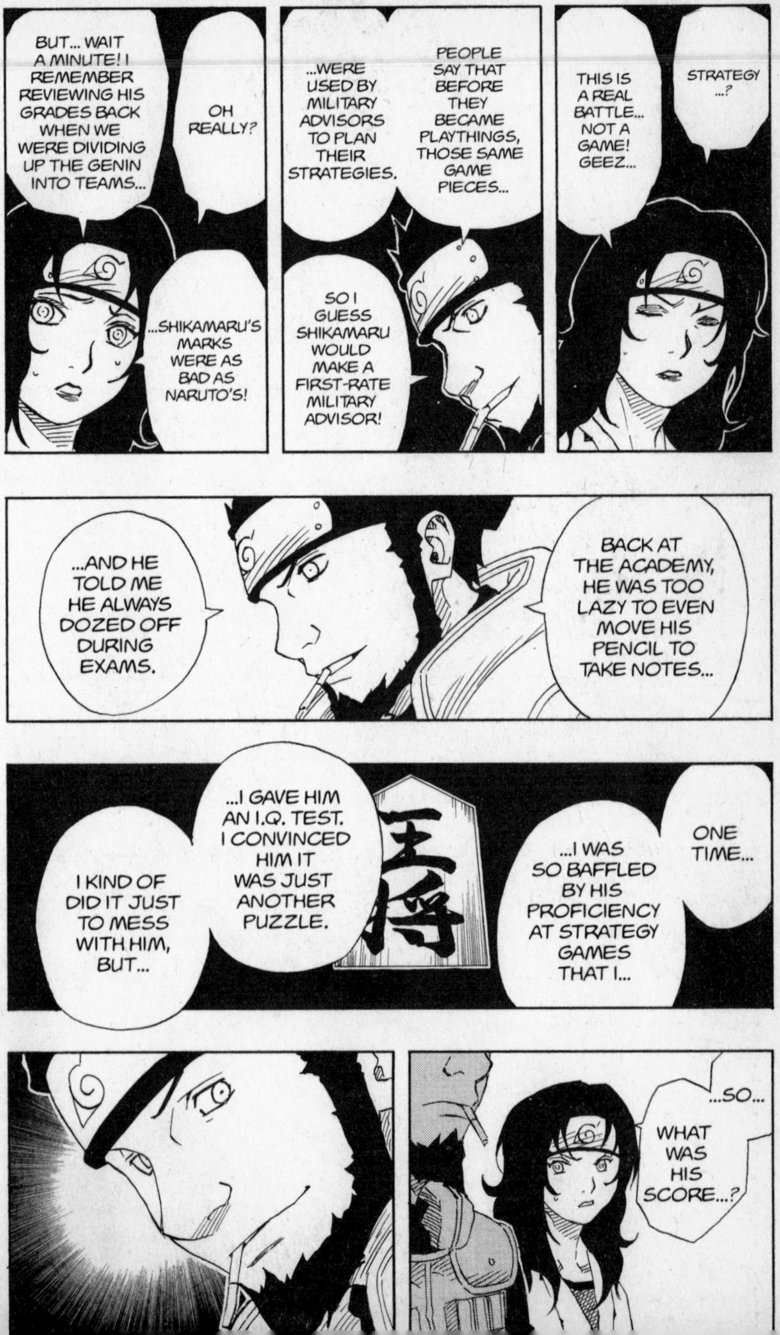
STRATEGY ...?
THIS IS A REAL BATTLE... NOT A GAME! GEEZ...
PEOPLE SAY THAT BEFORE THEY BECAME PLAYTHINGS, THOSE SAME GAME PIECES...
...WERE USED BY MILITARY ADVISORS TO PLAN THEIR STRATEGIES.
SO I GUESS SHIKAMARU WOULD MAKE A FIRST-RATE MILITARY ADVISOR!
OH REALLY?
BUT... WAIT A MINUTE! I REMEMBER REVIEWING HIS GRADES BACK WHEN WE WERE DIVIDING UP THE GENIN INTO TEAMS...
...SHIKAMARU'S MARKS WERE AS BAD AS NARUTO'S!
BACK AT THE ACADEMY, HE WAS TOO LAZY TO EVEN MOVE HIS PENCIL TO TAKE NOTES...
...AND HE TOLD ME HE ALWAYS DOZED OFF DURING EXAMS.
ONE TIME...
...I WAS SO BAFFLED BY HIS PROFICIENCY AT STRATEGY GAMES THAT I...
王将
I KIND OF DID IT JUST TO MESS WITH HIM, BUT...
...I GAVE HIM AN I.Q. TEST. I CONVINCED HIM IT WAS JUST ANOTHER PUZZLE.
...SO...
WHAT WAS HIS SCORE...?

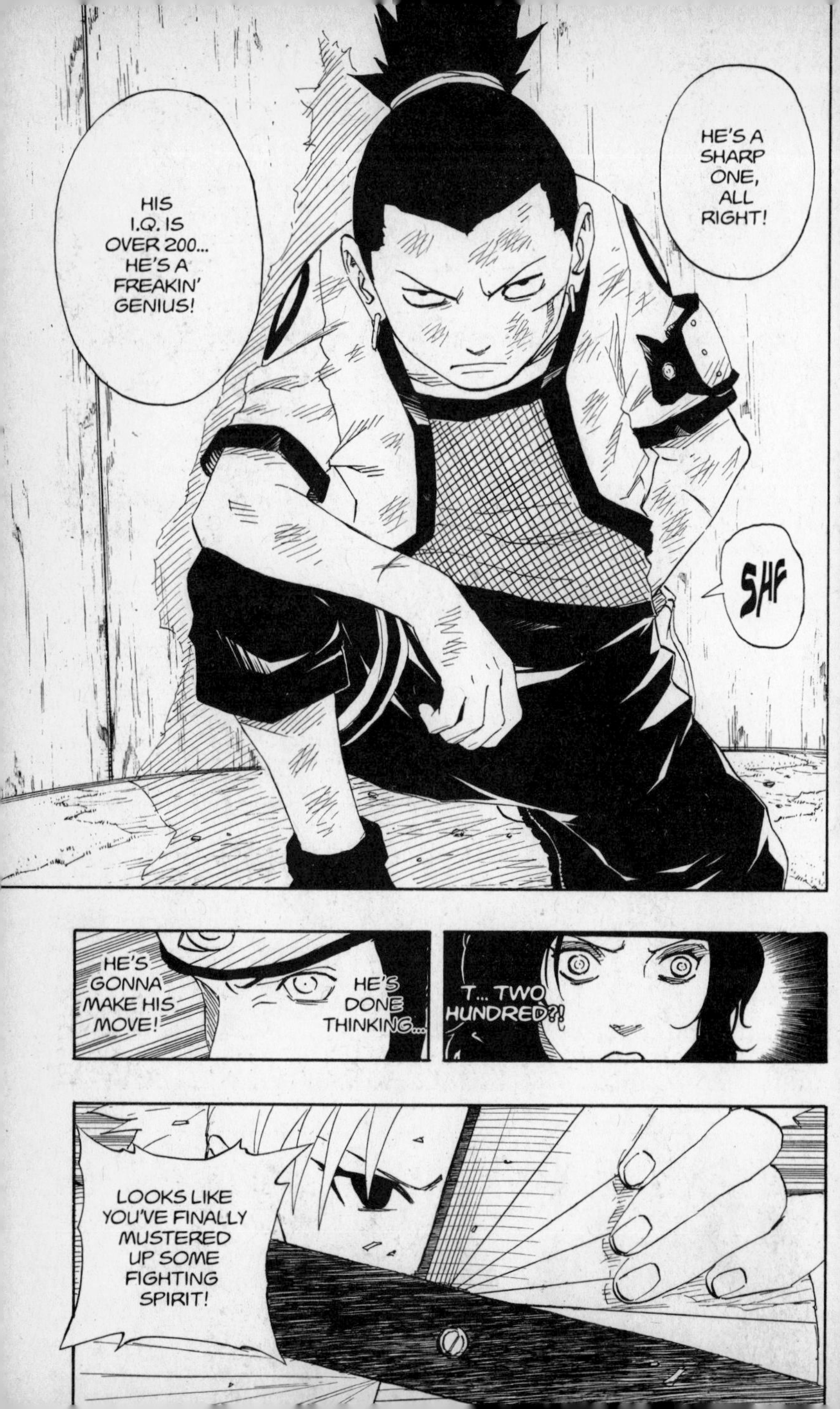
HE'S A SHARP ONE, ALL RIGHT!
HIS I.Q. IS OVER 200... HE'S A FREAKIN' GENIUS!
SHF
T... TWO HUNDRED?!
HE'S DONE THINKING...
HE'S GONNA MAKE HIS MOVE!
LOOKS LIKE YOU'VE FINALLY MUSTERED UP SOME FIGHTING SPIRIT!

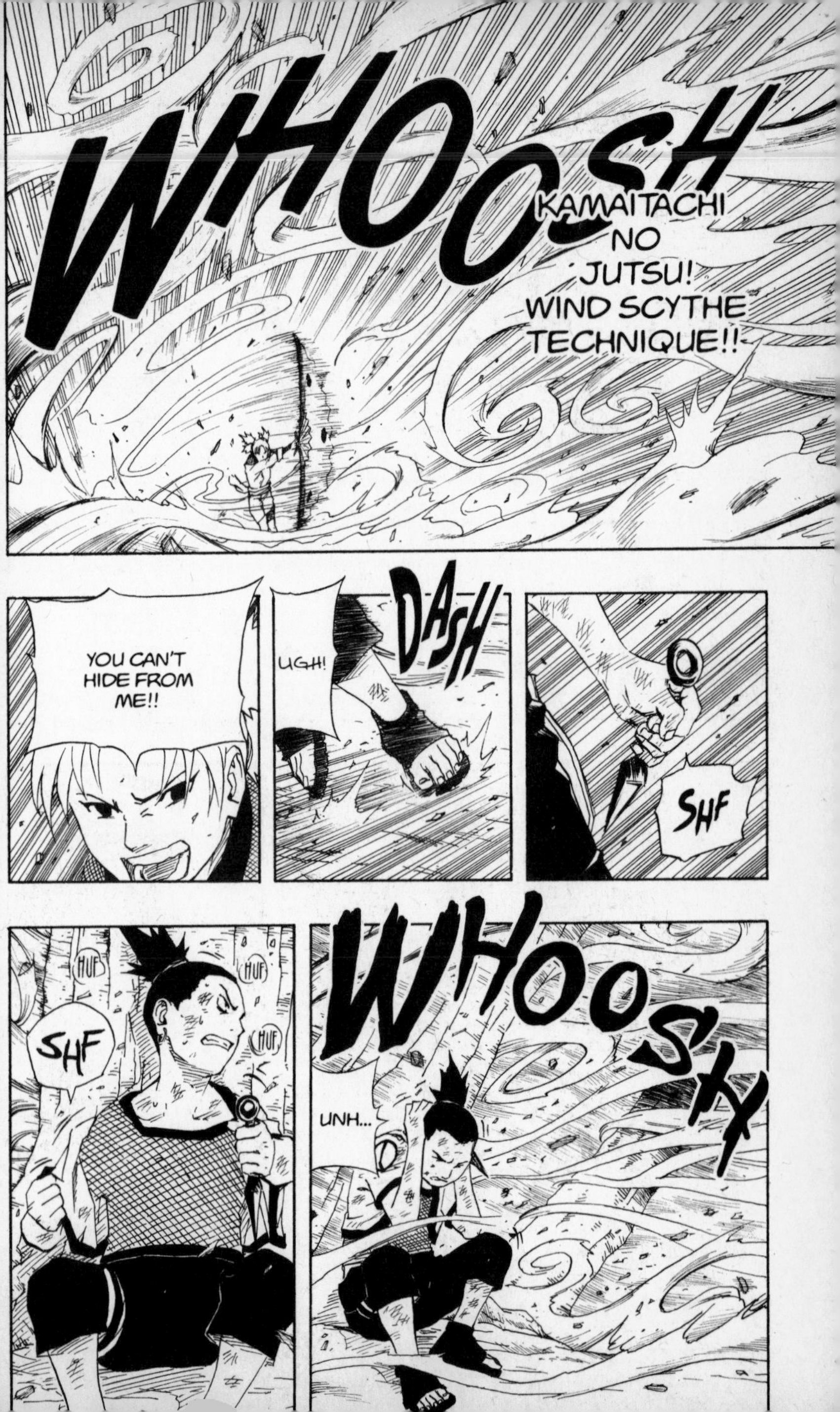
WHOOSH
KAMAITACHI NO JUTSU! WIND SCYTHE TECHNIQUE!!
SHF
DASH
UGH!
YOU CAN'T HIDE FROM ME!!
WHOOSH
UNH...
HUF
HUF
HUF
SHF

READ THIS WAY

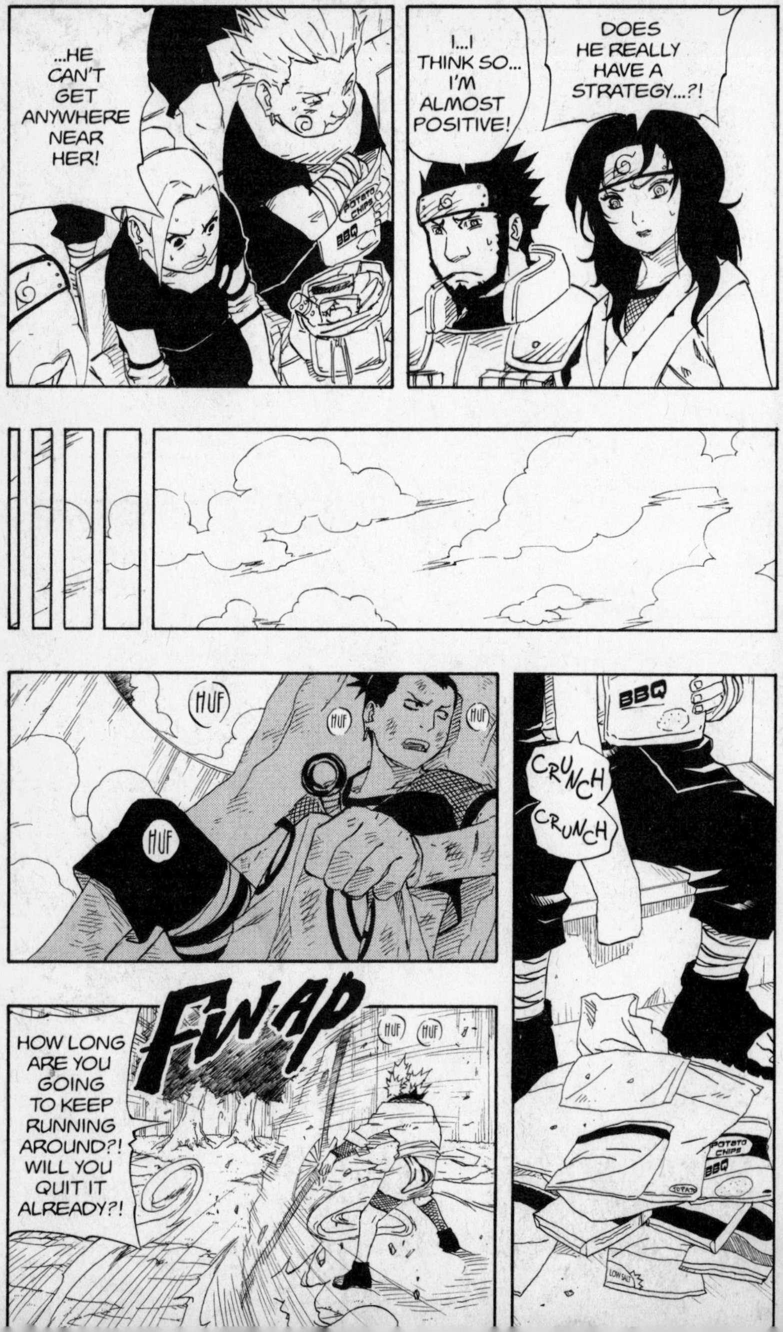
DOES HE REALLY HAVE A STRATEGY...?!
I...I THINK SO... I'M ALMOST POSITIVE!
...HE CAN'T GET ANYWHERE NEAR HER!
POTATO CHIPS
BBQ
BBQ
CRUNCH
CRUNCH
POTATO CHIPS
BBQ
LOW SALT
HUF
HUF
HUF
HUF
FWAP
HUF
HUF
HOW LONG ARE YOU GOING TO KEEP RUNNING AROUND?! WILL YOU QUIT IT ALREADY?!

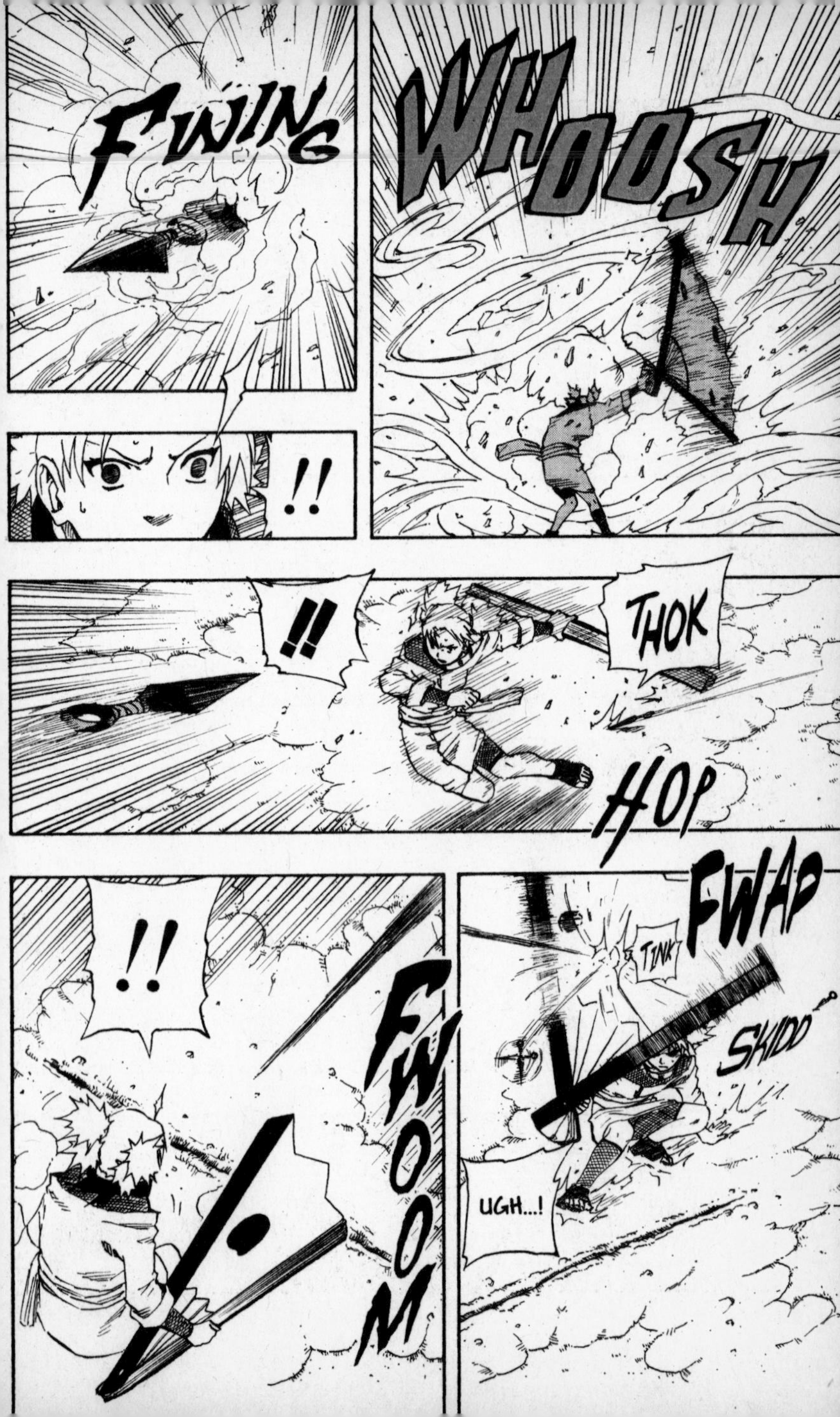
WHOOSH
FWING
!!
THOK
!!
HOP
FWAP
TINK
SKIDD
UGH...!
!!
FWOOM

READ THIS WAY

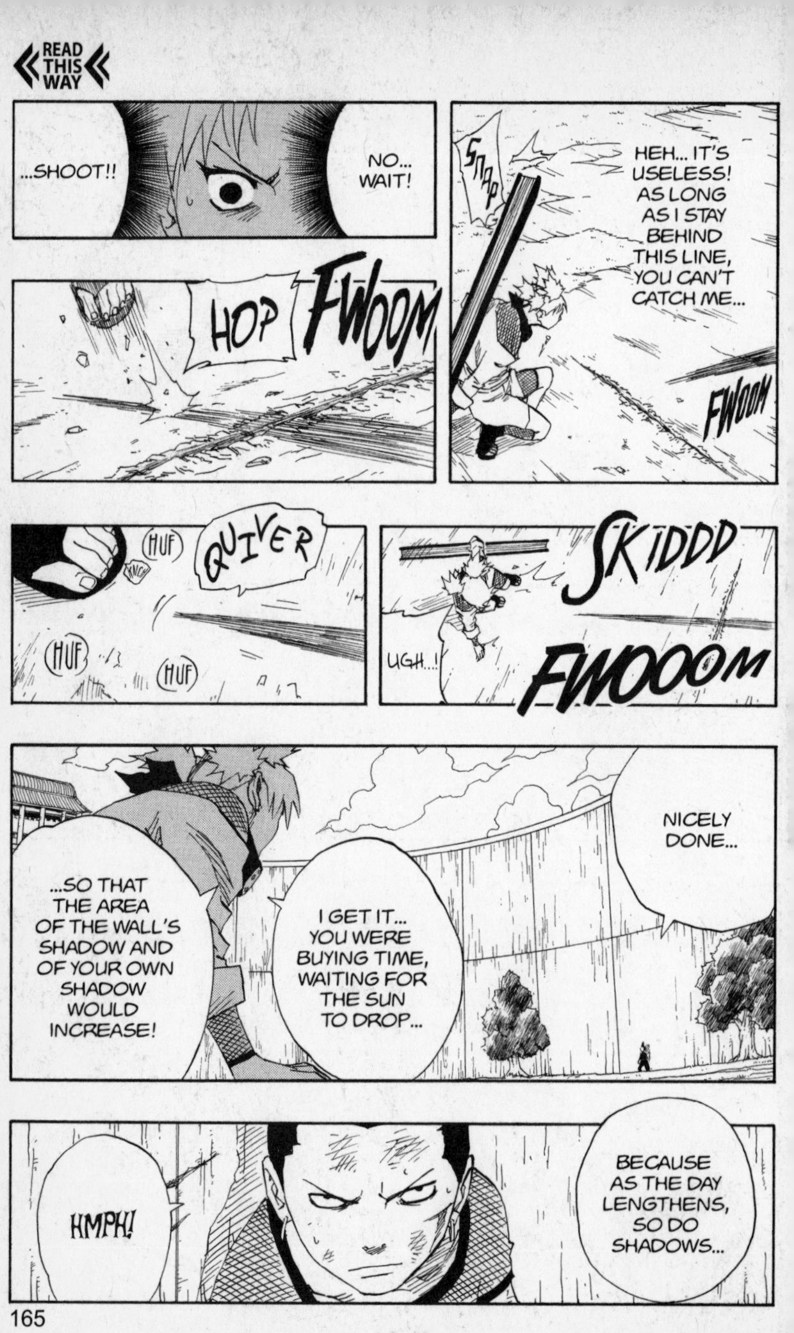
SNAP
HEH... IT'S USELESS! AS LONG AS I STAY BEHIND THIS LINE, YOU CAN'T CATCH ME...
FWOOM
NO... WAIT!
...SHOOT!!
FWOOM
HOP
SKIDDD
UGH...!
FWOOOM
QUIVER
HUF
KNCH
HUF
HUF
NICELY DONE...
I GET IT... YOU WERE BUYING TIME, WAITING FOR THE SUN TO DROP...
...SO THAT THE AREA OF THE WALL'S SHADOW AND OF YOUR OWN SHADOW WOULD INCREASE!
BECAUSE AS THE DAY LENGTHENS, SO DO SHADOWS...
HMPH!

CELEBRATE!!
SECOND
ANNIVERSARY!!

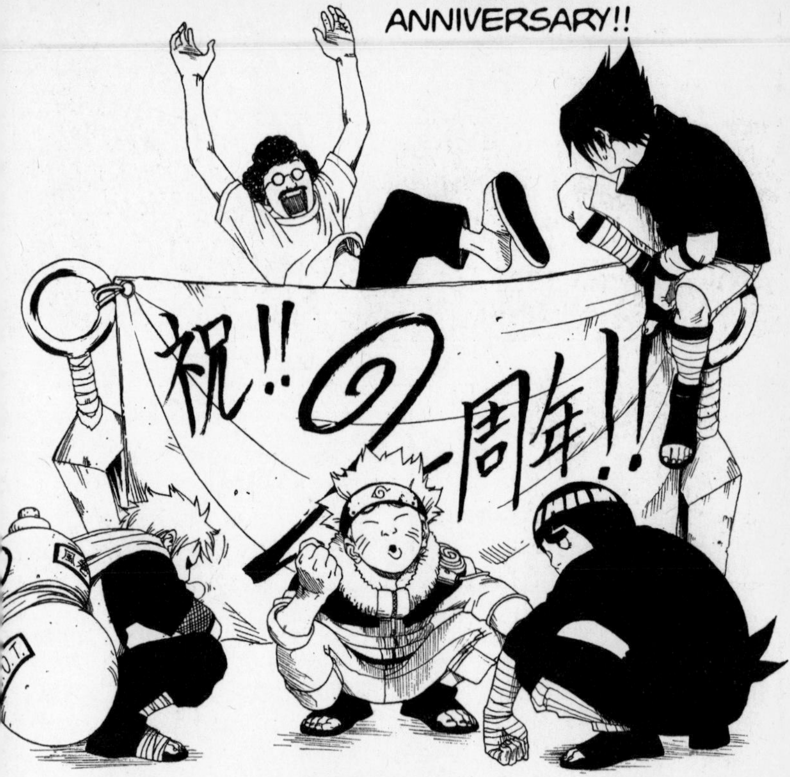
祝!!2周年!!

KISHIMOTO-SAN!
HAPPY BIRTHDAY AND HAPPY *NARUTO* SECOND ANNIVERSARY!!
PLEASE KEEP UP THE GOOD ENERGY AND GOOD WORK!!!

岸本さん! 誕生日&「NARUTO」
連載2周年 おめでとー!!
これからも気合いいれて頑張って!!!

H.13 11.8. 河原武美 KAWAHARA TAKEMI

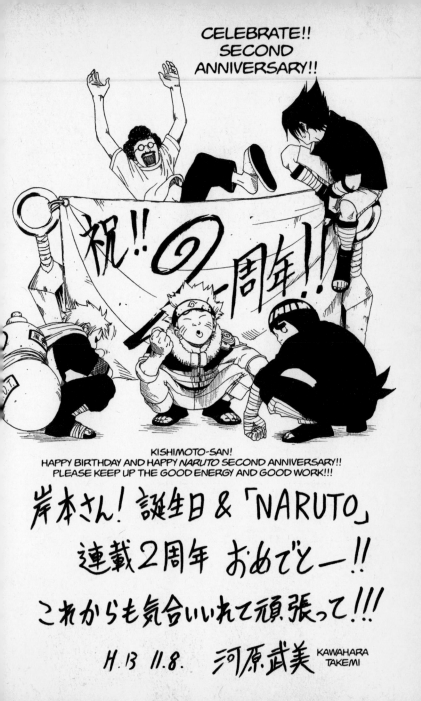

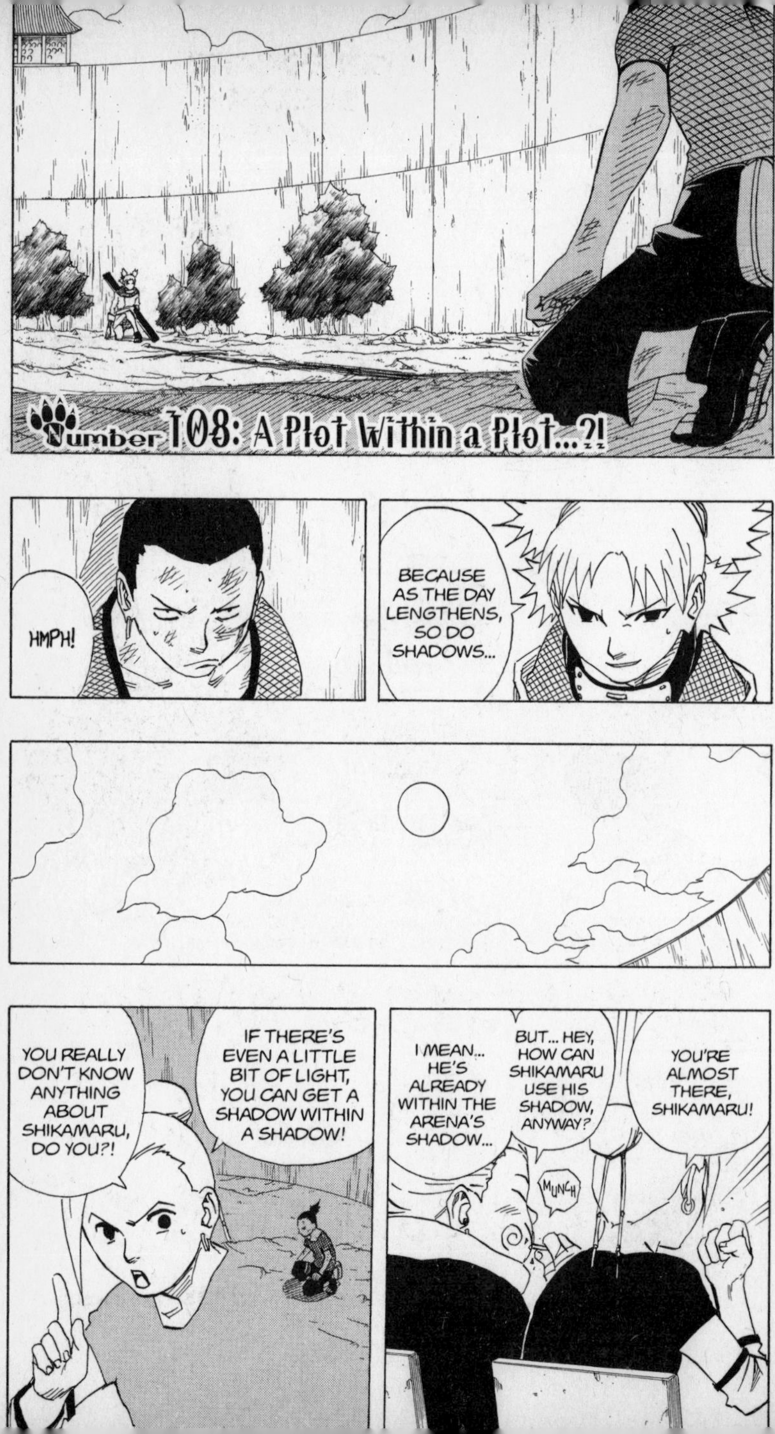
Number 108: A Plot Within a Plot...?!
BECAUSE AS THE DAY LENGTHENS, SO DO SHADOWS...
HMPH!
YOU'RE ALMOST THERE, SHIKAMARU!
BUT... HEY, HOW CAN SHIKAMARU USE HIS SHADOW, ANYWAY?
I MEAN... HE'S ALREADY WITHIN THE ARENA'S SHADOW...
MUNCH
IF THERE'S EVEN A LITTLE BIT OF LIGHT, YOU CAN GET A SHADOW WITHIN A SHADOW!
YOU REALLY DON'T KNOW ANYTHING ABOUT SHIKAMARU, DO YOU?!

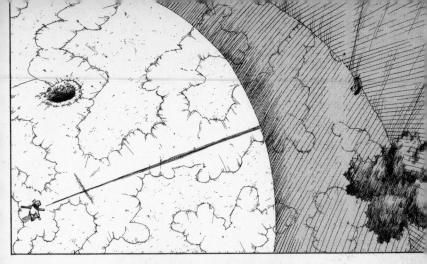

TAKING INTO ACCOUNT THE SUN'S CURRENT POSITION AND HIS LAST MAXIMUM ATTACK DISTANCE...

I'M DEFINITELY SAFE HERE... FOR SURE!

BRILLIANT...

!

TEMARI! LOOK UP!!

!!

!

READ THIS WAY

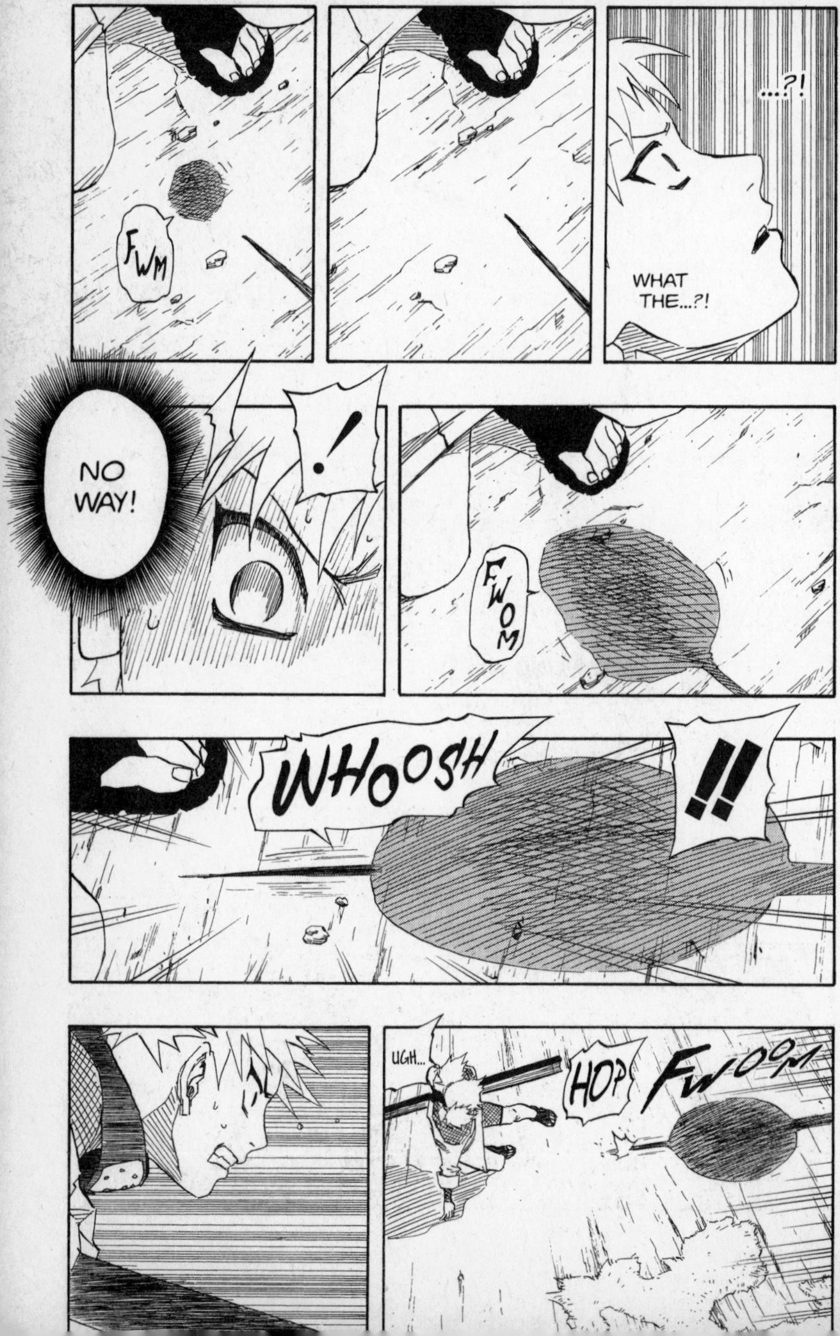

...?!
WHAT THE...?!
FWM
FWOM
!
NO WAY!
WHOOSH
!!
FWOOM
HOP
UGH...

Number 108: A Plot Within a Plot...?!

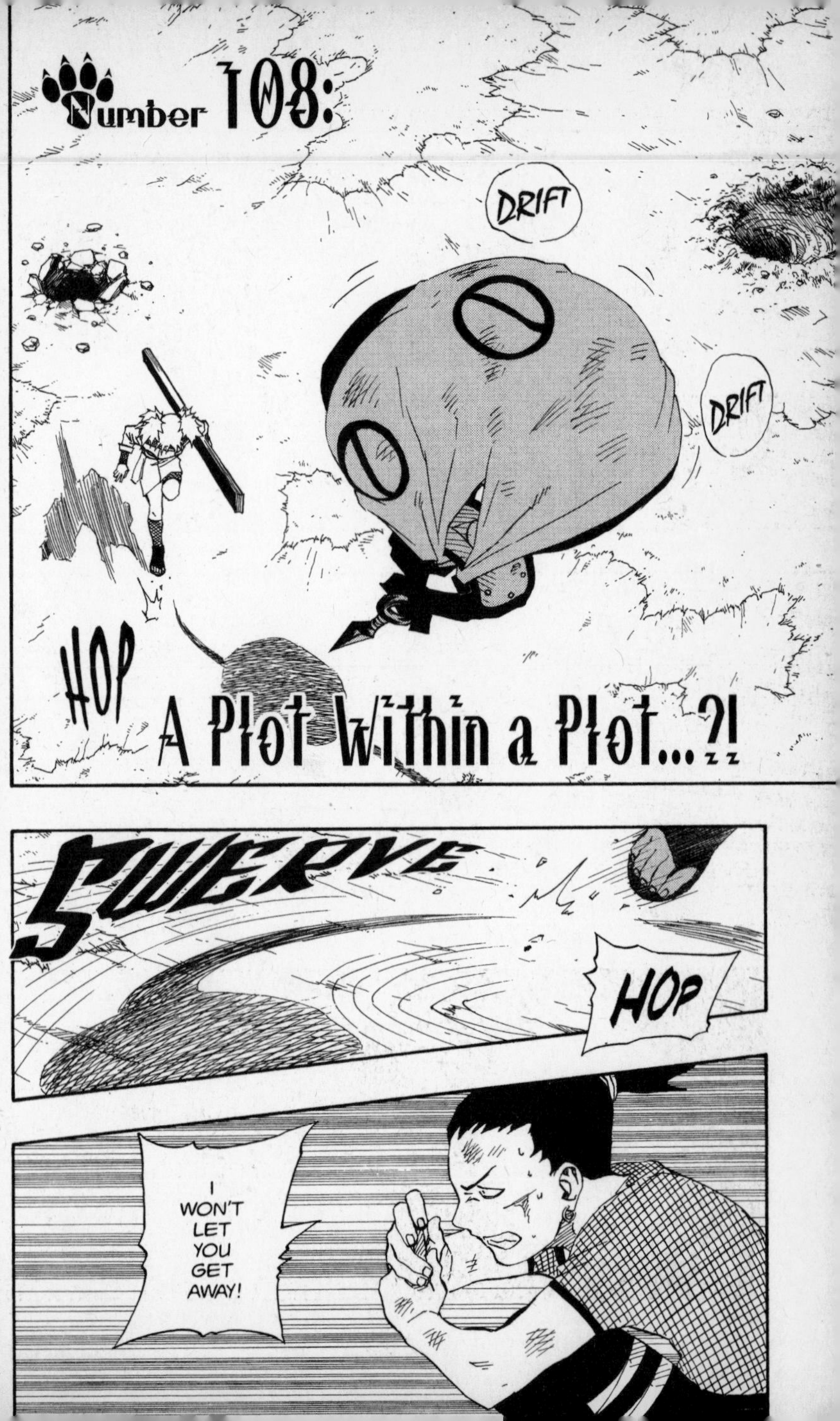
DRIFT
DRIFT
HOP
SWERVE
HOP
I WON'T LET YOU GET AWAY!

READ THIS WAY

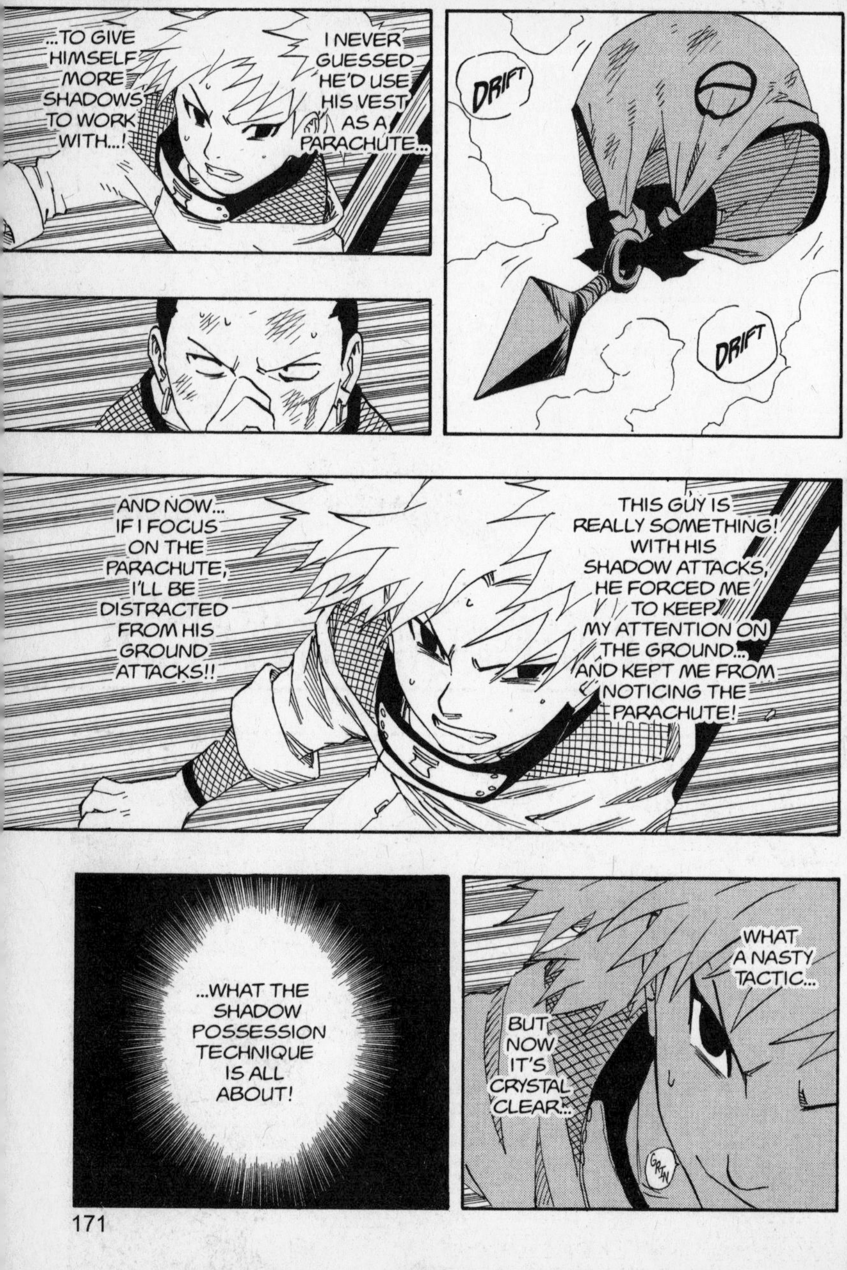

DRIFT
DRIFT
I NEVER GUESSED HE'D USE HIS VEST AS A PARACHUTE...
...TO GIVE HIMSELF MORE SHADOWS TO WORK WITH...!
THIS GUY IS REALLY SOMETHING! WITH HIS SHADOW ATTACKS, HE FORCED ME TO KEEP MY ATTENTION ON THE GROUND... AND KEPT ME FROM NOTICING THE PARACHUTE!
AND NOW... IF I FOCUS ON THE PARACHUTE, I'LL BE DISTRACTED FROM HIS GROUND ATTACKS!!
WHAT A NASTY TACTIC...
BUT NOW IT'S CRYSTAL CLEAR...
GRIN
...WHAT THE SHADOW POSSESSION TECHNIQUE IS ALL ABOUT!

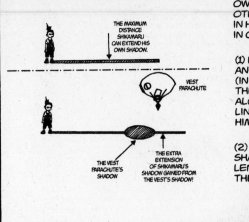

SHIKAMARU CAN USE HIS OWN SHADOW AND ANY OTHER AVAILABLE SHADOWS IN HIS ATTACK! IN OTHER WORDS...
(1) HE CAN UTILIZE ANY OTHER SHADOWS (IN THIS CASE, THE PARACHUTE'S SHADOW) ALONG THE STRAIGHT LINE BETWEEN HIM AND HIS TARGET.
(2) HE CAN EXTEND HIS OWN SHADOW THE ADDITIONAL LENGTH PROVIDED BY THE OTHER SHADOW.
THE MAXIMUM DISTANCE SHIKAMARU CAN EXTEND HIS OWN SHADOW.
VEST PARACHUTE
THE EXTRA EXTENSION OF SHIKAMARU'S SHADOW GAINED FROM THE VEST'S SHADOW!
THE VEST PARACHUTE'S SHADOW
HOWEVER... OTHER THAN THE CHANGES CAUSED BY THE MOVEMENT OF THE SUN, THE SHAPE OF BOTH THE WALL'S AND THE VEST'S SHADOWS HAVE BEEN FIXED.
(3) SHIKAMARU CANNOT FREELY CHANGE THE SHAPE OF SHADOWS OTHER THAN HIS OWN.
THEREFORE, I MUST CONCLUDE THAT...
...THE PARACHUTE'S SHADOW DOES NOT CHANGE.
EVEN IF HE CHANGES HIS OWN SHADOW TO A WAVY LINE...
AND FROM OBSERVING HIS PREVIOUS BATTLES...
(4) ONLY WHEN HE HAS CAPTURED HIS TARGET'S SHADOW WITH **HIS OWN SHADOW** CAN HE STOP HIS TARGET'S MOVEMENTS!
SNAP
UNH!
SHIKAMARU
TARGET

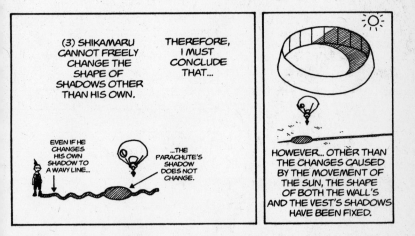

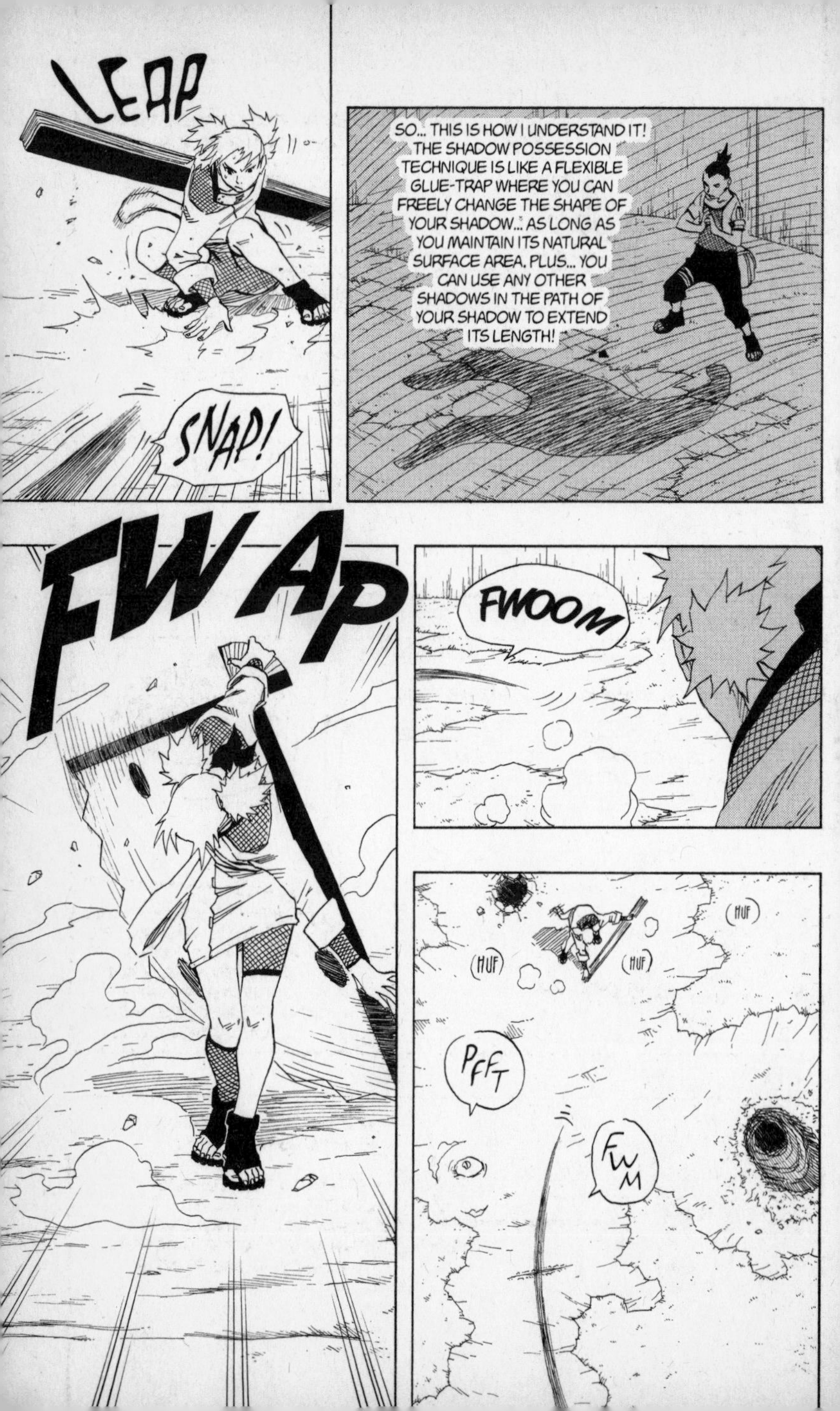
SO... THIS IS HOW I UNDERSTAND IT! THE SHADOW POSSESSION TECHNIQUE IS LIKE A FLEXIBLE GLUE-TRAP WHERE YOU CAN FREELY CHANGE THE SHAPE OF YOUR SHADOW... AS LONG AS YOU MAINTAIN ITS NATURAL SURFACE AREA. PLUS... YOU CAN USE ANY OTHER SHADOWS IN THE PATH OF YOUR SHADOW TO EXTEND ITS LENGTH!
LEAP
SNAP!
FWOOM
HUF
HUF
HUF
PFFT
FWM
FWAP

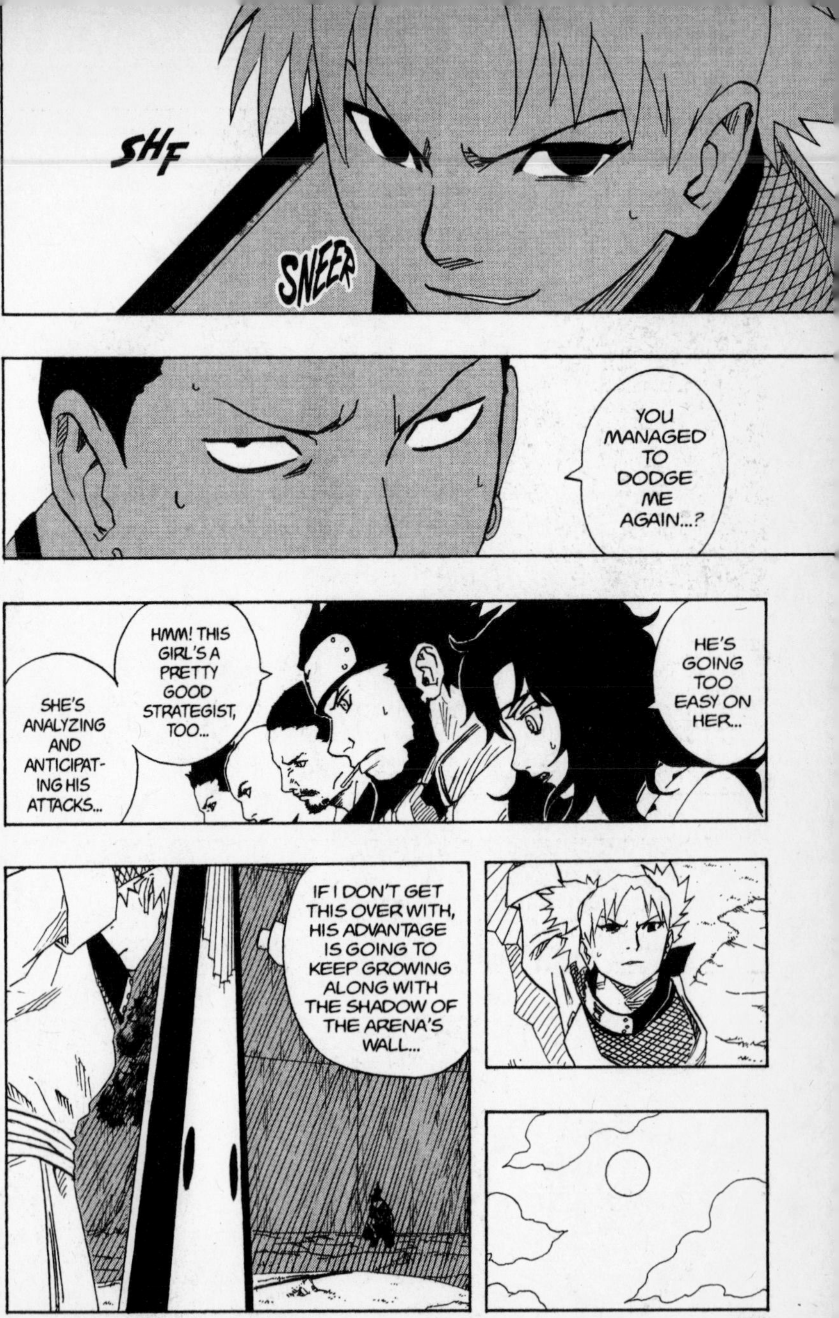
SHF
SNEER
YOU MANAGED TO DODGE ME AGAIN...?
HE'S GOING TOO EASY ON HER...
HMM! THIS GIRL'S A PRETTY GOOD STRATEGIST, TOO...
SHE'S ANALYZING AND ANTICIPATING HIS ATTACKS...
IF I DON'T GET THIS OVER WITH, HIS ADVANTAGE IS GOING TO KEEP GROWING ALONG WITH THE SHADOW OF THE ARENA'S WALL...

READ THIS WAY

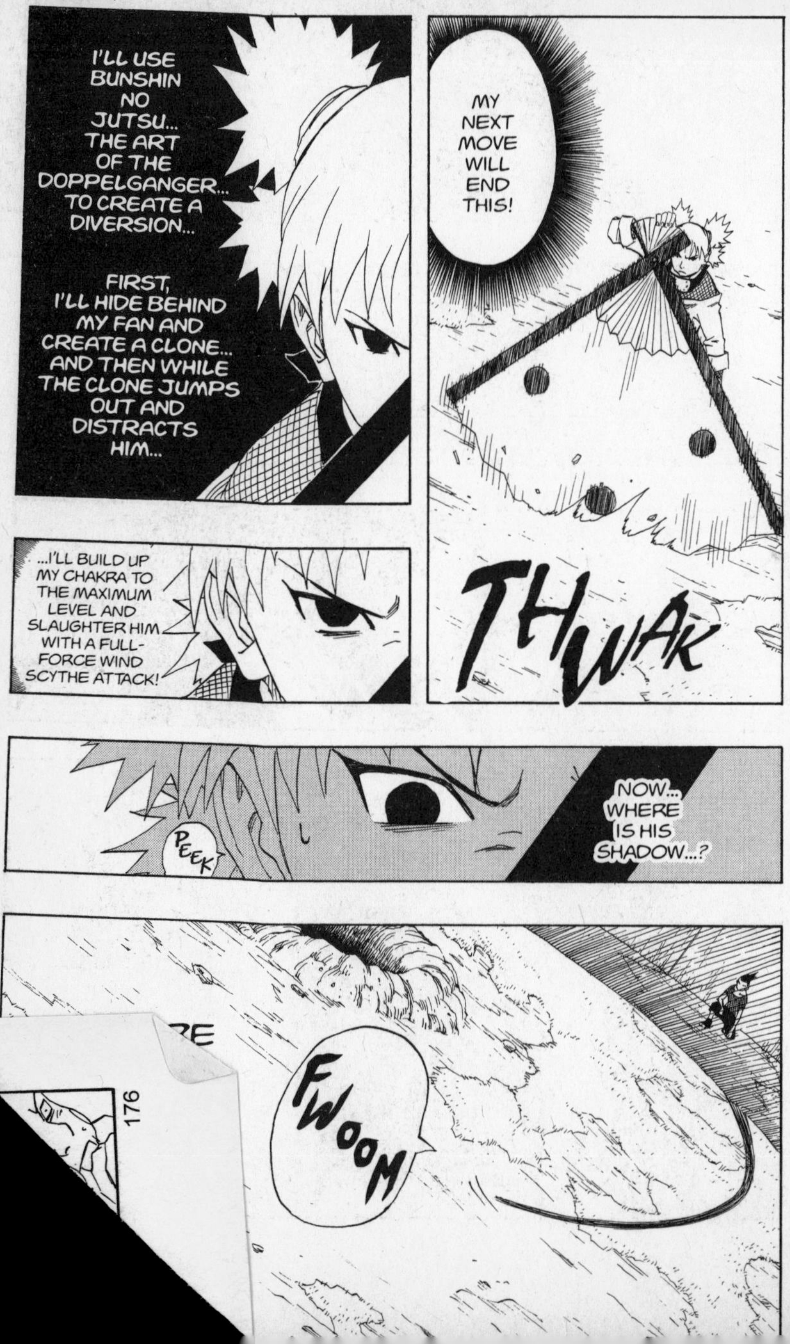
MY NEXT MOVE WILL END THIS!
THWAK
I'LL USE BUNSHIN NO JUTSU... THE ART OF THE DOPPELGANGER... TO CREATE A DIVERSION...
FIRST, I'LL HIDE BEHIND MY FAN AND CREATE A CLONE... AND THEN WHILE THE CLONE JUMPS OUT AND DISTRACTS HIM...
...I'LL BUILD UP MY CHAKRA TO THE MAXIMUM LEVEL AND SLAUGHTER HIM WITH A FULL-FORCE WIND SCYTHE ATTACK!
NOW... WHERE IS HIS SHADOW...?
PEEK
FWOOM

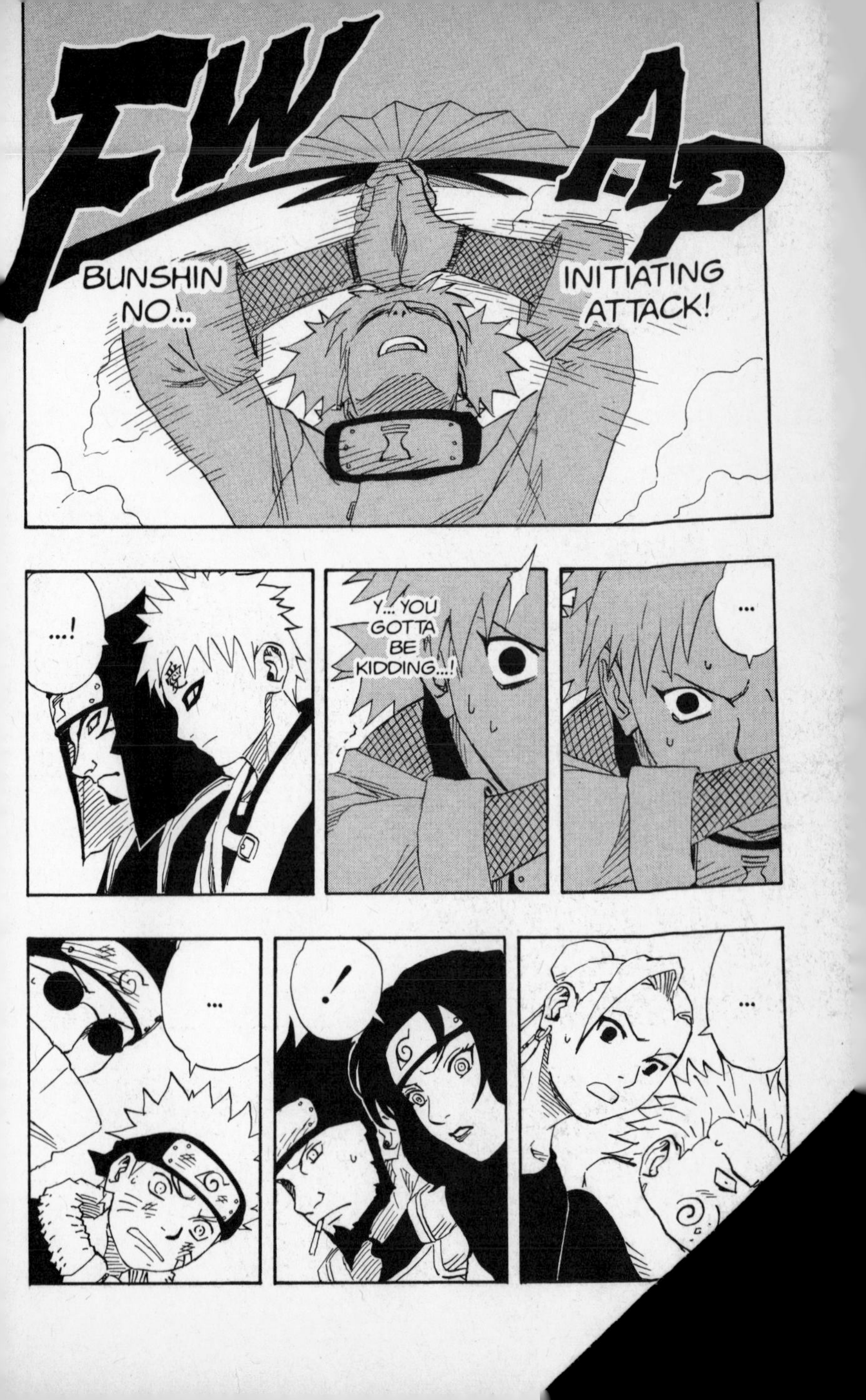
FWAP
INITIATING ATTACK!
BUNSHIN NO...
...
Y... YOU GOTTA BE KIDDING...!
...!
...
!
...

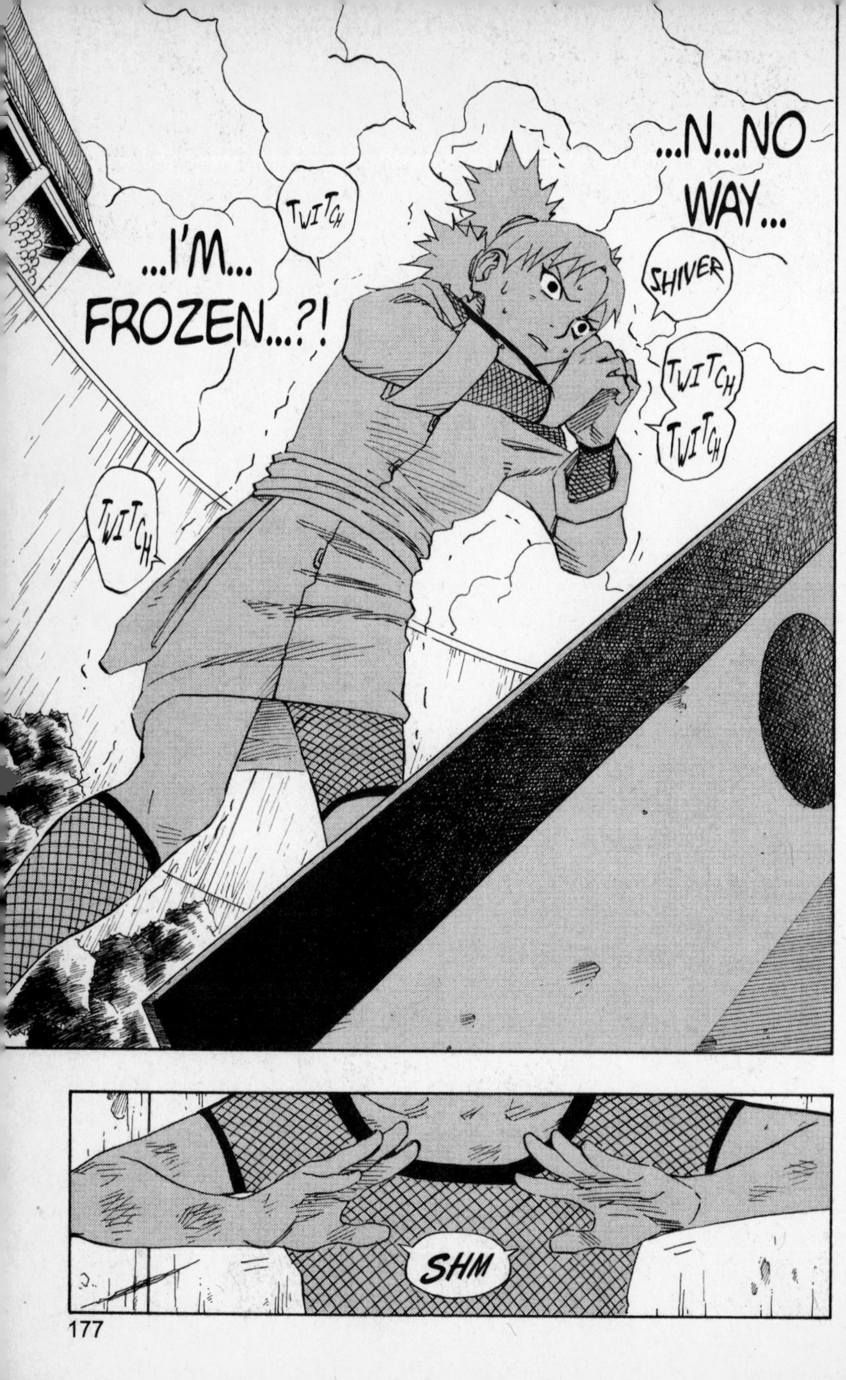
...N...NO WAY...
SHIVER
TWITCH
TWITCH
TWITCH
...I'M... FROZEN...?!
TWITCH
SHM

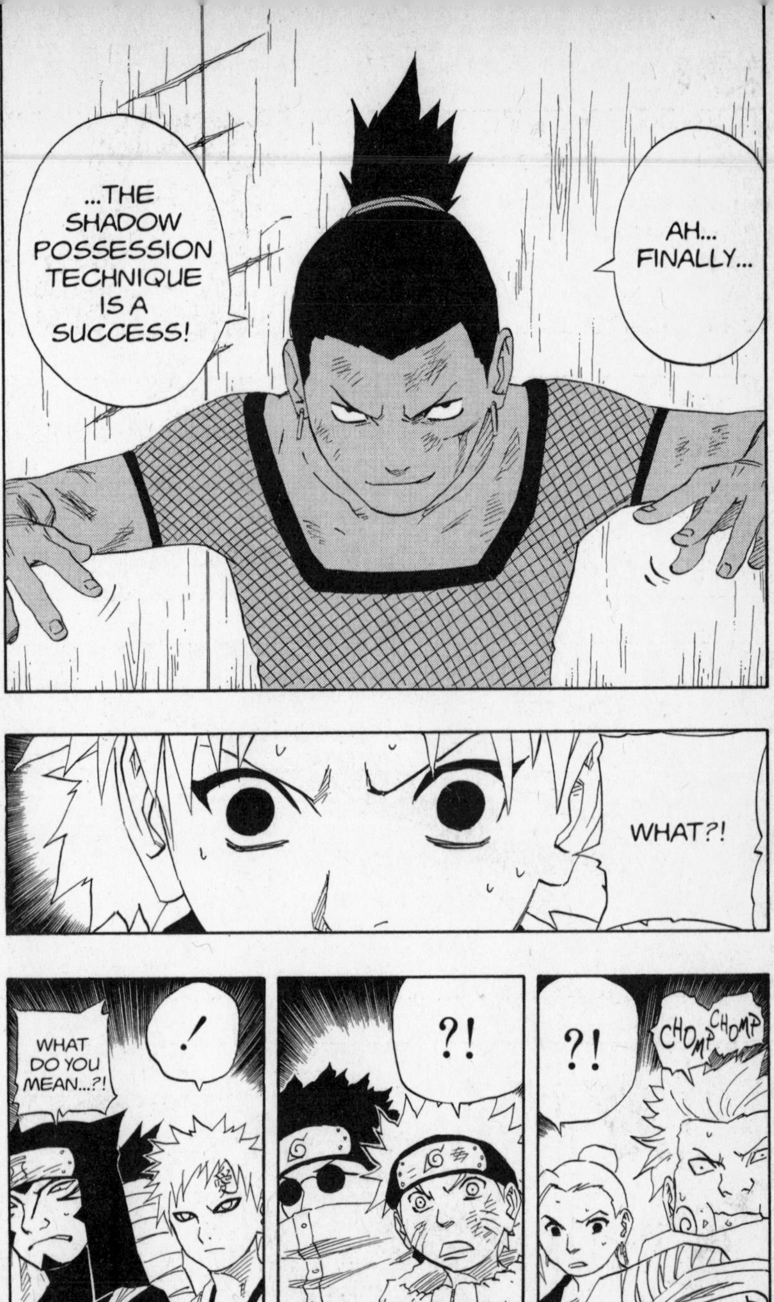
AH... FINALLY...
...THE SHADOW POSSESSION TECHNIQUE IS A SUCCESS!
WHAT?!
CHOMP CHOMP
?!
?!
!
WHAT DO YOU MEAN...?!

READ THIS WAY

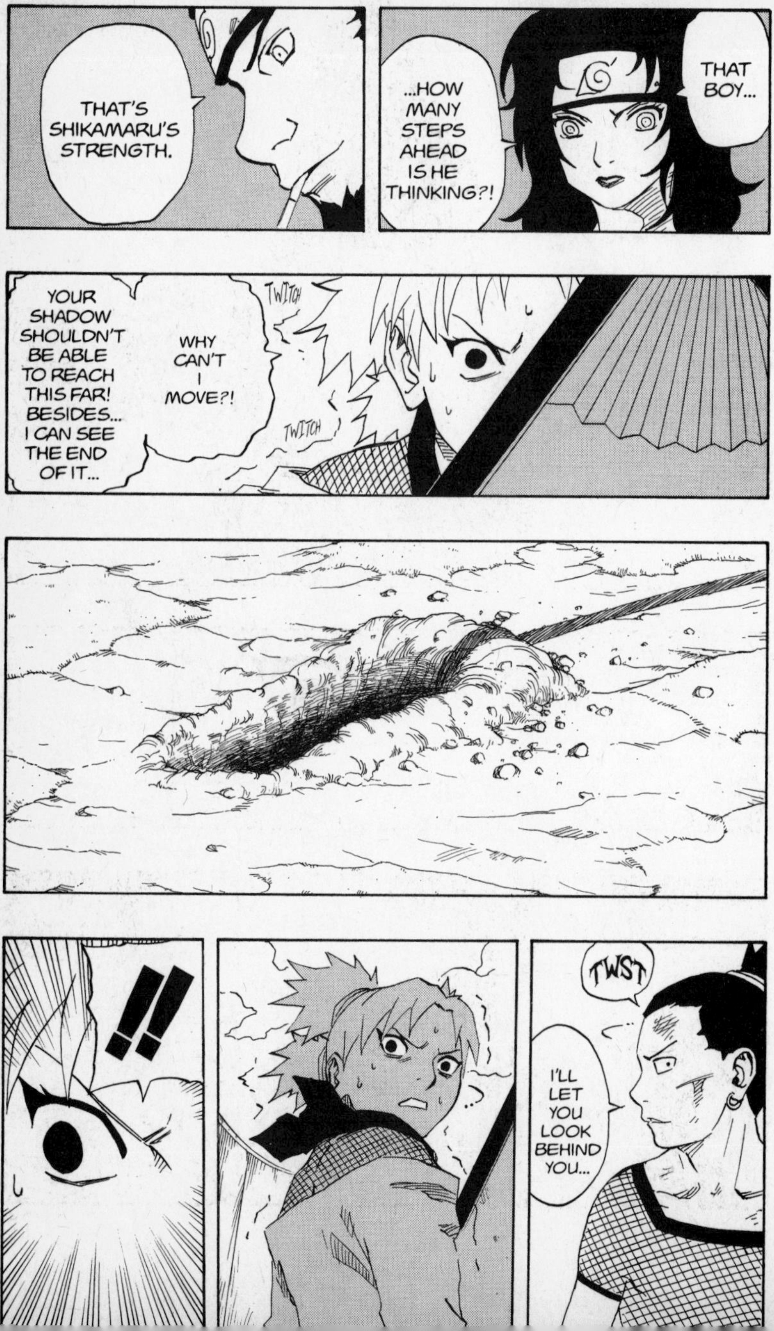
THAT BOY...
...HOW MANY STEPS AHEAD IS HE THINKING?!
THAT'S SHIKAMARU'S STRENGTH.
TWITCH
WHY CAN'T I MOVE?!
YOUR SHADOW SHOULDN'T BE ABLE TO REACH THIS FAR! BESIDES... I CAN SEE THE END OF IT...
TWITCH
TWST
I'LL LET YOU LOOK BEHIND YOU...
...
!!

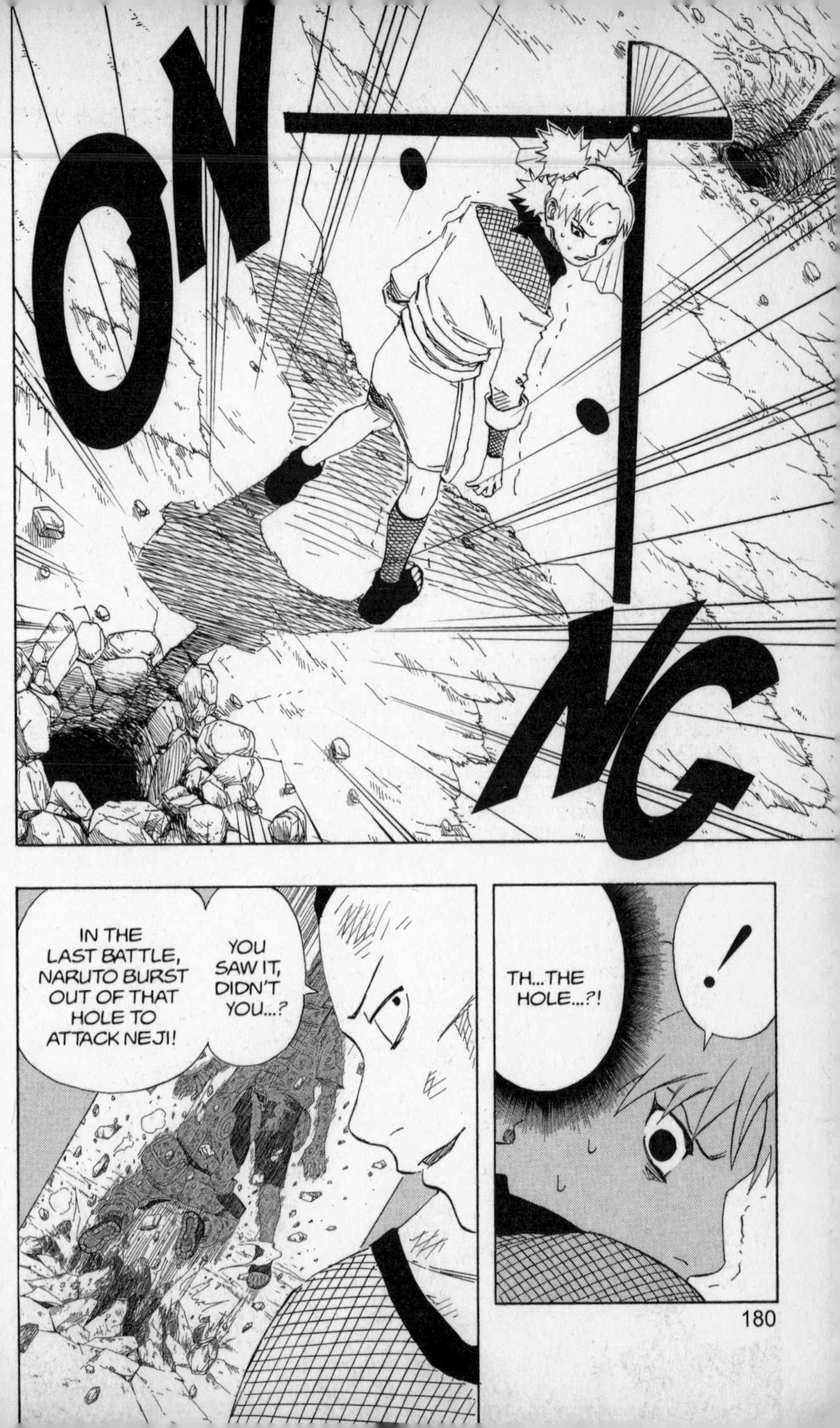

ON...T...NG
!
TH...THE HOLE...?!
YOU SAW IT, DIDN'T YOU...?
IN THE LAST BATTLE, NARUTO BURST OUT OF THAT HOLE TO ATTACK NEJI!

READ THIS WAY

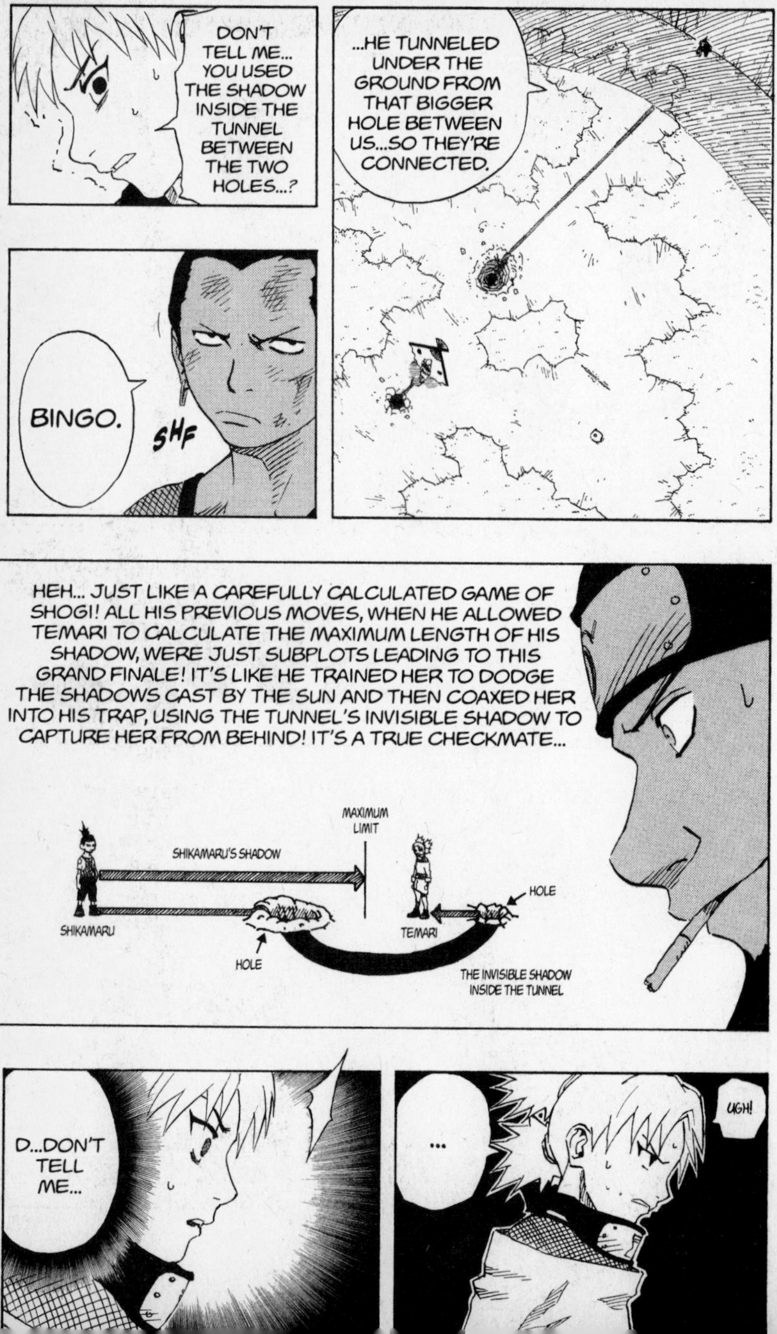
...HE TUNNELED UNDER THE GROUND FROM THAT BIGGER HOLE BETWEEN US...SO THEY'RE CONNECTED.
DON'T TELL ME... YOU USED THE SHADOW INSIDE THE TUNNEL BETWEEN THE TWO HOLES...?
BINGO.
SHF
HEH... JUST LIKE A CAREFULLY CALCULATED GAME OF SHOGI! ALL HIS PREVIOUS MOVES, WHEN HE ALLOWED TEMARI TO CALCULATE THE MAXIMUM LENGTH OF HIS SHADOW, WERE JUST SUBPLOTS LEADING TO THIS GRAND FINALE! IT'S LIKE HE TRAINED HER TO DODGE THE SHADOWS CAST BY THE SUN AND THEN COAXED HER INTO HIS TRAP, USING THE TUNNEL'S INVISIBLE SHADOW TO CAPTURE HER FROM BEHIND! IT'S A TRUE CHECKMATE...
MAXIMUM LIMIT
SHIKAMARU'S SHADOW
HOLE
SHIKAMARU
TEMARI
HOLE
THE INVISIBLE SHADOW INSIDE THE TUNNEL
UGH!
...
D...DON'T TELL ME...

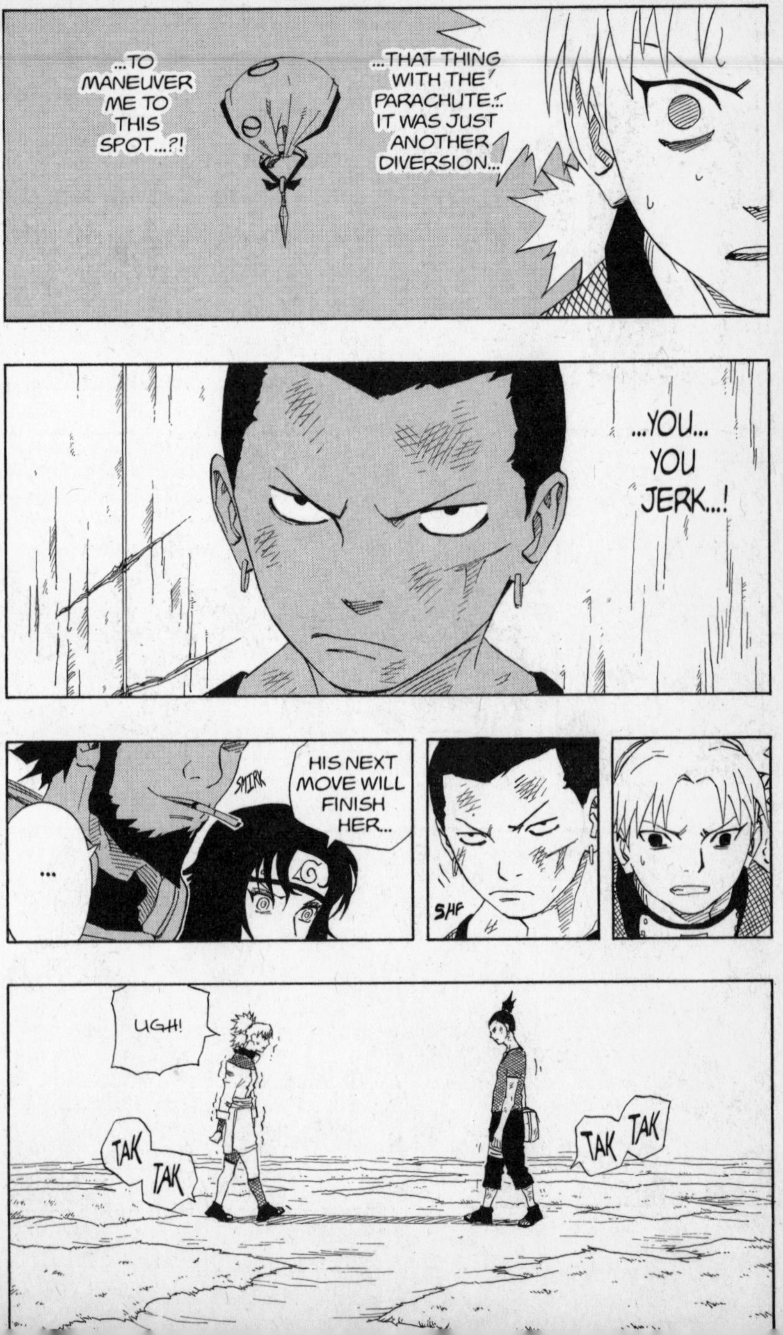
...THAT THING WITH THE PARACHUTE... IT WAS JUST ANOTHER DIVERSION...
...TO MANEUVER ME TO THIS SPOT...?!
...YOU... YOU JERK...!
SHF
HIS NEXT MOVE WILL FINISH HER...
SMIRK
...
TAK TAK
UGH!
TAK TAK

READ THIS WAY

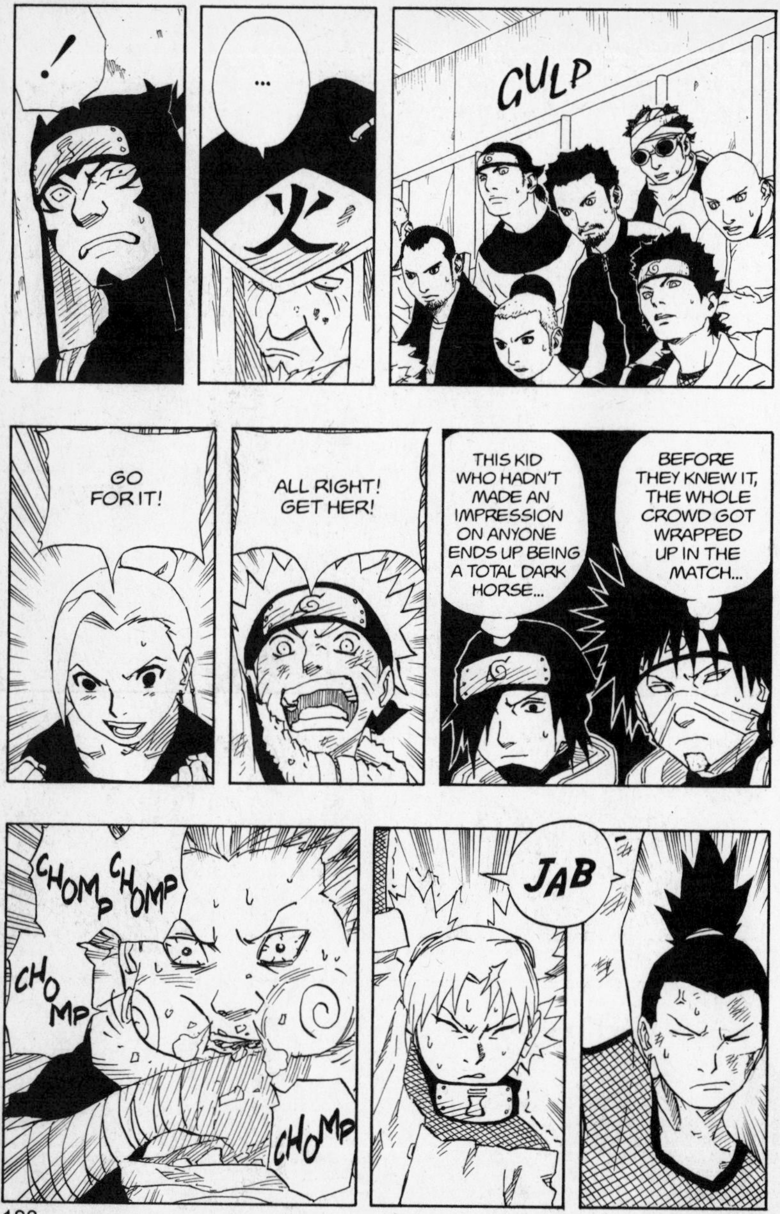
GULP
...
!
BEFORE THEY KNEW IT, THE WHOLE CROWD GOT WRAPPED UP IN THE MATCH...
THIS KID WHO HADN'T MADE AN IMPRESSION ON ANYONE ENDS UP BEING A TOTAL DARK HORSE...
ALL RIGHT! GET HER!
GO FOR IT!
JAB
CHOMP CHOMP
CHOMP
CHOMP

THAT'S IT... I'M DONE...
NG
!!
...
HUH?
WHAT THE HECK DID YOU SAY?!
I TOLD YOU HE WAS GONNA QUIT...
BURP
YOU REALLY DON'T KNOW ANYTHING ABOUT SHIKAMARU, DO YOU, INO?!
WH...
WHAT?!

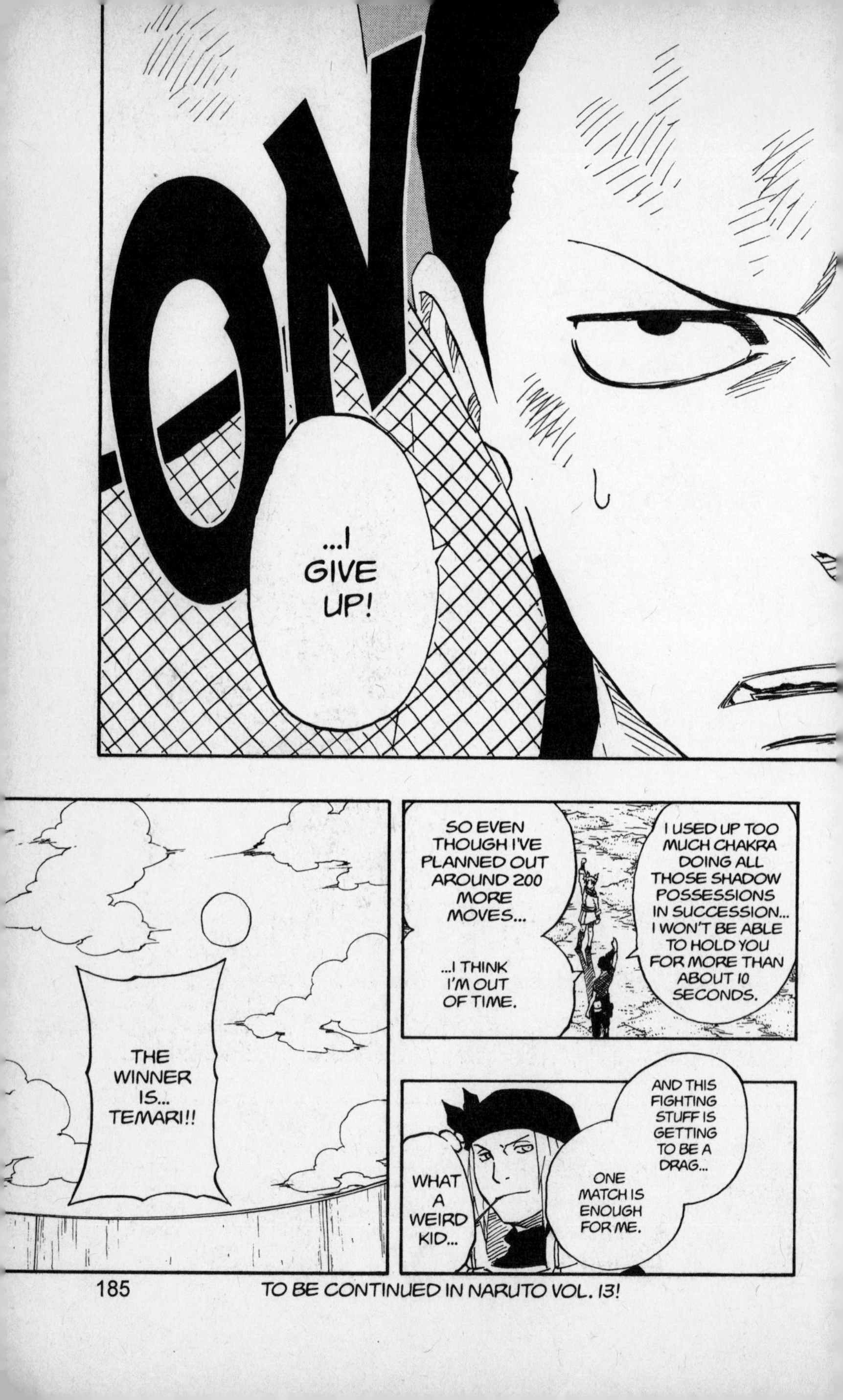
...I GIVE UP!
I USED UP TOO MUCH CHAKRA DOING ALL THOSE SHADOW POSSESSIONS IN SUCCESSION... I WON'T BE ABLE TO HOLD YOU FOR MORE THAN ABOUT 10 SECONDS.
SO EVEN THOUGH I'VE PLANNED OUT AROUND 200 MORE MOVES...
...I THINK I'M OUT OF TIME.
AND THIS FIGHTING STUFF IS GETTING TO BE A DRAG...
ONE MATCH IS ENOUGH FOR ME.
WHAT A WEIRD KID...
THE WINNER IS... TEMARI!!

TO BE CONTINUED IN NARUTO VOL. 13!

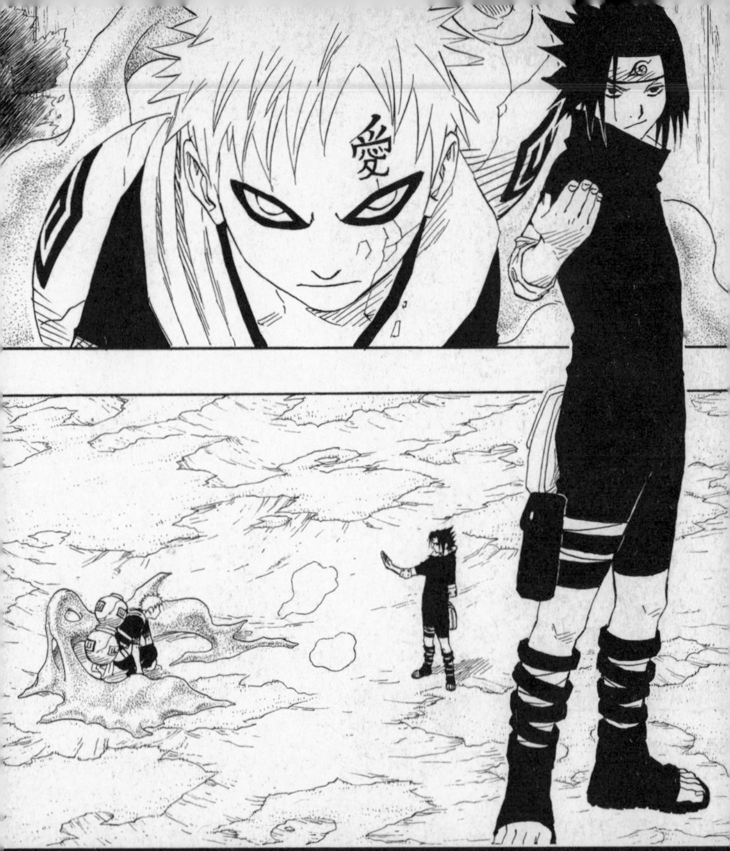

IN THE NEXT VOLUME...

Sasuke shows up for his battle with Gaara just in the nick of time after a month of training intensively with Kakashi. With a new move up his sleeve, Sasuke is ready to face his strongest opponent. But can mere training prepare him for the madness of Gaara? Look out, Sasuke, treasure's not the only thing that gets buried in the sand!

AVAILABLE MARCH 2007!

Read it first in SHONEN JUMP magazine!

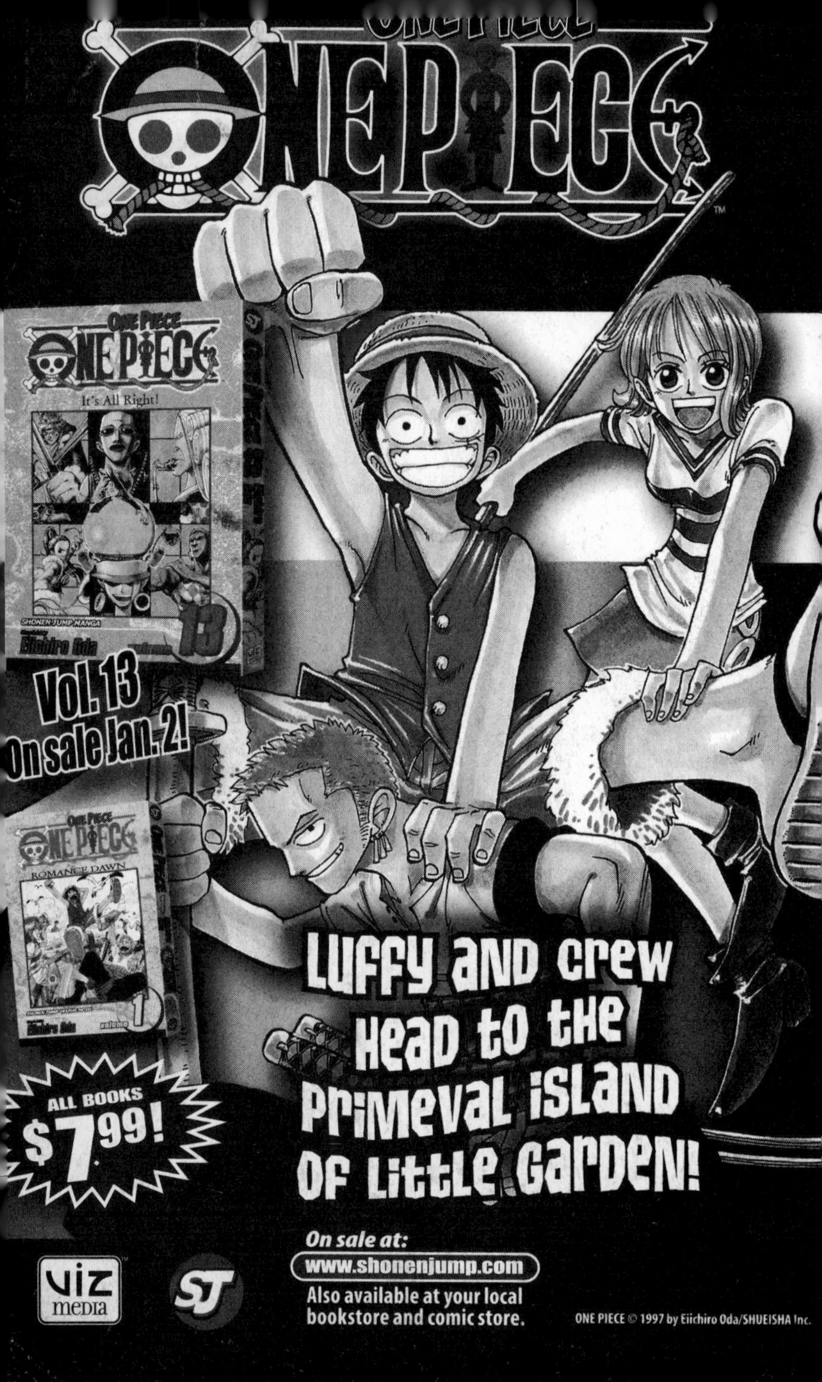
ONE PIECE
ONE PIECE
It's All Right!
SHONEN JUMP MANGA
13
Vol. 13
On sale Jan. 2!
ONE PIECE
ONE PIECE
ROMANCE DAWN
ALL BOOKS
$7.99!
LUFFY AND CREW
HEAD TO THE
PRIMEVAL ISLAND
OF LITTLE GARDEN!
On sale at:
www.shonenjump.com
Also available at your local
bookstore and comic store.
VIZ media
SJ
ONE PIECE © 1997 by Eiichiro Oda/SHUEISHA Inc.

Tell us what y
SHONEN JUMP manga!

[redacted]

Our survey is now available online.
Go to: ***www.SHONENJUMP.com/mangasurvey***

Help us make our product offering better!

[redacted]

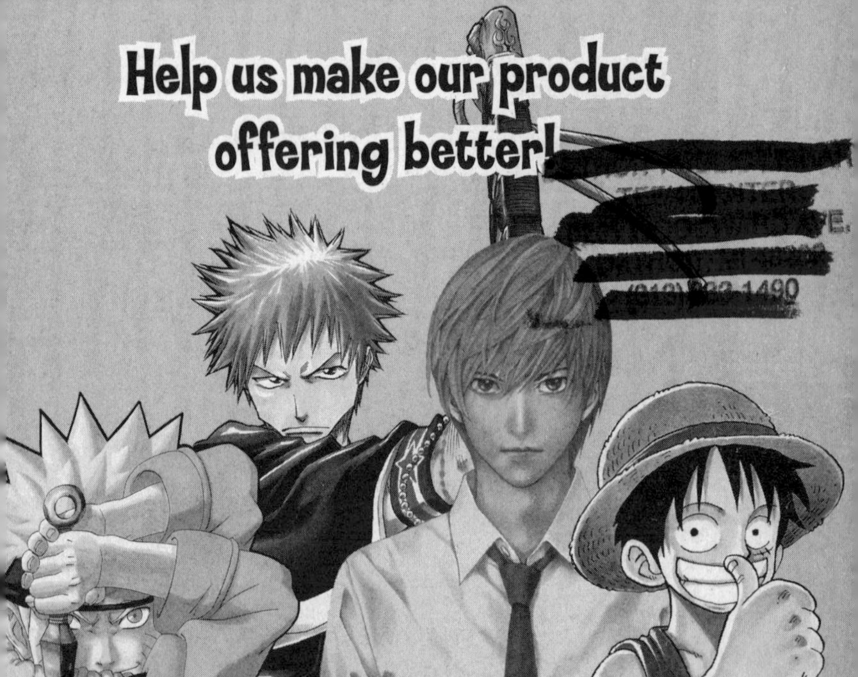
THE REAL ACTION STARTS IN...